RETHINKING ORGANIZATION

RETHINKING ORGANIZATION

New Directions in Organization Theory
and Analysis

edited by
Michael Reed and Michael Hughes

SAGE Publications
London • Newbury Park • New Delhi

Editorial arrangement © Michael Reed and Michael Hughes 1992
Chapter 1 © Michael Reed 1992
Chapter 2 © Howard E. Aldrich 1992
Chapter 3 © Barry A. Turner 1992
Chapter 4 © Colin Brown 1992
Chapter 5 © Nick Perry 1992
Chapter 6 © Stephen Ackroyd 1992
Chapter 7 © Richard Whitley 1992
Chapter 8 © Mark Wardell 1992
Chapter 9 © Gibson Burrell 1992
Chapter 10 © Alan Whitaker 1992
Chapter 11 © Kenneth J. Gergen 1992
Chapter 12 © Marta B. Calás and Linda Smircich 1992
Chapter 13 © Robert Cooper 1992
Chapter 14 © Frank Blackler 1992
Chapter 15 © Michael Hughes 1992

First published 1992

SAGE Publications Ltd
6 Bonhill Street
London EC2A 4PU

SAGE Publications Inc
2455 Teller Road
Newbury Park, California 91320

SAGE Publications India Pvt Ltd
32, M-Block Market
Greater Kailash – I
New Delhi 110 048

British Library Cataloguing in Publication Data

Rethinking organization: new directions in
organization theory and analysis.
I. Reed, Michael   II. Hughes, Michael
658.001

ISBN 0–8039–8287–9
ISBN 0–8039–8288–7 pbk

Library of Congress catalog card number 91-50970

Typeset by Mayhew Typesetting, Rhayader, Powys
Printed in Great Britain by Biddles Ltd, Guildford, Surrey

Contents

Notes on the Contributors

Stephen Ackroyd is a Lecturer in the Department of Behaviour in Organisations, The Management School, University of Lancaster, and an organizational consultant. His current research interests concern change processes in private and public sector organizations as well as the philosophy and methodology of social scientific inquiry.

Howard E. Aldrich is Professor of Sociology, Department of Sociology, University of North Carolina. He has made major contributions to the development of the Population Ecology framework in organizational analysis.

Frank Blackler is Professor of Organisational Behaviour, Department of Behaviour in Organisations, The Management School, Lancaster University. He is best known for his contributions to organizational psychology in the fields of work design, organization change and advanced technologies.

Colin Brown is a Lecturer in the Department of Behaviour Organisations, The Management School, Lancaster University. Currently, he is working on the interconnections between the philosophy/sociology of science and organizational analysis.

Gibson Burrell is Professor of Organisational Behaviour, School of Industrial and Business Studies, Warwick University. He is currently interested in 'pre-modern' organizational forms and their articulation in 'modern' and 'postmodern' settings.

Marta B. Calás and Linda Smircich are faculty members at the School of Management of the University of Massachusetts. Marta and Linda have been writing together for the past six years, exploring connections among culture, feminism, post-structuralism, postmodernism, and organization and management theory.

Robert Cooper is Reader in Organisation Theory, Department of Behaviour in Organisations, The Management School, Lancaster University. He has played a pivotal role in exploring the implications of post-structuralist concepts and methodology for the study of organizations.

Kenneth J. Gergen is Professor of Psychology at Swarthmore College, Pennsylvania. He has been at the forefront of recent innovations in social psychology concerned with the development and application of a social constructionist approach to the study of human behaviour in a wide range of social and organizational contexts.

Michael Hughes is Professor of Management in the Department of Business Studies, The School of Management, University of Stirling. His research interests lie in the fields of multinational corporations, comparative management structures and the political economies of Central and Eastern European societies.

Nick Perry is Senior Lecturer in Sociology, Department of Sociology, University of Auckland. He has published extensively in the fields of organizational analysis, popular culture and total institutions.

Michael Reed is Senior Lecturer, Department of Behaviour in Organisations, The Management School, Lancaster University. He has published in the fields of organizational analysis and the sociology of management. His current research interests centre on the emergence and management of 'knowledge workers' in advanced industrial societies.

Barry Turner is Research Professor of European Business, Middlesex Business School, Middlesex Polytechnic. He is a central figure in the 'culture and symbolism' movement in contemporary organizational analysis. He has also carried out in-depth field research on expert systems and the management of man-made disasters in modern societies.

Mark Wardell is Associate Professor of Sociology, Virginia Polytechnic Institute and State University. His research interests lie in the area of labour process analysis and the labour movement, with particular reference to the mining industry within an international context.

Alan Whitaker is a Lecturer in the Department of Behaviour in Organisations, The Management School, Lancaster University. His research interests include the sociology of work, industrial relations and comparative organizational change.

Richard Whitley is Professor of Organisational Sociology, Manchester Business School, University of Manchester. He has published extensively in organizational analysis, the sociology of science, managerial behaviour, and comparative organizational structures. He is currently researching 'business recipes' in East Asian Enterprises.

1

Introduction

Michael Reed

Since the end of the 1960s organizational studies has become much more pluralistic – some might even say anarchistic (Donaldson, 1985) – in terms of its central themes or problems and the theoretical frameworks through which they are analysed. This transformation in problematics, theories and methodologies also reflects deep-seated changes taking place in the actual organizational forms through which social behaviour is structured and controlled, as well as the wider institutional settings in which these forms are located. In short, most of the crucial theoretical questions and substantive issues which define organizational analysis as an identifiable and viable field of study seem to be matters of considerable dispute, not to say deep controversy.

Some welcome this state of affairs with open arms, seeing it as an over-due vindication of a long intellectual march from sterile and stultifying orthodoxy which has finally culminated in an historical juncture characterized by considerable theoretical and methodological diversity and the innovative developments that the accelerated pace of intellectual change releases. Others see it as a sign of a once well-regarded discipline in a state of potentially terminal disarray and dissolution. For them, any overarching sense of intellectual coherence and practical relevance is lost beneath the welter of disputation and controversy released by the decay and eventual decomposition of theoretical orthodoxy. The desire to retrieve and recover the comforting embrace of established thought is still a very powerful force in contemporary organization theory. However, it sits rather uneasily with an historical juncture characterized by debates over philosophical and theoretical fundamentals which inevitably question and undermine conventional modes of thought and analysis.

Whatever response one makes to this current state of affairs, there is general agreement that the 1970s and 1980s were a period of considerable intellectual instability, not to say upheaval, within the field of organiza-tional studies. The purpose of this volume is to map some of the key move-ments experienced over this period and to assess the impact of the theoretical debates and controversies that have crystallized around them. The following chapters also provide an evaluation of where these debates may be leading, in terms of outlining future decisions for a field of study that has experienced considerable movement since the break-up of 'ortho-dox consensus' (Giddens, 1979) from the late 1960s onwards and the plural-ity of theoretical approaches that have entered the field since that time.

This introductory chapter aims to provide an overview of the major developments that have occurred in organization theory since the end of the 1960s and to locate the chapters of the book in relation to the analysis that the former provides. It is organized in three major sections, which provide the overarching classificatory framework in which individual contributions are situated and interrelated within a wider structure. First, a review of the most significant *theoretical developments* that have taken place in organizational studies during the 1970s and 1980s. This section will focus on changes in the way in which 'organization' has been conceptualized and their implications for the manner in which organization theory or analysis is conceived and practised. Second, a discussion of the putative emergence of unconventional *organizational forms* in advanced industrial societies, as reflected in the decay of rational bureaucratic structures and the rise of flexible, network-based configurations. Third, an explanation of new *problematics* – that is, conceptual schemes organized around a core idea (Benson, 1977) – that seem to signify rupture with the 'modernist project', which has provided the dominant ideological framework and intellectual rationale for theoretical orthodoxy in organizational studies since its origins in mid/late nineteenth century speculations concerning the development of an 'administered' or 'organized' society (Wolin, 1961).

A brief conclusion will outline some of the underlying intellectual tensions which the above analysis has revealed and their implications for longer-term development within the field – as taken up in more detail in the final chapter of this book.

Theoretical Developments: From Orthodox Consensus to Pluralistic Diversity

Since the end of the 1960s there have been very significant changes in the way in which the concept of 'organization' is defined and the practice of 'organizational analysis' conceived. Broadly speaking, one can divide the period into three phases of theoretical change and development during which different conceptions of organization and organizational analysis have been dominant. Overall, the underlying intellectual trajectory revealed through an examination of the three phases of theoretical development seems to press in the direction of increasing diversity, plurality and controversy, as well as the fragmenting dynamic which they have set in motion.

By the late 1960s, various strands of theoretical development in organizational analysis seemed to be converging towards a systems-based contingency approach that focused on the adaptability of organizational designs to environmental imperatives of one sort or another (Reed, 1985; Thompson and McHugh, 1990; Mills and Murgatroyd, 1991). However, the subsequent decade witnessed a sharp move away from this presumptive orthodoxy in the shape of critiques and alternative formulations that substantially devalued the theoretical capital on which systems-based approaches had traded. In particular, the latter were seen to rely on static conceptions of 'organization' as distinctive, indeed separable, social units that were constrained, if not determined, by the larger environmental settings in which they operated. Alternative formulations suggested that organizations were reproduced and transformed through cultural and political processes that could not be caught in the analytical net provided ✓ by systems theory, with its theoretical trawl for isolatable 'dimensions' of formal organizational structure and environmental context which could be aligned through an assumed 'logic of effectiveness' (Child, 1972, 1973). Instead of a presumed logic of organizational adaptation that reinforced an ingrained theoretical predilection favourably disposed towards environmental determinism, alternative perspectives – the action frame of reference (Silverman, 1970), negotiated order (Strauss, 1978), ethnomethodology (Cicourel, 1968) and political theories of organization decision-making (Pettigrew, 1973; Pfeffer, 1981) – promulgated conceptions of 'organization' that highlighted the *construction* of organizational reality by means of power processes and symbolic interventions, which manipulated and interpreted 'external' demands and pressures in such a way that they either buttressed or undermined established arrangements. Consequently, organizational design was perceived not as the outcome of an impersonal, objective force but more as a constructed and manipulated social artefact. In turn, this development seriously undermined the conceptual separation between 'organization' on the one hand and 'environment' on the other.

Ten years later, by the late 1970s, the retreat from systems-based conceptualizations of organization and the scientific legitimations of organizational analysis which they reinforced – that is, the commitment to organizational studies as a social *science* geared to the identification of causal relationships between 'organization' and 'environment' – had turned into a rout. By this time, orthodox organization theory was increasingly perceived as being in a state of intellectual crisis, or paralysis, in which the once solid conceptual foundations of systems orthodoxy had all but been eaten away in the 'locust years' of deepening dissension and counter-movement (Donaldson, 1985). Thus, systems orthodoxy, by the late 1970s, was perceived to have no answer to the mounting clamour for theoretical frameworks which could effectively deal with

> the social production of organizational reality, including the reality-constructing activity of the organization scientist; the political bases of organizational realities, including the ties of theorists to power structures; the connection of organizations to the larger set of structural arrangements in the society; and the continuously emergent character of organizational patterns. (Benson, 1977: 16)

Around these strategic conceptual and methodological issues, a series of theoretical streams began to coagulate that considerably widened the agenda for organizational studies. They also presented an often bewildering array of alternative approaches that could not be accommodated within the once impregnable aegis of intellectual orthodoxy. As the latter began to dissipate, the ability to establish a, or *the*, defining problematic and framework for organizational analysis became increasingly difficult, if not impossible, to achieve. Organization theory seemed to be moving into a state of intellectual anomie. The *fin de siècle* condition of intellectual orthodoxy coincided with a proliferation of theoretical options which created a deepening sense of academic 'normlessness'.

Between the late 1970s and the late 1980s an ever-widening range of theoretical perspectives were offered as alternatives to the unacceptable constrictions of orthodoxy and as potential palliatives for the conceptual profusion into which organizational theory was being seduced. First, there was an increasingly potent emphasis on the cultural and symbolic processes through which organizations were socially constructed and organizational analysis academically structured (Turner, 1990a: 90). Second, the macro-level power relations and ideological systems through which organizational forms were shaped became a central theme for analysis (McNeil, 1978). Third, the retreat from natural science conceptions of organizational analysis seems to make intellectual and institutional space available for approaches that focused on the complex interaction between theoretical innovation and social context (Morgan, 1990). At one level, these developments seemed to signify the dissolution of organizational analysis as an identifiable field of study and body of knowledge. At another level, they seemed to open up attractive possibilities for research and explanation that forged connections between philosophical debate, theoretical development and institutional change – connections that had either been ignored or inadequately treated in previous work. Organization theory seemed to have finally left its period of 'intellectual innocence' far behind; by now, it was engaging in debates about the nature of social scientific research and explanation that moved beyond the narrow confines of established disciplinary discourse.

The chapters included in the first part of this book can be located in relation to this wider background of intensifying theoretical debate, diversity and innovation within organizational studies. Aldrich reviews three approaches to understanding organizational change that have become influential in the 1980s: population-ecology, institutional and interpretive perspectives respectively. While there are very important divergences between these three approaches in terms of their treatment of strategic conceptual issues concerned with agency, structures and levels of analysis, he argues that their complementary aspects outweigh their points of conflict. In this way, he argues against those who have previously advocated paradigm incommensurability and closure (Burrell and Morgan, 1979). Instead, he stresses the collective contribution that these three general approaches have to make by illuminating contrasting, but related, aspects of a diverse and complex organizational reality.

Turner concentrates on the cultural and symbolic dimensions of organizational life. While supporting a broad move towards greater emphasis on the qualitative aspects of organizational reality and research, he maintains that the cultivation of 'connoisseurship' in organizational studies – that is, the capacity to make informed judgements of complex relationships and practices – can only be developed if middle-range theories of organizational change, which are sensitive to actual practices, are advanced on a wider empirical front. He recommends recent work on the complexities and contradictions of organizational culture as one way of developing 'connoisseurship' in organizational analysis. This work, he suggests, 'stays close to' the multiple rationalities that inform social life in complex organizations, while illuminating the more general processes of symbolic and cultural production in which they are implicated.

Chapters 4, 5 and 6 focus on the academic organization of organizational studies and the way in which it influences, and is influenced by, theoretical developments within the field itself. Brown attempts to steer a middle course between the extreme relativism propounded by those who have emphasized the ideological and political interests which determine the conduct of organizational analysis, and the unreflective scientism of those who assume that the latter can be treated as an objective, value-free discipline. In contrast to either of these extremes, he advocates an approach to the theorization of organization and the practice of organizational analysis which attempts to unearth the complex interaction between the institutional arrangements of a particular discipline or field of study and the advancement of claims for accredited knowledge made with the domain that it occupies. Consequently, he calls attention to the intimate relationship between epistemological claims and disciplinary practices which unavoidably shapes the way in which a field of study develops. Latour's 'actor network theory' (Latour, 1982) is offered as one of the most promising approaches for understanding this complex relationship between academic organization and intellectual advance in organization theory.

Both Perry and Ackroyd follow the broad guidelines laid down by Brown. Perry suggests that developing patterns of disagreement and debate within organization theory – such as that between contingency theory and Marxist theory – can only be understood in terms of the wider configurations of cultural norms and institutional arrangements in which they progress. He concentrates on the forms of intellectual legitimation which different schools of thought or research programmes – such as the Aston School research programme – rely on to secure cognitive and institutional control within an increasingly fluid and pluralistic field of study. The upshot of his analysis is to advance an interpretation of 'theory making' in organizational analysis as an active process which necessarily reflects, but cannot and should not resolve, the endemic conflicts and resulting tensions between competing lines of inquiry. It is these conflicts and tensions which provide organization theory with its underlying impetus for change and innovation.

Ackroyd completes the set of chapters in this first part by recognizing the reality of institutionally located theoretical conflict and controversy, while arguing strongly against the 'paradigm mentality' which has been such a pervasive feature of organizational analysis in recent years. He maintains that this 'paradigm thinking' – and the overriding emphasis on incommensurability and resulting polarization which has flowed from it – has had a debilitating impact on producing organizational knowledge that is simultaneously insightful and useful. Consequently, organizational studies has conspicuously failed to identify and cultivate a professional-cum-managerial group or cadre that will provide a receptive audience for, and advocate on behalf of, its intellectual wares. Rather, organizational analysis has fragmented and fractured into a competing set of theoretical factions that stand in the way of disciplinary institutionalization and legitimation. In this sense, Ackroyd reminds us of the practical – that is, political – price that has been paid – in terms of declining academic legitimation and the material support which usually flows from it – for the theoretical excitements and innovations of more recent times. Yet, he clearly recognizes that some kind of enforced unity around a tired and worn theoretical dogma will not provide the necessary intellectual foundations for disciplinary coherence. These can only be found in limited synthesis between competing approaches and the engagement in empirical research projects that demonstrate their relevance to improved organizational practice. Only in this way, Ackroyd argues, can organization theorists establish a firm social base for their intellectual activities.

Changing Organizational Forms: From Bureaucracy to Networks

Intensified debate and controversy over the theoretical foundations of organizational studies has been paralleled by growing awareness of and sensitivity to substantive changes in those organizational forms that provide the empirical focus for research and analysis. Whether these structural changes should be regarded as signifying a fundamental transformation in the institutional fabric of advanced industrial societies, or more appropriately as the working through of older, well-established forms to their more developed state, is a moot point (Reed, 1991a, forthcoming). Nevertheless, however these changes in organizational forms are characterized and explained, there is general agreement that they signify the theoretical importance and practical relevance of a far wider range of structural options than were considered under the rational systems perspective.

The belief that rational bureaucracy, as exemplified in formal organization structures characterized by extreme internal differentiation and rigid hierarchical control, constituted a universalizable solution to the problem of achieving operational efficiency and effectiveness in conditions of environmental uncertainty had petrified into a rigid orthodoxy that the dominant systems perspective maintained (Clegg, 1990). While such structures required some 'fine tuning' to align them more closely with specific configurations of environmental contingencies, they were assumed to provide a core repertoire of universalizable principles and mechanisms that equipped organizations to face competitive pressures and the implacable demands that the latter generated for effective coordination of large-scale, complex operations.

Since the early 1980s historical and comparative research on organizational forms has revealed the inherent limitations and inadequacies of this 'universalistic' thesis. It has shown that different historical periods and institutional locations within and between different societies produce and reproduce a wide range of organizational forms which cannot be accommodated within the rational/systems model (Clark and Starkey, 1988; Clegg, 1990; Lane, 1989). Indeed, this research has shown that the conventionally accepted functional relationship between highly differentiated and formalized organizational structures, and socio-economic contexts defined by competitive pressures pressing in the direction of market efficiency, may be much more tenuous than supporters of the dominant orthodoxy have suggested. In addition, such research has also called into question the conventional conceptual and methodological apparatus through which comparative organizational forms have been studied within the analytical confines presented by the rational/systems approach. Thus, a growing interest in the *social* rationalities and practices which shape economic organization, the power struggles through which they are formulated, implemented and contested, and the conceptions of historical and institutional time in which such rationalities and struggles are contextualized, all signal a dramatic shift of emphasis in the study of organizational forms towards the dynamics of change and the 'logics' through which it proceeds.

Each of the chapters in the second part of this book addresses the multiplicity of theoretical, substantive and interpretive issues raised by the theme of changing organizational forms. They also suggest that the trajectories of organizational transition and institutional change followed by both Western industrialized societies and Eastern political economies have to be accounted for within a comparative/historical framework that is theoretically and methodologically equipped to cope with the complex mix of processual discontinuities and structural continuities which shape longer-term developments. Whitley provides an extremely detailed review of the various theoretical perspectives available for the comparative study of economic organizations. He argues against the 'culture free' thesis of organizational change and development advocated by researchers such as Williamson (1975) and Chandler and Daems (1980). Neither is he enamoured with the 'cultural determinism' offered by those who stress the ways in which business structures and practices come to reflect the beliefs and ideologies of dominant elites within different countries (Ouchi, 1981). In direct contrast to the extremes of economic rationalism and cultural relativism, Whitley offers an approach to the comparative analysis of 'business recipes' focused on the organizing rationalities pursued by dominant economic groups and the particular institutional configurations in which they operate. These dominant conceptions of organizational practices and rationalities crystallize in the form of different 'logics of action' or 'rules of the game' which have an elective affinity with the societal and institutional contexts in which they are mobilized. The comparative explanatory power of this approach is then displayed in Whitley's review of the different social recipes and structural arrangements for economic organization found in Japan, Korea, China and Taiwan.

If Whitley provides a top-down, comparative analysis of different forms of economic organization shaped by elite ideologies and practices, Wardell approaches historical transformations in workplace organization and control in the USA between the late nineteenth and mid twentieth centuries from a 'bottom-up', case study perspective. The latter concentrates on workplace-based struggles to control the labour process through a succession of organizational forms adapted by management to cope with the practical or operational autonomy of labour from the 1880s onwards. What emerges as Wardell's central theme is the way in which the forms of organizational coordination and control utilized by management in their attempt to subordinate labour to the dictates of the production process mediate the social dependency of capital on labour. Wardell maintains that a focus on the way in which various struggles over labour's effort at the points of production shape historical transformations in the organization of capitalist workplaces can correct for the explanatory deficiencies of structural approaches that minimize the impact of collective consciousness and agency on institutional forms and the underlying 'logic of development' which they are presumed to follow.

This approach is then applied to changes in workplace organization in the USA taking place between the dominance of craft workplaces up to the middle of the nineteenth century and their eventual deterioration and break-up under the impact of subcontracting and foreman control systems which gave capitalist owners a formal representation at points of production. These, more intensive and structured, control systems provided an embryonic administrative framework for hierarchical domination and coordinated work discipline, but they simultaneously opened up new 'arenas of struggle' that workers could exploit and attempt to turn to their own advantage.

Burrell turns his attention to the various philosophies of time which have underpinned different approaches to the analysis of changing organizational forms. He adumbrates three major conceptions of time – linear, cyclical and spiral time – which respectively inform different, and often competing, theoretical approaches to the analysis of 'new' organizational forms and the developmental trajectories which they are presumed to follow. Much of his chapter is taken up with a review of the putative emergence of 'Post-Fordist' forms of work organization and their explanation through theoretical frameworks that assume a total 'rupture' with the past. These interpretations, he maintains, stand in sharp contrast to evolutionary theories of organizational forms based on a linear view of time and the steadily unfolding progression of structural patterns which it purports to reveal.

Burrell suggests that a synthetic conception of time – based on the notion of time as a never-ending spiral which continually turns back on itself – may provide a more appropriate theoretical basis for analysing changing forms of organizing and organization. This is so to the extent that spiral time can provide a better understanding of the 'heterogeneous time codes' which shape organizational change and development, and the way in which this conception resonates much more strongly with the 'postmodernist' turn in contemporary organizational analysis. A tempered view of the latter, Burrell argues, can provide much greater insight into the multiple histories which shape organizational transformation and the need to locate these in shared narratives that make communication and discourse across 'paradigm boundaries' possible.

Whitaker's chapter, the last in this part, provides a detailed overview and assessment of the overarching debate about changing forms of work organization in advanced industrial society. In so doing, he pulls together many of the substantive and analytical threads evident in the previous three chapters, such as culturally embedded rationalities, workplace struggles and novel control strategies. In particular, Whitaker focuses on the currently influential theoretical frameworks and interpretations of those who have argued for a fundamental break with established bureaucratic forms of organization and the rise of innovative 'network structures' based on opposing principles of decentralization, deregulation and de-differentiation. However, he finds these novel interpretations wanting in several respects: unexamined theoretical contradictions; unsupported empirical assertions; unrecognized elisions between abstract theorizations and reported empirical trends.

Rather than identify a 'sea-change' or 'epochal movement' in the institutional and organizational fabric of contemporary capitalist economics in the West, Whitaker takes a much more temperate and cautious line which highlights the continuing strategic role of multi-national corporations in restructuring the established relationships within and between 'capital' and 'labour'. He sees, not a fragmentation of organization and control through dispersed and flexible structures, but a further extension and strengthening of Fordist structures brought about by the restructuring initiatives in which multinationals have become increasingly involved, both in relation to their own internal systems and external relations. This, he contends, will lead to a more tightly integrated international system dominated by a relatively small number of multinational corporations working towards a 'globally networked economy'. The latter becomes much more desirable and feasible for socio-economic elites in contemporary and prospective political conditions that are very different from those prevailing under the post-Second-

World-War Keynesian consensus and the relative stability which it provided.

At the level of work organization, a more globally networked international economy, dominated by increasingly powerful multinationals, encourages management to experiment with control strategies seeking 'the mobilization of consent' through ideological manipulation and cultural indoctrination, as well as more flexible production systems and wage-payment structures. Without denying the reality of structural change in institutional systems and organizational forms, Whitaker attempts to locate and explain these developments within an analytical framework that calls attention to the underlying *continuities* that shape contemporary developments which are highly complex and often push in contradictory directions.

Emerging Problematics: From Organization to Disorganization

As well as internal theoretical innovation and external institutional change, contemporary organizational analysis has also witnessed significant movement in the central 'problematics' which give the field some kind of coherent identity and shape as a going intellectual concern. If we regard a problematic as a general conceptual scheme organized around a core idea or problem which then provides a range of specific issues or puzzles for people working within the framework to get their intellectual teeth into, then it is possible to trace the emergence of alternative problematics since the end of the 1960s that have challenged the intellectual status quo in varying ways and to different degrees.

By the late 1960s the problematic of order had structured the field to the virtual exclusion of alternative formulations. This problematic centred on the question of how organizational survival was possible in the face of environmental forces and pressures which threatened the organization's very existence as a viable social unit (Thompson, 1967). The conceptual framework woven around this core problem rested on an ontological commitment to 'organization' as a distinctive and separate entity, dependent on certain stability-maintaining and integrating mechanisms facilitating long-term survival in a potentially hostile environment (Gouldner, 1971). These mechanisms were presumed to facilitate the fine tuning in organizational design that equipped them to cope with uncertain and complex environments.

Ten years later, the problematic of order had been largely displaced by the problematic of domination – that is, a significant shift away from a primary concern with survival and stability towards an emphasis on the social and political processes through which organizational power is mobilized and legitimated (McNeil, 1978). This movement entailed a drastic reappraisal of the explanatory priorities which had traditionally shaped the substantive agenda for organizational analysis, as well as the theoretical and methodological tools thought most appropriate to the working through of that agenda. Instead of concentrating theoretical resources and methodological strategies around the establishment of causal relationships between environmental contingencies and formal organizational designs, the focus of attention shifted to an unearthing of the political and ideological manipulations which operated behind the public facade of stability and order (Clegg, 1975; Pfeffer, 1982). The power of non-decision-making (Lukes, 1974) and institutional bias became the orienting themes in organizational analysis.

The 1980s saw another transition in problematic in which the construction of organizational reality, through the skilled utilization of largely arbitrary linguistic and cultural representations or 'language games' (Power, 1990), has become the central concern (Turner, 1990b; Reed, 1991b). This has given added intellectual momentum to approaches which reject the rationalistic predilections of earlier formulations and call attention to the complex negotiating processes through which a precarious, and unavoidably unstable, collective sense of organizational reality is sustained (Mills and Murgatroyd, 1991).

This third movement in problematics – the linguistic or cultural 'turn' in contemporary organizational analysis – also owes much to the widening impact of postmodernist thinking within the field. This latter development – and its far-reaching implications for the way in which we conceptualize 'organization' – provides the central theme for the groups of chapters included in the penultimate part of this book. Thus, Gergen argues that a recognition that our theories of organizations are, 'first and foremost', linguistic constructions or devices striving to achieve better understanding or intelligibility in the face of an increasingly fragmented and disorganized cultural order, draws attention to the wider discursive contexts in which these theories take on meaning and significance for action. Whereas the modernist discourse in which organization studies originally developed based itself on the search for rational scientific theories of a distinctive object which would facilitate general social progress and political stability, postmodernist thinking reverses the relationship between theoretical language and 'objective' reality by treating the former as master of the latter. Belief in an independently existing and objective 'organizational reality', knowable through scientific reasoning and discourse, is replaced by a conception of theories as self-justifying representational forms or 'intelligible narratives' which allow groups or communities of researchers and scholars to make shared sense of their collective engagement with a predefined phenomenon. Ironic self-reflection and 'playful seriousness' replace the quest for universal objective truth through the application of scientific method and reason as the appropriate cognitive strategies and cultural discourses for organizational analysis in a postmodern world.

However, Gergen draws back from the seductive allure of the 'relativist vortex' which beckons him; the modernist meta-narratives of organizational rationality and inexorable social progress may have been shattered by postmodernist argumentation and insinuation, but this does not render the theorist voiceless – 'objective truth is not the only game in town'.

Indeed, Gergen suggests that the strength and depth of the challenge which new theories offer to the taken-for-granted 'truths' of intellectual orthodoxy offers an alternative ground on which to evaluate competing theorizations of organization. The capacity of the new theories to generate novel and innovative discursive formations that counteract the intellectual inertia and conservatism encouraged by a slothful acceptance of the theoretical status quo provides an acceptable epistemological basis for resisting the worst excesses of cultural and cognitive relativism.

Each of the three subsequent chapters explores in greater detail some of the issues raised by Gergen. Calás and Smircich assess the potential offered by feminist theory for 're-writing' organization theory against the wider intellectual and cultural background provided by postmodernist discourse. They deploy feminist theory and its analytical focus on the core idea of gender to question what has conventionally been represented as 'organization theory' and the way in which this privileges – both epistemologically and politically – distinctive ways of conceptualizing 'organization'. Their analysis reveals the subtle, and not so subtle, ways in which the male-gendered bias of organization theory is insinuated through the modes of theoretical representation – or repression – and forms of research practice that present themselves in the guise of objective science. They show how the production and evaluation of knowledge about organizations and organization theories are dependent on implicit exclusionary practices and categories based on patriarchy and the 'de-gendering' of organizational reality which it encourages.

They see some positive signs of change in more recent analyses and critiques of deep-seated gender-bias entailed in much current organizational theorizing and practice. But they also maintain that feminist theory and scholarship must move beyond this strategy of argumentation to develop forms of research and teaching which would more fully embrace the political consequences of having recognized exclusion and limitations under feminist tenets. Such a development, they insist, would require a more thoughtful exploration of the ambiguous relationship between feminism and postmodernism at the time of 'paradigm plurality' and its inherent de-politicizing and relativizing tendencies. While they share a self-conscious critical intellectual space and historical location, feminism and postmodernism must maintain a relationship of managed distance if the former is to sustain its political momentum and force within the expanding and enabling, but ideologically fragile, critique of the totalizing aspirations of modernist discourse offered by the latter.

Cooper deploys three key concepts from postmodernist and post-structuralist forms of organizational analysis to explore the representational practices through which organizations achieve 'control at a distance'. He examines remote control, displacement and abbreviation as three interrelated techniques of representation which allow organizational elites to construct 'organizations' as active conversion processes that transform geographically remote events or supposedly intractable realities into visible and controllable objects. The explanatory potential of this framework is then illustrated by reference to three empirical examples of 'control at a distance': the development of advanced navigational technologies by the Portuguese East India Company in the fifteenth century; Pasteur's construction of a mobile laboratory technology to isolate and counteract the anthrax virus in nineteenth century France; finally, the development and implementation by French and British administrators of vision-oriented administrative techniques that regulate the potentially dislocating and disruptive effects of rapid demographic expansion in the eighteenth and nineteenth centuries.

The penultimate section of Cooper's chapter considers how this type of analysis can fundamentally transform the way in which conventional approaches to formal organization structure proceed by way of statistical representations and operationalizations of supposedly fixed and unchanging dimensions. In its place, Cooper's focus on the representational technologies facilitating control at a distance transforms these structures into dynamic socio-technical networks along which 'the organization' travels.

Finally, Blackler's chapter turns to the problem of planning and managing organizational change in a postmodern world characterized by the seemingly intractable instabilities and uncertainties released by 'disjunctive' or transformative institutional change. He draws on Unger's theory of formative contexts and Vygotsky's activity theory to provide a conceptual framework that will integrate an interest in the strategic role of human agency and a concern with the constraining impact of structural arrangements as they simultaneously shape the trajectories of social and organizational development followed in postmodern societies. This framework, Blackler suggests, will facilitate a sustained focus on the processes that link cognitions with social contexts at different levels of analysis. It is likely to reveal the essential 'arbitrariness' of social institutions and organizational realities; that is, the manner in which they are held together by rules and practices that assume a 'false necessity' as indispensable and unavoidable mechanisms and devices, rather than as ideologies and arrangements that obscure and protect certain sectional interests and values rather than others. By 'de-naturalizing' formative contexts and activity systems through a social constructivist perspective, Blackler anticipates that we may be better placed to provide a practical and empowering theory of managing organizational change in highly unstable and turbulent social conditions.

Conclusion: Beyond Incommensurability

The overriding impression which emerges from reading the chapters of this book is of a field of study that has been transformed beyond all recognition from that which existed in the late 1960s. Diversity, plurality, uncertainty and fragmentation seem to be the epithets which most easily and readily spring to mind when attempting to provide a general characterization of the current state of play in, and future prospects for, organizational analysis. In this respect, fundamental and far-reaching discontinuity in concerns, conceptualizations and conditions seems to be the dominant theme underlying the analyses presented between these covers. Indeed, most of them consistently identify a trend towards polarization within the intellectual and institutional structure of organization theory and the supposedly unmanageable tensions which this trend generates. Thus, Brown and Whitley emphasize the polarization between scientific or economic rationalism on the one hand and epistemological or cultural relativism on the other. Burrell and Gergen point to the growing tension between conceptions of time and history based on a belief in unilinear progression towards universal order and stability, as opposed to those highlighting the episodic or fractured nature of time and the essential undecidability of human history. Aldrich, Turner and Blackler contrast approaches to organizational analysis in which the 'logic', or rather 'logics', of institutional change and development assume explanatory priority as opposed to those perspectives that stress the centrality of social construction and action. Ackroyd argues for a re-ordering of academic priorities away from scientific generalization towards action-oriented research, while Perry reminds us of the cultural and institutional constraints which inevitably shape the trajectory of intellectual development in any field of study or discipline.

However, an interpretation of the arguments presented in this book which gave overriding emphasis to discontinuity and incommensurability between competing or conflicting 'paradigms' and their respective communities (Bernstein, 1983) would provide a very superficial and distorted reading of the overarching theoretical trajectories which these arguments reveal. Each of the contributors to this volume recognizes the very real differences of theoretical orientation, substantive focus and ideological preference which now prevail – and are likely to prevail for the foreseeable future – in organization theory. Yet, the overwhelming aspiration motivating their efforts is to provide theoretical frameworks, methodologies and substantive interpretations which avoid the 'paradigm mentality' that dominated the field in the 1970s and that threatens to make a comeback if the revivified guardians of positivistic rectitude or ideological acceptability get their way. The need to entice supposedly opposed philosophies, theories and methods into a more fruitful dialogue which explores common ground and shared interpretations, without looking for, much less imposing, false integration or bland synthesis, is a recurring feature of this volume. Rather than emphasize the impossibility of meaningful dialogue across paradigm boundaries and rely on internal self-development as the basis for intellectual growth and innovation, the analyses conducted in this book strive to exploit opportunities for developing mediating links between different perspectives which enable them to maintain their own integrity, whilst expanding the points of contact with other approaches (Gioia and Pitre, 1990).

As a result, there are very strong and distinctive continuities between the attempts made in this book to sustain dialogue between a range of perspectives or paradigms which play different parts in a shared narrative, and earlier struggles to maintain a coherent and viable discourse. As Burrell reflects, 'if one gives up the search for narratives, one gives up the search for academic understanding'. But the latter can only be sustained if the willingness to engage in the making and remaking of intelligible narratives evident in the pages of this book is echoed elsewhere.

The longer-term directions in which these more recent and innovative attempts to sustain the narrative drive and analytical complexity of organizational analysis may be pressing are explored in greater detail in the concluding chapter of this book. In particular, it highlights the over-arching significance of the modernist/postmodernist debate as providing a wider theoretical context in which the individual contributions reviewed above can be located and assessed.

References

Benson, J.K. (ed.) (1977) *Organisational Analysis: Critique and Innovation*. London: Sage Contemporary Social Science Issues, 17.

Bernstein, R. (1983) *Objectivism and Realism*. Oxford: Basil Blackwell.

Burrell, G. and Morgan, G. (1979) *Sociological Paradigms and Organizational Analysis*. London: Heinemann.

Chandler, A. (1977) *The Visible Hand*. Cambridge, MA: Harvard University Press.

Chandler, A. and Daems, H. (eds) (1980) *Managerial Hierarchies: Comparative Perspectives on the Rise of Modern Industrial Enterprise*. Cambridge, MA: Harvard University Press.

Child, J. (1972) 'Organizational structure, environment and performance: The role of strategic choice', *Sociology*, 6 (1): 1–22.

Child, J. (1973) 'Organization: A choice for man', in J. Child (ed.), *Man and Organization*. London: Allen and Unwin, pp. 234–55.

Cicourel, A. (1968) *The Social Organization of Juvenile Justice*. New York: Free Press.

Clark, P. and Starkey, K. (1988) *Organization Transitions and Innovation Design*. London: Pinter Publishers.

Clegg, S. (1975) *Power, Rule and Domination*. London: Routledge.

Clegg, S. (1990) *Modern Organizations: Organization Studies in the Postmodern World*. London: Sage.

Donaldson, L. (1985) *In Defence of Organization Theory*. Cambridge: Cambridge University Press.

Giddens, A. (1979) *Central Problems in Social Theory*. London: Macmillan.

Gioia, D.A. and Pitre, E. (1990) 'Multiparadigm perspectives on theory building', *Academy of Management Review*, 5 (4): 584–602.

Gouldner, A. (1971) *The Coming Crisis of Western Sociology*. London: Heinemann.

Lane, C. (1989) *Management and Labour in Europe*. Aldershot: Edward Elgar.

Latour, B. (1982) *Science in Action*. Milton Keynes: Open University.

Lukes, A. (1974) *Power: A Radical View*. London: Macmillan.

McNeil, K. (1978) 'Understanding organizational power: Building on the Weberian legacy', *Administrative Science Quarterly*, 23 (1): 65–90.

Mills, A.J. and Murgatroyd, S.J. (1991) *Organizational Rules: A Framework for Understanding Organizational Action*. Milton Keynes: Open University Press.

Morgan, G. (1990) *Organisations in Society*. London: Macmillan.

Ouchi, W.G. (1981) *Theory Z*. Reading, MA: Addison Wesley.

Pettigrew, A. (1973) *The Politics of Organizational Decision-Making*. London: Tavistock.

Pfeffer, J. (1981) *Power in Organizations*. Boston: Pitman Press.

Pfeffer, J. (1982) *Organizations and Organization Theory*. Boston: Pitman Press.

Power, M. (1990) 'Modernism, postmodernism and organization', in J. Hassard and D. Pym (eds), *The Theory and Philosophy of Organizations*. London: Routledge, pp. 109–24.

Reed, M. (1985) *Redirections in Organizational Analysis*. London: Tavistock.

Reed, M. (1991a) 'The end of organized society: A theme in search of a theory?', in P. Blyton and J. Morris (eds), *A Flexible Future?* Berlin: de Gruyter.

Reed, M. (1991b) 'Scripting scenarios for a new organization theory and practice', *Work Employment and Society*, 5 (1): 119–32.

Reed, M. (forthcoming), *The Disorganized Society and the Future of Organizations* London: Sage.

Silverman, D. (1970) *The Theory of Organizations*. London: Heinemann.

Strauss, A. (1978) *Negotiations*. New York: Wiley.

Thompson, J.D. (1967) *Organizations in Action*. New York: McGraw Hill.

Thompson, P. and McHugh, D. (1990) *Work Organizations: A Critical Introduction*. London: Macmillan.

Turner, B. (1990a) 'The rise of organizational symbolism', in J. Hassard and D. Pym (eds), *The Theory and Philosophy of Organizations*. London: Routledge, pp. 83–96.

Turner, B. (ed.) (1990b) *Organizational Symbolism*. Berlin: de Gruyter.

Williamson, O.E. (1975) *Markets and Hierarchies: Analysis and Anti-Trust Implications*. New York: Free Press.

Wolin, S. (1961) *Politics and Vision*. London: Allen and Unwin.

DEVELOPMENTS IN THEORY

2

Incommensurable Paradigms? Vital Signs from Three Perspectives

Howard E. Aldrich

In this chapter, I review two fairly new approaches to the understanding of organizational change – the ecological and institutional approaches – as well as a third which is enjoying continued vitality – an interpretive approach. I do not claim to synthesize the three; rather, I examine the extent to which they differ because they make different assumptions about the nature of social and organizational reality. I also examine the extent to which they are complementary, because they treat similar problems at a different level of analysis, or invoke in an implicit way principles that are explicit in another perspective. I build on the work of others who have noted the mutual contributions, as well as the conflicts, characterizing the three.

Preparing this paper took me into territory I had not anticipated visiting. Indeed, I considered at least two alternative titles for my paper: 'Confessions of a disillusioned positivist', and 'Pursued by the post-modernist panic'. The first title reflects my sense that the promise of the 1960s – when organizational sociology began a substantial expansion – remains unfulfilled. The major research programs generated by enthusiastic teams of investigators ultimately did not spawn the long-term cumulative growth of theorizing and research glimpsed as a possibility in 1970. The second title reflects my belief that language is, indeed, more than words. Developments in the arts and humanities have been filtering into the social sciences, generating concern over the form our discourse takes and the power that language has to shape our ways of seeing the world (Botti, 1990; Clegg, 1975). *Modes* of theorizing may be as important as *models* of theory, as several other chapters in this book make clear.

At its heart, each perspective contains a core metaphor (or a few related ones) which organizational theorists have used in making sense of their world. On some level, these perspectives are 'fashions' – symbol systems used to make sense of a more fragmented world. Why these perspectives have become fashionable at this juncture in organizational studies is a fascinating question.[1] I cannot, however, contribute anything new to this debate – other contributors to this volume deal with theorizing as an intellectual activity. I concentrate on an examination of theories as products, rather than the process of their construction. I take them for what they purport to be – theories casting light on organizations and their forms. In my conclusions, I take up the question of what the future holds for the three perspectives: integration, coexistence, or oblivion.

Three Approaches

I assume most organizational researchers are familiar with the three approaches, so I only highlight the central themes of each.[2] The first – the ecological approach – explains organizational change by focusing on the distribution of environmental resources and the terms on which they are available. It emphasizes foundings and dissolutions as sources of population level change, and down-plays transformations. The second – the institutional approach – explains organizational change by focusing on the objectified and taken-for-granted nature of organizational environments, as perceived by participants. It emphasizes the value-laden character of institutions and the way in which organizational actions are legitimated when cloaked in an institutionally acceptable rhetoric. The third – the interpretive approach – explains organizational change by focusing on the meaning social actions have for participants. It emphasizes the socially constructed nature of organizational reality and the process by which participants negotiate the meanings of their actions. I turn now to a fuller exposition of some recent themes in these three approaches, as well as an examination of their underlying assumptions.[3]

The Ecological Approach

Ecological approaches to organizational analysis have posed an across-the-board challenge to traditional approaches. Traditional approaches focused primarily on social relations *within* organizations, whereas ecological approaches focus on relations *between* organizations. Ecologists assume that organizations are grouped into populations that share a common fate *vis-à-vis* resources which define niches. Because they compete for resources within the same environment, organizations in a population are in a state of competitive interdependence. Organizations often make common cause with one another as they compete with other populations, thus creating a state of mutual interdependence, or cooperative relations. Competitive and cooperative interdependencies jointly affect which organizations survive and prosper, resulting in a distribution of organizational forms adapted to a particular environmental configuration (Hannan and Freeman, 1977).

   Several assumptions guide ecological analyses.[4] First, ecologists assume that organizational populations can be identified which have 'unit character', responding in similar ways to environmental forces. Populations are dependent upon distinct combinations of resources – called niches – which support them. Populations form as a result of processes that segregate one set of organizations from another, such as incompatible technologies, market demands, or institutional actions such as governmental regulation (Hannan and Freeman, 1986). Populations are also subject to blending processes which blur the boundaries between them, such as the rise of shared technologies, common markets, and institutional actions such as deregulation.

Second, ecologists assume that essential differences between types of organizations can be captured with the concept of organizational form. Debate has raged over whether forms need to be defined a priori, rather than invoked pragmatically in the context of each empirical study (McKelvey and Aldrich, 1983; Carroll, 1984). A common dimension to organizational forms running through many studies is that of specialism versus generalism, which is the scope of the environment claimed by organizations as their domains. Specialists concentrate on a narrow range of their environments, whereas generalists spread themselves out over a broader range. Neither organizational forms nor environmental conditions are studied separately; the interaction of the two is what interests ecologists.

Third, ecologists assume that organizations are relatively structurally inert. This assumption undergirds the principle that selection, rather than adaptation, drives population level change. Populations change because of differential mortality, not because organizations live for ever by adapting to each change as it comes along. Hannan and Freeman (1984) argued that the combination of external selection of organizations displaying reliable and accountable structures *and* the power of internal institutionalization produces structurally inert organizations. Moreover, *if* organizations attempt to change, later in their life cycles, such changes are risky enough to raise their probability of dissolution. *If* organizations survived such risky moves, they could lower their probability of dissolution. Freeman and Hannan's (1989) study of semiconductor firms, for example, shows such an effect.

Fourth, ecologists assume that the most important processes to follow in understanding organizational changes are population demographics: patterns of foundings, transformations, and disbandings. For example, Carroll's (1984) review of three levels of ecological analysis – community, population, and organization – focused heavily on these vital events at each level of analysis.[5] The models ecologists build thus tend to neglect individuals in organizations, decision-making processes, and the microprocesses linking 'environments' to 'organizations'. Most analyses have been at the population level, as Astley (1985) pointed out, and ecologists have mostly neglected the community level, preferring to focus on intrapopulation dynamics rather than on the origins of new populations. However, some theorists have paid more attention to the community level than others (Aldrich and Mueller, 1982; Hage et al., 1989; Tushman and Anderson, 1986).

Fifth, ecologists appreciate, and even celebrate, the high level of volatility found in organizational communities. In studying volatility in populations, ecologists have paid a great deal of attention to one dimension of the life cycle of organizations – the association between organizational age and dissolution in a population of business organizations. Research has found that dissolution rates are high initially, in the first few years after organizations are founded, with rates then dropping as organizations age. Typically, as many as fifty per cent of organizing efforts that get to the founding stage are dissolved within the first two years.[6] In the business sector – but not necessarily in the non-business sector – the dissolution rate then drops substantially for many, but not all, industries. Some of this liability of newness reflects the extreme heterogeneity of foundings: many are quite small, founded by inexperienced persons, and attempt to combine incompatible competencies (McKelvey and Aldrich, 1983; Staber, 1989b). Some of the early dissolutions reflect the effects of youth itself (Aldrich and Auster, 1986), although appropriate controls for organizational characteristics remove much of the liability of newness in many populations (Aldrich et al., 1990; Halliday et al., 1987; Fichman and Levinthal, 1988; Staber, 1989a).

Ecologists, then, focus on populations, rather than individual organizations as their level of analysis, and explain the distribution of organizational forms across populations. Because ecological research is primarily concerned with aggregates of organizations, it down-plays the role of individual actors and their interpretations. Because they assume organizations tend toward structural inertia, ecologists believe foundings and dissolutions, rather than transformations, account for most population level changes. The *assumption* of structural inertia has blinded most ecologists to the need for an empirical examination of the question, and most research has been on foundings and dissolutions, rather than on the likelihood of transformation and the conditions under which it occurs.

Ecologists have built very sophisticated models of population dynamics, using large data sets covering large spans of time. Because their data sets encompass such a broad historical sweep, ecologists typically obtain only limited information on the internal structural features of the organizations in a population. Few studies include information on decision-making processes or strategy formulation.

The Institutional Approach

'Institutionalization' has a number of meanings, depending on which institutional theorist one reads, although the meanings are certainly complementary. Zucker (1987) pointed to the exterior and objective/nonpersonal character of something that has been institutionalized: it takes on rule-like, social fact quality, and when it is embedded in a formal structure, its existence is not tied to a particular actor or situation. She noted that both environments and organizations have been analyzed as 'institutions'. When environments are treated as institutions, an analyst typically adopts a reproductive theme, focusing on how system- or sector-wide social facts are copied on the organizational level, with governmental units seen as the usual source of such facts (Hinings and Greenwood, 1988). One consequence of adopting externally generated facts in pursuit of legitimacy is the decoupling of the technical core of an organization – its operating level – from direct evaluation on the grounds of efficiency.

When organizations are treated as institutions, analysts adopt a generative theme, examining the creation of new cultural elements by organizations, with small groups and/or managers often acquiring new facts by imitating other organizations. Internal organizational processes and the example set by similar organizations are the spark generating new cultural elements. One outcome of successful institutionalization is enhanced organizational stability, and perhaps also a higher level of efficiency (Tolbert, 1988).

DiMaggio (1988) proposed a more imaginative way of describing the essence of the institutional approach. He suggested that a consequence of institutionalization is that individuals do not recognize their own objective interests in a situation. If they do recognize them, they still fail to act upon them. Both consequences follow from people accepting an externally imposed taken-for-granted view of the world.

As with other rather diffuse theoretical perspectives, institutional theory has many faces (Scott, 1987). First, Selznick (1957) originally developed the theme of institutionalization as a process of instilling values, and this line of inquiry was subsequently pursued by his students and intellectual heirs (Clark, Perrow, Zald). Second, Berger and Luckmann (1966) elaborated the theme of institutionalization as a process of creating reality, and they depicted actors as creating an external reality which was subsequently objectified, taken as 'real', and internalized by others.[7] Zucker (1977) and Kurke (1988) tested this notion experimentally.

Third, some analysts treat institutional systems as a class of elements to be investigated, focusing on the role played by cultural elements – symbols, cognitive systems – in organizations. Observers are concerned with why organizations change their structures to conform to an institutionalized pattern (DiMaggio and Powell, 1983; Orru et al., 1991). Scott argued that in modern societies, symbolic systems have become more formally rationalized, with government and the professions playing a key role. Fourth, some analysts treat 'institutions' as distinct societal systems, in keeping with a long tradition in sociology which explores the character of the family, religion, the economy, government and education.

A common theme running through all faces of institutional theory is the power which environments have over organizations, as Scott (1987) made clear. He identified seven different forms of institutional explanation, differing by which types of institutional elements were examined and which causal mechanisms were posited. Most of the verbs used to describe organization–environment relations carry the connotation that environments dominate or overpower organizations, and in this respect, institutional theory resembles population ecology. Organizational structures may be: *imposed* by a higher authority, such as via the coercive power of government (Dobbin et al., 1988); *authorized* by a higher authority when a subordinate unit voluntarily seeks its approval (Singh, Tucker and House, 1986); *induced* when a higher authority offers incentives or sets conditions for recipients of funding (Meyer et al., 1988; Powell, 1988); *acquired* when organizations deliberately choose a structural model, such as via imitative or normative isomorphism (DiMaggio and Powell, 1983); *imprinted* when organizations take on the attributes of their surroundings at the time of their founding (Stinchcombe, 1965); *incorporated* when organizations adapt to the degree of differentiation in their environments (Selznick, 1957); and *by-passed* when lower-level participants pay more attention to normative pressures than technical requirements (Meyer and Rowan, 1977).

I have been struck by how much these descriptions of the institutional approach and its agenda overlap with what I have always thought of as 'just plain sociology'. Consider its message: reality is socially constructed; social life is governed by taken-for-granted rules and norms; symbol systems in modern societies have become increasingly rationalized; and so forth. These assumptions form the core of most introductory textbooks in sociology. The broad reach of the institutional perspective is its major strength, as it is potentially relevant to all levels of analysis and all spans of time, from micro-level interactions to large-scale change in nation-states.

However, this same broad sweep also blurs the boundaries between the institutional perspective and other mainstream sociological views. Commenting on Scott's portrayal of institutional explanations, Heydebrand (1989: 333) argued that 'while the scope of institutionalism has been widened, its internal coherence and precision has been weakened by incorporating various strands of traditional sociology, although omitting the most obvious progenitor of institutionalism: Parsonian systems theory'.[8] Perhaps the perspective will have accomplished its goal when organizational studies takes fuller account of what a thoroughgoing sociological perspective has to offer.

The Interpretive Approach

Organizations are in environments, but environments are also in organizations, as the institutionalists remind us. Once we allow environments and organizations to become intertwined in our theories, we make a place for cultural/interpretive approaches. Institutional analyses tend to emphasize the exteriority and objectivity ('facticity') of institutions, arguing that people experience them as taken-for-granted constraints within which they must live. In their simpler models, ecologists treat populations in an analogous fashion, arguing that organizations are relatively powerless against the combined weight of their competitors. But facades of objectivity sometimes crack, and organizations sometimes take collective action to mitigate competition. Both processes require a new definition of the situation, which actors must construct. Hence, interpretive theorists argue that a fuller understanding of the conditions under which such discontinuities occur requires an interpretive account of social action.[9]

I have taken the liberty of assembling under one heading a variety of approaches, variously headed 'cultural', 'interpretive', 'cognitive', and so forth. The term 'cultural' is more encompassing, but because the institutional approach has strong elements of a cultural approach within it, I chose not to use that label.[10] The various interpretive views have in common their focus on an actor's perspective on life in organizations, and they stress that organizational members must take into account the constraints of their social and physical environments (Fine, 1984).[11]

Some persons who call themselves 'cultural' researchers study values or cognitive interpretations, focusing on the stories, myths, ceremonies and rituals they collect through field work or surveys within organizations. Other who label what they do as 'cultural' focus more on observed behavior, rather than on stories (Van Maanen and Barley, 1984). Some cultural researchers argue very strongly against a purely cognitive approach and take a more materialist approach, maintaining that considerations such as power and privilege heavily affect culture (and an observer's ability to understand it).

Meyerson and Martin (1987) reviewed three different views of organizations and cultural change, and their overview provides an excellent portrait of the interpretive perspective's themes. They labelled the three views *integration*, *differentiation*, and *ambiguity*. The first posits that organizations have unitary cultures, the second assumes multiple cultures, and the third begins with the assumption that there is no such thing as a fixed 'culture' in organizations.[12]

The Unitary View: Cultures as Integrated Entities The *integrationist* view emphasizes consistency and organization-wide consensus, and neglects ambiguity. Organizational culture is usually defined in terms of shared values or cognitions, emphasizing those cultural manifestations that can be interpreted as consistent with, and reinforcing, one another. For example, Fine (1984: 239) pointed out that 'organization structure' has a special meaning in the interpretive perspective: 'a relationship among members, produced and created so that the organization becomes constitutive of the members' provinces of meaning' (Fine, 1984: 239). The ecological perspective does not probe so deeply into the foundations of organizations, whereas the institutional perspective – in most guises – seems quite compatible with such a view.

Meyerson and Martin label this the integration view because it assumes that almost all members share the same taken-for-granted interpretations.

'Culture' is therefore an arena of clarity, a 'clearing' in the jungle of meaninglessness (Wuthnow, 1987). Cultural elements are assumed to have a single, dominant interpretation – typically, that provided by leaders or top managers (Clark, 1972; Ouchi, 1981; Peters and Waterman, 1982). The unitary organizational culture metaphor focuses on myths, symbols, and ceremonies in organizations, and their consequences for participants and organizations. Leaders are responsible for typifying policy and inducing commitment to it (Selznick, 1957). Leaders must demonstrate action on collectively valued purposes, and build community and thus organizational coherence.

Investigators often link cultural strength and consistency to organizational profitability (Kilmann et al., 1985; Schein, 1985). The methodological sophistication of much integrationist research is quite thin, as researchers rely on superficial interviews with small samples of leaders, and define culture as those elements everyone agrees on.

The Multi-culture View: Differentiation and Multiple Meanings The *differentiation* paradigm on organizational culture recognizes lack of consensus across organizational sectors or clusters, coupled with consensus within subcultures. Researchers in this view emphasize how various cultural manifestations are directly inconsistent with each other, such as the different feelings about time held by research versus production departments. To the extent that different clusters of shared values and meanings are found in distinct sub-units, they mark the existence of discrete subcultures. Ambiguity arises when subcultures clash, swirling around the islands of clarity provided to members by their separate subcultures (Van Maanen and Kunda, 1989).

Because researchers using this view are highly cognizant of discrepancies across sub-units, they often use a critical-conflict perspective to interpret their findings (Young, 1989). Others, however, simply note the fact of different subcultures (Martin and Siehl, 1983). Much of the research on multiple cultures within organizations is based on careful participant observation, in the anthropological tradition.

The Ambiguity View: Meanings Are Always in Flux The *ambiguity* view – the third cultural paradigm – emphasizes the intrinsic and inescapable ambiguities in all organizational cultures. Cultural manifestations may be interpreted differently by different people – what is consistent according to one person's view may be inconsistent according to another's (Martin and Meyerson, 1988). Whereas the unitary view assumed consensus as the order of the day, the ambiguity view sees consensus as ephemeral, fluctuating across issues, individuals and organizational life cycles (Meyerson, 1990, 1991). Culture is *not* the island of clarity within a jungle of meaninglessness – it is the jungle itself.[13]

Fine (1984) called this the 'negotiated order view' because it is based upon the way in which actors perceive the structure in which they are embedded (Granovetter, 1985), and assumes that change is inevitable and continuous, though often slow. This latter assumption is a bedrock premise of the evolutionary perspective (Aldrich, 1979), and of the newer though not the older version of population ecology (compare Hannan and Freeman, 1986, with Hannan and Freeman, 1977). Individuals and groups continually make adjustments to the situations in which they find themselves, and relations in organizations ultimately depend on agreement between the participants.

All three culture paradigms assume that people's lives in organizations depend on their sense-making abilities (Fine, 1984). Thus, to study organizations, an analyst must – among other things – understand an organization as its members do. In practice, this means conducting unstructured interviews, doing field work, participant observation, and collecting archived information (Aldrich, 1972; Kleinman, 1984). The expressive side of participation is as important as the task-related side, as organizations do not operate solely on the basis of a rational economic model. As March and his many collaborators have argued, bounded or cognitive rationality governs a great deal of organizational behavior: people behave in ways that seem appropriate at the time (March, 1981).

The three different views of organizational culture differ in several ways that are highly relevant to researchers studying organizations. First, the unitary culture metaphor tends to assume a collective order in which an organization's culture is widely shared, whereas the differentiation and ambiguity views examine the accommodations made by interacting groups and individual members to what they perceive as 'the order'. Integration paradigm researchers focus primarily on organization-wide change caused by external environmental changes or internal changes generated by management. The differentiation paradigm focuses on intergroup conflicts as sources of change, as individuals shift group allegiances or the mix of groups changes. From this view, changes occur in piecemeal fashion, as conveyed by the notion of 'loose coupling' in organizations (Weick, 1976).

Institutional and ecological theories have generally taken an integrationist perspective, though on a different level of analysis than most interpretive researchers. Organizations and their surrounding environments are treated as unitary objects, containing a single view of what is legitimate. In this respect, the ambiguity and multiple cultures views contain a major challenge to the ecological and institutional perspectives, for how can organizations be institutions if they have multiple or ambiguous cultures? If organizations do not cohere as unitary entities, then the 'object' or 'target' of selection by external forces is no longer clear.

Second, researchers using the unitary culture metaphor tend to focus on the fixed or formal genres of folklore studies, examining narratives, rituals and artifacts (Martin, 1982), whereas ambiguity paradigm researchers focus on more ordinary behaviors and the meaning embedded in routine transactions (Boden, 1984).[14] The ambiguity paradigm draws

attention to cognitive, value and behavioral changes at the individual level
of analysis, which then create temporary clusters of issue-specific shared
perceptions at the group or organizational level.

Third, an interpretive perspective is particularly appropriate for studying organizational socialization, and power and conflict in organizations
(Fine, 1984). From an institutional perspective, recruits learning their
roles – the how and the why – are being initiated into the taken-for-
granted aspect of their organizations. From an ecological perspective, the
occasional surprises newcomers encounter (Louis, 1980; Young, 1989) and
slip-ups in cultural transmission (March, 1981) may raise an organization's risk of transformation or dissolution. Misunderstandings and
communication failures are sometimes the cause of conflict in organizations, but deliberate distortions of meanings and withholding of information are also strategies to gain power (Welsh and Slusher, 1986).

Agency and Interest

Points of agreement as well as divergence are apparent from my review
so far. Let me turn now to some specific issues for which a forced
juxtaposition of the three perspectives generates some discomfort and
hence some possible insight.

The Neglect of Agency and Interest

One convergence between population ecology and institutional approaches
is that both relatively neglect the issues of agency and interest, as
compared to the interpretive perspective, and as Reed (1988) noted, the
problem is widespread in organization studies.[15] That is, who or what is
responsible for the structure of the field, or the forms in the population?[16] How did things come to be this way? Who benefits? Institutional
theory concentrates more on reproduction than on creation of organizational fields, and ecology concentrates more on selection than variations.
I note, however, that people who call what they are doing 'institutional
analysis' often differ substantially from one another. DiMaggio (1988),
for example, felt that the key problem in institutional theory is explaining
why things ever change, whereas Zucker (1988b), in the same volume, felt
that the key problem is how social systems maintain some stability![17]

I think the rhetoric of institutional theory, to use DiMaggio's (1988)
phrase, is particularly good at hiding who is responsible for action. Catch
phrases and passive constructions disguise the need for actors who have
taken an interest in a particular social construction, and lead to a neglect
of the organizational entrepreneurs (DiMaggio, 1988) who create the
organizations and associations that ultimately coalesce into a field.
Ecological models attribute agency to forces external to organizations,
and their language empowers 'selection forces' as the driving force behind
change.

Clegg, often using an interpretive approach, has long argued for the importance of agency, although I think he tends to overstate the extent of struggle over control in most organizations. He depicts organizations as engaged in a battle for the 'hearts and minds' of employees, against other actors, such as political parties, the various organs of the state, popular discourse in the media, employers' federations, and trade unions. He recently argued (Clegg, 1989b: 102) that 'organization [note the singular, not the plural] encounters agency in at least two prototypic forms: the person as an agent of signification and the person as an agent of production. Both meaning and body, fused in the person, are capacities for resisting the encroachment of organization control on the discursive play of individuals as well as on their capacities to work'.[18] To achieve control, organizational elites must overcome the resistance of employees. But of course, resistance is variable, and as organizational culture theorists remind us, may be insignificant.

Explicit consideration of the agency and interest question raises several issues that I will address in the remainder of this chapter: what model of organization is assumed by the various perspectives, to what extent do they stress competition as opposed to mutualism, and how predetermined are outcomes?

Two Models of Organizations as Entities

All models of organizations as coherent entities can be reduced to two basic views: organizations as *social systems*, sustained by the roles allocated to their participants, and organizations as *associations* of self-interested parties, sustained by the rewards the participants derive from their association with the organization (Lammers, 1987). These two views have a venerable heritage in the social sciences, going back hundreds of years. Regardless of subtle variations, all perspectives on organizations ultimately use either one or both of these models. The two models are *not* logically mutually exclusive, as each can be used to shed light on some – but not all – aspects of organizational change.

The various institutional approaches, as well as the ecological perspective, rely more on a systemic than an associative model, viewing organizations as relatively coherent, stable entities. The differentiation and ambiguity views of the interpretive perspective – based more on an associative model – lead to the expectation that organizations are constantly at risk of dissolution. Reproduction of structure depends on participants re-subscribing to a shared view of what they jointly are doing. The differentiation perspective emphasizes that different, conflicting views coexist, and that there are differing views in organizations and environments over what is legitimate.

By contrast, an institutional approach, because it emphasizes socialization and other processes that make the transmission of shared meaning easier, helps us understand the usually successful daily reproduction of organizations. An institutional approach also shores up the ecological approach, as it highlights the forces that create and maintain organizations as coherent, integral units. Ecology usually takes organizations as the units that are being selected for/against, and such a technique *must* assume that the organizations cohere as units.

In this respect, an institutional approach is also a challenge to two views which see organizations either as epiphenomena – with no clear distinction between organizations and their environments – or as simply the site upon which various contending societal forces are worked out. Clegg (1989b) expressed such a view, and Burrell (1988), in his appreciative remarks on Foucault, also came close to this position.

Views of organizations as market-places of incentives (Dow, 1988; Georgiou, 1973), bundles of transactions (Williamson, 1981), or arenas of class conflict are in harmony with interpretive views, in so far as they focus on actors' contributions to keeping interaction going. However, the ambiguity view highlights a problem with these views, because they assume negotiation takes place between actors with fixed preferences. A more realistic view incorporates a learning model, in which people discover or modify their preferences as they interact.[19] Organizations, whether unified or differentiated in their cultures, can socialize individuals into accepting a new meaning of their behaviors.

The Assumption of Structural Inertia

Ecological models implicitly assume a systematic model of organizations, reinforced by the assumption that organizations are structurally inert – changing at rates slower than their environments. Many institutional analyses also contain an implicit assumption that organizations only change when it is forced upon them – witness five of the seven verbs used in the explanations Scott (1987) cited: change is imposed, authorized, induced, imprinted, and incorporated. The various paradigms in the interpretive perspective imply a much lower degree of inertia, although they differ substantially in how they account for it.

What is the direct evidence for structural inertia? The best evidence would be based on studies of the same organizations over time, to see *if* they change, what parts change, and at what rate. Unfortunately, we have few such studies. The longest time series are on very simple things, such as size and administrative ratios.

Studies of size changes which use a representative sample of organizations – covering the entire size range – find a pattern of nearly random change (Leonard, 1987). Studies of administrative ratios must, by definition, use only surviving organizations. With that caveat, studies show that ratios do change over time, in predictable ways (the more employees hired, the more managers hired, up to a point). These studies don't really reach the heart of the inertia issue, however.

The key question is, do the things that matter to organizational identity or survival change very much over time, or more precisely, does the rate of change vary over time? That is, are organizations more likely to change their goals, technology, or chief executive earlier in their life than later? And are such changes more frequent in the earlier years than in the later years of organizations' life cycles? We are all familiar with case studies of organizations that have changed – the exposé tradition in sociology (Perrow, 1986) and the case-writing tradition in business schools have seen to that – but large-scale studies of repeated observations on the same organizational attributes over time are rare. Singh et al. (1988), for example, in their study of voluntary social service organizations, found that the rate of change in core features did not vary much over time, and the rate of change in peripheral features actually went up. Their study covered only a fairly short time span of 13 years, however, which may be too short to observe opportunities for major changes.[20]

Broadening our search, we could look in the business strategy literature for studies of changes. However, most strategy studies make dynamic inferences from cross-sectional data, and so they are not of much help. During the 1980s growing awareness of techniques for performing dynamic analysis produced some useful studies, such as those on diversification, top executive changes, and changes in corporate form (Fligstein, 1990). These studies tell us that changes *do* occur, though they do not report whether *rates of change* go up or down over time. Again, most of these studies are of the very largest business firms, for which data is publicly available, and *not* for representative samples.

Levels of Analysis: Opportunity and Constraint

Returning now to the issue of agency and interest, we can posit four levels of analysis of organizational change: group, organization, population and community. At each level, the units of analysis are the constituent components and the agents of change at that level. The types of relations between units that are relevant to social change differ across levels: at the group level, we examine relations between individuals; at the organizational level, relations between groups; at the population level, interorganizational relations; and at the community level, relations between populations. This nesting of levels and components is shown in Table 2.1.

Agency, then, arises from the collective actions of interested parties (individuals, groups, organizations, populations) at each level.[21] These actions have the potential of transforming relations at the next highest level, *depending on whether the action is successfully institutionalized*. Thus, collective action by organizations can transform a population, as when the individual firms in an industry's early days succeed in forming an employers' association to deal with workers' wage demands, and thus standardize costs across the industry (Staber and Aldrich, 1983). Or, cooperative alliances between populations of producers, suppliers, and distributors can transform a community from a set of fiercely competing

Table 2.1 *Levels of Analysis, Agency, Structure, and Relations Examined*

Level of analysis	Components	Agency	Structure	Relations examined
Community	Populations			Between populations
		↑	↓	
Populations	Organizations			Between organizations
		↑	↓	
Organizations	Groups			Between groups
		↑	↓	
Groups	Individuals			Between individuals

populations to a set of mutually regarding populations (Lorenzoni and Ornati, 1988). Collective action in such cases will only persist if institutionalized, and the barriers to it are formidable (Olson, 1965). Interpretive approaches might ask how the actors in a situation begin to share a collective sense that joint action is necessary and feasible – why is meaningful action no longer individual but instead collective?

Seen from the top down, the levels can be viewed as setting constraints or posing opportunities for the components below them. Constraints may be set at population or community levels if a competence-destroying innovation in an organization or competing population transforms the conditions of existence for other organizations in the population or a neighbor population (Tushman and Anderson, 1986). Examples include new product classes developed, such as automobiles for horse-drawn wagons (Lawrence and Dyer, 1983), or substitutes for existing products, such as diesel for steam locomotives (Marx, 1976). At the organizational level, the institutionalization of standard operating procedures in a population may preclude *local* adaptations that would be more effective, as occurred in the economies of Soviet bloc countries after World War II.

An example of increasing opportunities for organizations produced by populations is often observed in the early stages of a population's expansion (Brittain and Freeman, 1980). As businesses grow, they hire many workers who are in the early stages of their careers, and eventually the youngest cohorts of such workers bump up against the cohorts immediately above them, who are also fairly young. Younger workers, in their attempts to make sense of their organizational experiences and plan their careers, realize that their chances for moving up rapidly in a company with such a young age structure are fairly low, and so some leave to join newly founded businesses, or even found their own. So, population growth fuels the organizational formation process, to the extent that workers *interpret* slow intra-firm promotions in a fast-growing industry as a signal to look elsewhere for opportunities.

The three approaches cut across all the levels of analysis identified in

Table 2.1, for they help us understand the conditions sustaining communities, populations, organizations, and groups. If we view the levels as nested, then the components from the 'lower' level are the agents for the reproduction of the 'higher' level. For example, the reproduction of populations depends on the persistence of individual organizations and the environmental conditions which support them. Simultaneously, the reproduction of individual organizations is contingent upon – depending upon which view of organizational culture one accepts – elites maintaining an integrated, unitary view *or* subgroups reaching a temporary accommodation *or* members finding grounds for shared commitment to the organization's existence, in spite of ambiguities and doubts.

Of course, external conditions at any particular level are also part of the structure of constraint sustaining that level. So, components are the agents, and the next higher level's components are the constraints on the agents. For example, Robins (1987), in his critique of transactions-cost theory, argued that analysts need to make a distinction between social and political conditions existing at a given time and place, and the economic/ organizational processes unfolding within their sociopolitical framework. Thus, in criticizing the priority Williamson (1981) gave to transactions-cost economizing, Robins argued that the history of the nineteenth century is not really a story of hierarchy displacing markets, but rather a story of social and political centralization creating the conditions making large-scale commerce and manufacturing possible. Robins is addressing the highest level in Table 2.1, conditions sustaining the community level.

Competition and Mutualism

The interpretive, ecological and institutional approaches diverge in the extent to which they emphasize competitive versus cooperative behavior within and between organizations and populations of organizations. As I have already reviewed the three varieties of the interpretive approach and the assumptions they make about internal consensus, I concentrate in this section on the other two perspectives. However, I draw on all three to show how an analyst might blend them to produce a more comprehensive understanding of organizational change than is possible with one perspective alone.

An ecological approach takes seriously the institutional argument that networks bind widely dispersed organizations together (Zucker, 1988b), though so far most ecological research has been directed toward competition rather than cooperation through networks. By contrast, institutional theory, in focusing on taken-for-granted aspects of reality and conformity to them, emphasizes mutualism or cooperation, rather than competition. Zucker (1986), for example, presented an extremely detailed historical account of the transformation of the USA's economic system, in which she stressed the creation of an active market for institutionally based trust. She stressed the spread of institutional mechanisms to produce trust and the extent to which modern economic life takes such mechanisms for granted, the 'external world known in common'.

We can distinguish between direct and indirect competition. *Direct* competition occurs between organizations in the same population (mutually supportive action may also occur in the same population). *Indirect*, or diffuse, competition occurs between organizations in different populations. Some indirect competition is between populations that are struggling for the same niche, but other forms are more diffuse. For example, many organizations in different populations seek college graduates as white-collar workers, and are thus competing with thousands of other organizations. In this sense, every organization added to the community of populations has a small, perhaps almost infinitesimal, effect on every other organization.[22] Some effects are negative, such as for workers, capital or members. Other effects are positive, such as organizations that create technological breakthroughs benefiting others, or organizations that train workers who subsequently disperse to other sites. Such positive interdependencies are a link between ecology and the institutional perspective.

The institutional perspective provides a framework for describing the collective action and institutional practices which sometimes protect organizations against the effects of competition, though they might not mitigate all of its effects. For example, several recent studies of organizational mortality have found a curvilinear relation between population density (number of organizations) and dissolution rates (for example, Carroll and Hannan, 1989a; Hannan and Freeman, 1988; Aldrich et al., 1990). Early in some populations' lives, dissolution rates *decrease* as the population grows, but then eventually rise again as the population grows further toward its carrying capacity. Hannan and Freeman (1988) interpreted this finding as a result of two processes: legitimacy and competition. Early in a population's life, such as for newspapers, trade unions or trade associations, the form is not yet perceived as completely legitimate by authorities or even the persons the organizations are created to serve. As the population grows, acceptance of the form spreads, especially if the early organizations take successful collective action. This legitimacy effect should decrease the indifference or even hostility faced by organizations, and thus dissolution rates would continue to drop, were it not for the intra-population competitive pressures organizations face as the population reaches its carrying capacity.

Delacroix et al. (1989) questioned the generality of this formulation, arguing that most *business* organizations in capitalist societies need not worry about their legitimacy in the eyes of governmental authorities or the general population. Perhaps a more general explanation, fitting both business and non-business organizations, can be derived from a blending of the interpretive, institutional, and ecological perspectives (Delacroix and Rao, 1989). Early in a population's life cycle, knowledge of the form is not widespread and entrepreneurs may not truly understand how to copy it. Many local variations are attempted, with mixed success. However, as information about successful forms spreads, as employees with experience of working for successful organizations are recruited, and as more prosperous entrepreneurs are attracted, dissolution rates in the population should drop.

Research on organizational and industry-wide learning curves suggests that successful routines *can* be transferred from one organization to another (Zimmerman, 1982). In their study of the construction of Liberty Ships during World War II, Argote et al. (1990) found that shipyards beginning production later in the war benefited from knowledge acquired from shipyards that had begun production earlier. However, once they had begun production, shipyards did not benefit from further transfers of knowledge as workers switched jobs between shipyards. Halliday et al. (1987) found that state bar associations founded later in the population's growth apparently benefited from the knowledge gained from earlier foundings. Similarly, Aldrich et al. (1990) found that trade association disbandings were reduced in industries which had large numbers of already existing associations.

The exchange between the ecological and institutional perspectives over the issue of mutualism versus competition has been very fruitful.[23] Ecologists are exploring other forms of mutualism, such as the relationship between large and small firms in the same industry (Barnett and Carroll, 1987; Barnett and Amburgey, 1990). Institutionalists are continuing to point out how difficult it is to assess the overall balance between such effects, simply because they are so diffuse. For example, DiMaggio (1988: 19) pointed out that creation of the Environmental Protection Agency (EPA) in the USA 'empowered, legitimated, and to some extent, institutionalized environmental interest groups, which were, in fact, necessary to bolster the claims of EPA staff to providing a service that the public demanded. Once legitimated, however, the environmental groups generated escalating demands for public action that tended to delegitimate the federal agency.'

Researchers using an interpretive perspective might approach this issue rather differently, especially if they assume organizations have multiple or ambiguous cultures. Whereas ecological and institutional theorists might look for isomorphism between environmental values/norms and organizational characteristics, these interpretive researchers would ask, 'isomorphic with what?' They would suggest studies of deviation and difference, in addition to the usual studies of conformity with unitary standards of the appropriate external structures. Ambiguity paradigm researchers might go further and ask how the interpretation and meaning of external forces is ambiguous across individuals and over time.

Indeterminacy

Another issue on which the three perspectives diverge somewhat concerns the extent to which social life is seen as indeterminate versus well-structured. The ecological perspective, because it ultimately is nested within an evolutionary perspective, treats the future as very much an open question. The interpretive perspective, because it sees social reality as built from the bottom up, also allows room for the play of chance, creativity and accidents. The institutional perspective is harder to place. Although several programmatic statements have included admonitions to produce more process-oriented research, actual studies to date have mostly taken the existence of institutions for granted and have examined their spread, adoption and the like, rather than their creation.

People do not construct institutions. Instead, they construct solutions to very specific problems, as the interpretive perspective reminds us. The accumulation of solutions – see Table 2.1 – may eventually result in organizations, then populations, then communities, but the process may require tens of thousands of trials and errors, occurring within historically conditioned constraints. This sense of indeterminacy is missing in most current institutional accounts.

Indeed, one of the hardest principles of ecological and interpretive theory for sociologists to accept is the indeterminacy of outcomes, which must be explained after the fact. Zucker (1988b: 27–8), in reviewing theories of institutional entrepreneurship, noted that such theories attribute a specific institutional framework to the relative success that competing groups of leaders have in imposing their preferred solutions on a situation, using individual or class-based power differentials. She was troubled by the difficulty of generalizing from such explanations, because 'the particular historical details that lead to the success of a given institutional entrepreneur or group of entrepreneurs and the failure of another, defy theoretical prediction'. She also observed that some collective action theorists build the accidental intersection of self-interest into their explanations, noting that when the interests of different collective actors converge, even by accident and only temporarily, radical change can occur (Skocpol, 1979). Zucker (1988b: 28) worried that 'convergence explanations lend themselves to post hoc theorizing because it is difficult to predict just which interests will converge and under what conditions convergence is more or less likely'. However, this is the nature of ecological and interpretive explanations: we can say that some outcome has occurred because of some prior sequence of events, even though we could *not* have foreseen, prior to the fact, that particular sequence unfolding (Aldrich, 1979: Chapter 2).

The openness of the ecological approach gives it a good fit with interpretive approaches. At the micro level, the future is always open (within limits, of course), and creativity, strategy, ambition, accidents, luck and other forces drive changes in social life. In this respect, the form of an ecological explanation and an interpretive explanation are isomorphic.

Persons unsympathetic to an evolutionary perspective often commit the retrospective fallacy, viewing earlier events as though they were controlled by their subsequent outcomes, even though at the time of their occurrence many other outcomes were equally probable. This tendency is illustrated in Perrow's (1985) reaction to Langton's (1984) evolutionary account of the founding of Josiah Wedgwood's pottery factory and the subsequent emergence of the British pottery industry. Langton, using detailed historical data, showed that the successful bureaucratization of Wedgwood's potbank resulted from the interaction of Wedgwood's strategy for organizational domination (using particular strategies to hire and train workers) and certain environmental changes (a rising standard of living, an increased demand for pottery, and improvements in transportation and communication). Langton treated Wedgwood as a creative actor who, by his successful example, influenced others in the industry to imitate him. He also tried to demonstrate that Wedgwood's ability to bureaucratize his firm was dependent upon his power to control a wide array of positive and negative sanctions over his workers. In keeping with evolutionary/ecological theory, Langton's was a non-teleological argument, with the outcome ultimately dependent on the interaction between Wedgwood's actions and the context of the times.[24]

Perrow, in his critique, used the benefit of historical hindsight to argue that Wedgwood was but the first step on the road to the coercion and exploitation of workers. Perrow treated Wedgwood *not* as a creative actor, but as an agent of historical forces, evidently playing out a role pre-ordained by his class position and the interests of the British State. Using a grand narrative, he painted a picture in which the whole was carved up into parts, each of which then was seen as contributing to a long-term outcome known to us today, but most assuredly not at all clear to Wedgwood, his workers, or British governmental elites. Elites were painted as all-powerful and all-knowing, manipulating workers and the State with some grand scheme in mind.

Imposing meaning on historical events from knowledge of outcomes is a tempting trap, but it is wrong. The interpretive perspective is one antidote to such folly, and the ecological perspective's clarity in providing falsifiable hypotheses is another. To the extent that the institutional perspective overlaps with traditional sociological approaches to explanation, it is subject to the retrospective fallacy.

Conclusion

I have reviewed three approaches to the understanding of organizational change – ecological, institutional and interpretive – in an attempt to show that each has something to contribute to our understanding of organizations. Some commentators have emphasized the conflicting assumptions of the three perspectives, whereas others have noted the complementarity, rather than conflict, characterizing the three. I reviewed the assumptions underlying each, and noted where two perspectives seemed to share a common theme, as well as points of conflict.

Two models of organization underlie all perspectives – a systemic and an associative model – with the ecological and institutional perspectives favoring the systemic model and the interpretive perspective favoring the associative model. In reviewing how each perspective treats issues of agency and interest, I proposed a simple scheme, showing how four levels of analysis are nested within each other, and argued that the perspectives cut across all levels. Ecological analyses have emphasized competitive more than cooperative interdependence, but as institutionalists make their case for the significance of collective action in organizational populations and communities, mutualism is achieving a more central empirical status. The ecological and interpretive perspectives have accorded greater theoretical primacy to the indeterminacy of organizational outcomes, and as such, pose a challenge to institutional explanations with an historical bent.

Paradigm Incommensurability

Are the three perspectives incommensurable? One's answer to this question depends upon one's assumption about the scientific and normative structure of our field. We can consider three possibilities, paralleling the three views within the interpretive perspective: a unitary, normal science view, a multiple conflicting paradigms view, and a totally pragmatic, anti-positivist view.

Unification?

First, if one adopts a 'normal science' approach to organizational theorizing, the question is unanswerable. What would a strict positivist conclude after observing the relation between research and theory in our field? Too often theoretical developments appear driven primarily by responses to other theorizing, rather than by the accumulation of empirically tested hypotheses and well-grounded generalizations. Organization studies resembles many other social sciences in the way that it systematically disdains the two processes central to scientific endeavor: attempted replication of previous findings, and publication of negative findings. Instead, we are treated to 'new' concepts and 'positive' findings, as authors try to differentiate their products from their potential competitors.

From this view, we will not be able to answer the question of paradigm incommensurability until the field takes a normal science approach to theorizing and research – replications, publishing negative findings, and so forth. Presently, we have persons calling themselves 'theorists' who need not take seriously the stream of contradictory research findings pouring out of various research programs (Stinchcombe, 1986: 84–5). 'Theorizing' is an activity divorced from 'research'. Can we judge incommensurability by only reading the theories? In actual research practice, do investigators find combining the perspectives a simple matter? We might never know.

Multiplicity?

Second, all of the perspectives I have reviewed have achieved significant standing today because, at their core, they have groups of dedicated researchers working on empirical research to test hypotheses derived from the perspectives. They read one another's papers, hold conferences, and issue edited volumes collecting recent empirical work (Carroll, 1987; Frost et al., 1985; Pondy et al., 1981; Powell and DiMaggio, 1991; Singh, 1990; Zucker, 1988a). In the process of constructing theory groups they have bounded themselves, and organizational boundaries can be extremely difficult to surmount. The groups work very hard at emphasizing how they differ from one another, and investigators have a stake in stressing their incompatibilities.

Multiple perspectives can have an invigorating effect on organizational research, causing investigators to stretch their minds to cope with apparently contradictory views. Investigators might ask themselves what someone from another perspective might do with the same information. Some might even argue that we are intellectually harmed by confining ourselves to one mode of thinking. Although we do not need to convert to every new perspective that comes along, we can at least acknowledge it.

Ambiguity?

Finally, if one adopts a more pragmatic – dare one say 'postmodern'? – approach, and asks simply, 'Do the three groups talk to each other?', the answer is 'Some of the time'. They even occasionally work on similar problems, though the similarity is often obscured by different descriptive vocabularies. Ecologists and institutionalists are arguing with one another, but they are also using one another's ideas. Some institutionalists seem quite sympathetic to the interpretive perspective, as both share a concern for the meaning of events in organizations for participants. Both the interpretive and institutional perspectives lend themselves more readily to a political analysis of organizations than does the ecological perspective.

Ecologists, however, appear wedded to a method of data collection and analysis that renders empirical concern for interpretive analysis very difficult. Similarly, interpretive researchers' passion for direct observation makes it difficult for them to accumulate the sorts of massive data sets that fascinate ecologists. Gioia et al. (1989: 524) contrasted an 'interpretive' with a 'positivist' paradigm and argued that 'When one adopts different "lenses" with which to view ostensibly the same organizational phenomena, one simply "sees" different things'.[25] From their point of view, paradigms should be chosen to match researchers' purposes.

Perhaps we should be content with analyses that interest, inform and provoke us. As our interests are constantly changing, we should not be surprised if authors of books and journal articles change their targets fairly frequently. If the latest developments in French post-structuralism find an audience in Lancaster, New Zealand and North Carolina, we should be pleased that people in different cultures have apparently found a common ground around which to organize their discourse.

Notes

Conversations with Nicole Biggart, Judith Blau, Paul DiMaggio, Mark Fruin, Sherryl Kleinman and Lynne Zucker helped me clarify my thoughts on some of the issues discussed in this paper. Joanne Martin, Hope Botti, Wolf Heydebrand, Gary Fine, Udo Staber and Gabriele Wiedenmayer provided extremely helpful and constructive written comments on earlier drafts.

1 I am indebted to Gary Fine for drawing my attention to this way of phrasing the question.

2 I noted with great interest that Reed's (1985) book on redirections in organizational analysis included *no* mention of the three perspectives I discuss in this chapter. Clearly, we have different conceptions of what constitutes modern organization theory, and this divergence will hopefully contribute to making this book challenging reading for people who wish to understand the current agitation in the organization studies field!

3 Nicole Biggart suggested I treat these three perspectives as representatives of a two-by-two classification scheme. On the first axis, we could classify perspectives as subjectivist or objectivist, and on the second axis we would classify them as micro or macro. The interpretive perspective is then representative of the micro-subjectivist view, the institutional perspective represents the macro-subjectivist view, and the ecological perspective is the macro-objectivist view. Missing, of course, is the micro-objectivist view. I concentrate on the first three because they are the most sociological – in the micro-objectivist category would fall behavioral psychology, agency theory, and probably transactions-cost economics theories.

4 Because ecological theory stands in the tradition of evolutionary theory, a fundamental grasp of the principles of evolutionary analysis is quite helpful in understanding what ecologists are trying to do (Dawkins, 1986).

5 I had initially envisioned the 'natural selection' approach as applicable to all levels of analysis, as it was described in Aldrich and Pfeffer (1976). However, with the publication of Hannan and Freeman's (1977) landmark and now dominant statement, the 'selection approach' became synonymous with 'population ecology'. Carroll (1984) used the term 'ecological models' to cover more levels of analysis than simply populations.

6 Finding new organizations and tracking their liability of newness is not an easy matter. Katz and Gartner (1988) pointed out four dimensions along which new organizations emerge. Their article is a nice example of how ecological, institutional and interpretive perspectives can be combined to shed light on a substantive issue. For an attempt to find new firms, see Aldrich et al., 1989.

7 Berger and Luckmann did not, however, identify what they were doing as 'institutional theory' – they were simply developing one of the core themes of sociology. Compare, for example, Berger and Luckmann to Berger's (1963) introductory sociology text, *Invitation to Sociology*.

8 One of the first explicit statements on organizational environments as institutional–cultural phenomena was contained in Talcott Parsons' two essays in the inaugural (1956) volume of the *Administrative Science Quarterly*. Parsons pointed out that institutional

patterns within organizations must be compatible with those of other organizations and social units within society as a whole. Parsons explored the various complexes of institutionalized rules governing organizational behavior, identifying supra-organizational societal norms as the context within which authority and contracts within and between organizations are carried out.

9 My observations in this section depend heavily upon Joanne Martin's extensive comments on an earlier version of this chapter.

10 The interpretive perspective includes many other schools of thought, of course. I have chosen only a few for ease of exposition. I define 'interpretive' quite broadly, and thus would include such classic studies as Blau's (1955) *Dynamics of Bureaucracy*, based on field work in several bureaucracies, as well as more recent monographs, such as Biggart, 1988, which uses a Weberian social action approach, Hochschild, 1983, which uses a symbolic interactionist approach, and Powell, 1985, which is more eclectic.

11 Interpretive theorists are not interested in actors as individuals but as members of social categories.

12 We might relabel them the mono-culture, multi-culture, and messy-culture views.

13 Joanne Martin provided this well-turned phrase.

14 The various versions of the interpretive perspective are well-displayed in a special issues of the *Administrative Science Quarterly* on 'organizational culture'. See Smircich (1983).

15 'Agency' is a fancy word meaning 'who does what to whom, and why'.

16 As Wolf Heydebrand reminded me, posing the issue as 'who is responsible' frames the question in a way that fits methodological individualism or even rational choice models, and is itself a theoretical statement. Sandelands and Drazin (1989), in their critique of the *language* in which many theories are cast, ultimately find themselves in this position, apparently willingly.

17 Heydebrand (1989: 333) agreed with DiMaggio, arguing that in practice, 'the institutional perspective focuses on the process of symbolic reproduction of form rather than on the nature [and] extent of change of the macrocultural, institutional environment. Whether there are few or many institutional environments, any one of them is seen as relatively stable and is largely taken for granted, although attempts have been made to distinguish technical from institutional environments' (Scott, 1983).

18 As with many other social scientists who sometimes treat sociology as a mode of philosophical discourse, Clegg occasionally reifies abstract categories. (But see his (1989a) book on power.) Thus, the substantial heterogeneity of organizational populations is reduced to 'organization'. 'Organization' is not an actor, and cannot 'confront' anything – organizational elites, of course, can. In an encounter such as 'Godzilla meets Bambi', the singular of each is quite appropriate. There is only one of each type, so far as I am aware, and readers are in no danger of overgeneralizing from the outcome. For a recent critique of overcategorization in the social sciences, see Bates and Peacock (1989).

19 Critical theorists might quality this statement further with the observation that people may be manipulated into a view of the world more compatible with the organization's interests, as opposed to their own (Perrow, 1986).

20 For example, in the United States, the March of Dimes and the YMCA survived for decades before changing circumstances compelled them to change their goals (Aldrich, 1979: 211–17). Similarly, in West Germany, an organization to assist persons disabled by the war was founded directly after World War II, and more than three decades later – in the early 1980s – it changed to representing *all* disabled persons.

21 Coleman (1957) made this point in his short monograph on community conflict.

22 I am indebted to Michael Hannan for this idea.

23 In the first direct clash between institutionalists and ecologists over how to interpret findings of density dependence, Zucker (1989) argued that Carroll and Hannan (1989a) were misinterpreting their results for several reasons, including (1) they did not directly measure legitimacy and its relationship to density; and (2) they mis-specified their models by not explicitly including historical events in them. In their reply, Carroll and Hannan

(1989b) pointed out that (1) finding reliable direct measures of legitimacy over long historical periods is nearly impossible; (2) they have extensive and rich historical detail on the early history of the newspaper populations they studied; (3) they were following the common practice of inferring legitimacy from its effects, a tactic practiced by institutionalists as well as ecologists; (4) to include unique historical events for each population would make it extremely difficult to generalize across populations; and (5) history *is* in their models, in the data structure and in the data analysis (as year). Of course, as Wolf Heydebrand reminded me, having an annual data set or time series does not necessarily make the data set historical – the analysis could still be genetic-structural, with little meaningful historical interpretation.

24 The word 'progress' never appeared in his article, and Langton was careful to point out the substantial changes wrought in workers' lives by the bureaucratization of work.

25 Unfortunately, they treated 'interpretive' as synonymous with 'qualitative', and 'positivist' as synonymous with 'quantitative'. Meanings, if properly coded, are every bit as subject to quantitative analysis as any other social science data.

References

Aldrich, Howard E. (1972) 'Sociability in Mensa: Characteristics of interaction among strangers', *Urban Life*, 1 (July): 167–86.

Aldrich, Howard E. (1979) *Organizations and Environments*. Englewood Cliffs, NJ: Prentice-Hall.

Aldrich, Howard E. and Pfeffer, Jeffrey (1976) 'Environments of organizations', in A. Inkeles (ed.), *Annual Review of Sociology*, 2. Palo Alto, CA: Annual Reviews, pp. 79–105.

Aldrich, Howard E. and Herker, Diane (1977) 'Boundary spanning roles and organization structure', *Academy of Management Review*, 2 (April): 217–30.

Aldrich, Howard E. and Mueller, Susan (1982) 'The evolution of organizational forms', in L.L. Cummings and Barry Staw, *Research in Organizational Behavior*. Greenwich, CT: JAI Press, pp. 33–87.

Aldrich, Howard E. and Auster, Ellen R. (1986) 'Even dwarfs started small', in L.L. Cummings and Barry Staw, *Research in Organizational Behavior*, 8: 165–98.

Aldrich, Howard E., Kalleberg, Arne L., Marsden, Peter V. and Cassell, James (1989) 'In pursuit of evidence: Strategies for locating new businesses', *Journal of Business Venturing*, 4 (November): 367–86.

Aldrich, Howard, E., Staber, Udo H., Zimmer, Catherine R. and Beggs, John J. (1990) 'Minimalism and organizational mortality: Patterns of disbanding among US trade associations, 1900–1983', in Jitendra Singh (ed.), *Organizational Evolution*. Beverly Hills, CA: Sage.

Argote, Linda, Beckman, Sara L. and Epple, Dennis (1990) 'The persistence and transfer of learning in industrial settings', *Management Science*, 36 (February): 140–54.

Astley, W. Graham (1985) 'The two ecologies: Population and community perspectives on organizational evolution', *Administrative Science Quarterly*, 30, 2 (June): 224–41.

Barnett, William and Glenn, Carroll R. (1987) 'Competition and mutualism among early telephone companies', *Administrative Science Quarterly*, 32: 400–21.

Barnett, William and Amburgey, Terry (1990) 'Do larger organizations generate stronger competition?' in Jitendra Singh (ed.), *Organizational Evolution*. Beverly Hills, CA: Sage.

Bates, Frederick L. and Peacock, Walter Gillis (1989) 'Conceptualizing social structure: The misuse of classification in structural modeling', *American Sociological Review*, 54 (August): 565–77.

Berger, Peter (1963) *Invitation to Sociology: A Humanistic Perspective*. Garden City, NY: Doubleday.

Berger, Peter and Luckmann, Thomas (1966) *The Social Construction of Reality*. New York: Doubleday.

Biggart, Nicole W. (1988) *Charismatic Capitalism*. Chicago: University of Chicago Press.

Blau, Peter M. (1955) *The Dynamics of Bureaucracy*. Chicago: University of Chicago.

Boden, Deidre (1984) 'The business of talk: Meetings as occasioned organizational events'. Ph.D. dissertation, Department of Sociology, University of California, Santa Barbara.

Botti, Hope (1990) 'My conversations in Pirelli: A research tale'. Paper prepared for presentation at the International Sociological Association meetings, Madrid.

Brittain, Jack and Freeman, John Henry (1980) 'Organizational proliferation and Density Dependent Selection', in John Kimberly, Robert Miles and Associates (eds), *Organizational Life Cycles*. San Francisco: Jossey-Bass, pp. 291–338.

Burrell, Gibson (1988) 'Modernism, post modernism and organizational analysis. 2: The contribution of Michel Foucault', *Organization Studies*, 9 (2): 221–35.

Carroll, Glenn R. (1984) 'Organizational ecology', *Annual Review of Sociology*, 10: 71–93.

Carroll, Glenn R. (ed.) (1987) *Ecology Models of Organization*. Cambridge, MA: Ballinger.

Carroll, Glenn R. and Hannan, Michael T. (1989a) 'Density dependence in the evolution of populations of newspaper organizations', *American Sociological Review*, 54 (August): 524–41.

Carroll, Glenn R. and Hannan, Michael T. (1989b) 'On using institutional theory in studying organizational populations', *American Sociological Review*, 54 (August): 545–8.

Carroll, Glenn R. and Hannan, Michael T. (1990) 'Density delay in the evolution of organizational populations: A model and five empirical tests', in Jitendra Singh (ed.), *Organizational Evolution*. Beverly Hills, CA: Sage.

Clark, Burton (1972) 'The organizational saga in higher education', *Administrative Science Quarterly*, 17 (June): 178–84.

Clegg, Stewart (1975) *Power, Rule, and Domination*. London: Routledge and Kegan Paul.

Clegg, Stewart (1989a) *Frameworks of Power*. London: Sage.

Clegg, Stewart (1989b) 'Radical revisions: Power, discipline and organizations', *Organization Studies*, 10 (1): 97–115.

Coleman, James S. (1957) *Community Conflict*. Glencoe, IL: Free Press.

Dawkins, Richard (1986) *The Blind Watchmaker*. New York: Norton.

Delacroix, Jacques and Carroll, Glenn R. (1983) 'Organizational foundings: An ecological study of the newspaper industries of Argentina and Ireland', *Administrative Science Quarterly*, 28 (2): 274–91.

Delacroix, Jacques and Rao, Hayagreeva M.V. (1989) 'Density dependence in the death rate of organizations: A critique'. Unpublished paper.

Delacroix, Jacques, Swaminathan, Anand and Solt, Michael (1989) 'Density dependence versus population dynamics: An ecological study of failings in the California wine industry', *American Sociological Review*, 54: 245–62.

DiMaggio, Paul (1988) 'Interest and agency in institutional theory', in Lynne G. Zucker (ed.), *Institutional Patterns and Organizations*. Cambridge, MA: Ballinger, pp. 3–21.

DiMaggio, Paul and Powell, Walter W. (1983) 'The iron cage revisited: Institutional isomorphism and collective rationality in organizational fields', *American Sociological Review*, 48: 147–60.

Dobbin, Frank, Edelman, Lauren, Meyer, John W., Scott, W. Richard and Swidler, Ann (1988) 'The expansion of due process in organizations', in Lynne G. Zucker (ed.), *Institutional Patterns and Organizations*. Cambridge, MA: Ballinger, pp. 71–98.

Dow, Gregory K. (1988) 'Configurational and coactivational views of organizational structure', *Academy of Management Review*, 13: 53–64.

Fichman, Mark and Levinthal, Daniel (1988) 'Honeymoons and the liability of adolescence: A new perspective on duration dependence in social and organizational relationships'. Paper presented at the Academy of Management meetings, Anaheim, CA.

Fine, Gary (1984) 'Negotiated order and organizational cultures', *Annual Review of Sociology*, 10: 239–62.

Fligstein, Neil (1990) *The Transformation of Corporate Control*. Cambridge, MA: Harvard University Press.

Freeman, John Henry and Hannan, Michael T. (1989) 'An ecological analysis of mortality in the semi-conductor industry'. Paper presented at the EGOS conference, West Berlin.

Frost, Peter, Moore, Larry, Louis, Meryl, Lundberg, Craig and Martin, Joanne (1985) *Organizational Culture*. Beverly Hills, CA: Sage.

Georgiou, Petro (1973) 'The goal paradigm and notes towards a counter paradigm', *Administrative Science Quarterly*, 18: 291-310.

Gioia, Dennis A., Donnellon, Anne and Sims, Henry P., Jr. (1989) 'Communication and cognition in appraisal: A tale of two paradigms', *Organization Studies*, 10 (4): 503-29.

Granovetter, Mark (1985) 'Economic action and social structure: The problem of embeddedness', *American Journal of Sociology*, 91: 481-510.

Hage, Jerald, Collins, Paul, Hull, Frank and Teachman, Jay (1989) 'Liabilities of organizational form in a family of populations: The case of capital intensive American manufacturing in 1973-87'. Unpublished paper, Center for Innovation and Department of Sociology, University of Maryland.

Halliday, Terence, Powell, Michael and Granfors, Mark (1987) 'Minimalist organizations: Vital events in state bar associations, 1870-1930', *American Sociological Review*, 52: 456-71.

Hannan, Michael T. and Freeman, John Henry (1977) 'The population ecology of organizations', *American Journal of Sociology*, 82: 929-64.

Hannan, Michael T. and Freeman, John Henry (1984) 'Structural inertia and organizational change', *American Sociological Review*, 49: 149-64.

Hannan, Michael T. and Freeman, John Henry (1986) 'Where do organizational forms come from?' *Sociological Forum*, 1: 50-72.

Hannan, Michael T. and Freeman, John Henry (1988) 'The ecology of organizational mortality: American labor unions, 1836-1985', *American Journal of Sociology*, 94: 25-52.

Hannan, Michael T. and Freeman, John Henry (1989) *Organizational Ecology*. Cambridge, MA: Harvard University.

Heydebrand, Wolf V. (1989) 'New Organizational forms', *Work and Occupations*, 16 (August): 323-57.

Hinings, Bob and Greenwood, Royston (1988) 'The normative prescription of organizations', in Lynne G. Zucker (ed.), *Institutional Patterns and Organizations*. Cambridge, MA: Ballinger, pp. 53-70.

Hochschild, Arlie (1983) *The Managed Heart: Commercialization of Human Feeling*. Berkeley, CA: University of California Press.

Katz, Jerome and Gartner, William (1988) 'Properties of emerging organizations', *Academy of Management Review*, 13 (July): 429-41.

Killman, Ralph, Saxton, M. and Serpa, R. (1985) *Gaining Control of the Corporate Culture*. San Francisco, CA: Jossey-Bass.

Kleinman, Sherryl (1984) *Equals Before God: Seminarians as Humanistic Professionals*. Chicago: University of Chicago Press.

Kurke, Lance (1988) 'Does adaptation preclude adaptability? Strategy and performance', in Lynne G. Zucker (ed.), *Institutional Patterns and Organizations*. Cambridge, MA: Ballinger, pp. 199-222.

Lammers, Cornelis J. (1987) 'Sociology of organizations around the globe: Convergences and divergences'. Unpublished paper presented at the Annual Meeting of the American Sociological Association, Chicago.

Langton, John (1984) 'The ecological theory of bureaucracy', *Administrative Science Quarterly*, 29: 330-54.

Lawrence, Paul and Dyer, Davis (1983) *Renewing American Industry*. New York: Free Press.

Leonard, Jonathan S. (1987) 'In the wrong place at the wrong time: The extent of frictional and structural unemployment', in Kevin Lang and Jonathan Leonard (eds), *Unemployment and the Structure of Labor Markets*. Oxford: Basil Blackwell, pp. 141-63.

Lorenzoni, Gianni and Ornati, Oscar A. (1988) 'Constellations of firms and new ventures', *Journal of Business Venturing*, 3 (Winter): 41-58.

Louis, Meryl R. (1980) 'Surprise and sense making: What newcomers experience in entering unfamiliar organizational settings', *Administrative Science Quarterly*, 25: 226–51.

McKelvey, Bill and Aldrich, Howard E. (1983) 'Applied population science', *Administrative Science Quarterly*, 28: 101–28.

March, James G. (1981) 'Footnotes to organizational change', *Administrative Science Quarterly*, 26: 563–77.

Martin, Joanne (1982) 'Stories and scripts in organizational settings', in H. Hastorf and A. Isen (eds), *Cognitive Social Psychology*. New York: Elsevier-North Holland, pp. 225–305.

Martin, Joanne and Siehl, Caren (1983) 'Organizational culture and counterculture: An uneasy symbiosis', *Organizational Dynamics*, (Autumn): 52–64.

Martin, Joanne and Meyerson, Debra (1988) 'Organizational culture and the denial, channeling and acknowledgement of ambiguity', in Louis R. Pondy, Richard Boland, Jr. and Howard Thomas (eds), *Managing Ambiguity and Change*. London: John Wiley, pp. 93–125.

Marx, Thomas (1976) 'Technological change and the theory of the firm: The American locomotive industry, 1920–1955', *Business History Review*, 50: 1–24.

Meyer, John W. and Rowan, Henry (1977) 'Institutionalized organizations: Formal structure as myth and ceremony', *American Journal of Sociology*, 83: 340–63.

Meyer, John W., Scott, W. Richard, Strang, David and Creighton, Andrew L. (1988) 'Bureaucratization without centralization. Changes in the organizational system of US public education, 1940–1980', in Lynne G. Zucker (ed.), *Institutional Patterns and Organizations*. Cambridge, MA: Ballinger, pp. 139–67.

Meyerson, Debra (1990) 'Uncovering socially undesirable emotions: Experiences of ambiguity in organizations', *American Behavioral Scientist*, 33 (3): 296–307.

Meyerson, Debra (1991) '"Normal" Ambiguity?: A glimpse of an occupational culture', in P.J. Frost, L.F. Moore, M.R. Louis, C.C. Lundberg and J. Martin (eds), *Reframing Organizational Culture*. Newbury Park, CA: Sage.

Meyerson, Debra and Martin, Joanne (1987) 'Cultural change: An integration of three different views', *Journal of Management Studies*, 24: 623–47.

Olson, Mancur (1965) *The Logic of Collective Action*. Cambridge, MA: Harvard University Press.

Orru, Marco, Biggart, Nicole and Hamilton, Gary (1991) 'Organizational isomorphism in East Asia', in Walter W. Powell and Paul J. DiMaggio (eds), *The New Institutionalism in Organizational Analysis*. Chicago: University Chicago Press.

Ouchi, William (1981) *Theory Z*. Reading, MA: Addison-Wesley.

Perrow, Charles (1985) 'Comment on Langton', *Administrative Science Quarterly*, 30: 278–83.

Perrow, Charles (1986) *Complex Organizations*. New York: Scott Foresman.

Peters, Tom and Waterman, Robert (1982) *In Search of Excellence*. New York: Harper & Row.

Pondy, Louis, Frost, Peter, Morgan, Gareth and Dandridge, Thomas (1981) *Organizational Symbolism*. Greenwich, CT: JAI Press.

Pondy, Louis, Boland, Richard and Thomas, Howard (1988) *Managing Ambiguity and Change*. New York: Wiley.

Powell, Walter W. (1985) *Getting Into Print: The Decision Making Process in Scholarly Publishing*. Chicago: University of Chicago Press.

Powell, Walter W. (1988) 'Institutional effects on organizational structure and performance', in Lynne G. Zucker (ed.), *Institutional Patterns and Organizations*. Cambridge, MA: Ballinger, pp. 115–36.

Powell, Walter W. and DiMaggio, Paul (eds) (1991) *The New Institutionalism in Organizational Analysis*. Chicago: University of Chicago Press.

Reed, Michael I. (1985) *Re-Directions in Organizational Analysis*. London: Tavistock.

Reed, Michael I. (1988) 'The problem of human agency in organizational analysis', *Organization Studies*, 9: 33–46.

Robins, James A. (1987) 'Organizational economics: Notes on the use of transaction-cost theory in the study of organizations', *Administrative Science Quarterly*, 32: 68–86.

Sandelands, Lloyd and Drazin, Robert (1989) 'On the language of organization theory', *Organization Studies*, 10 (4): 457–77.

Schein, Edgar (1985) *Organizational Culture and Leadership*. San Francisco, CA: Jossey-Bass.

Scott, W. Richard (1983) 'The organization of environments: Network, cultural, and historical elements', in John W. Meyer and W. Richard Scott, *Organizational Environments*. Beverly Hills, CA: Sage, pp. 155–75.

Scott, W. Richard (1987) 'The adolescence of institutional theory', *Administrative Science Quarterly*, 32: 493–511.

Selznick, Philip (1957) *Leadership in Administration*. New York: Harper & Row.

Singh, Jitendra (ed.) (1990) *Organizational Evolution*. Beverly Hills, CA: Sage.

Singh, Jitendra, House, Robert and Tucker, David (1986) 'Organizational change and organizational mortality', *Administrative Science Quarterly*, 31: 587–611.

Singh, Jitendra, Tucker, David and House, Robert (1986) 'Organizational legitimacy and the liability of newness', *Administrative Science Quarterly*, 31: 171–93.

Singh, Jitendra V., Tucker, David and Meinhard, Agnes (1988) 'Are voluntary organizations structurally inert? Exploring an assumption in organizational ecology'. Academy of Management, Anaheim, CA, August.

Skocpol, Theda (1979) *States and Social Revolutions*. Cambridge: Cambridge University Press.

Smircich, Linda (1983) 'Concepts of culture and organizational analysis', *Administrative Science Quarterly*, 28 (September): 339–58.

Staber, Udo H. (1989a) 'Age-dependence and historical effects on the failure rates of worker cooperatives: An event-history analysis', *Economic and Industrial Democracy*, 10: 59–80.

Staber, Udo, H. (1989b) 'Organizational foundings in the cooperative sector in Atlantic Canada: An ecological perspective', *Organization Studies*, 10: 383–405.

Staber, Udo and Aldrich, Howard E. (1983) 'Trade association stability and public policy', in Richard Hall and Robert Quinn (eds), *Organizational Theory and Public Policy*. Beverly Hills, CA: Sage, pp. 163–78.

Stinchcombe, Arthur (1965) 'Social structure and organizations', in James March (ed.), *Handbook of Organizations*. Chicago: Rand McNally, pp. 142–59.

Stinchcombe, Arthur (1986) *Stratification and Organization: Selected Papers*. Cambridge: Cambridge University Press.

Tolbert, Pamela (1988) 'Institutional sources of organizational culture in large law firms', in Lynne G. Zucker (ed.), *Institutional Patterns and Organizations*. Cambridge, MA: Ballinger, pp. 101–13.

Tushman, Michael and Anderson, Philip (1986) 'Technological discontinuities and organizational environments', *Administrative Science Quarterly*, 31: 439–65.

Van Maanen, John and Barley, Stephen (1984) 'Occupational communities: Culture and control in organizations', in Barry Staw and L.L. Cummings (eds), *Research in Organizational Behavior*. Greenwich, CT: JAI Press, pp. 287–366.

Van Maanen, John and Kunda, Gideon (1989) 'Real feelings: Emotional expression and organizational culture', in Barry Staw and L.L. Cummings (eds), *Research in Organizational Behavior*, vol. 11. Greenwich, CT: JAI Press, pp. 43–103.

Weick, Karl (1976) 'Educational organizations as loosely coupled systems', *Administrative Science Quarterly*, 21 (March): 1–19.

Weick, Karl (1979) *The Social Psychology of Organizing*. Reading, MA: Addison-Wesley.

Welsh, M. Ann and Slusher, E. Allen (1986) 'Organizational design as a context for political activity', *Administrative Science Quarterly*, 31: 389–402.

Williamson, Oliver (1981) 'The economics of organization: The transaction cost approach', *American Journal of Sociology*, 87: 548–77.

Wuthnow, Robert (1987) *Meaning and Moral Order: Explorations in Cultural Analysis*. Berkeley, CA: University of California Press.

Young, Ed (1989) 'On the naming of the rose: Interests and multiple meanings as elements of organizational culture', *Organization Studies*, 10 (2): 187–206.

Zimmerman, M.B. (1982) 'Learning effects and the commercialization of new energy technologies: The case of nuclear power', *Bell Journal of Economics*, 13: 297–310.

Zucker, Lynne G. (1977) 'The role of institutionalization in cultural persistence', *American Sociological Review*, 42: 726–43.

Zucker, Lynne G. (1986) 'The production of trust: Institutional sources of economic structure, 1840–1920', in Barry Staw and L.L. Cummings (eds), *Research in Organizational Behavior*, vol. 8. Greenwich, CT: JAI, pp. 53–112.

Zucker, Lynne G. (1987) 'Institutional theories of organization', in W. Richard Scott (ed.), *Annual Review of Sociology*, 13: 443–64.

Zucker, Lynne G. (ed.) (1988a) *Institutional Patterns and Organizations*. Cambridge, MA: Ballinger.

Zucker, Lynne G. (1988b) 'Where do institutional patterns come from? Organizations as actors in social systems', in Lynne G. Zucker (ed.), *Institutional Patterns and Organizations*. Cambridge, MA: Ballinger, pp. 23–49.

Zucker, Lynne G. (1989) 'Combining institutional theory and population ecology: No legitimacy, no history', *American Sociological Review*, 54 (August): 542–5.

3

The Symbolic Understanding of Organizations

Barry A. Turner

Energy is the only life, and is from the Body and Reason is the bound or outward circumference of Energy. Energy is pure delight. (William Blake, cited by Capra, 1989: 84)

Writing about new directions in organizational theory and analysis is like tipping promising scholastic runners in the next theoretical race. In an uncertain field it is not too difficult to act as a tipster; the problem is to come up with tips which are of good quality. For someone like myself who has maintained that there is an important place for theory which is grounded in data – theory which in large part is only 'discovered' or created by a process of abduction as the investigator moves back and forth between data and theory during an investigation – the task of naming a future winner in the theoretical stakes appears as a doubly difficult one. Moreover, we may have reached a time when the next race will not be run. The idea of naming a single option to mark out our future understanding of behaviour in organizations itself has an old-fashioned air to it. So I can only offer here speculations about future issues in organizational studies, looking in particular at some symbolic issues in the field, and also taking a look at some of the dangers of an excessive fascination with symbols.

It seems likely to me that in the near future organizational research will display the following characteristics. It will be in large part participative; it will be predisposed to qualitative rather than exclusively quantitative methods; it will be both wary and skilful in its use of language; and it will be unlikely to produce a single, unified, coherent theory. Some aspects of organizational behaviour can be explored and understood by means of questionnaire surveys, by indices and by attitude measurement, but the topics likely to raise the most interest will not be readily or wholly accessible through such techniques. To gain access to such material, research inquiries will involve meeting and talking to people in organizations, entering into and understanding their way of life. Such qualitative inquiries are conducted and reported through the medium of language, and researchers are becoming more aware of both the manner in which language inserts a classificatory barrier between us and our experience of the world, and the impossibility of getting around this barrier.

Part of this growing sophistication in the use of language is a recognition, as Ash (1990) has phrased it, that language breaks down, and that the idea of coherence which it offers is illusory, although it is all that we have. In a parallel way, we become more aware of similar properties associated with theory. The search for the single, overarching theory which will explain all of organizational (and thus all of social) life has been abandoned, or should have been. But since we cannot live in the world at all without creating degrees of coherence, without constructing the appearances of certainty, the outcomes of future theoretical discussion are likely to be extensions of these bulwarks against chaos – situated, context-related typifications and generalizations, which are to varying degrees both time- and culture-bound.

Almost inevitably, then, this kind of research will lead the organizational investigator to two sets of preoccupations. The first is a concern with cultural and symbolic environments: environments to which the participative researcher must be sensitive. The second concern is with issues of practical import to actors in the organizations studied, with the praxis of the members; and, inevitably, this is tied up with the intended praxis of the investigator. Theoretical jottings made up of circumscribed, context-bound typifications, categorizations or propositions may be of limited use to those seeking to produce a 'unified field theory' of organizations, but they will be of much more absorbing interest to those attempting to live, work and operate in the organizational context in question. This kind of theorizing is likely to be precisely that needed to produce what Schon (1987) has so aptly labelled 'the reflective practitioner'.

Style and Identity

What kind of theoretical approaches will be thrown up by such inquiries into organizations? The participative researcher, concerned with entering the way of life of an organization and with getting to grips with its culture, will immediately encounter issues of style, will sense the aesthetic qualities of a way of life, and will have to recognize and understand how groups and factions within the organization generate and maintain their identity.

Several recent developments seem to offer ways of deepening or enhancing our understanding of the significance of such matters in the organizational domain. Attention is already being paid by some writers (Strati, 1990; Witkin, 1990) to precisely *how* people behave in organizations. These researchers have looked at the style, emotion and aesthetics of organizational life, and considered how these serve to express individual and collective identity. Building in part upon contemporary studies of style in youth culture, such accounts of the sensuous and stylistic qualities of collective life have already started to uncover interesting, relevant and previously neglected aspects of the way in which modes of behaviour in organizations are constituted, conveyed and lived for the participants.

A slightly different way of viewing group identity is provided by recent attempts by cultural anthropologists to understand and analyse the symbolic construction of community (Cohen, 1982). These studies, which give particular importance to boundary conditions, have examined small villages or other settlements within contemporary industrial society, but although they originate outside the organizational tradition, they are not irrelevant to organizations. The way in which Cohen, for example, looks at the symbolic construction of community (Cohen 1986) could readily be transferred to organizational settings. He regards 'community' as a relational idea, a community defining itself in opposition to other communities or social entities, and establishing a boundary to express this relationship. Such a view can readily be applied to perceptions of organizational identity.

Cohen focuses his attention on how the boundary is marked, and what this demarcation means to people, or, rather, what meanings they give to it. Since the boundaries are symbolically constructed, those which are important for some people may be imperceptible to others. However, public acknowledgement of such symbolic constructions helps to register them within members' experience. Rituals provide social markers for boundaries and identify the community of meaning within the perimeter. These communities of meaning symbolize the past, and then create from it classifications and identities as a basis for a response to the present.

Archetypes and Hermeneutics

An alternative way of coming to grips with the deeper meanings of symbols in contemporary organizational life is, of course, that offered by Jungian inquiry. Although there have been very few attempts to apply such an approach to organizations, work on archetypes has developed and revealed aspects of symbols which other cultural approaches have sometimes neglected, even though some aspects of these analyses may not always be wholly persuasive to the outsider. Beyond the well-known work of Mitroff (1984) in this field, I am aware of only three analyses – all stimulating accounts – which use a Jungian or a hermeneutic approach in an organizational context: those of Tatham, Bird and Aredal.

Tatham (1981), in a verbal conference presentation, offered an allegory of the phases of progress and development in organizational life based upon the cycle of the experiences of Icarus. His flight towards the sun, his fall and his emergence after immersion in the sea are taken to represent a recurrent pattern of human experience, supplying a guide to and an interpretation of developmental problems encountered by managers in contemporary organizational life. More recently, Bird (1989) has convincingly argued that the mythical figure of Hermes/Mercury offers an archetype of the kinds of behaviour expected of contemporary entrepreneurs, as opposed to leaders or executives. They share an extensive cluster of characteristics including ingenuity, nimbleness, subtle cunning, deceitfulness and an ability to see and to transform hidden value. They also have a special affinity for areas of marginality and transition.

A hermeneutic approach to the analysis of myth has been used in the study of a Swedish organization by Aredal (1989), who unearths a myth from his data and then uses it to aid his understanding of that data. Hermeneutics is the theory of rules of interpretation, and Aredal places emphasis upon this type of interpretation which he believes is likely to assist us in understanding contemporary organizations. He comments (1989: 163):

> Within organizations, it is often not understood just to how great an extent rationalism has destroyed the ability to reflect on ideas and to interpret symbols, and how this rationalism has left the organization exposed to unconscious mental powers.

All of these writers, however, pose for the organizational investigator the question of how their diagnostics might illuminate our understanding of symbolic features of organizations. They may offer persuasive pictures of the patterns of human behaviour and human propensities through their *archetypes* – an archetype referring to 'a transpersonal pattern of energy, meaning and value related to instincts, a pattern which crosses history and culture' (Bird, 1989: 3). However, to discern a deeper significance in these diagnoses, we have to accept the Jungian view that such a pattern, related to instinct, is constituted by important regularities which hold constant, not only across history but also across cultures. This then constitutes a claim for a degree of theoretical coherence which jars with the doubts about the possibility of universal social theories which I have already expressed.

To explore this point a little further, Aredal's methodological approach to the problem of uncovering the enduring messages which he finds within organizations is, following Ricoeur, to regard organizations as 'symbolically mediated interactions' which can be examined by hermeneutic interpretations of organizational documents. Specifically, he studied the texts of the proceedings of a committee concerned with the Swedish dental service. His interpretations make use of myths which, he believes, explain organizational interactions, make them meaningful and comprehensible, and relate them to what he considers to be fixed, trans-historical, mythical paradigms. Starting with a search for polarized oppositions in the texts, he proceeds to examine the material in a *hermeneutic circle*, seeking to understand the whole from the parts and the parts from the whole and thus to uncover a consistent and comprehensible structure. He assumes that there is 'logic of double meaning' (1989: 156), the literal meaning of the data constituting its first-order meaning, and the symbolic or metaphoric level constituting the second order. A symbol is an indirect representation characterized by double meaning.

As a result of this analysis, Aredal argues that the symbolic key to the understanding of the committee which he is studying is the myth of

Theseus and Procrustes, the latter with his single-sized bed into which short and tall travellers were all equally and brutally fitted. The activities of the committee demonstrate a process of standardization, in pursuit of mediocrity: 'extremely high incomes will disappear; extremely low incomes should be raised' (1989: 158). Using the 'transferred meaning' of this mythical picture he throws light on something which otherwise he would be unable to realize or express. I find this proposition fascinating, but I have to say that I resist accepting wholeheartedly the results of the interpretation. I feel constrained to ask why *this* myth, at *this* time, for *this* organization? And I harbour doubts about the degree to which all myths offer fixed, trans-historical patterns for the interpretation of human behaviour.

Aredal sees myth as a symbolic language which reflects the basic needs, functions and features of human life and which for this reason has persisted from century to century. 'The symbolic language of myths is always modern' (Aredal, 1989: 160). Such archetypes are also held to constitute 'a way for the collective unconscious to enter the phenomenal world' (Bird, 1989: 16), and although I am intrigued by these kinds of analyses, and although the aspects of symbolism in organizations with which they deal will continue to be important, I cannot endorse without qualification the idea of the collective unconscious. I would though, like to see more studies based upon archetypal approaches to organizations, to provide a wider range of cases exploring this approach.[1]

As an aside, given that future studies of organizational contexts may consciously turn away from aspects of the rational–mechanical model of social life, we might mention here another aspect of Jungian thought: that is, its relation to the tradition of hermetic inquiry, submerged as the Renaissance gave way to the Enlightenment (Yates, 1974). New directions in organizational analysis may require us to look again at alternative styles of reasoning to consider for such tasks. The mode of presentation in this tradition (Hillman, 1980/1981; Eckman, 1986) is not that of a single, linear, deductive sequence of argument, but of a myriad of characteristics, of parallels, of similarities, of allusions which induce at first a feeling of scorn and disbelief or even vertigo in someone nurtured in the Enlightenment tradition, but which on occasion assemble such an accumulation of evidence, construct such a web of linkages, parallels and cross-associations that it becomes difficult to dismiss.

Anyone wishing to sample this form of discourse could do worse than to look at the example offered by Hillman in his essay 'Silver and the white earth' (Hillman, 1980/1981), a persuasive and extended examination of the symbolism of *silver*, as both a relatively neglected stage in the hermetic process; and as an analogue of certain psychological conditions. I refer to this tradition here because, if we are to take seriously the task of understanding symbols in our contemporary organizations, and of making links between individual development and collective behaviour, the contemporary, functional language in which we are accustomed to argue may be inherently unsuitable for our task (Adams and Hill Ingersoll, 1990). So we may have to reassess other traditions of understanding and perception which have been swept aside by the orthodoxies of industrial thought.[2]

Symbols in the Imaginary: The Structural Option and Alternatives

A number of writers have sought to make distinctions between different types of symbols and myths, and this seems to me to be an area where more reflection is needed, for all that is symbolic is not necessarily pregnant with meaning. Gadda (1989) distinguished second-hand myths, 'poppy-seed dreams', from those which transform in a pragmatic tension the most profound instincts of our being, among the latter being the psychodynamic myth which is the 'authenticity of a consciousness'. In a similar way, Aredal offers Ricoeur's distinction between the three levels of: *sedimented symbolism*, made up of stereotypes, fairy tales and old, worn metaphors; *everyday, functional, useful symbols*; and *prospective symbols*. These latter:

> 'are creations of meaning that take up the traditional symbols with their multiple significations and serve as the vehicles of new meanings'; this creation of meaning is at the same time a 'recapture of archaic fantasies and a living interpretation of this fantasy substrate'. (Aredal, 1989: 161, citing Ricoeur, 1977)

One problem for analyses based on an examination of myths and symbols, then, is to distinguish between the types of myths which are to be considered significant and worth investigating, and those which are merely second-hand, worn-out metaphors.

Recognizing that symbols may come in different forms, and casting about for writers who may help us to relate these forms to organizational activities, the French post-Marxist writer Cornelius Castoriadis seems to be worthy of more than passing attention, though, at least in English translation, his message is not always uniformly accessible. Castoriadis presses himself upon our attention on two counts. First, he is concerned not only with symbols, but also with praxis, and a particularly enabling, participative form of praxis at that. Second, he has been for several years engaged in an extended critique of the postmodernist or structuralist writers whose approach to symbols, language and the interpretation of the social world I have so far studiously avoided mentioning.

The growth of interest in symbolism in organizations has occurred during the period when the advocates of what has been called 'the structural allegory' have been attempting to revise the way in which we might think. Writers of the various structuralist schools refuse to accept conscious, intentional sources of meaning; tell us, one way or another that the medium is the message; and would transform inquiry about the 'reality' of 'things' into an exploration of codes. If we are concerned to further our interpretation of the cultural patterns of organizations, the structural option of transforming things into codes might seem to be an appealing one. But the anti-empiricist tendencies of structural analysis lie uneasily with some of the issues which seem to me to be of importance in organizational theory, and for this reason I do not look for new directions of inquiry within 'the solipsism of self-referentiality in which the structural allegory has tended to become trapped' (Fekete, 1984: xvii).

At the other extreme, it is not intellectually sufficient to look solely at the manner in which symbols contribute to the functioning of an organization. For their own reasons, the 'corporate culture' writers promote the use of symbols to achieve functional change, while taking as given the symbolic constitution of an organization. Paradoxically, there is a limit to which such analyses can deal with their own ostensible goals of promoting change, for the partial picture which they have of why and how organizations function can only be completed by looking outside the framework of functionality.

Castoriadis' critique (1984, 1987) of the structuralist trend, in which he talks about 'the imaginary institution of society' and highlights some key issues in the study of symbolism, offers a provocative challenge to structuralism. Even though he does not offer immediate, practical prescriptions for research, his discussion of symbolism raises matters which can helpfully be explored in the context of organizations; and, in spite of the limitations which we shall identify in his approach, he does press us to think anew about the symbolic texture of organizations. It seems to be important, therefore, to try to assess the implications of his thought for the study of organizations and to see if his work could be used to point organizational analysis in a new direction.

To offer a brief summary of relevant aspects of his approach,[3] Castoriadis argues that although institutions are unavoidably symbolic, they cannot be *reduced* to the symbolic. Every functionalist, he says, is aware of the role of symbolism in social life. But he argues that such views do not normally recognize the importance of symbolism, or that if they do, they usually try to limit it. Symbolism in such cases is thus seen either as a neutral instrument which merely serves to express the existing content of a situation, or as a phenomenon with its own logic which, once understood, can be inserted into an existing rational order to produce deducible consequences. However, 'one cannot interpret [a] ceremony by reducing it to its functionalist dimension' (Castoriadis, 1984: 13).

For Castoriadis, the imaginary capacity is of key importance, though this concept of his may give us some trouble. The imaginary capacity he identifies as the ability to evolve images and to link terms such that one 'represents' the other. And, while the imaginary (*l'imaginaire*) is not the symbol, it is inseparable from the generation of the symbol. Symbolism inescapably presupposes this imaginary capacity,[4] so that when we talk about symbols we are referring to an 'elementary and irreducible capacity for evoking images' (Castoriadis, 1984: 10). This giving of meaning does not occur at the behest of 'real factors', because prior to the attribution of meaning, such factors have no place or importance for the society; the meaning of the society itself determines what is real. Thus the 'problems' of a society depend upon how people in that society define themselves.

We can see here Castoriadis' concern to identify an aspect of social institutions not picked up by many existing analyses, a concern that there must be some hidden mental and social capacity, a creative, image-making potential which underpins the ability to make symbols. A professional musicologist can only operate because other people, creative musicians, have taken an alternative path (Castoriadis, 1987: 137). Accordingly, studying symbols, we depend upon the abilities of those people or groups who create them. The essence of human creative abilities, the capacity to make something out of nothing, to invent, to grant to the creators something which was not, clearly beguiles Castoriadis, and his fascination with it carries over into his discussion of symbols. Faced with the primordial inchoateness of an unclassified world – what Castoriadis calls a 'magma' – the invention of a symbol is a creative act which rests upon the ability to see a thing as what it is not. Such an ability defines the 'social imaginary'.

In what seems like a post-Marxist return to Durkheim's 'collective representations', Castoriadis then focuses attention on the possibility of assembling many of the symbols associated with an institution, together with their inseparable, imaginary component. The synthesis of these symbolic elements, he argues, these 'partial totalities' that make up an institution's or a society's life and structure, constitute what he calls 'a culture's central imaginary'. The imaginary of a society is implicated in the constitution of its general mode of being, in defining issues of collective identity, collective needs and wants, and collective interpretations of how people should properly deal with each other.

The imaginary capacity is prior to definitions of function; it is involved in the specification of what we collectively value and what we want to aim for. Symbols can never be explained away merely because they serve to resolve certain practical problems such as matters of coordination, distribution or the division of labour. And this is the reason why approaches which regard the significance of institutions as *merely* functional offer only a partial truth about them. Institutions regarded in such a manner become nothing but projections of the ideas of rationality, utility and commodity fetishism which pervade the Western capitalist world. Equally, though, attempts to conceptualize institutions only in terms of the symbolic also turn out to be partial.

To understand symbolism for Castoriadis is to understand the significations which symbols carry. A structure in itself (*pace* McLuhan) does not convey messages; for this we need discourse. The types of relationships which may exist between a set of symbols and any perceived, calculated or imagined meanings within them are then what differentiates discourse from delirium. The symbols which carry meanings within social institutions are not fixed, inevitable or necessary, but neither are they merely haphazard or conventional. By the operation of the social imaginary, symbols within a social institution are selected because they are, in Lévi-Strauss's phrase, 'good to think with'. The usefulness of symbols lies partly in their ability to offer a bridge between various meanings, allowing us to cross and recross from one meaning to another, making it possible to live with ambiguity without the need to choose between its elements (Duncan, 1969). '[T]he symbolic's most profound trait – its relative indetermination' (Castoriadis, 1984: 22; see also Johnson, 1989; Ricoeur, 1986), though this advantage is bought, of course, at the expense of precision (Turner, 1990).

An organization's life and structure will therefore be bound up with its 'central imaginary'. These symbolic elements constitute its general mode of being; and to understand how people in a given organization define their needs and wants as a group, specify their collective identity and formulate their understanding of the style by which people should properly deal with each other, we need to pay attention to the symbolic clusters that make up what Castoriadis would call the imaginary of the organization. For Castoriadis, institutions, and thus organizations, are socially sanctioned symbolic networks in which a functional component and an imaginary or symbolic component are combined in variable proportions. This view mirrors his proposition that all social institutions combine both logic and action. They are concerned with thoughtful doing, which must embody both the ability to 'distinguish–choose–posit–assemble–count–speak' and the ability to 'assemble–adjust–fabricate–construct'. This position, with which I sympathize, rejects the reduction of the institution to a *mere* symbolic structure.

Castoriadis has an amalgam of concerns. In institutional analysis, he is *interested in meaning*. For example, commenting that, 'Ancient views about the "divine" origins of institutions were, under their mythical shell, closer to the truth' (1984: 14), he wants to determine, say, in what sense Sophocles' discussion of Oedipus and the incest taboo goes beyond being a mere account of a mythical story with a given structure and instead initiates and embodies a meaningful discourse on the important topic of incest. His concern with significance means that he is *committed to an anti-structuralist critique*. Recognizing the mythical nature of the story of God giving the Law to Moses he wants to focus on the *content* and the *meaning* of this account, rather than merely see it as something which can be explained away by a reduction to a set of patterns and relationships. He is also concerned to *develop human autonomy through praxis*, seeking ways of liberating individuals from the control of others. And finally, he is preoccupied with *specifying and defining the hidden components in symbol creation*. It is in this sphere that he wants to focus attention on those hidden origins, generators and keys to action which lie beyond our lucid organizing consciousness.

Castoriadis' formulations are attractive because he is concerned to link the symbolic with the world of action, the world of praxis, the world of meaning. He retains a materialist regard for nature, for action and for technology, and he also refuses to deny or to give up our potential ability to distinguish the meaningful from the meaningless; though he acknowledges that it is impossible in advance to provide complete theoretical guidance for practical action, so praxis must be based upon fragmentary knowledge. In his advocacy of praxis, he sees it as not only thoughtful action in the world, but also as a political act, an act which aims to recognize, to respect and to facilitate people's autonomy, and their ability to operate 'free of control by the other, even in the subconscious'.

However, Castoriadis' discussion, already having some utopian elements, acquires romantic or mystical overtones when he insists upon the imaginary as the source of meaning. Mystical approaches involve a dualism between the visible and the hidden, and for Castoriadis the hidden components of this opposition are the imaginary and the creative capacities. Their elusive, distant, romantic quality becomes evident when we try to work out how we would apply such ideas to specific organizational analyses. We realize then the difficulty, or perhaps the impossibility, of working with such hidden and essentially unknowable elements. If we are going to extend our understanding of symbols in organizations we must look for alternative ways of doing so.

In assessing what Castoriadis might have to offer to organization theory, therefore, I have to conclude that, however intriguing the idea of a *social imaginary*[5] might be, we would be wise to reject it as a basis for future directions in organizational analysis, on the grounds that it mystifies the process of symbol generation and use. This crucial process can be studied and understood in other, more accessible ways. If the important feature of symbolism is the giving and sustaining of meaning, it is necessary to try to locate and to understand the full significance of that meaning by participating in the discourse to which it contributes. In the process, we do not simply *recognize* an organization as an institution constituted by a symbolic network, we try to *understand* why this system of symbols was chosen and not another, what these symbols convey or signify, and why and how the symbol in question has managed to become relatively autonomous. The requirement is thus not to analyse in a manner which will eliminate the meaning of organizational structures and practices by reducing them to a formula, but to uncover, to discover and to use meaning.

Selecting Castoriadis as a guide to the understanding of organizations generates difficulties for us which are not merely methodological ones. We can agree that the symbolic aspects of organizations and institutions are too important to be viewed merely as interesting codified patterns, but Castoriadis implies that there is something deep and basic there to be explored, even though it is inaccessible. But symbol use, though fascinating and complex, is much less mysterious than that. We have to exhaust explanations based upon the way in which people order and categorize the world, and cluster together those things which are thought to demonstrate perceptual or conceptual similarities before we resort to theories with inaccessible components.

So, in using the writings of Castoriadis to provoke thought about the directions in which symbolic organizational analysis might move, the primary theme which I would draw from his writings is the assertion that it is important to move away from the kind of structurally induced relativism which sees all cultural and symbolic patterns as simply re-arrangements of signs and relations. Instead, in response to his analyses, 'attention is redirected to questions of meaning, reason and history in contrast to a structuralism that treats meaning as epiphenomenal, rationality essentially as a problem of form and history as an accumulated jumble of combinations and their ruptures' (Singer, 1984: 4).

Reality and Illusion: Symbols in Modernity

If, however, we share Castoriadis' more general concerns to try to explore linkages between symbols and functionality, or, in some senses, the imaginary and the real, we need to review what we consider this latter, 'real' element might be, and to see how we could relate this to contemporary organizations. As with the analysis of myth, we have again to recognize that we are no longer in a traditional society, and that the characteristics of contemporary society modify the nature of the symbols that we try to deal with. Curiously, one of the clearest expressions of some of these problems is to be found in an essay by the science fiction writer, Philip Dick:

> But the problem [of defining reality] is a real one, not a mere intellectual game. Because today we live in a society in which spurious realities are manufactured by the media, by governments, by big corporations, by religious groups, political groups and the electronic hardware exists by which to deliver those pseudo-worlds right into the heads of the reader, the viewer, the listener . . . the matter of defining what is real – that is a serious topic, even a vital topic. And in there somewhere is the other topic, the definition of the authentic human. Because the bombardment of pseudo-realities begins to produce inauthentic humans very quickly, spurious humans as fake as the data pressing at them from all sides . . . Fake realities will create fake humans. Or, fake humans will generate fake realities and then sell them to other humans, turning them, eventually, into forgeries of themselves . . . It's just a very large version of Disneyland. (Dick, 1986: 10–13)

Theories which help us to cope with the symbolic aspects of organizations have to take account of this very modern symbolic environment, and of its relationship to other aspects of reality. The symbolic concern is shared by Baudrillard (1984), who looks at how signs and symbols evolve, concatenate, and produce themselves. His discussions centre on the power which we now have to fake or to simulate reality, and he offers the disturbing but perceptive dictum, perhaps a kind of symbolic Gresham's

Law, that 'In a society of simulation, the simulacrum rules' (Baudrillard, 1988).

In the spirit of Philip Dick's comments, Baudrillard wants to understand how we come to create conditions where reality is the effect of the sign – in the stock market, in the appeal of a leader, in marketing. The brand endorsement reported in the Italian press recently, by a man who was killed at a police road-block shortly after hijacking a car at gunpoint from a Milan showroom – 'If I am going to die, I want to die in a Ferrari!' – must represent a kind of ultimate limit, or an ultimate accolade, to this power of commercial sign-making. Surely this is a point at which symbolic discourse slips into delirium?

Some aspects of reality are pushed into the background and become increasingly difficult to track down in our contemporary world, where the appearance of things, their simulation via the media, especially television, can often come to seem more significant than the original. Baudrillard suggests that the dominance of simulation through the media leads to a collapsing of those discursive polarities which previously sustained meaning – imaginary/real, subjective/objective, private/public and, presumably, life/death. Such distinctions as original/copy also become eroded or outmoded. But Baudrillard concludes, or appears to conclude, that these developments point to the extinction of referentiality and to a move towards a state of 'hyper-reality' in which we can discern no referents at all, only simulacra,[6] giving us the illusion that we have moved completely to a world of symbols, and that functionality has been extinguished. To counter this illusion, we have to assert that Baudrillard's insights into our world of symbols do not wholly deplete our possibilities for understanding.

Baudrillard (1988) makes a distinction between illusion, which challenges our notion of what is real, neither unreality nor irreality but a play (*ludere*) upon reality; and what he called the 'seduction of reality'. The seduction of reality presents us with simulation, and meaning evaporates. In this condition, making the identical contrast to Castoriadis, he observes that delirium replaces discourse. The meaning of the holocaust is absorbed, he suggests, into the television series of the same name, and the reality of the Vietnam War into *Apocalypse Now*. Shattuck (1981), in his discussion of the Wild Boy of Aveyron, observed how historians he spoke to had come to believe that the ostensibly documentary sequence of events in the boy's life shown in a biographical film by Truffaut represented the true state of affairs. They thought this even though they were familiar with original accounts to the contrary, and even though Truffaut had openly acknowledged that, in his largely faithful reconstruction, he had had to edit certain events together because of constraints in the structure of the film.

Many of the organizations we are concerned to understand and analyse are major protagonists in these processes of simulation and seduction, and they are also penetrated by them. So in our attempts to locate and understand significant clusters of symbols in organizational culture and organizational practice, in our attempts to search for the appropriate way of locating and comprehending an organization's cultural domain, we enter into this vortex of symbols and symbol transformations. Looking backwards, attempting to codify and to classify, we can identify those elements of the culture of an organization which have been embodied in training or set out in official handbooks. But once a culture is imposed in this way, it is already a collection of worn metaphors, a sedimented symbolism. It represents a 'game of the boundary rather than a game of the horizon' (Carse, 1986). These impositions already represent a simulation and a seduction of the reality of organizational culture.

By contrast, if we try to turn our attention to the processes by which reality emerges in the continuously created culture of an organization, we realize that we are dealing with the playfulness of people and with the evolution, the concatenation, the gambolling together of their symbols. Just as the symbolic life of an organization merges with wider societal symbolisms, so the creative, cultural 'game of the horizon' within an organization merges with the wider 'game of the horizon' of society.

The world as we deal with it is always *constituted* by those in it so that it can always be *re*viewed, *re*constituted and thus transcended by making use of possibilities for reframing or for redefining the way in which the world is understood. This has always been the case, but we are now presented, thanks to modern technical rationality, with a whole array of new possibilities for reframing and redefining which succeed one another in a bewildering spiral. The creative possibilities are increased, and the difficulties of analysis are compounded when we realize that although we try to impose rules upon it, the process of symbol transformation does not follow rules – we can do whatever we like, repeatedly.

Eventually, attempts to look for laws in this area break down because of the realization that language is infinitely malleable and the transformations unconfined. Hence some of the difficulties of identifying symbols and discerning their meaning: rather than rigorous laws of structural transformational relationships at the roots of a symbol system, we find instead what I once heard called a 'holiday among the rhizomes'. And, even in conversation with members of organizations, we have to recognize that they themselves may well be living out their own media-acquired images of the organization that they imagine themselves to be in. As Philip Dick and Baudrillard have both observed, it's just a very large version of Disneyland. The problem for the organizational researcher is to try to find the best way of standing, inside, outside or on the borders of this Disneyland in order to try to create new meanings for the events within it.

Participation and Praxis

The creative possibilities of symbol use, symbol play and symbol transformation, however, do not arise autonomously from a sovereign world of symbols. As we have seen, Castoriadis and Fekete, among others, are determined to point out the significance of both the material and the value base from which symbols spring. The only genuine symbol generators which we know are ourselves, and we are all biological organisms. When there is speech, it is always one of *us* who speaks, using our own breath in our own body. Logic as a process appears to separate our symbols from our body, from our person, from our place (Capra, 1989; Ash, 1990), but in spite of the games that can be played with them, the symbols are none the less dependent upon us.

The meanings and the knowledge which are associated with organizational milieux must be understood in the context of, and related to the biological condition of, the people who populate organizations. If we remind ourselves of this human character of organizational activity and take care not to regard this character as something to be modified in a utopian search for human perfection of one kind or another, we will also have to acknowledge that the cultural environment encountered by the student of organizations must be related in some way to the physical presence of the human beings involved. We must then, as Castoriadis does, regard the capacity to create symbols and to spin culture as integral to this humanness.

But, equally, we need to recognize that much of human life is pursued, not by the application of logic, but through the acquisition and the application of skills. Skills are integral to any form of praxis, and much of the knowledge associated with skilled behaviour, while not instinctive, is none the less more available to the human organism as a whole than to the conscious mind. The participative, qualitative organizational investigator must thus take account of the major significance of the part played by what Polanyi (1958) calls personal knowledge in organizational behaviour. People know more than they can say, Polanyi observes, and this kind of tacit knowledge outflanks many of the structuralist debates, because it deals with knowledge which lies outside the explicitly analytic mode of thought.

Not only do people in organizations – in a variety of manual and non-manual jobs – develop skills, judgements and other forms of tacit knowledge, but many of them also develop second-order skills and judgements which enable them to appraise the quality of their own knowing and their own performance. They develop, to use Polanyi's term, 'connoisseurship' (Polanyi, 1958; Turner, 1988). Understanding and knowing are not passive processes, but active ones: *understanding* organizational environments and *knowing* work-related topics involves passionate participation. The connoisseur, in these terms, is anyone who not only participates passionately in acts of knowing, but also appraises at the same time the quality of that which is known, bridging, in doing so, 'the disjunction between subjectivity and objectivity' (Polanyi, 1958: 16).

The implications of this for the organizational investigator are, first, to recognize his or her own skills and connoisseurship in the processes of investigation (Turner, 1988). Second, to realize that people in organizations participate, work, communicate and relate in ways which also involve such elements of passionate and tacit knowing which may not be readily accessible at an analytical level. And third, to recognize that much of the knowledge which enables organizations to operate is knowledge obtained by doing, knowledge which is built in to the behaviour of the people concerned and is not merely part of their cognition. The partial, situated theories which might be sought in future organizational inquiries are of interest precisely because they hold the potential to influence the manner in which people in those contexts behave. This potential will not be fully realized, however, if the elements of skill, connoisseurship and tacit knowledge in the actions of the people concerned are neglected. It is an open question how far the development of culture and symbol use overlaps with such tacit processes. What is clear is that whether or not they operate in separate realms, the future organizational investigator has to cope in some way with the influence in organizations of both symbolism and tacit, personal knowledge.

Another, related, question to ask about likely future theories is how far they facilitate the development of 'reflective practitioners' (Schon, 1987), organization members who themselves have acquired a sensitivity to the cultural, symbolic and skill-related aspects of their behaviour within the organization. Gagliardi (1986, 1990) has for some years seen the development of such sensitivities as part of his institute's management training programmes, and Johnson's (1989) pursuit of a strategic role for organizational symbolism has a similar reflexive goal. Johnson gets managers to construct their own 'cultural paradigm' of their organization. He asks them to describe, and subsequently to link, *symbols*, *stories*, *rituals and routines*, *power structures*, *cultural systems* and *organizational structure*. As a consultant he then reinterprets these managers' accounts of cultural linkages within their organization and uses them as a basis for an enhanced understanding of strategic change.

In this form of intervention, the special capacity of symbols to deliver powerful, strategic signals makes such reflexive awareness of symbolic action of particular value to managers. In an echo of the comments of Duncan noted above, Johnson observes that symbols are able to create links both to the past and to an indeterminate future, in ways which are at the same time mundane and profound, thereby offering means for dealing with the uncertainty of change. Symbolic acts within an organization can, he comments, be totemistic, embodying the 'corporate soul',[7] and they can be powerful, because of the manner in which they link the mundane and the substantial. As interpretations they are vivid, emotive and are able to embrace excessive ambiguity, and, in appropriate settings, seem to have a life of their own.

The Perils of Symbolism

If we are correct in our guess that organizational inquiries will, in the near future, be preoccupied with situationally bounded, context-specific 'theories of the middle range', with issues of participation, and with the qualitative, symbolic, sensuous experiences of entering into the life of those others who are being studied, we should also be aware of certain dangers which may be associated with such trends. There are the dangers of 'going native' – not so much the danger of forgetting about organizational research and never returning, but the danger of becoming so successfully absorbed into a culture that delirium is mistaken for discourse: as, in an extreme example, in the recording of sadistic initiation ceremonies and aggressive sexual harassment in a relativistic fashion, as though they are merely another variant of subcultural patterning which can be noted without comment (Vaught and Smith, 1980). But there are also the dangers of becoming overattached to the romantic qualities of symbols. The subject-matter of symbolism is potentially perilous and we need to be aware of the nature of the risks which we run in dealing with it. As with any quest, there is an element of romanticism in the search (Ebers, 1985), and one of the dangers of romanticism is that it may be ill-equipped to resist the embrace of fascism or other forms of authoritarianism.

Such dangers become evident in connection with just that ambiguous appeal of symbols whose positive qualities we have already noted. A related danger arises in the marginalizing anarchy of structuralism which, as Fekete (1984) notes, means not only that is it unable to make *new* proposals but that it is defenceless against the 'will-to-will'. Evidence that this unease may be more widely felt came at a recent conference on the 'symbolics of leadership'[8] when participants protested about contributions which seemed to glorify 'leaders' too much, and objected that to talk of managers as charismatics or as magicians was unduly mystifying. Such contributions, if allowed to flourish unchecked, were seen as a potential new route by which the self-image of those with power could be aggrandized, and by which they could be assisted in remystifying their power.

The potential for giving assistance to mystification contrasts with the strong, anti-romantic theme of social science since the Enlightenment, of challenging and unmasking myths and ideologies in order to sweep away what was seen as the previous obscurantism and to help to create more realistic knowledge about society. Elias, once a refugee from Nazi Germany, has commented that people need myths, but that they should embody them in poetry rather than giving them form in social life, because myths always eventually exact a penalty of us (Elias, quoted in Mennell, 1989, Chapter 1).

We must, of course, be wary of any penalty which we may ultimately have to pay, but as we have seen in our discussions of the seduction of reality, we are less secure than we used to be about just what is reality and what is myth.[9] Even though the romanticism of symbols perpetuates dualism (Ash, 1990), it may be equally dangerous to neglect the sensuous, aesthetic and stylistic character of our organizations, and to regard them as rational authority machines, their members acting as mere nodes of communication, command and control. While being vigilant about re-legitimizing a new authoritarianism we also have to acknowledge the central place held by myths and potent symbols in every societal construct, for humans spin about them their web of myth as the cater-pillar spins its cocoon (MacIver, 1947). Whom should we be more con-cerned about, the martyrs to reason or the martyrs to symbolism (Gorky, 1979: 41)?

Concluding Discussion

During the 1980s the growth of interest in matters of culture and symbolism in organizations made this approach to the study of organiza-tions an accepted option, if not yet quite an orthodoxy. I have tried to review here, in an inescapably idiosyncratic way, some possible directions for organizational studies which recognize the significance of symbolism and culture.

Every organization is a jungle of symbols – symbolic fields, symbolic acts and symbolic games. All of life, inside or outside organizations, is symbolic, even the biological process of transmitting hereditary informa-tion from one generation to another.[10] Communication between individual human beings is a symbolic process, and all culture is predicated upon such symbolic interaction. The way in which we under-stand the operations of the individual human mind, in psychology or psychoanalysis, is symbolic, as is the way in which we interpret the struc-ture and behaviour of social groupings and phenomena. Just to talk about an organization is therefore to create a nested set of symbolic accounts, which contain each other. But instead of remaining inert and neatly tucked inside one another like a set of wooden Russian dolls, these accounts incessantly interweave and interact.

Moreover, the relation of an organization to the market and to the economy is also, in part, a symbolic matter. Although the market is sometimes talked about as a kind of final substratum of reality, with the implication that this is where reality testing will ultimately take place, the market itself is a complex symbolic construct. The creation and the sustenance of a market requires a realm of discourse which depends upon skilled accomplishments by participants who have particular sets of symbolic knowledge and beliefs (Mauss, 1954 [1925]; Weber, 1979; Castoriadis, 1987; Rosen, 1990).

Human beings engage compulsively and continuously in activities which create both culture and myth. However, the forms emerging from this incessant human activity are conditioned by the surroundings and the context. For contemporary citizens, the context is not that of a traditional, non-literate, hunting-and-gathering or agricultural society, but that of the legal–rational organization and, increasingly, the environment of the chaotic iterations and interpenetrations of the market, of telecommunications and of modern media. So we can expect local cultural and mythical agglomerations to be more fragmentary, more disrupted, less dense than the clusters of cultural symbols in traditional settings. The rational, linear, denotative style of thought prevalent in contemporary industrial society thins out the symbolic density of cultural meaning arrays, which are then further fragmented by the prolific and sometimes incestuous transformations which we daily inflict upon all kinds of symbolic representations.

Organizations cannot exist without being generated by and being able to use various forms of symbolic orders, though the problem of making sense of some of these symbolic manifestations is rather more difficult. In spite of the dangers of a preoccupation with such topics, we cannot neglect them. A concern with such characteristics is also important because of the circumscribed potential, even the breakdown, of existing modes of understanding organizations and related social phenomena. Given this need, I have tried to look over some possible options which might take existing investigations a little further.

Symbolic aspects of organizations are worth exploring to understand the aesthetic and stylistic identities which are generated within them, to increase our knowledge of how boundaries are constituted around organizational identities and to promote strategic change. More studies are needed to explore the available possibilities of archetypal or even hermetic investigations of organizational phenomena – the material available here is usually fascinating and intriguing, but not always convincing.

We turn to the more elusive aspects of mythical and symbolic constructions in the context of organizations because of a concern, shared with Fekete and Castoriadis, that beyond structuralism there is, or there should be, a region with space for concern about how the modern organizational world and its surroundings are instituted, a space where it is possible to consider approaches to creative and transformist praxis. Undue and uninformed passivity in the face of the complex subtleties of worlds and organizations potentially ruled by simulacra can only lead to an acceptance of that overarching power structure which limits the explorations of structuralism. An alternative, having sought to understand the situation of organizational practice, is to look for ways of changing it, not merely in a functional manner, but also in a participatory one.

Notes

I would like to acknowledge helpful discussions with Silvio Funtowicz, Massimo Paruccini and Bob Witkin in the preparation of this paper. The responsibility for the outcome, of course, is entirely my own.

1 It is interesting, in view of the discussion below of both hermetics and hermeneutics, to note that Hermes is also at the source of both of these terms, with slightly different constellations of characteristics attributed to him:

> The etymology of the term hermeneutics carries an obvious relation to Hermes, the messenger god of the Greeks, and suggests a multiplicity of meanings . . . He had to understand and interpret for himself what the gods wanted to convey before he could proceed to translate, articulate and explicate their intention to mortals. (Mueller-Vollmer, 1986: 1)

2 For social scientists, the idea that we should consider the world as a rational, determinist machine, with wholly straightforward laws and wholly predictable outcomes, is a fantasy which also displays a cultural lag in relation to the scientific models it emulates. Discussions of theories which involve chaos and fractals show that natural scientists are now having to get to grips with natural systems which are unpredictable, chaotic and which never repeat themselves (Davies, 1987; Barnsley, 1988; Gleick, 1988; Prigogine and Stengers, 1989). Physicists such as Bohm (1980) are now seeing their ideas, once considered mystical, moving nearer to the centre of advanced thought in natural science, as are the evocative explorations of natural patterns based upon Rudolf Steiner's philosophy produced by Schwenck (1976). However, see Adams and Hill Ingersoll, 1990, for a strong argument that the attempt to study culture in organizations has failed because of an inability of researchers to escape the pressures of the functional, and the patterns and directions of thought typical of utilitarian rationality.

3 The following discussion draws extensively upon Castoriadis (1984, 1987).

4 ' "To metaphorize well," said Aristotle, "implies an intuitive perception of the similarity in dissimilars" ' – quoted by Ricoeur (1986: 6) while pointing out that metaphorical statement is the power to redescribe reality.

5 In relation to the 'imaginary', it is possibly relevant to mention the account by science fiction writer Philip Dick of his first response on encountering a Gnostic codex called *The Unreal God and the Aspects of His Nonexistent Universe*:

> What kind of person would write about something he knows doesn't exist, and how can something that doesn't exist have aspects? But then I realized that I'd been writing about these matters for over twenty-five years. . . . And yet the strange thing is, in some way, some real way, much of what appears under the title 'science fiction' is true. . . . The basic tool for the manipulation of reality is the manipulation of words. (Dick, 1986: 14–15)

6 For a useful discussion of some of the properties of replicas in the physical world, see Kubler, 1962.

7 Cf. the comment by Sievers (1990) that it is possible to consider the soul as a metaphor for transcendence.

8 SCOS Conference on 'The Symbolics of Leadership', INSEAD, Fontainebleau, June 1989.

9 'Reality is that which, when you stop believing in it, doesn't go away' (Dick, 1986: 10). Perhaps.

10 In referring to the idea of the record which is necessary for the biological transmission of hereditary information, H.H. Pattee (1971, quoted by Davies, 1987: 178), comments: 'It is my central idea that the matter–symbol problem and the measurement or recording problem must appear at the origin of living matter.'

References

Adams, Guy B. and Hill Ingersoll, Virginia (1990) 'Painting over old works: The culture of organisation in an age of technical rationality', in Barry A. Turner (ed.), *Organizational Symbolism*. Berlin: de Gruyter, pp. 15–31.

Aredal, Ake (1989) *Invisible Social Control: A Hermeneutical Study of Social Control in the Swedish Dental Administration* (in Swedish, *Den Osynliga Styrningen*, with an English summary and discussion). University of Stockholm.

Ash, Maurice (1990) *Journey Into the Eye of a Needle*. Hartland, Bideford, Devon: Green Books.

Barnsley, Michael (1988) *Fractals Everywhere*. San Diego: Academic Press.

Baudrillard, Jean (1984) 'The structural law of value and the order of simulacra', in J. Fekete (ed.), *The Structural Allegory*. Manchester: Manchester University Press, pp. 540–73.

Baudrillard, Jean (1988) *Selected Writings*, ed. M. Poster. Cambridge: Polity Press. See especially 'Simulacra and simulations', pp. 166–84, and 'Symbolic exchange and death', pp. 119–48.

Bird, Barbara (1989) 'The Mercurial entrepreneur: A Jungian look at the venture process'. Paper presented to 'The Symbolics of Leadership', 4th International Conference on Organisational Symbolism and Corporate Culture, Fontainebleau, June 28–30.

Bohm, David (1980) *Wholeness and the Implicate Order*. London: Routledge & Kegan Paul.

Capra, Fritjof (1989) *Uncommon Wisdom: Conversation with Remarkable People*. London: Fontana.

Carse, James P. (1986) *Finite and Infinite Games*. New York: Free Press.

Castoriadis, Cornelius (1984) 'The imaginary institution of society', trans. Brian Singer, in J. Fekete (ed.), *The Structural Allegory*. Manchester: Manchester University Press, pp. 6–45.

Castoriadis, Cornelius (1987) *The Imaginary Institution of Society*, trans. Kathleen Blamey. Cambridge: Polity Press.

Cohen Anthony P. (ed.) (1982) *Belonging: Identity and Social Organisation in British Rural Cultures*. Manchester: Manchester University Press.

Cohen, Anthony P. (1986) *The Symbolic Construction of Community*. Chichester: Ellis Horwood and Tavistock.

Davies, Paul (1987) *The Cosmic Blueprint*. London: Heinemann.

Dick, Philip K. (1986) 'Introduction: How to build a universe that doesn't fall apart two days later', in Philip K. Dick, *I Hope I Shall Arrive Soon*, ed. M. Hurst and Paul Williams. London: Gollancz, pp. 7–34.

Duncan, H.D. (1969) *Symbols and Social Theory*. New York: Oxford University Press.

Ebers, Mark (1985) 'Understanding organisations – the poetic mode', *Journal of Management*, VII (2): 51–62.

Eckman, Barbara (1986) 'Moon colonization and the imagination', in Charles H. Holbrow, Allan M. Russell and Gordon F. Sutton (eds), *Space Colonization: Space Technology and the Liberal Arts*. AIP Conference Proceedings, 148. New York: American Institute of Physics, pp. 105–13.

Fekete, John (1984) 'Descent into the new maelstrom: Introduction', in J. Fekete (ed.), *The Structural Allegory: Reconstructive encounters with the new French thought*. Manchester: Manchester University Press, pp. xi–xxiv.

Gadda, Carlo Emilio (1989) [1944] *I Miti de Somaro*. Schweiller: Milano.

Gagliardi, Pasquale (1986) 'The creation and change of organizational cultures: A conceptual framework', *Organizational Studies*, 7 (2): 117–34.

Gagliardi, Pasquale (1990) 'Culture and management training: Closed minds and change in managers belonging to organizational and occupation communities', in Barry A. Turner (ed.), *Organizational Symbolism*. Berlin: de Gruyter, pp. 159–71.

Gleick, James (1988) *Chaos: Making a new science*. London: Sphere.

Gorky, Maxim (1979) *My Universities*, trans. R. Wilks. London: Penguin.

Hillman, James (1980/1981) 'Silver and the white earth', *Spring: An Annual of Archetypal Psychology and Jungian Thought*, ed. James Hillman. Part I, 1980; part II, 1981. Dallas: Spring Publications.

Johnson, Gerry (1989) 'Leadership, symbolic action and strategic change'. Paper presented to 'The Symbolics of Leadership', 4th International Conference on Organisational Symbolism and Corporate Culture, Fontainebleau, June 28–30.

Kubler, G. (1962) *The Shape of Time: Remarks on the History of Things*. New Haven: Yale University Press.

MacIver, R.M. (1947) *The Web of Government*. New York: Macmillan.

Mauss, M. (1954) [1925] *The Gift Relationship*. New York: Free Press.

Mennell, S.J. (1989) *Civilization and the Human Self-Image*. Oxford: Basil Blackwell.

Mitroff, I. (1984) *Stakeholders of the Mind*. San Francisco: Jossey-Bass.

Mueller-Vollmer, Kurt (1986) *The Hermeneutics Reader*. Oxford: Basil Blackwell.

Pattee, H.H. (1971) 'Can life explain quantum mechanics?' in T. Bastin (ed.), *Quantum Theory and Beyond*. Cambridge: Cambridge University Press.

Polanyi, M. (1958) *Personal Knowledge: Towards a Post-Critical Philosophy*. London: Routledge & Kegan Paul.

Prigogine, Ilya and Stengers, Isabella (1989) *Order Out of Chaos: Man's New Dialogue with Nature*. London: Fontana.

Ricoeur, P. (1977) *Freud and Philosophy. An Essay in interpretation*. New Haven: Yale University Press.

Ricoeur, P. (1986) *The Role of Metaphor: Multidisciplinary Studies of the Creation of Meaning in Language*. London: Routledge & Kegan Paul.

Rosen, M. (1990) 'Crashing in eighty-seven: Power and symbolism in the Dow', in B.A. Turner (ed.), *Organizational Symbolism*. Berlin: de Gruyter, pp. 115–35.

Schon, Donald (1987) *Educating the Reflective Practitioner: Toward a New Design for Teaching and Learning in the Professions*. San Francisco: Jossey-Bass.

Schwenck, Theodor (1976) *Sensitive Chaos*. New York: Shocken.

Shattuck, R. (1981) *The Forbidden Experiment: The Story of the Wild Boy of Aveyron*. London: Quartet.

Sievers, Burkard (1990) 'Zombies or people: What is the product of work?' in Barry A. Turner (ed.) *Organizational Symbolism*. Berlin: de Gruyter, pp. 83–93.

Singer, Brian (1984) 'Introduction to Castoriadis', in J. Fekete (ed.), *The Structural Allegory*. Manchester: Manchester University Press, pp. 3–5.

Strati, Antonio (1990) 'Aesthetics and organisational skill', in Barry A. Turner (ed.), *Organizational Symbolism*. Berlin: de Gruyter, pp. 207–22.

Tatham, P. (1981) 'The myth of Icarus'. Oral presentation to SCOS Workshop on Organisational Symbolism, Exeter University, June.

Turner, Barry A. (1988) 'Connoisseurship in the study of organizational cultures', in A. Bryman (ed.) *Doing Research in Organizations*. London: Routledge, pp. 108–22.

Turner, Barry A. (1990) 'Introduction', in Barry A. Turner (ed.), *Organizational Symbolism*. Berlin: de Gruyter, pp. 1–11.

Vaught, C. and Smith, D. (1980) 'Incorporation and mechanical solidarity in an underground coal mine', *Sociology of Work and Occupations*, 7: 159–87.

Weber, M. (1979) *Economy and Society* (2 vols), ed. G. Roth and C. Wittich. Berkeley: University of California Press.

Witkin, R.W. (1990) 'The collusive manoeuvre: A study of organisational style of work relations', in Barry A. Turner (ed.), *Organizational Symbolism*. Berlin: de Gruyter, pp. 191–205.

Yates, Frances A. (1974) *The Art of Memory*. Chicago: University of Chicago Press.

4

Organization Studies and Scientific Authority

Colin Brown

The focus of this chapter is an examination of the relationship between organization studies and the cultural authority of science in Western society. As this authority undergoes challenge, and perhaps decline, fresh opportunities are opened up for cross-fertilization between organization and science studies. Since the early 1980s theoretical and methodological research on the history and sociology of scientific knowledge has provided a stream of fresh insights into the structure, function and possibilities of science as a key institution of modernity. However, most of this work has had little impact upon developments in organization studies. Most writers on organization have either accepted the authority of science as unproblematic or have rejected such a chain as imperialistic, as a form of unacceptable scientism. Neither response seems ideal. By uncritically accepting traditional views of science or scientific knowledge-claims, some students of organization have idealized conceptions of science as models for organizations and people. To adopt this stance is to accept the cultural importance of science and the privileging of science as a unique force for knowledge generation and moral progress. The popular alternative position stems from an outright rejection of such scientistic views. Here, advocates suggest that freedom from a reliance upon scientific idealism and imagery should be welcomed as emancipatory. Drawing support for their position from an emasculated reading of Kuhn and Feyerabend, they claim that there are no secure grounds for attaining objective truth in principle or in practice. Consequently, it is argued that paradigms in organizational theory are incommensurable (Burrell and Morgan, 1979; Jackson and Carter, 1991), metaphors are infinitely exchangeable (Morgan, 1986), and that all judgements of the adequacy of different theories and methods are inherently relativistic. On this view, all judgements of adequacy between paradigms, metaphors, theories, models and methods reduce to questions of 'subjective taste'.

It is perhaps not surprising, given this schizoid reaction of contributors to organization studies concerning the nature or value of science, that several commentators on the state of the discipline show signs of discomfort or uncertainty. For example, Pfeffer (1982) observes: 'It is often difficult to discern in what direction knowledge of organisations is progressing – or indeed if it is progressing at all.'

For Weick (1987), it is imperative that we preserve a faith that progress is being made towards unification in organization theory in spite of contradictory evidence:

> If I cannot see the coherence in organisation theory and neither can Whitley, Mcguire or Astley, that does not mean it is not there. Coherence may exist collectively even though our limited rationality cannot grasp it. If individuals can never know their field in its entirety, then theorising boils down to an act of faith that collective omniscience is significant and growing. Faith is required because no-one will ever know for sure whether it is.

For Weick, if we lose that faith then all we can do is 'give up'. Notions of unity and progress are of course central to the enterprise of science.

The central contention of this chapter is that recent work in the history and sociology of science offers insights and perhaps a resolution of this confused state of affairs as to the nature and importance of science in organization studies. Actor network theory, as developed by Latour (1986) and Callon et al. (1986), suggests that both scientism and relativism stem from misunderstandings as to the nature and practice of science. In developing a specifically even-handed approach to social, technical and political factors or 'forces', important distinctions both between science and other knowledge-generating activities, and between different scientific theories, can be made.

From the suggestion that organization studies has much to gain from attention to such work, it should not be concluded that the relationship between organization and science studies cannot be reciprocal. In the work of Mitroff (1974) on the activities of the NASA scientists, Perrow (1984) on the organization and management of different technologies, or Whitley (1984) on the social organization of management science, we have excellent examples of important interdisciplinary contributions. But it should be noted that these are exceptional cases and that there are several areas in the history and sociology of science where insights into the nature of scientific organization are of key importance. In the context of this chapter, analysis of the cultural authority of science is an obvious example where organizational analysis would be relevant. The emphasis here, however, is only incidentally how analysis of organization might contribute to the study of science, since the central concern is the possibility of beneficial influence in the other direction. An understanding of science is important to students of organization for several reasons, not least because scientific images invade our conceptions of what is possible and desirable in organizations, and we justify our own knowledge-claims in terms of their (social) scientific adequacy. There now follows an analysis of the cultural authority of science in Western society, and an examination of the responses of organization theorists to that authority, followed by a presentation of some key ideas from the work of Feyerabend (1975, 1978) and Latour (1986), which I suggest has strong heuristic potential for organization studies.

The Cultural Authority of Science

Whilst it may be more usual to contrast science with culture, work on the development of modernity (Vattimo, 1988), as well as analyses of the current ideology and trajectory of contemporary society (Robins and Webster, 1988), make clear that science and technology, together with commonly held beliefs about their transformational power, in large part constitute modern culture. Our culture is a scientific one, in which our icons of progress are drawn from science, technology or medicine. In such a culture the rational is sharply demarcated from the emotional, and the influence of science is best illustrated in the power it exhibits to 'make natural' specific social, political or cultural differences (see, for example, Scarr, 1985, on the claimed advantages of the nuclear family on child development in post-war America, or Hajek's (1979) analysis of the superiority of the free market economy). The power of science in our culture is also demonstrated by the persistent faith in expertise as superior to common sense in shaping our visions of what is both desirable and possible.

In the modern era, then, science has come to be viewed as the dominant means by which reason could be harnessed to secure the Enlightenment belief in societal progress. Reason, or rationality, was to be understood as the application of scientific or true rules to particular cases. Progress was conceived of in a general sense as the development of human consciousness and culture to a stage where we are better able to cope with our economy, technology, psychology and biology. More specifically, scientific progress entailed growth in accredited knowledge or in problem-solving abilities (Laudan, 1977). It has been claimed that all societies could and should be changed by the use of science and reason, and thus the power of science was seen as universalistic – not limited to particular contexts but equally applicable to all people at all times.

Adas (1989) has forcibly argued that the domination and colonization of large areas of the globe by a relatively small number of Europeans since the seventeenth century was based not so much upon a racist ideology but upon the assumed neutrality and superiority of Western science and technology. The influence of these forces upon local habits and behaviour, including conceptions of time and space, was truly imperialistic. Science, as Weber (1961) noted, was 'chained to the course of progress'.

The persistence and fragility of the Enlightenment project, based upon scientific research, political emancipation and ethical responsibility, has attracted much analysis in recent years. Harvey (1989), in his comprehensive analysis of the twists and turns in modernist developments, argues that faith in the idea that there was only one possible adequate answer to any one question declined sharply in the period following the First World War. That faith, however, revived strongly in the USA during the period of high modernism following the Second World War, as a 'corporate capitalist version of the Enlightenment project of development for progress and human emancipation', where it was centred upon 'the belief in linear progress, absolute truths and rational planning of ideal social orders under standardised conditions of knowledge and production'.

Enlightenment visions of the emancipatory power of science and rationality have been strongly criticized, most notably by Horkheimer and Adorno (1972), as likely to lead to universal oppression rather than liberation. Weber argued that purposive–instrumental rationality would lead to the creation of an 'iron cage' of bureaucratic rationality. Others, whilst accepting the disappointments associated with the outcomes to date, have argued for the need to reform the project. Thus Habermas (1983), whilst acknowledging 'the deformed realisation of reason in history', argues for the possibility of achieving a universalizing reason through appropriate 'communicative action'. Yet in spite of such doubts, the important sociological issues centre upon the reasons for the hegemonic success of science as a social movement over a 300-year period.

Yearley (1988) suggests that there are three main characteristics of science that explain its dominance. In the first place, Western science has exhibited continuing cognitive viability over an extended period. It has transformed our understanding of the natural and social worlds, consistently undermined beliefs concerning religious certainties, and demonstrated continual innovative potential. Such innovations have been particularly notable in times of war. Jones (1978) described how, over a seven-month period, British scientists successfully detected, characterized and then developed and implemented countermeasures against three separate German bomber guidance systems. The success of industrial psychologists in devising selection tests for service personnel in both world wars is a less dramatic example. A myriad of other examples, developed in peace time, covering health and disease, the basic forces in the universe, the principles of space flight or genetic engineering, could also be cited as evidence of scientific originality.

Secondly, science has demonstrated considerable flexibility in terms of its institutional and ideological resources. These resources have been utilized both to heighten feelings of professional solidarity and cohesion and to promote the interests of science to outside groups. Ben David (1971) has shown how the institution of science became separated from the Church and State in the nineteenth-century Germany. Merton (1942) highlighted claims made by scientists as to the moral appropriateness of the socialization processes of their profession. Gilbert and Mulkay (1984) have illustrated how charges of confusion and conflict resulting from the competing claims of different scientific workers, and hence doubts about claims to progressiveness, are countered by reference to the 'truth will out device'. Latour (1986) suggests that the power and uniqueness of 'techno-science' derives from its ability to build strong alliances out of heterogeneous components, to enrol allies in all areas of society by translating their interests and imposing severe costs for resistance, thus establishing ever more powerful actor networks.

Finally, science has achieved dominance because of its adaptability to a variety of legitimizing roles in society, both idealist and utilitarian. Tobey (1971) claimed that 'American democracy is the political version of the scientific method'. The history of scientific contributions to programmes of social engineering (Skinner, 1976), and the importance of science as an essential component in State and economic growth (Frame, 1979) or as a force shaping national identity (Mitroff, 1974), all attest to its utilitarian functions. MacIntyre (1988) shows how science and rationality have been utilized to support and operationalize a social utilitarian philosophy. Schon (1983) neatly summarizes the long-standing success of the technoscientific culture as follows:

> Since the Reformation the history of the west has been shaped by the rise of science and technology and by the industrial movement which was both the cause and consequence of the increasingly powerful scientific world view. As the scientific world view gained dominance so did the idea that human progress would be achieved by harnessing science to create technology for the achievement of human ends. This technological programme which was firstly vividly expressed in the writings of Bacon and Hobbes became a major theme for philosophers of the Enlightenment in the 18th Century and by the late 19th Century had been firmly established as a pillar of conventional wisdom.

The gradual but persistent growth in the cultural authority of Western science has led to the achievement of a privileged status at both epistemological and ethical levels. The most dramatic example of the epistemological privileging of science were the claims of the logical positivists. These claims became well known in Britain through the influential book *Language, Truth and Logic* by A.J. Ayer (1936). Ayer claimed that only empirically verifiable knowledge and deductive knowledge made any sense at all. This proved an unsustainable point of view. So to privilege science epistemologically does not entail that *only* science gives access to valid or useful knowledge but that science is the best, or more weakly probably the best, way of gaining reliable knowledge about the world. But privileging historically has a sociological as well as a philosophical basis. Mulkay (1979) has shown how in the history of the sociology of knowledge there has been a loose consensus amongst the main contributors: namely, that the sociological analysis of scientific knowledge-claims was seen as either unnecessary or severely restricted in comparison with other forms of human knowledge. This was because it was accepted that scientists had, by means of their particular methods, found ways of ensuring that their knowledge was uniquely determined by the state of the physical or social world. This in turn led to assumptions about the characteristics of the scientific community that must necessarily exist if such knowledge was to be realized in practice (Merton, 1942).

These last points illustrate an often neglected aspect of the scientific project: that is, the ethical component. Gans (1988: 11), in his presidential address to the ASA, pointed out that 'idealized natural science is a kind of civil religion in modern America, and there may be a quasi-religious element both in the ideal and the consensus behind it'. Hence the ideal of societal progress entails moral progress and is to be accomplished by means of universalistic rational criteria of method. This specifically modern conception challenges alternative faiths, categorizing them as mere customs or contingencies. To engage in an activity which leads to increased knowledge and possible control over the natural and social worlds is often held to be a means of overcoming earlier, more traditional, forms of dogma and superstition. As Vattimo (1988) has observed, this progressive notion in modernity becomes 'both a secularised faith and a faith in secularisation'. Science on this view became ethically privileged, and whilst its houses of worship took a different form from those of the faiths it replaced, its function was similar. Touraine's (1973) work on the changing strategic loci of society, the sites of change, development and transformation, considers that the monastery, cathedral, palace and industrial firm have now been superseded by the scientific laboratory as the current locus of crucial social power, an argument forcibly developed by Latour and Woolgar (1979).

Organization Theory and Visions of Science

For some involved in the study of organization the use of idealized scientific models and procedures is entirely appropriate and should be further encouraged. Thus Donaldson (1985) or Aldrich, in this volume, wish to see more empirical work involving better sampling, more replicative studies and the publishing of negative findings in order to better establish valid generalizations about organizational life. Others, in seeking to develop desirable models of people or organizations, import specific scientific images or structures into the discipline (Nisbett and Ross, 1980; Argyris et al., 1985).

The study of organization has historically been closely linked to the rise of science. Organizations, from Comte until the present day, have conventionally been seen as a manifestation of scientific analysis. For Comte, organizations were a form of instrumental rationality, a means of achieving particular purposes by means of rational analysis and design. For Weber (1961), the ideal bureaucracy was a key example of both scientific rationality and efficiency, in which 'there are no incalculable mysterious forces which come into play, but rather that one can in principle master all things by calculation. This means the world is disenchanted.' Scott (1987) traces the development of this approach to organization, and whilst demonstrating the emergence of the competing natural system and open-system approaches leaves the reader in little doubt as to the continuing popularity of the idea that organizations are a means of achieving particular aims.

We can further develop this idea of the ways in which scientific imagery and ideals have guided organizational theory and behaviour. It appears that there are very few areas of intellectual concern to the discipline that have not been so influenced. Psychological models of human capacities and interests emphasize the idea of people as inquiring organisms who structure their understandings and practices much as an ideal scientist is supposed to behave (Kelly, 1955). Cognitive psychologists have spent the best part of two decades working out the consequences of viewing humans as complex information-processors in the image of the computer (Nisbett and Ross, 1980). Action-oriented psychologists (Argyris et al., 1985), in attempting to generate knowledge useful for guiding action in organizational settings, have set out to identify the *causes* of action which an organization's members are assumed to be seeking, as an aid to understanding organizational life (see also other theories of causal attribution; Kelley, 1972). Indeed most input from psychology to organization studies, but excluding the action approach mentioned above, have assumed a traditional model of expertise in which the application of the laws of human or organizational functioning can be unproblematically applied. Bakan's (1966) analyses of the growth in popularity of psychology in America is a particularly clear example.

The analysis of management, including notions both of best practice and appropriate development strategies, is suffused with scientific imagery. Faced with the problem of how to manage organizations effectively, the primary tasks are seen as the establishment of essential facts of the situation, how to identify the key problems, and then how to objectively apply and evaluate the range of possible solutions. Chaffee (1985), and Blackler and Brown (1986), demonstrate the vitality of this approach in current attempts to manage the impacts of information technology on organizations. Bell (1980), in projecting towards a future based on the centrality of knowledge, argues that a major role of such knowledge will be 'to substitute an algorithm for intuitive judgements' in the management of complex organizations and systems.

Argyris et al. (1985) provide a key example in organization studies of dissatisfaction with the outcomes of traditional scientific activity, leading to a suggested programme as to how scientific practice might be reformed so as to become more effective in achieving emancipatory ends. The aim here is to reform organizational science rather than to debunk or reject it. Collins (1985) has noted that 'a loss of confidence in the scientific enterprise is a disaster we cannot afford. For all its fallibility science is the best institution for generating knowledge about the natural world that we have.' Working within a similar perspective, Argyris and his co-workers develop a programme for 'action science' that is a bold attempt, in the critical tradition, to produce knowledge that is directly relevant to action in organizations. Yet it remains largely uninformed by recent work in the history and sociology of science, conceptualizing human agents as hypothesis-testers seeking causal explanations for social events, and focusing upon the epistemological aims for an action science at the expense of its social organization. Similar objections can be raised against other attempts to redirect modern science such as those of Maxwell (1984), Lyotard (1984), and Lovelock (1990).

In contrast to such attempts to redirect scientific activity whilst retaining the legitimacy of its authority, other writers in organization studies have rejected scientific imagery in organization theory or have given up any claims to objective knowledge. From this perspective, scientism is seen as a real but unacceptable bias. (Scientism may be characterized as the making of exaggerated claims for the sphere of competence of scientific procedures, often involving the inappropriate use of natural scientific methods and imagery in the study of the social world, and necessarily entailing the privileging of science in an uncritical fashion.) Such a rejection of scientism has become associated with a relativistic approach to organization theory and practice. Within organization studies, differing reactions against scientism have grown rapidly since the early 1980s. Thus Weick (1985) argues that behaviour in organizations is not primarily goal-directed, that goals are discovered by action, that rational accounts are used to justify actions retrospectively rather than to direct them initially, and that the rational talk by managers about the world is merely rhetorical. Ambiguity not certainty is seen as characterizing loosely coupled systems in which action, interaction and discourse are means of securing order. Such analysis leads to a focus on the process of organizing rather than organization.

In a similar vein, post-industrial and 'end of ideology' theories (Bell, 1959, 1980), which postulate that political issues in organizations can be transformed into an activity concerned with rational–scientific issues, are rejected by many theorists who argue for the centrality of power and control as key concepts (Robins and Webster, 1988). One of the most effective demonstrations of the inadequacy of attempts to 'scientize' politics has been the study of public inquiries into the use of nuclear and chemical technologies (Wynne, 1982, 1989). Wynne shows how public inquiries conducted according to the scientific ideal usually function. The notion of rational individuals possessing expert knowledge and reaching consensus through appropriate analysis is transferred from the arena of science to that of political decision-making. In this way, an idealized model of scientific consensus provides a model for political consensus. The rationale here is described by Gouldner (1967; the emphasis is mine):

> Reason as method dis-establishes inner conviction, or strength of feeling as the basis of a claim to knowledge. The truth of reason is no longer held to be vouched for by a sense of intuitive certainty . . . Reason as method says that people are not right because born to high station and further neither does majority agreement among the many make something right. In this way reason is both anti-aristocratic and has begun to become *depoliticised in principle*.

But, as Wynne shows, to the objectors rationality is strongly politicized in practice. In recent public inquiries in the UK, the social assumptions of the experts, which cover organizations and their members, are exposed in a piecemeal fashion if at all. Objectors, whilst often impotent to resist the legitimacy of expert claims, still refuse to accept them, and thus a cycle of alienation is created, in which an expert group berates anti-scientific fundamentalists, and an objector group challenges what is seen as politicized rationality masquerading as expertise. The consequence on all sides is suspicion, mistrust and an absence of social learning.

Bernard Doray (1988), in a recent book focused on work organization, has summarized many such objections to scientific cultural imperialism as objections to a form of 'rational madness'. This occurs when purveyors of 'logical' scientific ideas become blind to their own preconceptions and to concern for their fellow human beings. Doray discusses Taylorism in these terms as establishing servitude and oppression as necessary conditions for efficiency. Current forms of such 'madness' are not difficult to discern in the claims of many of the advocates of the new industrial revolution based upon artificial intelligence and other forms of computerization (Robins and Webster, 1988). It seems clear that the Argyris et al. (1985) account of much organizational behaviour, based upon the ideal of controlling and winning unemotionally by means of 'rational' activity, is closely related to Doray's analyses. Argyris goes on to point out how difficult it is for individuals, who have been socialized into this view of appropriate behaviour, to change. We should not, therefore, underestimate the difficulties of avoiding such scientistic thinking and action in our culture.

Other objections have been lodged against the view that science is a valid form of progressive activity in society. Feyerabend (1975) views modern Western science as a form of trained incapacity. MacIntyre (1985) characterizes modern society as morally fractured and implicates social science, and particularly social psychology, as an important instrument in this state of affairs through its challenge to all forms of authoritative utterance. Such analysis give rise to some pressing problems, for if science is not a source of progressive ideas in society then the question arises as to what else might be. This problem haunts students of organization, for there seem to be few answers and some despondency on this issue, as the earlier quote from Pfeffer indicates. But just as scientists worked on happily for many years unaffected by the challenge which Hume's analysis of the problems of induction posed for their claims to verifiable certain knowledge, so many writers are content to pursue the 'scientific' study of organizations and leave it to others to resolve the difficulties posed by current challenges to scientific imagery and authority.

By contrast, others enthusiastically accept as liberating this challenge to scientific authority. There are a growing number of such discontents with modernity. For Feyerabend (1975), release from the strictures of scientific method will result in social emancipation. For Lyotard (1984), the 1980s was characterized by the end of the grand narratives – reason and science being the key. For Salman Rushdie's mouthpiece of Islamic fundamentalism in the *Satanic Verses*, the greatest of lies are 'progress, science and human rights'. For each, a celebration is in order if resistance is effective. A similar flavour is found in the organizational literature. Mangham (1987), for example, in an introduction to a collection of papers offered guidelines to the reader on the objectives of the work. These were 'to give offence': 'I want the readers to be made uncomfortable by what they read, to become angry and to react sharply'. Similarly, Kenneth Gergen (1985), discussing the consequences of social constructivist accounts in psychology, suggests that 'the success of such accounts depends primarily on the capacity to invite, compel, stimulate or delight the audience and *not on criteria of veracity*' (my emphasis).

Much writing on organization sees paradigms (Burrell and Morgan, 1979) and metaphors (Morgan, 1986) in such relativistic terms. If paradigms are characterized as incommensurable or metaphors as infinitely exchangeable, then a relativistic discipline is defined in which there are no secure grounds for selecting, using or valuing one approach over another.

The further elaboration and defence of this position is often traced to the seminal work of Feyerabend (1975). This, it is claimed, justifies the assertion that no rational criteria exist for choosing between theories within science, nor for choosing between science and other forms of life. Thus if there are no external or universal intellectual standards then it appears to follow that 'subjective taste' is all there is, and that there is no circumstance in which rules or standards can be unambiguously applied. Such an interpretation amounts to the view that each theory, paradigm or metaphor is as good, or bad, as any other. Woolgar's (1988) deconstruction of the representational practices of scientists appears to further support this position.

Any student of organization, therefore, now appears to be faced with a fundamental and unavoidable choice; either to continue within a science-privileging framework, conscious perhaps that this has created problems to date, but holding to a faith that with more effort and better practice any difficulties will be overcome and unity will emerge from apparent fragmentation; *or* alternatively to break away from all forms of perceived scientism to embrace relativism and to give up any claims to the scientific legitimacy of any particular knowledge-claim in the discipline.

In the final section of this chapter I want to challenge this dichotomy by suggesting a way forward which focuses upon the social and organizational basis of modern science and which offers opportunities for organization studies to contribute to a deeper understanding of the key institution of modernity.

Avoiding the Rock and the Hard Place

In this final section I suggest that reference to recent work in the history and sociology of science offers a way of avoiding both the scientistic and relativistic emphases in much organization theory. In the space available I can only hope to identify the key areas that are relevant here rather than fully develop their consequences. The two main sources are Feyerabend (1975, 1978) on different conceptions of relativism, and Latour (1986, 1989) for his radical programmatic for the characterization and study of all forms of science. Drawing upon these and other sources it can be argued that scientistic tendencies depend upon a discredited and unsupportable view of science based upon an ideology of representation (Woolgar, 1988), whilst relativistic stances in organization theory are primitive and poorly developed because they systematically ignore the social and organizational characteristics of differing theoretical and methodological positions.

As other contributors to this volume suggest (see in particular Stephen Ackroyd and Nick Perry), many current misunderstandings and difficulties stem from an emasculated conception of the concept of paradigm. If as Masterman (1970) suggests, Kuhn in his original formulation of the concept manipulated its meaning in 21 different ways it is perhaps unsurprising that confusions exist. The conventional interpretation in organization theory is that paradigms differ in terms of their epistemological characteristics, or the philosophical positions that they imply. Thus paradigms encapsulate irreconcilable or incommensurable differences, and judgements as to paradigm adequacy can only be made in terms of criteria internal to any particular paradigmatic framework. Two important consequences follow from such an analysis. Firstly, a clear sharp separation can be made between epistemological and sociological phenomena, and this in spite of Kuhn's characterization of paradigm in terms of metaphysical, exemplary and sociological factors. Secondly, since there are no secure grounds for judgements to be made between competing paradigms, relativism is unavoidable. Kuhn's gradual retreat from a wholehearted embrace of relativism and his retrenchment to a semi-rationalist position in which the *socialization* of scientists is the key, seems largely ignored; and instead Feyerabend's work is utilized to support and develop the inevitability of incommensurability, but only at an epistemological level. Feyerabend is thus viewed as a philosopher; his claim also to be an historian is forgotten, and 'epistemologicalism' is born in which the social is strangely overlooked.

Detailed examination of this received wisdom on Feyerabend soon shows the paucity of such an analysis. Feyerabend (1978) offered the principle 'anything goes' as the only defensible principle that a rationalist can be certain of, as the only universal rational rule of scientific content. 'Anything goes' is thus a summary of the predicament of the rationalist who searches for a universal standard. It serves as such a standard even though it is 'empty, useless and pretty ridiculous'. When charged that this meant selection between theories or methods thereby became impossible, he explicitly rejected that view. 'The epistemological anarchist has no compulsion to defend the most trite or the most outrageous statement' (Feyerabend, 1975). The history of science shows that scientists consistently select between competing views, and Feyerabend's point was that such choice depends upon values, not upon universal rational criteria. The pertinent values change depending upon culture, and may or may not include rational criteria as a relevant value. An important distinction is thus made between an unacceptable and an acceptable form of relativism: judgemental relativism, which claims all forms of knowledge are equally valid or invalid; and epistemic relativism.

> Epistemic relativism is not committed to the idea that there is no material world, or that all knowledge claims are equally good or bad, or to the idea that meter readings can be made to our liking. It is only committed to the idea that what we make of physical resistances and of meter signals is itself grounded in human assumptions and selections which appear to be specific to a particular historical place and time. (Knorr-Cetina, 1982)

It therefore becomes not only possible but essential for the full force of sociological analysis to be brought to bear to show how value judgements and decisions concerning choices in science are made and how the particular institutional and organizational arrangements of a particular discipline shape and order knowledge-claims. Such an analysis allows an appreciation of the adequacy of any particular knowledge-claim to be made. Epistemological claims therefore arise from social practice and not simply from legitimation or otherwise by philosophers. As Yearley (1988) claims, there is nothing in the physical or social world that uniquely determines scientific conclusions and hence the social organization of science is the key. Thus the cognitive, technical and organizational resources of scientists are open to sociological analysis much as any other form of human knowledge might be. Judgements between paradigms, metaphors or theories are to be understood as value judgements sustained by particular social arrangements but open to revision and debate.

This conclusion is well supported and documented in the sociology of science. Barnes (1974) states that 'Belief systems cannot be objectively ranked in terms of their proximity to reality or their rationality. This is not to say that practical choices between belief systems are at all difficult to make or that I myself am not clear as to my own preferences.' And Edge (1979), writing of the sociological task involved in characterizing the chain of decisions which lead to scientific knowledge-claims, holds that 'Each decision brings together cognitive, intellectual, technical, cultural, and social and historical factors. One task of the historian or sociologist of science is to explicate such decisions and to explore the grounding of their rationality.'

It seems, then, that taken seriously such a programme invites a reappraisal of science within organization studies. Discussion of the epistemological incommensurability of our paradigms (see Jackson and Carter, 1991) or assumptions about the epistemological equivalence of metaphors seems limited and misplaced. More importantly, we should be more reflexive and examine the justifications in value terms for different approaches, their relevance to different audiences and the organizational and institutional support each receives.

Bloor (1976) has neatly characterized the sociological contribution to the analysis of science in terms of the principle of symmetry. In traditional accounts of science, social factors are only introduced to explain events when things go wrong, when the true path of reason or the adequacy of representational activity becomes distorted. Bloor criticizes such asymmetry in the use of rational and social factors and argues that social factors should be used to account for instances of both successful and unsuccessful scientific outcomes. Furthermore, social factors can also properly be used to account for both scientific and non-scientific activities. In this way, science apparently becomes no different from other forms of knowledge-generating activity. Yet given the earlier analysis of the cultural authority of science, Bloor seems to offer no clear analysis as to the importance or uniqueness of science in modern society, since by claiming to reveal the similarity between science and other knowledge-generating activities such sociology of science cannot pursue the key question raised by Gieryn (1982): 'What makes science unique among culture producing institutions?'

In contrast, Latour's radical programmatic for the study of science, technology and society, or 'technoscience', offers an answer to that question as well as identifying the limitations of both rationalistic and relativistic conceptions of science. Latour outlines a research programme for the study of all sciences – natural, social or organizational – which avoids problems of disciplinary specialization ('this Babel of disciplines'), collapses conventional boundaries between science, technology and society into a seamless web of stronger or weaker associations, and conceptualizes technoscience as a unique activity which builds strong networks of association out of 'heterogeneous elements'. Latour invites us to apply this programme to any aspect of 'science in action' and to assess its potency and limitations. What follows is the beginnings of such a project for organization studies.

For Latour, science is a form of paper war, with its key feature the organization of persuasion through literary inscription (Latour and Woolgar, 1979). This is achieved by enrolling and controlling physical and social resources, or allies, into strong networks of association. Fact-making becomes a collective business in which resistance must be overcome or realigned. Interests must be translated if the key objective of making one's own work indispensable, or 'blackboxed', is to be attained. The contents of actor networks are surprisingly varied: technoscience includes 'all the elements tied to scientific contents no matter how dirty, unexpected or foreign they may seem', and this contrasts sharply with conventional accounts of science and technology which are only 'what is kept of technoscience once all the trials of responsibility have been settled'. Scientific truth or reality is that which resists the several trials of strength to which it is subjected. Thus assertions 'do not catch on because they are true but are held to be true because they catch on'. Science and scientists are imperialistic, conducting a paper war to allow action at a distance. 'Every time you hear about a successful application of science look for a progressive extension of a network.'

In order to study science, then, we should focus on following the diverse actors as they contribute to the growth or decline of networks. It is the formation and durability of those networks that is the key to understanding, not the epistemological characteristics of knowledge-claims. In describing networks, Latour recommends that we should consider a whole range of unexpected physical and social entities. 'Those that are really doing science are not all at the bench; on the contrary there are people at the bench because many more are doing science elsewhere.' Perhaps the key exemplar of this mode of analysis is the account of the 'Pasteurization' of France. Here the focus is upon the way in which Pasteur developed control over bacilli in the laboratory and on the farm, and over hygienists, government agencies and others with social power so as to be able to enrol all necessary allies into a network of association that becomes increasingly costly to resist. The importance and uniqueness of science in our society, on this analysis, lies in the particularly strong set of heterogeneous associations that has made scientific claims less resistible than others. The cultural authority of science is understood in terms of the very limited scope for negotiation available to new recruits.

In his most recent work (Latour, 1989), the actor network model is elaborated in terms of its ability to offer a new perspective on the issues of rationality and relativism which I have argued are central to established positions in organization theory. Both are examined and found wanting, in large part because they both insist upon too homogeneous a set of factors relevant to the resolution of disputes. Thus for the rationalists, those accused of a scientistic bias in organization theory, disputes are resolved solely by recourse to logical rules and methodologies for exact representation of reality. On this view, to allow social factors to dictate outcomes is pathological. On the other hand, relativists claim that only social factors determine outcomes and that constraints of the physical or social worlds are immaterial. Each group, then, is seen as having too restricted a conception of reality.

This analysis also casts fresh light upon the issue of symmetry and asymmetry in the explanation of outcomes (Bloor, 1976). For the rationalist, Pasteur, Einstein and Diesel succeeded *because* they were more rational, their opponents being led from the path of truth by social intrusions. For the relativist, a more symmetrical examination of the winners and losers in scientific disputes is needed. Both sides must be treated equally to discern the social and organizational factors at work. For Latour, however, the establishment of a new asymmetry is required. If we want to understand how Pasteur, Einstein or Diesel triumphed over their respective oppositions, then we need to establish the strength of the respective actor networks that are established, including the costs of opposition and resistance.

Pasteur is a member of The Academy; his opponent is not. He can expound his own point of view at length in the house journal; his opponent cannot. The commission set up by the academy to judge their two claims is made up only of Pasteur's colleagues and admirers; his opponent has no-one on the commission sympathetic to his claim. Pasteur invokes God, the support of the church, Law and Order, on behalf of his demonstration that spontaneous generation cannot occur; his opponent is associated with atheism, Darwinism and social revolution. Pasteur traces a complete dichotomy between his religious or political opinions and his science, his opponent . . . mixes moral argument with his experimental set up . . . (Latour, 1989)

Scientific truth, then, is not the result of just representational activity or just social definitions, but rather is the outcome of struggles between competing actor networks in which the weight of allies, both physical and social, determines outcomes. Only after the outcome is decided can the label 'truth' be attached. On this view, to see different knowledge-claims as somehow equivalent, as judgemental relativists claim, is to ignore all the efforts entailed in building stronger networks of association. Such a relativism implies that Pasteur's and others' huge efforts to establish powerful networks are all a waste of time because their knowledge-claims are in reality indistinguishable from those of their defeated opponents.

It has been possible only to point to the range of new perspectives opened up by actor network theory and its relevance to contemporary concerns in organization theory. Much systematic research efforts will be required before an adequate evaluation of this approach could be offered. In conclusion I suggest three possible avenues for future development.

First, since actor network theory depends upon the establishment and organization of networks of association, theorists of organization would appear to have an important role in developing the analysis. Deeper understanding of the organizational characteristics of successful and unsuccessful networks might then be forthcoming. Latour's work is first and foremost an invitation to scholars from a variety of disciplines to develop and criticize the programmatic that he offers. The contribution of students of organization could be central to that project.

Secondly, actor network theory offers us an opportunity to be more reflexive concerning our own activities. New avenues of inquiry into the characteristics of preferred paradigms and metaphors are suggested. Rather than focus upon incommensurability we should study how extensive and heterogeneous are the networks which support and define the functionalist paradigm or the organic metaphor. The structure, development and longevity of the appropriate network would be the focus. This would not necessarily threaten the viability or legitimacy of any particular paradigm or metaphor, but would usefully examine the justification in value terms of different approaches, their relevance to different audiences and the institutional support that each receives.

Finally, I do not wish to be understood as taking an uncritical view of actor network theory. Although it appears that this work is theoretically rather innovative, with the rejection of sociological and methodological reductionism and advocacy of a seamless web approach to explanation, it is not clear to what extent an explanation or a description of the nature of science is being offered. Deep at the heart of the approach lies the notion that science is a form of paper war fought out between conflicting armies. If this characteristic were to be confirmed, disillusion with the progressive aims and ideals for science might have to be accepted. Earlier in this chapter I argued for the link between modernity and certain beliefs about the epistemological and ethical characteristics of science. Denial or rejection of that link opens up a wholly new set of problems and possibilities.

References

Adas, M. (1989) *Machines as the Measure of Men: Science, Technology and Ideologies of Western Dominance*. Ithaca: Cornell University Press.

Argyris, C., Putnam, R. and Smith, D. (1985) *Action Science*. San Francisco: Jossey-Bass.

Ayer, A.J. (1936) *Language, Truth and Logic*. London: Gollancz.

Bakan, D. (1966) 'Behaviourism and American urbanism', *Journal of the History of Behavioural Sciences*, 2: 5–28.

Barnes, B. (1974) *Scientific Knowledge and Sociological Theory*. London: Routledge & Kegan Paul.

Bell, D. (1959) *The End of Ideology*. New York: Free Press.

Bell, D. (1980) 'The social framework of the information society', in T. Forester (ed.) *The Microelectronic Revolution*. Oxford: Blackwell.

Ben David, J. (1971) *The Scientist's Role in Society*. Englewood Cliffs, NJ: Prentice-Hall.

Blackler, F. and Brown, C. (1986) 'Alternative models to guide the design and introduction of the new information technologies into work organisations', *Journal of Occupational Psychology*, 59: 287–313.

Bloor, D. (1976) *Knowledge and Social Imagery*. London: Routledge & Kegan Paul.

Burrell, G. and Morgan, G. (1979) *Sociological Paradigms and Organisational Analysis*. London: Heinemann.

Callon, M., Law, J. and Rip, A. (eds) (1986) *Mapping the Dynamics of Science and Technology*. London: Macmillan.

Chaffee, E.E. (1985) 'Three models of strategy', *Academy of Management Review*, 10 (1): 89–98.

Collins, H.M. (1985) *Changing Order: Replication and Induction in Scientific Practice*. London: Sage.

Donaldson, L. (1985) *In Defence of Organisation Theory: A Reply to the Critics*. Cambridge: Cambridge University Press.

Doray, B. (1988) *From Taylorism to Fordism: A Rational Madness*. London: Free Association.

Edge, D. (1979) 'Quantitative measures of communication in science', *History of Science*, 17: 102–34.

Feyerabend, P. (1975) *Against Method*. London: New Left Books.

Feyerabend, P. (1978) 'From incompetent professionalism to professionalised incompetence – The rise of a new breed of intellectuals', in P. Feyerabend, *Science in a Free Society*. London: New Left Books.

Frame, J.D. (1979) 'National economic resources and the production of research in lesser developed countries', *Social Studies of Science*, 9: 233–46.

Gans, H.J. (1988) 'Sociology in America: The discipline and the public', *American Sociological Review*, 54 (1): 1–16.

Gergen, K. (1985) 'The social constructionist movement in modern psychology', *American Psychologist*, 40 (3): 266–75.

Gieryn, T.F. (1982) 'Relativist/constructivist programmes in the sociology of science: Redundance and retreat', *Social Studies of Science*, 12: 279–97.

Gilbert, N. and Mulkay, M. (1984) *Opening Pandora's Box: A sociological analysis of scientists' discourse*. Cambridge: Cambridge University Press.

Gouldner, (1967) *Enter Plato*. London: Routledge & Kegan Paul.

Habermas, J. (1983) 'Modernity: An incomplete project', in H. Foster (ed.), *The Antiaesthetic: Essays on Postmodern Culture*. Washington: Bay Press.

Hajek, F.A. (1979) 'Coping with ignorance', in C.A. Yarchis (ed.) *Champions of Freedom*. Michigan: Hillsdale College Press.

Harvey, D. (1989) *The Condition of Postmodernity*. Oxford: Basil Blackwell.

Horkheimer, M. and Adorno, T. (1972) *The Dialectic of the Enlightenment*. London: Allen Lane.

Jackson, N. and Carter, P. (1991) 'In defence of paradigm incommensurability', *Organization Studies*, 12 (1): 109–27.

Jones, R.V. (1978) *Most Secret War*. London: Hamish Hamilton.

Kelley, H.H. (1972) *Causal Schemata and the Attribution Process*. Morristown, NJ: General Learning Press.

Kelly, G. (1955) *The Psychology of Personal Constructs*. New York: Norton.

Knorr-Cetina, K.D. (1982) 'The constructivist programme in the sociology of science: Retreats or advances?' *Social Studies of Science*, 12: 320–4.

Latour, B. (1986) *Science in Action*. Milton Keynes: Open University Press.

Latour, B. (1989) 'Clothing the naked truth', in H. Lawson and L. Appignanesi (eds), *Dismantling Truth*. London: Weidenfeld & Nicolson.

Latour, B. and Woolgar, S. (1979) *Laboratory Life: The Social Construction of Scientific Facts*. Beverly Hills: Sage.

Laudan, L. (1977) *Progress and its Problems*. London: Routledge & Kegan Paul.

Lovelock, J. (1990) 'The greening of science', *Resurgence*, 138: 12–19.

Lyotard, J.F. (1984) *The Postmodern Condition: A Report on Knowledge*. Manchester: Manchester University Press.

MacIntyre, A. (1985) 'How psychology makes itself true or false', in S. Koch and D. Leary (eds), *A Century of Psychology as Science*. New York: McGraw-Hill.

MacIntyre, A. (1988) *Whose Justice? Whose Rationality?* London: Duckworth.

Mangham, I. (1987) *Organization Analysis and Development*. London: Wiley.

Masterman, M. (1970) 'The nature of a paradigm', in I. Lakatos and A. Musgrave (eds), *Criticism and the Growth of Knowledge*. Cambridge: Cambridge University Press.

Maxwell, N. (1984) *From Knowledge to Wisdom: A Revolution in the Aims and Methods of Science*. Oxford: Basil Blackwell.

Merton, R.K. (1942) 'Science and technology in a democratic order', *Journal of Legal and Political Sociology*, vol. 1. Republished in R.K. Merton (1967) *Social Theory and Social Structure*. London: Free Press.

Mitroff, I. (1974) *The Subjective Side of Science*. Amsterdam: Elsevier.

Morgan, G.M. (1986) *Images of Organization*. London: Sage.

Mulkay, M. (1979) *Science and the Sociology of Knowledge*. London: George Allen and Unwin.

Nisbett, R.E. and Ross, L. (1980) *Human Inference: Strategies and Shortcomings of Social Judgement*. Englewood Cliffs, NJ: Prentice-Hall.

Perrow, C. (1984) *Normal Accidents: Living with High Risk Technologies*. New York: Basic Books.

Pfeffer, J. (1982) *Organisations and Organisation Theory*. Marshfield, MA: Pitman Press.

Ravetz, J. (1971) *Scientific Knowledge and its Social Problems*. Oxford: Oxford University Press.

Robins, K. and Webster, F. (1988) 'Athens without slaves . . . or slaves without Athens? The neurosis of technology', *Science as Culture*, 4: 7–50.

Scarr, S. (1985) 'Constructing psychology: Making facts and fables for our times', *American Psychologist*, 40: 499–512.

Schon, D. (1983) *The Reflective Practitioner*. London: Temple Smith.

Scott, W.R. (1987) *Organizations: Rational, Natural and Open Systems*. Englewood Cliffs, NJ: Prentice-Hall.

Skinner, B.F. (1976) *Walden Two*. London: Macmillan.

Tobey, R.C. (1971) *The American Ideology of National Science*. Pittsburgh, PA: University of Pittsburgh Press.

Touraine, A. (1973) *Production de la Société*. Paris: Le Seuil.

Vattimo, G. (1988) *The End of Modernity: Nihilism and Hermeneutics in Post-modern Culture*. Cambridge: Polity Press.

Weber, M. (1961) 'Science as vocation', in H.H. Gerth and G.W. Mills (eds), *For Max Weber: Essays in Sociology*. London: Routledge & Kegan Paul.

Weick, K. (1985) 'Sources of order in underorganized systems: Themes in recent organisational theory', in Y. Lincoln (ed.), *Organization Theory and Inquiry: The Paradigm Revolution*. Beverly Hills: Sage.

Weick, K. (1987) 'Theorising about organizational communication', in F. Jablin, L. Putnam and L. Porter (eds), *Handbook of Organizational Communication*. Beverly Hills: Sage.

Whitley, R. (1984) 'The development of management studies as a fragmented adhocracy', *Social Science Information*, 23: 775–818.

Woolgar, S. (1988) *Science – The Very Idea*. London: Tavistock.

Wynne, B. (1982) *Rationality and Ritual*. Chalfont St. Giles: British Society for the History of Science.

Wynne, B. (1989) 'Frameworks of rationality in risk management: Towards the testing of naive sociology', in J. Brown (ed.), *Environmental Threats: Analysis, Perception and Management*. London: Belhaven.

Yearley, S. (1988) *Science, Technology and Social Change*. London: Unwin Hyman.

5

Putting Theory in its Place:
The Social Organization of
Organizational Theorizing

Nick Perry

One might describe organization theory as that discipline which moves between the discussion of what Max Weber's writings can be made to mean and the exploration of what computers can be made to say. Such a caricature does have its uses. It bears a recognizable relation to what practitioners have identified as the theoretical foundations of the subject and its subsequent technical elaboration. Like all caricatures, it has the legitimate and conscious intention of distorting its subject in order to reveal it, and the incidental effect of revealing the preoccupations of its producer.

It is just such 'distortions' – in the form of conceptual choices and technical operations – which are the subject matter of this chapter. More specifically, my interest is in trying to explain why the patterns of disagreement and debate that are endemic to organizational analysis take the form that they do. My argument is that since organizational theorizing is at once cognitive and social, it is neither unsullied by social interests nor unproblematically deducible from them. As such, organization theories are neither the product of immaculate conception nor reducible to ideological conspiracies. They are rather constitutive of differing configurations of interests, symbolic resources through which a sense of commonality is recognized and constructed. This claim is advanced by investigating how differences in cultural style and in disciplinary background are expressed, and then probing how such expressions relate to notions of communal use, professional closure, paradigm elaboration and institutional context. And since the ghost of Weber and the machinery of computation have already been invoked, they can serve to provide the examples with which this inquiry can begin.

Cultural Style and National Differences

Those examples occur in the published proceedings of what would seem to be two very different international conferences. One was based in Germany (Stammer, 1971) and one in the United States (Greenberger, 1962). The Heidelberg conference purportedly harked back to Max

Weber's birth, whereas the American colloquium was dedicated to probing into the future of computers and management. But as David Lodge's
recent satire (1985) has elegantly exposed, academic conferences are small
worlds unto themselves, in which their typical patterns of 'internal'
differences are actually suggestive of the structural similarities between
them. In the examples I want to cite, it is variations in national
background and disciplinary allegiance which offer a preliminary
purchase in understanding the patterns of debate and contestation that are
characteristic of such gatherings.

Consider, for example, the reaction of American political scientist Karl
Deutsch to an interpretation by French sociologist Raymond Aron which
had emphasized the nationalist underpinnings of Weber's thought. It is
worth quoting Deutsch's observations (1971: 120) at length:

> Government, for Weber, is the chance of getting obedience. A chance is a
> probability, and the answer to the question: what is chance? is a number. So
> Weber's concept of sovereign power is a matter of the frequency of men's
> compliance or submission . . . This idea of Weber's can be operationalised.
> There are methods of measuring . . .
>
> One could go further . . . We can try to express the interaction of rates of
> submission, transgression and enforcement by a system of equations. Weber's
> theory, thus explained and enriched by the factor of the autonomous
> probability of relevant behaviour, forms a mathematical model of four equa-
> tions . . .

Which prompted Aron to respond (1971: 131–2):

> Professor Deutsch has told me more or less plainly that I translated Weber into
> French. That may be so but he can be translated into American too, even with
> a certain German thoroughness. But whether the American or the French
> translation is better is not to be determined in a 'value free' way . . . It is quite
> possible that one can measure legality mathematically, but . . . that is Max
> Weber translated into American: it may be an improvement, but it is not the
> Max Weber I have read . . .

This British-based (and basically British) account of a Franco-American
exchange, made in the context of a conference organized under German
auspices, merits comparison with Galtung's essay on different intellectual
styles. For Galtung, stylistic variations are not decorative epiphenomena,
but the very way in which different modes of cultural understanding find
expression. He sees them as most clearly displayed in the form of national
differences in the typical question that is posed when social scientific practitioners are faced with a proposition. In Galtung's pithy and sardonic
formulation (1981: 838):

> – saxonic style: how do you operationalize it? (US version)
>   how do you document it? (UK version)
> – teutonic style: wie können Sie das zurückführen – ableiten? (how can you
>   trace this back – deduce it from basic principles?)
> – gallic style: peut-on dire cela en bon français? (is it possible to say this in
>   French?)

Why Weber Matters: The Transition from Meaning to Use

My condensed version of a single academic skirmish can do no more than illustrate Galtung's thesis. But it does allow us to view his argument as prima facie plausible rather than outrageously speculative. As such, it offers valuable leverage in explaining the strange fate of Weber's ideas within organization theory and the curious intensity of the attendant debate. For what proves to be at stake is not just the correct exegesis of a dead scholar but the appropriate agenda for engaging with a live issue.

Let me elaborate. The puzzle is that in the development of American-inspired bureaucratic theory and the contingency theory which succeeded it, it was the least original aspects of Weber's work which received most attention – that is, his inventory of bureaucratic characteristics. The significance of that inventory in Weber's own work derived from its relation to other organizational forms and its place in his comparative schema. Its significance in the development of organization theory, however, appears to lie in its affinities with the maxims of classical management theory. Despite the exasperation (Bendix and Roth, 1971: 122) or bemusement (Albrow, 1970: 54–66) of Weberian scholars, there seems no necessary reason to interpret this development as unproductive. Such a partial and partisan account of Weber's ideas becomes explicable as soon as one interprets Weber's role as catalytic or legitimatory rather than epigenetic. The exigencies of Weber's translation into English no doubt played a part in this, as did Parsons' (1947, 1949) Whiggish interpretation of him as an incipient functionalist. However pertinent these, and related, historical contingencies may have been, what merits emphasis and requires explanation is how the reference to Weber came to seem obligatory. In other words, what kind of cultural work got done through such a standardized social practice? How did meaning connect with use?

It is Weber's own account of the relation between the protestant ethic and the spirit of capitalism which can furnish a clue. His project was to explain how the other-worldly orientation of a handful of Puritan divines might none the less be connected to the this-worldly practices of an economic system that had become global in its reach and self-sustaining in its modes of legitimation. My much more mundane (if no less esoteric) concern is to account for the initially significant, and now declining, ritual invocation of Weber's scholarly writing within the otherwise pragmatically operationalist and technique-oriented practices of contemporary organization theory in its mainstream American variant.

The development of bureaucratic case studies in the USA was marked by a partisan interpretation of Weber which provided a creative working solution to contradictory cultural pressures. It premise was that there was an elective affinity between his concerns and those of his American interpreters; these latter offered a reading of Weber's work which endeavoured to reconcile their ideal interests with their material location. What distinguished these case studies, therefore, was the striving to reconcile the

antinomies of armchair reflection and empirical observation, European
social thought and American can-doism, the scholarly ethic and the spirit
of pragmatism. The resulting indeterminacies and ambiguities in such
texts are precisely what accounts for their continuing appeal to many
European readers (Perry, 1979; Reed, 1985). For the subsequent generation of American and American-oriented researchers, however, it was that
very same openness which they sought to overcome. The latter's response
to the perceived limitations of this body of work was the development and
elaboration of the operationalist strategies of contingency theory. The
authors of this initiative none the less continued to cast Weber in the
legitimatory, if progressively more honorific, role of founding father of
the discipline. In so doing they effectively laid the groundwork for the
kind of critique to which contingency theory was subjected during the
1970s and early 1980s.

Weber had been the means of resolving a dilemma for the immediate
post-war generation of American authors; for their successors he was
(eventually) to pose a problem. Given contingency theory's pragmatic
movement towards theoretical and methodological closure, the Weberian
bridge now assumed a different and more subversive role. It was available
to maintain the link with wider debates in European social and political
thought, and especially a revitalized Marxism. It could therefore be used
to open up closure, to legitimate critique, to sanction the return of the
repressed (see, for example, Clegg and Dunkerley, 1980).

Viewed against this background the exchange between Deutsch and
Aron becomes rather more than a debate about the relative merits of
patricide and ancestor worship. It can be read as an encapsulated moral
homily on the development of organization theory as a discipline and its
relation to different cultural traditions. It's a development in which the
general issue of how the parameters of a discipline should be defined was
expressed by and through the specifics of authorial interpretation. In
understanding that process it is more instructive to probe the various
discrepant uses to which Weber has been put than to seek to adjudicate
on what he might really have meant.

Disciplinary Differences and the Uses of Metaphor

Such a foregrounding of the effect of national differences on translation
is consistent with the (editorial) conclusion of the Hofstede and Kassen
anthology (Hofstede, 1976: 21) that the most meaningful classification of
organization theory in Europe is by culture area. In Crozier's (1976)
contribution to the same volume, however, it is discipline and methodological preference which are given priority. Such an emphasis on the
consequences of variations in disciplinary allegiance is also evident in the
American colloquium which I want to consider next. This involves cross-
ing from Heidelberg to MIT, and replacing Weberian controversy with
speculation about computers. There is none the less a clear continuity

between the anxieties expressed by the American historian of technology Elting Morison, and the exchange between Deutsch and Aron. Morison's concerns appear in his account of how his most able engineering students responded to the most famous play in the English language. The trouble with Hamlet, in their view, was that:

First, he had too much feedback on his circuits, and second he was only 16.7 percent efficient because he had one person to kill and he killed six. This, purely incidentally, is about the thermal efficiency of the average internal combustion engine. (Morison, 1962: 17)

What makes such an interpretation appear so exotic is the cultural distance between the disciplines of engineering and dramatic criticism; between our received notion of the centrality of a ghost and its effective displacement by a machine. Read one way, the engineers' view marks the subordination of the culturally indeterminate and morally ambiguous to cognitive power; read another, it vindicates critical claims about the limits of technical reason. It thus echoes the Aron/Deutsch exchange but transcribes national differences and epistemological distinctions into questions of methodology and disciplinary preference. It is also rather funny.

For present purposes, however, its prime significance is that for all its quirkiness it nevertheless dramatizes a more general cognitive practice – that is, the migration of guiding metaphors from one disciplinary context to another, with all their attendant productive possibilities and dislocative effects. The enthusiastic and selective appropriation of Kuhn's imagery of natural science by contemporary social scientists seeking to interpret – or change – their activities is a well known and much debated example of this process. In the development of organization theory, however, the most consequential case is probably the emergence of the 'Pareto circle' at Harvard. Under the leadership of physiologist L.J. Henderson and taking Cannon's *The Wisdom of the Body* as its model, its systematization of biological imagery exerted a crucial influence on, and through, Chester Barnard's *The Functions of the Executive*, the work of Elton Mayo and the writings of Talcott Parsons (Russett, 1966: 141–2). Whilst most such instances of cognitive transfer do not prove to be as influential as the Pareto circle was, some such patterns do none the less seem to be endemic to most of the social and at least some of the natural sciences (Mullins, 1972; Mulkay, 1972). When successful, it may require a conscious effort to recover their metaphoric origins. For example, an entire discipline has been built upon Freud's attempt to understand the psyche through the language of hydraulics (blockages, discharges, drains and so on), and yet what it takes for granted was once as arcane as positing a link between systems engineering and Shakespearian heroes.

From Discipline as Product to Discipline as Process

Thus far I have sketched out some of the characteristic effects upon organization theory of the apparent intractability of national frontiers and cultural traditions and of the apparent permeability of the discipline's cognitive boundaries. This should at least displace any lingering assumption that its findings are given by, or unproblematically deducible from, the nature of the external world. This is not, of course, to say that cognitive commitments can simply be read off from national background or disciplinary location. Practitioners' communities of orientation remain stubbornly discrete from their communities of origin. Allegiance to such communities of orientation is none the less not to be thought of as random but rather as structured in quite definite ways and in accordance with discernible interests. A more systematic and comprehensive mapping would therefore depend upon investigating the full range of cultural sites at which such commitments are both tested and contested, the terms under which those engagements occur, and their social and intellectual effects. Its correlate is a conception of the discipline not as an established datum but as a social process of structuration (Giddens, 1979). One effect of this is to decentre the tendencies of some practitioners to interpret the development of the discipline in terms of successive approximations to the presumed characteristics of natural science. In Donaldson's (1985) case the relevant authority and claimed source of indebtedness is the writing of Popper, whereas for Burrell and Morgan (1979) it is the work of Kuhn. However great the resulting differences, what such authors none the less share is the presumption that an understanding of how physics achieves its accomplishments has salience for the practice of social science. An emphasis on structuration is not only consistent with the substance (but not the tone) of Donaldson's scepticism about Burrell and Morgan's use of Kuhn (compare Perry, 1977). It also extends that scepticism to Donaldson's own (necessarily selective) recourse to other more socially reputable or cognitively powerful practices in his attempt to provide a mandate for the specificity of his own. His strategy of appealing to an externally derived scientific standard is both explicable and double-edged. For example, Popper's strictures on the scientific defects of sociological holism and the protracted defence of methodological individualism by him and his followers (compare O'Neill, 1973) make it wholly improbable that Donaldson's defence of functionalism would be supported by his philosophic mentor. For present purposes, therefore, Donaldson's 'scientific' strategy, like Burrell and Morgan's, is to be seen as just one amongst others. It is the strategies themselves which are the focus of inquiry, rather than the standard by which inquiries are to be judged.

A partial precedent and relevant parallel for this way of proceeding is given by Johnson's (1972) reworking of the concept of profession as a system of occupation *control* rather than an occupation *per se*. The effect was to free the academic study of professionalism from the so called 'trait approach', a methodology in which selected attributes of such traditional professional practices as law and medicine provided a benchmark against which aspirants for professional status could be measured. What Johnson demonstrated was that this unilinear approach was misconceived, and that the strategies available to, and deployed by, professional groups not only varied systematically, but were contingent upon the historical and institutional conditions under which those groupings had emerged. By extension, therefore, the concept of a discipline is here thought of *not* in terms of the extent to which it possesses a series of attributes associated with prestigious modes of inquiry, but rather as an historically and institutionally conditioned attempt to secure cognitive control.

This emphasis on cognitive, rather than occupational, control is a means of according full weight to the specificity and relative autonomy of academic inquiry and intellectual endeavour. (One of the ways in which such autonomy is signalled is that scholarly reputation can always be distinguished from both hierarchical position and institutional location.) But as is now widely recognized, relative autonomy (Althusser, 1971) is a description, rather than an explanation, of the relation between institutional orders. As such, the extent of that autonomy is not a theoretical given, but a matter of empirical investigation. The work of Richard Whitley provides a definitive demonstration of this. Thanks to him we now have both a map of the patterned variations as between the various sciences (including the social sciences) and an exploration of some of their intra-disciplinary effects (Whitley, 1984a). He categorizes management studies as a 'fragmented adhocracy' (Whitley, 1984b), in which not only are levels of dependence between researchers low, but also controls over objectives and techniques are dispersed and rudimentary. Whitley goes on to interpret these structural properties as contingent upon a series of contextual features such as the organization of audiences. With what may well be self-conscious irony, he thus deploys the very approach associated with contingency theory as a means of investigating the conditions of its own practice and in order to reveal the limitations on its development.

Given Whitley's comparative purpose, his structuralist emphasis is wholly appropriate. It's also particularly pertinent as a way of characterizing those disciplines or specialities which exhibit high levels of cognitive and social integration and which enjoy long periods of structural stability. My own emphasis on the notion of a discipline as a process, and on structuration rather than structure *per se*, is therefore governed not by a rival epistemological commitment but by a pragmatic methodological complementarity. Rather than reaffirming how the overall organization of organization theory, its fluidity and plurality, is itself structurally conditioned, my focus is on probing some of the specifics of this pattern of contestation, with an eye to their cognitive consequences and structural effects. It's a method which is foreshadowed by the examples with which this chapter began. Up until this point, however, I've been content to simply display the presence of variability and to describe some of the forms it takes. That procedure was sanctioned by the Wittgensteinian maxim of asking not for the meaning of a proposition but for its use. The next step is to demonstrate how the notions of use and interest are linked.

This involves tracing the trajectories of particular initiatives in terms of the interests which are at once immanent in their formulation and which coalesce around their representation in symbolic form. This emphasis on the production and reception of such representations as an active process recognizes that such initiatives are to be understood not as merely reflective of pre-existing interests but as constitutive of emergent ones; it carries the implication that the development of such interests and the development of the discipline are of a piece. Such an approach therefore defers and problematizes, but does not preclude, recourse to the notoriously slippery notion of real interests.

In this way, the contrasting uses made of Weber's work within contingency theory and radical organization theory respectively can be conceptualized as both cause and symptom of contrasting configurations of interest. These two approaches exemplify, but do not of course exhaust, the range and variety of contemporary organizational analysis. The contrast between them is at once cognitive and social; the differences in the content of their theories echo differences in their modal patterns of production and in the characteristic organization of their distribution and reception.

From Theory Production to Theory Reception – the Case of the Aston Paradigm

Let me develop this assertion primarily, but not exclusively, with reference to contingency theory. This is because, of the two approaches, it has been contingency theory which has most clearly made the transition from isolated contribution(s) to institutionalized orthodoxy. From his London Business School base in 1975 Derek Pugh (and others) referred, somewhat diffidently perhaps, to organization behaviour (in which Pugh held a chair) as an 'emergent quasi-independent sub-discipline' (Pugh et al., 1975: 58), but by 1988 his North American based co-worker Bob Hinings (1988) was confidently arguing that 'traditional organization theory', oriented towards questions of organizational design, is now a separate discipline, complete with its own doctoral programmes, journals and problematics. This American based organization theory is wider and more diverse than contingency theory (see, for example, Perrow, 1986) and contingency theory itself is more than the Aston version of it (Kast and Rosenzweig, 1973). Aston's approach has, however, been a particularly influential formulation, and the four volumes of collected papers from the Aston school are both a testimonial to, and can be made to provide a commentary on, the transition to institutionalized status. The volumes contain, in turn: the original studies on organizational structure and context based on a sample from the English Midlands (Pugh and

Hickson, 1976); a series of replications and extensions with other samples and other types of organization (Pugh and Hinings, 1976); studies which examined the relations between organizational context and structure and aspects of group structure and individual behaviour (Pugh and Payne, 1978); and cross-national studies (Hickson and McMillan, 1981).

This pattern of lateral and vertical expansion suggests that the original research instrument was, in some meaningful sense, paradigmatic. Having already expressed scepticism about the over-enthusiastic use of Kuhn's work by those in other disciplines (Perry, 1977), I have no wish to smuggle in by the back door what I was reluctant to let in at the front. Thanks to Masterman's (1970) crucial reformulation, however, it is possible to employ Kuhn's profoundly ambiguous term in a way which avoids using it as a classification device, in which science is on one side and non-science on the other.[1] Masterman identified 21 different meanings of the term 'paradigm' in the first edition of Kuhn's most famous work. She suggested they could be grouped as metaparadigms, sociological paradigms and construct paradigms. A metaparadigm is wider than, and ideologically prior to, a theory; it is a *Weltanschauung*, a way of seeing. A sociological paradigm is also prior to theory but is something concrete and observable, the set of habits actually adopted by the practitioners being considered. A construct paradigm is anything which can cause actual 'puzzle solving' to occur. It is 'the-practical-trick-which-works-sufficiently-for-the-choice-of-it-to-embody-a-potential-insight'   (Masterman, 1970: 70). It is this last, this 'concrete picture of something A, which is used analogically to describe a concrete something else B' (Masterman, 1970: 77), which is the primary meaning of the term. It is a trick, a picture, together with the insight that it is applicable to a given field. If delimited in this way, then mapping:

> The process of paradigm elaboration becomes a source of ideas and suggestions rather than a Procrustean bed, [allowing] differences in developmental sequences . . . [to be] detected . . . [This is because] the presence of a metaphysic and a set of community habits is not limited to scientific communities any more than acquisitiveness is peculiar to capitalism . . . [But] one cannot infer from the presence of common structural features in different specialist communities that their relative importance is the same or that the strains and linkages between them are the same . . . By asking what does a paradigm do? (it solves puzzles) attention is shifted from a static analysis of a community's characteristics towards the processes whereby change occurs. (Perry, 1977: 48).

Each of the four Aston volumes contains an introduction which briefly sketches out the historical circumstances and institutional arrangements which allowed the studies to develop across a ten-year time span and four 'generations' of researchers. The emphasis in these historical notes is on the contingent, idiosyncratic, and serendipitous characteristics of the Aston unit; a research grant designated for one purpose but employed for another, a cramped and isolated basement room with five desks in it, and so on. What emerges is a contrast between the type of explanation offered for the origins of the programme (institutional, historical, contingent, contextual) and the type of explanation offered for its subsequent academic reception – the centrality of the concepts, the intrinsic interest of the findings, and the explicitness of the methodology (Pugh and Hinings, 1976: viii). Against such a stylized contrast between the contexts of discovery and validation, I want to stress the commonalities and continuities between explaining how the Aston programme was produced and explaining how it was received. For what the fate of Weber's writing illustrates is that an exemplary or paradigmatic work is not to be understood as given only by some property or set of properties internal to the work itself, but by that active relation which is the process of its interpretation by others.

Why then was the Aston paradigm both noticed and taken up? What 'puzzle' did it solve? Why did it not, in David Hume's famous phrase, 'fall dead born from the presses' – the reception first accorded to his own definitive philosophical defence of empiricism? McMillan (1981: xvii) notes that the Aston researchers 'had to market themselves in the USA to get recognition (hence the shrewd idea of publishing the original work in the *Administrative Science Quarterly*)'. The *ASQ* is organization theory's most influential journal and the mid-1960s saw a dramatic surge in its sales figures. Although the first issue had appeared in 1956, by 1963 the average sales were a still modest (by American standards) 1595 copies with a further 150 copies distributed gratis. Yet over the next four years, sales more than doubled, so that by 1967 the corresponding figures were 3690 and 117. Thereafter growth was incremental, 3972 and 198 in 1973, 4587 and 124 in 1977, 4965 and 121 in 1980. By 1987 there were 5024 paying subscribers and some 318 free copies distributed (*Administrative Science Quarterly*, various years). Moreover, the dramatic increase during the sixties predates the *ASQ*'s various experiments with format and design (and which presumably signalled the arrival of marketing consultants).[2]

A casual comparison[3] of the 1963 and 1967 volumes shows a marked increase in the number of articles congruent with the Aston 'house style' – that is, comparative studies using scaling techniques and a variety of statistical procedures. In 1967, during Lodahl's editorship, there were some thirteen statistical/quantitative articles, ten of them comparative, as distinct from just three statistical/quantitative contributions under Presthus in 1963. Infrastructural support for this trend derived not just from the increased availability of computers but the increased accessibility of computer programs designed for the social sciences.

Such factors go some way to explaining how the Aston approach got on to the research agenda, but they are not in themselves sufficient to account for it. The study of sociological measurement by Bonjean et al. (1967) showed both how frequently the central concepts of American sociology are given operational measures and how infrequently the resulting scales attract even a modest level of consensus. Their analysis of contributions to four major American sociological journals between 1954 and 1965 documented the use of some 2080 different scales, of which only 589 (28.3 per cent) were employed more than once and just 47 (or 2.26 per cent) more than five times (Bonjean et al., 1967: 9). Within their subcategory of 'characteristics of complex organizations', there are no less than 34 scales but only 56 citations (Bonjean et al., 1967: 76–80).

In striving to construct acceptable measures, Aston's combination of overlapping groups of multiple authors and a long-term research programme in itself created both the nucleus of a constituency and the possibility of in-house criticism. An influential, if less developed, precedent for this strategy within British social research was the social mobility studies by David Glass and his colleagues at the LSE (Glass, 1954). 'Less developed' because of differences between the respective academic infrastructures and relevant audiences for the two programmes. The Glass studies engaged with issues associated with the pattern of post-war reform in Britain and thus were both directly linked to specifically local social and political concerns and predated the academic expansion of the social sciences in the 1960s. By contrast the Aston programme was from the outset: guided by 'internally' generated (that is, professional/technical) criteria of relevance; oriented towards an 'international' (that is, North American) academic audience; and coincidental with both the rapid expansion of the social sciences in Britain and the emergence of local business schools based on the American model.

The social organization of the Aston programme both marked a break with the conventional British pattern of social research and constituted a link with the pattern characteristic of the American system. But although it was distinguishable from both of these models and reducible to neither, the group remained British in spite of itself. Up until their diaspora, they had their heads in one place but their feet in another – a condition that is potentially conducive to conceptual innovation and technical ingenuity (Perry, 1984, 1987). Without leaving the country, the Aston researchers played out their own distinctive permutation on *Changing Places*, David Lodge's satirical account of an Anglo-American academic exchange.[4]

What the plot line of *Changing Places* successfully traded on was what Halsey and Trow's (1971) study had documented – that is, the continuing salience in the British system of a conception of the academic as artisan and the pressures to which that conception is subject. It is a model derived from the organization of the humanities and its central elements are a craft-based emphasis on tacit knowledge and the solitary teacher/researcher, involved with undergraduate teaching and administration, in which the pertinent social relations are those of journeyman and apprentice or perhaps a pair of colleagues. The associated division of labour seems quite rudimentary when compared with its American counterpart. This general pattern is obliquely recognized by the Aston researchers (Pugh and Hinings, 1976: xiii) and they interpret it as a barrier; British social research occurs more in spite of it than because of it. By distancing themselves from both undergraduate teaching and the project for which they were purportedly funded, they were able to create a functional analogue to the professional closure of the American model.

Among the distinguishing characteristics of the American system are: the number of participating organizations, its sheer institutional density; the graduate school as locus of both professional closure and competitive struggle within that system; and (of course) the association between unit size and the bureaucratic organization of work. Its correlate is a conception of research whose products and practice are more nearly isomorphic with other forms of large-scale organization – especially modern science (de Sola Price, 1963) – than is the British pattern. And as Brian Barry (1974: 79) notes, 'One important manifestation of the self-conscious professionalism of American academics is the way in which a corpus of ideas – often in severely stripped down form – is at any given time common property.' In order to enter the corpus an idea 'must have the dual characteristic that its essence can be expressed very simply while at the same time its ramifications are very great' (Barry, 1974: 79). The characteristic American conception of social research in thus constructed around the notion that there are broadly based, common 'research fronts', and these are coordinated and sustained by a dense pattern of formal and informal communication and an emphasis on the journal article rather than the discursive book. Kimberley's (1976) documentation of the exponential growth of studies of organizational size as it relates to structure provides an illustration from within the organizational analysis field.

Limitations of Theory and the Social Limits on Theorizing

Mullins (1973) has explicitly sought to map such social and cognitive practices in his account of theory and theory groups in American sociology; and Aldrich (1988) is amongst those who have extended the term 'theory groups' (and the assumptions of the model) to include organization theory. Mullins makes use of a structural model initially developed for understanding natural science and finds it generally applicable to American sociology. The difficulty with his otherwise illuminating account is that it collapses the distinction between those processes which are (merely) consistent with professional closure and akin to Simon's (1957) satisficing behaviour, and those which (might) actually enhance the discipline's cognitive power, its social relevance or both. Within Mullins' (1973: 270–93) inventory of theory groups, what he calls 'radical critical theory' occupies an anomalous position. Not only does it deviate from his model of sociological practice, but both the category and its purported representatives are highly problematic. Such cohesion as the category has derives from what its members are against; the only place where one can envisage them making common cause is within the pages of Mullins' text. The smaller, and arguably more cohesive, grouping of 'critics of organization theory' in Aldrich's (1988) brief paper were also seen as anomalous. They had 'little effect on the research programmes of the (dominant) groups . . . but they *have* enriched paradigmatic controversy among people applying organization theory to problems in education, social welfare, planning and other fields' (Aldrich 1988: 19).

But anomalies can be instructive in unanticipated ways – both for social science advocates of, or adherents to, the normal science path, and for their sociological critics. What Kuklich (1980) has pointed out for sociology is what Whitley (1988) has pointed out for the management sciences, namely, that 'the relationship between the discipline's scholarly obsessions and its institutionalized form has been highly tenuous' (Kuklich, 1980: 211). Kuklich notes the vast gap between undergraduate and professional sociology in the USA and argues (1980: 210) that:

> Sociologists might protest that their field is defined by its theoretical framework rather than by the social welfare problems 'residual' to the other social sciences, [but] their interests would not be served if their arguments proved persuasive. Were universities to reallocate consideration of social problems to other fields . . . sociology's bureaucratic base would be destroyed.

And Whitley's account (1988: 50) of the management sciences notes that:

> Academics are more concerned to affect colleagues' research strategies and priorities rather than managers' beliefs. This means that detailed knowledge of how organizations function is of less interest than general conclusions about managerial problems which have implications for theoretical issues.

He concludes (1988: 61) that:

> The more that abstraction and universality are emphasized, the less relevance the outcomes of research will have for managerial skills and the greater the disjunction between scientific knowledge and managerial accounts.

The implication, then, is that in seeking to negotiate a space for themselves, the authors of contingency theory may in practice be as much concerned to try and distance themselves from the needs of capitalism as to serve them. In so far as radical organization theorists take contingency theory at its own valuation, they will be predisposed to overemphasize its contribution to the reproduction of existing social relations.[5]

Yet neither sociology nor the management sciences can be protected from public scrutiny or the impact of non-academic influences. They lack the social mandate accorded to some forms of natural scientific (and professional) practice. In Kuhn's (1970b: 254) somewhat overdrawn but pithy summation, the contrast is between:

> An esoteric, isolated and largely self-contained discipline and one that still aims to communicate with and persuade an audience larger than its own profession. (Science is not the only activity the practitioners of which can be grouped into communities but it is the only one in which each community is its own audience and judge).

The *Administrative Science Quarterly* (1982, 1983) has directly signalled such concerns through its special issues on utilization, and more obliquely

– but in its own special way – through the publication of material on the readability of introductory textbooks in public administration (Bowman and Saylor, 1977; Hinajosa et al., 1980). One wonders what the protagonists of a David Lodge satire would make of the use of the Flesch readability index, complete with consonant and word counts of randomly sampled sentences (including standard deviations).[6]

Although radical organization theory is more typically produced through the artisan system that was sketched out earlier, it is arguably more directly dependent on, and vulnerable to, the dominant order, because of its characteristically greater reliance on the production of books (and hence the interests of publishers) rather than articles in research journals. The latter, when established, constitute 'semi-programmed' issues that are relatively insulated from market pressures (but not, of course, hierarchical controls) due to the assured spending of institutional purchasers. The primary constituency of radical organization theory is therefore the undergraduates and postgraduates of the social sciences, whose incipient membership of the service class(es) is broadly congruent with a distrust of commerce and business. An emerging main line of tension within the discourse of radical organization theory derives from the possible erosion, or at least internal differentiation, of its client base. This is displayed, for example, in the different trajectories followed by Morgan (1985) and Burrell (Cooper and Burrell, 1988) since their initial collaboration in 1979.

The overall thrust of this chapter is therefore at odds with Karpik's claim that the contrast between different forms of analysis is 'overdetermined by a more fundamental opposition between knowledge for its own sake and practical knowledge' (1988: 26). Organization theories are neither quite that disinterested nor quite that efficacious. But the argument of this chapter is wholly consistent with Karpik's general theme that the discipline is so permeated by a wider social, economic and political context that 'the defence of a strict academic specialization seems completely unrealistic . . . [and] that the unity of the discipline is nothing other than the debate between competing lines of analysis' (1988: 27–8). And just as one strand of organizational theorizing emphasizes the contingent, so others reveal that we cannot escape from either history or the game of culture. All theorizing is therefore partial; all theorizing is selective.[7] It should be put in its place.

Notes

1 Three of Kuhn's own remarks may help to place this in context. First of all, there is his suggestion that 'If the notion of paradigm can be useful to the art historians it will be pictures not styles that serve as paradigms' (Kuhn, 1969: 412). Second, we have his autobiographical observation that it was the contrast between the social scientists he encountered at Stanford, and the physicists with whom he had trained, that was instrumental in triggering the paradigm notion (Kuhn, 1970a: x). Third, there is his

insistence that 'If . . . some social scientists take from me the view that they can improve the status of their field by legislating agreement on fundamentals and then turning to puzzle solving, they are badly misconstruing my point' (Kuhn, 1970b: 245).

2 There is a paper to be written on the semiotics of the *ASQ* in its various transmutations. The shift in ambience signalled by changes of paper, the use of art work, the revamped cover, the reordered relation of text to page, of articles to reviews, of form to content, all merit investigation. Such a project might begin from Bourdieu's (1984: xiii) maxim that 'the mode of expression characteristic of a cultural production always depends on the laws of the market in which it is offered'.

3 There is a more systematic longitudinal analysis by Richard Daft (1980), the results of which are consistent with those given above.

4 The novel's British setting is the University of Rummidge which British readers will recognize as a play on Brum(miggen), the local term for Birmingham. American readers will know that the Euphoria campus is a (California) state of mind. See Carter (1990) for a sociologically informed discussion of the university novel as a genre.

5 Such a critique could no doubt be salvaged by recourse to a notion like 'structural silences'.

6 A case of Zapping it to them, perhaps?

7 My own chapter might be regarded as an instance of what I have elsewhere called 'antipodean camp' (Perry, 1990). Its main characteristics are a sardonic distancing and stylized subversion; the use of serious playfulness as a way of dealing with cultural dominance and peripheral location. It is what makes it possible for one former New Zealand prime minister (Sir Robert Muldoon) to act as compere for the local stage version of *The Rocky Horror Picture Show* (itself written by a New Zealander); and for another prime minister (David Lange) to remark on breakfast time American television that he 'had been four times to Disneyland but never to the White House' although invitations to the latter had been extended to 'all sorts of hoods'. For my own part I have twice been to Disneyland but never to Harvard. Like David Lange, I am open to offers.

References

Administrative Science Quarterly (various years).

Albrow, Martin (1970) *Bureaucracy*. London: Pall Mall.

Aldrich, Howard (1988) 'Paradigm warriors: Donaldson versus the critics of organization theory', *Organization Studies*, 9 (1): 19–25.

Althusser, Louis (1971) 'Ideology and ideological state apparatuses', in his *Lenin and Philosophy and other essays*. New York: Monthly Review Press, pp. 127–86.

Aron, Raymond (1971) 'Conclusion: Discussion on Max Weber and power politics', in O. Stammer (ed.), *Max Weber and Sociology Today*. Oxford: Basil Blackwell, pp. 131–2.

Barry, Brian (1974) Review article: 'Exit, voice and loyalty', *British Journal of Political Science*, 4: 79–107.

Bendix, Reinhard and Roth, Guenther (1971) *Scholarship and Partisanship*. Berkeley: University of California Press.

Bonjean, Charles M., Hill, Richard J. and McLemore, S. Dale (1967) *Sociological Measurement*. San Francisco: Chandler.

Bourdieu, Pierre (1984) *Distinction*. Cambridge, MA: Harvard University Press.

Bowman, James S. with Saylor, Donald (1977) 'The readability of introductory textbooks in public administration', *Administrative Science Quarterly*, 22: 373–6.

Burrell, Gibson and Morgan, Gareth (1979) *Sociological Paradigms and Organizational Analysis*. London: Heinemann.

Carter, Ian (1990) *Ancient Cultures of Conceit*. London: Routledge.

Clegg, Stewart and Dunkerley, David (1980) *Organisations, Class and Control*. London: Routledge & Kegan Paul.

Cooper, Robert and Burrell, Gibson (1988) 'Modernism, postmodernism and organizational analysis', *Organization Studies*, 9 (1): 91–112.

Crozier, Michel (1976) 'Comparing structures and comparing games', in G. Hofstede and M.S. Kassem (eds), *European Contributions to Organization Theory*. Amsterdam: Van Gorcum, Assen, pp. 193–207.

Daft, Richard L. (1980) 'The evolution of organizational analysis in *ASQ*, 1959–1979', *Administrative Science Quarterly*, 25: 623–36.

Deutsch, Karl W. (1971) 'Discussion on Max Weber and power politics', in O. Stammer (ed.), *Max Weber and Sociology Today*. Oxford: Basil Blackwell, pp. 116–22.

de Sola Price, Derek (1963) *Little Science, Big Science*. New York: Columbia University Press.

Donaldson, Lex (1985) *In Defence of Organization Theory*. Cambridge: Cambridge University Press.

Galtung, Johan (1981) 'Structure, culture and intellectual style: An essay comparing Saxonic, Teutonic, Gallic and Nipponic Approaches', *Social Science Information*, 20: 817–56.

Giddens, Anthony (1979) *Central Problems in Social Theory*. London: Macmillan.

Glass, David (ed.) (1954) *Social Mobility in Britain*. London: Routledge & Kegan Paul.

Greenberger, Martin (ed.) (1962) *Management and the Computer of the Future*. New York: MIT Press and John Wiley.

Halsey, A.H. and Trow, Martin (1971) *The British Academics*. London: Faber and Faber.

Hickson, David J. and McMillan, Charles J. (eds) (1981) *Organization and Nation: The Aston Programme IV*. Farnborough, Hants: Gower Press.

Hinajosa, Jose R., Miller, Lawrence W. and Noyes, Lillian F. (1980) 'The readability of introductory textbooks in public administration: An update', *Administrative Science Quarterly*, 25: 158–9.

Hinings, C.R. (1988) 'Defending organization theory: A British view from North America', *Organization Studies*, 9 (1): 2–7.

Hofstede, Geert (1976) 'A guide through this volume', in G. Hofstede and M.S. Kassem (eds), *European Contributions to Organization Theory*. Amsterdam: Van Gorcum, Assen, pp. 18–22.

Johnson, Terence J. (1972) *Professions and Power*. London: Macmillan.

Karpik, Lucien (1988) 'Misunderstandings and theoretical choices', *Organizational Studies*, 9 (1): 25–8.

Kast, Fremont R. and Rosenzweig, James E. (eds) (1973) *Contingency Views of Organization and Management*. Chicago: Science Research Associates.

Kimberley, John R. (1976) 'Organizational size and the structuralist perspective: A review, critique and proposal', *Administrative Science Quarterly*, 21: 571–97.

Kuhn, Thomas (1969) 'Comment', *Comparative Studies in Society and History*, 11: 403–12.

Kuhn, Thomas (1970a) *The Structure of Scientific Revolutions*, 2nd edition. Chicago: University of Chicago Press.

Kuhn, Thomas (1970b) 'Reflections on my critics', in Imre Lakatos and Alan Musgrave (eds), *Criticism and the Growth of Knowledge*. Cambridge: Cambridge University Press, pp. 231–78.

Kuklich, H. (1980) 'Boundary maintenance in American sociology: Limitations to academic "professionalization"', *Journal of the History of the Behavioral Sciences*, 16: 201–19.

Lodge, David (1975) *Changing Places: A Tale of Two Campuses*. London: Secker and Warburg.

Lodge, David (1985) *Small World*. Harmondsworth: Penguin.

McMillan, Charles J. (1981) 'Introduction', in David J. Hickson and Charles J. McMillan (eds), *Organization and Nation: The Aston Programme IV*. Farnborough, Hants: Gower Press, pp. xiii–xviii.

Masterman, Margaret (1970) 'The nature of a paradigm', in Imre Lakatos and Alan Musgrave (eds), *Criticism and the Growth of Knowledge*. Cambridge: Cambridge University Press, pp. 59–89.

Morgan, Gareth (1985) *Images of Organization*. London: Sage.

Morison, Elting E. (1962) 'Scientists and Decision Making', in M. Greenberger (ed.), *Management and the Computer of the Future*. New York: MIT Press and John Wiley, pp. 13–21.

Mulkay, Michael J. (1972) *The Social Process of Innovation*. London: Macmillan.

Mullins, Nicholas C. (1972) 'The development of a scientific specialty: The Phage Group and the origins of molecular biology', *Minerva*, 10 (1): 51–82.

Mullins, Nicholas C. (1973) *Theories and Theory Groups in Contemporary American Sociology*. New York: Harper and Row.

O'Neill, John (ed.) (1973) *Modes of Individualism and Collectivism*. London: Heinemann.

Parsons, Talcott (1947) 'Introduction' to Max Weber, *The Theory of Social and Economic Organization*. London: Hodge, pp. 1–86.

Parsons, Talcott (1949) *The Structure of Social Action*. Glencoe, IL: Free Press.

Perrow, Charles (1986) *Complex Organizations: A Critical Essay*, 3rd edition. New York: Random House.

Perry, Nick (1977) 'A comparative analysis of paradigm proliferation', *British Journal of Sociology*, 28 (1): 38–50.

Perry, Nick (1979) 'Recovery and retrieval in organizational analysis', *Sociology*, 13: 259–73.

Perry, Nick (1984) 'Catch, class and bureaucracy: The meaning of Joseph Heller's Catch-22', *Sociological Review*, 32 (4): 719–41.

Perry, Nick (1987) 'Flying by nets: The social pattern of New Zealand fiction', *Islands*, 38: 161–77.

Perry, Nick (1990) 'Review Essay on "The American Connection" and "A Foreign Egg in our Nest": American Popular Culture in New Zealand', *Landfall*, 173: 88–92.

Pugh, Derek, Mansfield, Roger and Warner, Malcolm (1975) *Research in Organizational Behaviour: A British Survey*. London: Heinemann.

Pugh, D.S. and Hickson, D.J. (eds) (1976) *Organizational Structure in its Context: The Aston Programme I*. Farnborough, Hants: Saxon House.

Pugh, D.S. and Hinings C.R. (eds) (1976) *Organization Structure: Extensions and Replications: The Aston Programme II*. Farnborough, Hants: Saxon House.

Pugh, D.S. and Payne, R.L. (eds) (1978) *Organizational Behaviour in its Context: The Aston Programme III*. Farnborough, Hants: Saxon House.

Reed, Michael (1985) *Redirections in Organizational Analysis*. London: Tavistock.

Russett, Cynthia E. (1966) *The Concept of Equilibrium in American Social Thought*. New Haven, CT: Yale University Press.

Simon, Herbert (1957) *Administrative Behaviour*. New York: Free Press.

Stammer, Otto (ed.) (1971) *Max Weber and Sociology Today*. Oxford: Basil Blackwell.

Whitley, Richard D. (1984a) *The Intellectual and Social Organization of the Sciences*. Oxford: Oxford University Press.

Whitley, Richard D. (1984b) 'The development of management studies as a fragmented adhocracy', *Social Science Information*, 23: 775–818.

Whitley, Richard D. (1988) 'The management sciences and managerial skills', *Organization Studies*, 9 (1): 47–68.

6

Paradigms Lost: Paradise Regained?

Stephen Ackroyd

The aim of this chapter is to provide some insights into the development of the area of knowledge variously described as organizational analysis or organizational studies, in a form that will assist the process of growth of the field. It is assumed at the outset that, potentially, the subject is one of immense practical value; and its emergence, along with a number of other new human disciplines, could well be held to mark a new phase in the development of the social sciences. In order for this potential to be realized, however, two developments have to take place. One concerns the paradigm idea referred to in the title of this chapter. Arguably, although it was among the most popular ways of thinking about the field during the 1980s, the paradigm idea, together with other ideas of a similar kind, has exerted a fateful influence over it. It will be argued that this sort of approach to organization must be fully and finally discarded, and new and more creative ways of thinking about the field devised. I also suggest an alternative to the paradigm idea, and outline some of its advantages.

The argument I will present suggest that what is needed is for more attention to be paid to the social and organizational aspects of organization studies. I argue that the way knowledge about organizations has been institutionalized is an important part of the reason why the subject has failed to develop, and this is partly in the control of those working in the field. There are other reasons which are also influential, but, in the present analysis, only institutional and organizational reasons for the backwardness of the discipline will be considered.[1] I will suggest that such factors continue to be formative not least because contemporary thinking about organization seems to be demonstrably concerned to defend existing institutional arrangements, and, in consuming energy in the defence of the status quo, limits are set on the time and attention that can be given to organizational research or attempts to induce organizational change. Because institutional structures are produced and reproduced by people, I will argue that the assumptions and ideas of many academics have perpetuated this situation and have been a positive brake on the development of a new discipline. There is every indication of an increasing appetite for knowledge about organization in the community, but academics in the field continue to write books aimed at student audiences, and deride those of their number who respond more directly.[2] Indeed, academics in the organizational field seek – by a number of contrived arguments and devices, some of which will be examined later in this chapter – to keep exclusive control of authoritative knowledge of the field.

It cannot reasonably be doubted that formalized knowledge of organizations has been slow to develop. In much of the West and certainly in Britain any recognizable general theory of organization only emerged after 200 or so years of industrial history, and then only as a specialist branch of social science. To the extent that such knowledge was developed and consolidated at all, within the universities, it was not until well into the present century. In this form, knowledge of organization was a branch of academic learning rather than a refinement of professional expertise. In most Western countries, organizational knowledge was first developed either as a series of offshoots of the social sciences or as an adjunct to technological studies like production engineering. More to the point, perhaps, in the context of this chapter, it was only after a comparatively long sojourn as a poor relation of sociology, psychology or engineering, that there was any perception that the subject could develop in different directions as an area of knowledge in its own right, and that it need not permanently remain a branch of specialized academic knowledge.[3]

It is less easy to establish that the development of academic knowledge is causally related to the failure of the development of practically useful knowledge. Until more research has been devoted to the question, one can only point to the arresting coincidence of a slow growth of theoretical knowledge within the academy and the failure of systematized practical knowledge to be developed anywhere. At many times before the present, the beginnings of a formalized and practical knowledge of organization has been set out. The writings and practice of Bentham, Chadwick, Taylor, Ford or Fayol, for example, seem to be likely starting points for a conceptually sophisticated and practically based knowledge of organization. Very little in the way of sustained research was actually developed from these initial statements, however, and knowledge of organization failed to grow from these beginnings. Through much of the Western world, management and administration remain the only important professions without a highly developed, formal knowledge base or professional organization. Hence, to the extent that professional or practitioner knowledge is given credence in this arrangement, it is seen as an inadequate approximation to academic knowledge, and academic criteria are the exclusive standard by which the value of knowledge is judged. Thus the classics of formalized practitioner knowledge only continue to be authoritative when they are reclaimed by academia as intellectually inadequate precursors of fully academic accomplishments.

One of the most enduring legacies of this pattern of development is the exaggerated importance attributed to general characterizations of organization. This has been variously labelled organizational theory or organizational analysis. In Britain, the very subject area itself has sometimes been equated with what is called organization analysis or theory (Silverman, 1970; Reed, 1985; Morgan, 1989). Research is seen as something that can only exemplify the characteristics of particular kinds of approach to subject matter. For a long time, the justification for this privileging of general characterizations of organization was that this was analogous to scientific theorizing. The fact that the way general ideas in the organizational field – as in much of social science more generally – were quite different in formulation and reference from theory in natural sciences, did not seem to discourage the belief. Following this, during the 1980s it was argued that the basis for the distinction between forms of organizational analysis is not only or even mainly scientific, but philosophical as well. This is the paradigm idea, which is the latest and most pernicious variant of the doctrine that the basis of organization studies must be general characterizations of organization. First used in the organizational context by Burrell and Morgan in 1979, the paradigm idea continues to be influential (Lincoln, 1985; Alvesson, 1987; Chanlat and Seguin, 1989). Even where the idea has been set aside as mistaken, it is by no means clear that an associated 'paradigm mentality' (Reed, 1985) has been entirely discarded.

In the remaining sections of this chapter, I take the following steps. First, I explore the idea that organizational analysis is a fit subject for organizational analysis. Although in a short space any such analysis will be rudimentary, some basic ideas are developed. Needless to say, perhaps, this analysis draws more on the sociology and anthropology of knowledge than on organizational analysis itself. However, a second task I undertake is to apply the concepts developed to a consideration of organizational analysis in Britain during the 1970s and 1980s. I argue that the origin of the paradigm idea, and some of the uses made of it, can be readily understood in terms of the institutional analysis deployed. My use of this perspective leads me to the conclusion that the paradigm idea, and kindred approaches to organizations produced at about the same time, were at least as much designed to defend threatened academic authority as to induce the development of the field. I argue that the paradigm idea applied to organizational analysis turns out to be a way of attempting to limit the number and type of approaches to organizations accepted as having any validity. In the final section of this chapter I argue that a more social and organizational approach to the subject of organization can yield a more promising way of thinking about the development of knowledge in the field. The analysis can point to ways in which the present boundaries of the subject might be extended, and also suggests ways of maximizing new audiences for organizational knowledge.

Towards an Organizational Analysis of Organizational Analysis

Organizational analysis is an organized and organizing institution. It exists at certain places and times and not others, it is constituted by distinct patterns of attitudes and behaviour, and adopts particular organizational forms in order to reach selected ends. Perhaps most importantly, against the background of this analysis, it is shaped by and shapes its social context. For these reasons the organizational properties of organization analysis can be analysed.

It is an ironic comment on the state of organizational analysis that it is difficult to see how one might base a fruitful analysis of the organizational characteristics of the subject on the perspectives of organizational analysis itself. In developing a way of thinking about and analysing the development of the subject, it is necessary to draw more generally on the insights and perspectives used in the analysis of ideas and culture.[4]

Many propositions derived from the sociology of science have an obvious relevance to the problem of the backwardness of organization studies. Being a specialist branch of social science – itself not an area of academic work generously funded – has meant that the requisite critical mass of researchers has not been available to sustain stable research networks and to produce cumulative growth. In recent years, cumulative research has been achieved only by very few groups of scholars, and debate in the field has continued without much reference to research findings. Such facts indicate very clearly that the problems in the development of the discipline are not simply intellectual, and that the consideration of the question of development is not only an intellectual problem. The suggestion that the problem of the field is simply that adequate theory has not been developed, or that scholars have been using the wrong paradigm or epistemologies, is at least partly misconceived. There are requisite social conditions for the development of disciplines that have not been met.

Among the more compelling conclusions of the empirical sociology of knowledge are findings concerning the extent and the manner to which academic studies are influenced by their context. Natural sciences are by no means autonomous, but connected to the general culture to an extent that has hitherto passed unrecognized (Mulkay, 1979; Brannigan, 1981). The social sciences are merely more extreme in the way that they actively and self-consciously select their subjects according to what is topical in general culture and shape their findings for target audiences (Mulkay, 1985). It also is for this reason – because they are aimed at least in part at a lay audience – that findings are usually formulated in less abstract ways than in natural science. For the purposes of this exercise, therefore, the social sciences – and organizational studies, as a particular case in point – will be considered in terms of the way that they select, handle and target the information with which they deal. The social sciences will, in fact, be considered as information loops, as one of the feedback mechanisms by which social groups become more self-conscious about their activities. As such, the social sciences select aspects of social behaviour and social organization for consideration; collect and deploy data about them; and, with the help of selected concepts and techniques, represent the data as information, as accredited and authoritative knowledge. At no point in this process can the selection of data and deployment of findings be seen as entirely disinterested, though social science can be seen to be less obviously interested in constructions of particular events than are other groups in society. Social science constructs supposedly general and typical events for social consumption.

In the way that they work as social information loops, the social sciences can be usefully compared with other institutions that have comparable qualities and functions. It is instructive to think, for example, following the seminal work of Wolf Lepenies (1988), of the social sciences being 'between literature and science' in their character, sharing some of the features of each and varying according to social context in the degree to which they model a quantitative and positivistic pattern or a more qualitative and interpretive one. A perceived need for social science is itself a product of a particular level and kind of social development. What are sometimes called sciences of social life are in most of their forms quite without the precise mathematical formulations typical of natural sciences like physics, chemistry or biology. They are much more obviously a kind of literature, in that they offer interpretations of events or collected data, and by pointing to the relevance of frameworks of ideas as contexts of judgement. In a sense, the social sciences are a species of bureaucratized literature, because they serve the purpose of attributing meaning to events as literature does; but unlike in literature, meaning is routinely produced, and the social sciences describe processes that are supposedly general and typical. The main function of social sciences is, like that of literature, to give meaning; but they do this in respect of common or familiar events and processes. In the case of organization studies, the knowledge concerned is bureaucratized in more than one sense: it is designed for the consumption of the bureaucratized society, and is about the bureaucratized society. From this point of view, differences of perspective in the social sciences are not only a matter of the logic of theoretical position, but a result of what is selected as a subject and of the choices made in the constitution of that data as knowledge. In addition, the authoritativeness and impact of the knowledge produced varies not only according to the correctness of its understanding, but also with the perceived appropriateness of its insights as judged by particular publics.

The processes by which organization studies has been constituted as an information loop by its practitioners – that is, as a branch of the social sciences – can be seen to have had, and to continue to have, profound effects on the status and efficacy of the discipline. These processes include tendencies towards the active shaping of knowledge for specifically academic contexts and audiences. Hence it is possible to identify, following the ideas of Quentin Skinner (1969; see also Ackroyd and Hughes, 1991), a specific 'problem context' in which the practitioners of organization studies in Britain operate. By this is meant the mixture of intellectual and practical concerns which shape the way that issues are conceived and problems identified. Broadly described, the problem context in which many organizational writers work involves a preference for academic rather than practitioner audiences. It is for this sort of reason that their work deliberately avoids non-academic outlets. It tends to defend the academic status quo, rather than actively seek new audiences in the world at large.

A major part of the reason that the status of the established social sciences is higher than organization studies, and that their development has been more secure, is that the former disciplines now serve professional cadres who use or depend on the authority of specialized academic knowledge. Thus the audience for the output of the social sciences does not just include students in training but also former students as practitioners. In economics there are employees of banks, financial institutions and crucially the government. For psychology there are the para-medical, para-penal and psychological professionals. For sociology there are social work and other State cadres, as well as the educated public at large. Particular enclaves of the labour market, such as social services and personnel administration, have been large consumers of educated man and woman power. Even where they are not employed for their professional expertise, social science graduates in support or training roles tend to define their activities at work partly in terms of ideas supplied by their academic education, and, in turn, continue to see the value of such knowledge.

Looked at in this way, the audience for organizational analysis is actually very small but potentially very large indeed. At present, it is made up of those specialist academics and students who have chosen to study in the field. The scale of resources devoted to it, and, to some degree at least, the limited interest in it, tend to be fixed by the slow development of the established social sciences of which it is taken to be an intellectually dependent offshoot. On the other hand, the potential audience for the subject encompasses the masses of middle managers and skilled functionaries of the public and private bureaucracies.

The development of this audience is not likely to be unproblematic, of course. One difficulty is that non-academic sources of supply of organizational knowledge have sprung up. There has been a great growth of private consultancy, serving the market without deference to universities and their claims to authority. Another crucial problem for organizational studies within the academy is the intellectual superiority of other, less specialized, social sciences and hence the relative dearth of academic talent in the organizational field. Yet another problem is the gulf between academic and practitioner knowledge referred to at the beginning of this chapter. This gap is unduly present in the private sector, which is the most important potential audience for organizational studies. These problems are to some extent mutually reinforcing. Finally, there is the point which is being laboured in this analysis: that few academics in the field actually see the present situation as a problem. And yet, despite these tendencies, the practitioner audience is there and ever more interested in developing points of contact with the academy. It is part of the present argument that one of the ways to develop the field is to actively seek ways of combining academic and practitioner knowledge of organization.

A final point to make before beginning substantive analysis – which will reveal the extent of the concern for general theories of an academic type in the discipline – is that organizational analysis which mainly considers the properties of general theories and concepts is unlikely to appeal very strongly to other than an academic audience, and so will not connect with other audiences, actual or potential; it will therefore also not deal with the failure of the discipline to develop.

Organizational Analysis Organizationally Analysed

Recent controversy in the field of organization studies can be seen as a disagreement over the nature of the subject, and this is certainly the way that practitioners would like the matter debated. On the other hand, if the ideas put forward in the last section have some relevance, disagreement can also be seen as a clash between different definitions of what is the appropriate kind of knowledge to have, given that one is speaking to a particular audience. Part of the reason for the different views about the discipline held by Donaldson (1985, 1989) and Hinings (1988) on the one side, and by Reed (1985, 1989) and Clegg (1988) on the other, concerns the different audiences they are assuming they should address. Thus, at one level, controversy has very little to do with academic issues at all. It has more to do with choices – made more or less self-consciously – about appropriate ways to formulate the subject. For much of the time, academics in the field have apparently chosen in favour of tradition. The paradigm idea can be seen as a last-ditch defence of traditional academic values.

Attachment to traditional academic values runs very deep in industrial sociology and related subjects. Despite the very considerable merits of the early work of the Tavistock Institute, its approach has been severely criticized for being applied and consultancy-based (Brown, 1967; Rose, 1979). The Aston approach was also given a cool reception on the ground that it was insufficiently theoretical and too positivistic (Whitley, 1977; Millar, 1978). The founding statements of the approach appeared in the late 1960s and made little impact on academic audiences in Britain. However, despite its limited appeal there, Aston nevertheless rose to importance because of its reception elsewhere – most notably in the USA. There is an interesting transition from the publication of the first articles in the journal of the British Sociological Association, to the appearance of many of the subsequent papers in the American journal *Administrative Science Quarterly* and similar American periodicals. Although they took longer to find, other receptive audiences for the Aston research were available in such places as Australia and Canada, where higher education had been strongly influenced by the American model. It was again in North America too that the approach was generalized into contingency theory. There was an audience in the USA for organization theory of this type, principally in the graduate schools of business. This audience and, in large part, the supporting institutions were simply not present in the UK.

It is well known that by the beginning of the 1970s, there was in Britain – and to a lesser extent elsewhere – a rising tide of dissatisfaction with both American functionalist sociology and the empiricism of the contingency approach to organizations, which was also increasingly seen as an American product. This dissatisfaction increased with some force towards the end of the decade. One thinks of the critical work of David Silverman (1970), J.K. Benson (1977a, 1977b), Nick Perry (1979) and Stewart Clegg (1979). There are several reasons for this rejection of contingency theory and functionalism. At the level of ideas, functionalism was seen to be theoretically flawed and ideologically compromised. Moreover, for the British, despite the rise of applied social science in business schools and elsewhere, there was no motivation to abandon traditional student audiences and conceptions of what was appropriate intellectual fare for such audiences. British university education in the arts has always had a general and liberal tone and a tradition of exposure of the young to the masters of social and political thought. The rise of Marxism in the social sciences during the 1970s – and especially in industrial sociology – did not, of course, threaten this tradition but perpetuated it. Even within the new business schools, which were springing up in Britain in the 1970s and 1980s as supposedly applied areas of management education, the teaching of Marxism and Weberianism was thought suitable as a basis for instruction.

The problem context for British academics in the late 1970s had some special features. There was, for example, mounting direct and indirect political pressure for 'relevance' in curricula. One of the effects of this was to give added force to the desire of academics to sustain traditional academic values and emphases. The importance of the functional tradition and the apparent pragmatism of contingency theory in this context was that they seemed precisely to fulfil political expectations current at the time. Unlikely though it may seem, theoretical functionalism was taken to be necessarily functional for capitalism. In these circumstances, the rising importance of functionalism and contingency theory was seen to be a considerable problem. The reputation and importance of these ideas of the field of organization studies was enhanced, as has been suggested already, by the existence of receptive international audiences. Indeed, the combination of such factors was threatening to allow a particular (and uncongenial) kind of approach to organizations to dominate the field and to submerge other traditions. Without any doubt, for those with the slightest concern for truth, the historical significance of functionalism and contingency theory would be impossible to ignore. At the same time, enclaves within industrial sociology in Britain, in common with much sociology more generally, was coming increasingly under the influence of neo-Marxist theory. In industrial sociology the dominance of labour process theory was complete by 1980 or so, and this seemed to be a clear alternative to functionalism and contingency theory.

The approach to organizational sociology that was devised by such writers as Burrell and Morgan (1979) and Clegg and Dunkerley (1980) in the late 1970s must be seen in considerable measure as responses to this problem of divergent subject matter and divergent audiences. It is important to note that what we have here is not a redefinition of the subject. One indication of this is that both pairs of authors declared that they were contributing to sociology and clung to this idea with remarkable tenacity. Similarly, they had highly traditional ideas about what should be the subjects for discussion in university courses of this type. What is novel about these writers is that they increased the variety of approaches they were willing to discuss, the detail in which they were willing to do so, and the lengths they went to in order to direct the choices that readers of their work were likely to make. These emphases were entirely new.

There had, of course, been textbooks in the field of organization before Burrell and Morgan that displayed the range of approaches historically extant. There is a recognizable tradition in the treatment of the history of ideas that may be called 'expository', and which has sometimes been used in the organizational field. A case in point is a modest text by Eldridge and Crombie, first published in 1974, in which a wide range of approaches to organizations is simply set out. However, the more usual account in the presentation of organization theory has been quite different from that used by Eldridge and Crombie, following what might be called the 'serial' approach. According to this, organization theories succeed each other in a series. Sometimes the series is limited to two, and the argument runs that the inadequacies of an initial theory were dealt with by a new theory which has more explanatory power. This mode of presentation is time-honoured in this field. More sophisticated accounts extend the series, offering more subtle accounts of evolution or development of organization theory. Nicos Mouzelis' *Organisation and Bureaucracy* (1967) offers a muted version of this in which schools are succeeded by each other. David Silverman (1970) suggests that the development from technical implications theory through varieties of functionalism and system theory to social action theory is a serial development.

The work of both Burrell and Morgan and Clegg and Dunkerley are syntheses of the expository and the serial accounts of organization theory, and in this lies their novelty and similarity. The length of their books is also substantially accounted for by this. In these books the simultaneous existence and viability of different kinds of theory is a key aspect. But the forebears of the ideas described are not neglected either. The intellectual origin and to some extent the historical integrity of different bodies of ideas are kept intact. Both Burrell and Morgan and Clegg and Dunkerley share the desire to be more adequately diachronic in their approach to ideas, without losing the fullness that is the attribute of synchronicity.

This combination leads them to suggest that more than one bundle of ideas – of equal intellectual if not empirical weight – had to be traced through from its origins, and this necessitated a much more detailed and lengthy exposition. Effective synthesis of diverse approaches to theory within the same general frame, denied exclusive authority to one approach to organization and effectively and neatly dealt with the problem of differences which arose with simpler expositions. On the other hand, it raised the problem of choice between alternatives in an acute form.

The argument is, then, that the idea of paradigm itself, and the use made of it with the suggestion of the desirability of paradigm closure, seems to be an intellectual answer to an urgent practical problem. It is a way of avoiding the imminent break-up of organizational sociology into disassociated specialisms, or of pre-empting the worse possibility of the subject being exclusively identified with the contingency–functional orthodoxy. The vigour with which Lex Donaldson's subsequent argument in favour of this latter possibility was rejected is indicative of the strength of this motivation against any such idea. In fact, Burrell and Morgan and Clegg and Dunkerley had, as might be expected in this problem context, no intention of giving up intellectual authority over the field as a whole: the expectation was that they should direct the choices between theories now that the recognition of the need for it could not be avoided. We see that both pairs of authors, by different devices, retain the intention of directing choice between competing theories. But the benefits of such a strategy might be less than the costs, unless some other factor or factors were in play. Unless very carefully handled, the admission that there are different traditions of thought is a perilous course. The existence of different audiences, however, placed the need to recognize different theories on the agenda; and also necessitated strenuous efforts to deal with the consequences of placing them there. In essence, both Burrell and Morgan and Clegg and Dunkerley made the same concession. This is the recognition that different accounts of organization are possible, but only a limited number – the different possibilities being defined primarily in terms of what is beyond theory itself.

Choice between theories, on this view, needs to be made by reference to criteria mainly external to the meaning of ideas specifically about organization. This view is substantially correct, but the number of possibilities is very wide and there is no obviously reliable guide to the way decisions should be made. The intellectual devices used to limit the range of meta-theoretical bases on which different theories might be built are different between authors, but the impulse is the same. This is to close down the range of choices to those few (in the case of Clegg and Dunkerley the one) legitimated by their own academic authority. Both make the choice between alternatives lie outside the discipline itself, to depend on ideas which are partly philosophical in character – a device which makes their ideas academically highly respectable, and simultaneously beyond empirical or theoretical discussion. At the same time organization studies is made potentially dependent on ideas within epistemology and ontology; that is, on metaphysics.

The uncompromising qualities of the positions established by Burrell and Morgan and Clegg and Dunkerley that staked out the difference between different positions in terms of philosophy were soon broken down. The focus soon shifted to the recognition of both the need for, and the desirability of, dialogue between different positions. In their various ways, the writings of Reed (1985), Alvesson (1987), Bouchiki (1989) and a number of others envisage the possibility of building synthetic theories from blocks provided by theories within different paradigms. The paradigm idea, despite some lingering support for it (Lincoln, 1985; Alvesson, 1987; Chanlat and Seguin, 1989) has been lost. Instead, there is a partial reinstatement of serialism in the presentation of the history of the field (Reed, 1985; Rose, 1979).

It cannot be too strongly emphasized, however, that several features of the paradigmatic approach, including much of its sterile academicism, remain. A central feature is the emphasis given to the production and restatement of general theory, and the acceptance that differences between theoretical positions are irreconcilable and fundamental.

The perceived threat of the imminent breakup of the subject has receded, owing largely to the demise of radical organization theory and labour process analysis, but the hegemony of academic values is still in place. The need to recognize the tensions and divisions in the field has become less urgent, and the process of imposing artificial order on diversity can be resumed on a routine basis rather than with a sense of urgency and crisis.

There has grown up a tradition in organization studies in recent years for writers to proclaim expansively and generally on the future of the discipline and to make discussions of theory central to these debates. Burrell and Morgan's book makes a contribution to this genre and gave considerable support to it. Reed has usefully collected together a variety of these general and programmatic statements which attempt to describe and direct the future of the discipline (1985: 174–209). Thus Reed distinguishes advocates of what he calls 'pluralism' from 'integrationism' and 'imperialism' and 'isolationism'. These are consciously recommended strategies offered by different authors in the expectation that they will be followed by others active in the field. Although Reed himself concludes his book by rejecting these positions and the 'paradigm mentality' implicitly involved in them, he does not develop his critique very far or indeed set out very fully what his alternative view might be. Indeed Reed's work is itself an essay in expansive writing on organization theory. Yet it is surely obvious that what is indefensible about these approaches to organization studies is that they can make no contribution to the development of knowledge in the field; they merely reorder what is already there.

Finally, it is important to underline that it is implausible to think of these disagreements in terms of conservatism versus radicalism as is sometimes implied. On the basis of the analysis of audiences, the radicalism of some organizational writers can be understood as an attempt to retain a particular (undergraduate student or academic) audience for the subject in the face of rising competition from those with other (graduate student or business) audiences in mind. The best that can be said is that the 'radicals' did not yield to rising pressures on academics to achieve more practical relevance in their work. In these circumstances, however, radicalism largely amounts to a desire to preserve a place for dissenting voices, and, through that, to maintain a secure attachment to traditional institutions. Since it has no aspiration whatever to change the world, but on the contrary to preserve aspects of the academic status quo, this approach actually turns out not to be radical at all and is in some respects very deeply conservative. This criticism applies with considerable force to the paradigmatic approach to theory.

An Alternative Future for Organization Studies?

Taking an organizational model of organization studies seriously has several direct implications for practitioners. Whilst it is probably fruitless to lay down the precise pattern of future development in any discipline, it is possible to describe the most likely sequences of development. The first point to make is that, although the professionals in social science seem to have all the power to decide what will happen, it would be wrong to restrict attention to this aspect of social organization. It is of course the academics, individually and collectively, who decide what work will be undertaken, what will be published and therefore what the main results of activities are. Superficially, the academics appear to be all-powerful. On the other hand, if the points made in earlier parts of this chapter have any validity, then a distinguishing feature of the social sciences is precisely the relative lack of insulation from the community, and the importance of certain forms of linkage between the academic community and the community more generally conceived. Ultimately, it is not the academics alone who decide whose work will attract prestige and be found significant.

I have emphasized that the success of the established social sciences has to do with the fact they have stable practitioner clienteles whose work-roles are seen to be increasingly dependent on the knowledge produced in the academy. It is fascinating to note that some of the more recent advanced work on science suggests, as in Bruno Latour's celebrated study of Pasteur (1988), that the sphere of influence of science when successful draws in and implicates quite other areas of social life, particularly aspects of the polity and the economy. To use an idea from the earlier discussion, political and economic institutions thus become part of the problem context for scientists. Of course, there will be relative autonomy in the relationship between practitioner and community definitions of what is appropriate to do in scientific work and what are the appropriate conclusions to draw from the work done. Indeed, it seems to be part of the essence of science as a social institution, according to Western definitions of it, that this independence should be present, and in cases of dispute that the views of practitioners should prevail. In relations between the scientific and the wider communities, however, it is the latter that has more power, and that can, in the last analysis, contrive retreat from traditional lines of research and the switching of resources in new directions. Pure science retains its position of almost complete independence, but there is a presumed functionality in this; that in some way pure research is an essential basis for all other science and knowledge-based work. The point to make, however, is that for the social sciences in particular, there is no *raison d'être* for them if their products are not in some way used by people. If it is correct, as has been argued here, that they mainly attribute meaning, then the social sciences must have an audience of some sort in order to work in this way.

At present, much debate on the stance that applied social sciences should take towards the community seems to be conducted on a very inadequate basis. There is apparently a belief that there are only two possible modes of engagement. The first is radical disengagement, which is the proper stance of the academic or scientist. This allows the fearless production and recording of (probably unpalatable) truths which would otherwise pass unnoticed. On this view, to the extent that the community can be interested in taking notice of the academic at all, then the social scientist is some kind of moral policeman whose work can potentially correct the worst excesses of politics and businesses. In contrast to this, there is for the academic the possibility of direct engagement with the world of politics and business, which must, inevitably – because of the greatly superior powers and resources of the latter – lead to academia taking a servile position. Social science is just another factor of production, or grist to the political mill. The choice posed is like that confronting the population in the south of occupied France during the Second World War – between joining the (noble, independent) local *maquis*, so engaging in a fitful guerrilla war with occupying powers; and joining the (servile, collaboratist) Petainist *milice*, so helping the Nazis to brutalize the population.

The parallel is just plausible enough to beguile the naive. On the other hand, the idea that careerist academics with leftist theoretical ideas are freedom fighters is wildly implausible. Similarly, those who have ever actively engaged in it will know that applied research in organizations is frequently very much like guerrilla war. Much of the time the researcher operates from a tenuous base camp in a jungle, trying gradually to win over the hearts and minds of the dwellers therein, whilst at the same time attacking their faith in the viability of their way of life and using destructive means to do it. The 'service to power' thesis depends on characterizing the practice of social research as being substantially without tensions – either within itself, or between it and its characteristic activities and values and those of the organizational community. Against this, a case can be made that growth areas in social science have always centred on points of intellectual as well as moral tension, and it is this that gives vitality to schools of thought.

For teaching purposes it is perhaps necessary to give the impression that models and perspectives on organizations are definite things with clear boundaries, and that adherents of theories believe given propositions as definite truths without dissent. Against this, any reasonably scrupulous examination of the history of social science will show the tensions and disagreements over basic issues at the very heart of the activity. See, for example, my analysis of the human relations school, which identifies very considerable differences of theoretical view amongst this very influential group of writers (Ackroyd, 1976). Differences of this very deep kind seem to have been at the core of all the more memorable growth points for industrial sociology since its beginnings. It can be argued that seeking some resolution of disagreements is what motivates both empirical research and the formulation of 'theoretical' statements. The latter, in particular, arise from the attempt to deal with anomalies, and explain the apparently incongruent. They are thus, when successful, the completion of any process of investigation rather than the starting point for it. Though they may initiate further investigations and provoke more thought, theoretical statements are best seen as the logical end-point in the involvement of the academic community, rather than the beginning. This is because the community produces problems which the academic community resolves. The paradigm idea is wrong because attempts to remove conflict from the human context place it substantially beyond the capacity of anyone to resolve either practically or intellectually.[5] It is in this sense profoundly unrealistic.

In this chapter, the analysis has been conducted on the assumption that there are two elements of social or organizational context within which social science operates. The first is the organization of social science itself, and it is obvious how influential this is in shaping the activities undertaken by the membership. On the other hand, there is also the more general social context. Analysts of organization studies usually simply overlook this, assuming, quite wrongly, that it can be safely ignored. This is an error for the simple reason that the discipline exists in and serves the community of which it is part. In all sorts of ways the existence of the community directly and indirectly shapes the activities of the practitioners themselves. Shaping occurs most directly through the definitions held by practitioners of how the discipline should work in relation to the community. But it does not cease to occur because practitioners do not have a highly developed conception of these influences. All social science is, more or less consciously, orientated towards its social environment and shaped by it. In this chapter I have identified and criticized the way that organization studies academics have simply assumed that they should only relate to the community in the traditional way of liberal arts academics

– sometimes masquerading as 'scientists'. Some very similar points are made by Donaldson in a review article (1989), specifically about Reed's work. It is difficult to appreciate that this orientation might be inappropriate, because the rhetoric of academia stresses the importance of independence so strongly. But, usually, academia is intent in some way to exploit its position of relative independence from the broad social context. Ultimately, however, the social context is as constitutive of a discipline as the professional organization.

If there is any validity in the analysis put forward here, several possible redirections for organizational analysis suggest themselves. Practically, there is much to be gained by attempting to make the source of data (organizations) and the audience for knowledge about it (organization members) correspond more closely. It is not easy to do this. It will not suddenly unlock vast stores of research funds, or bring dramatic changes to society as a result of intervention. The chief benefit in the short term is likely to be an increased practitioner audience, which, when it rivals the size of the cadres that constitute the main audience for other branches of social science, will greatly enhance the prestige and importance of the subject. Theoretically, organizational professionals would do well to attempt to open the conventional boundaries of their subject and to explore the connections between the constitutive theories which make up professional definitions of the discipline. This analysis, like the paradigm idea that it takes as its critical target, also asserts that the discipline is best defined meta-theoretically; that is, in other than theoretical terms. But, unlike the paradigm idea, which locates the differences of forms of thought in what are taken to be elemental or basic differences, the social organization thesis draws attention to the variability and plasticity of forms of knowledge, and points to the extent to which knowledge has been shaped into particular forms. Without for a minute conceding that forms of organizational knowledge can be constructed to reflect the social scientist's precise desires, this is a better basis on which to plan than the idea that there are fundamental philosophical limits which thought cannot transcend.

Notes

1 There are various lines of inquiry by which this puzzle might be more fully explored. One is that the nature of organization as a rational device has actually been substantially misconceived (see Gergen (this volume) who raises the possibility of organizations not being mechanisms).

2 An example is Gibson Burrell's recent dismissal of popular books as 'Heathrow organization theory'; that is, only fit to fill in the otherwise wasted hours in flight or transit lounge.

3 A key development in this respect has been the emergence of more than one perspective on organization. In America, the human relations viewpoint had to be superseded by functionalism, and functionalism by general systems theory, before organization could begin to be perceived as a potentially separate subject. In Britain, despite the enormous

sophistication of sociotechnical writing on organization and the international recognition found by contingency theory, the idea that organization studies could have a future separate from other social sciences has also been slow to take hold. Organizational knowledge has been consolidated as a minor branch of the established social sciences.

4 One of the most notable growth points in the social sciences of the 1970s was the sociology, anthropology and psychology of knowledge (see, for example, Barnes, 1974; Mulkay, 1979; Woolgar, 1980; Douglas, 1986). The sociology of academic knowledge, which has been a key source of inspiration in the present account, was in fact given considerable impetus by the work of Kuhn (1962). In sociology, after some equivocation (Perry, 1977; Harvey, 1979), the critical appraisal of the ideas of Kuhn, added to ideas from diverse sources like the anthropology of knowledge (Horton, 1967) and ethnomethodology (Sacks, 1963), led to a very fundamental reappraisal of our understanding of science (Latour and Woolgar, 1979; Woolgar, 1980; Latour, 1987; Mulkay, 1985). The approach also began to find applications in many other areas, such as professional and other occupational knowledge creation (Silverman and Jones, 1976; Hughes et al., 1989). Recently, the same kind of highly revealing perspective on knowledge has been applied to the social sciences themselves (Mulkay, 1985; Hughes et al., 1989). By contrast, as I have already indicated and will later exemplify, in organization studies the use of the paradigm idea has not opened up but has closed down the scope of the discipline. Despite the fact that there have been attempts to develop organizational sciences based on paradigms, any such thing failed to develop.

5 This is not the place to undertake a detailed critique of the paradigm idea as used by Burrell and Morgan and others. For one thing, the social scientific uses of the paradigm idea have been considered extensively by others. However, it is worth stating – very baldly – the basic objection that seems to apply here. This is that these authors appear to suggest that the differences between perspectives on organization do not arise from differences of perception and use. They are defined elementally as basic differences, as much by opposition to each other as by any other criterion. The difference between paradigms is simply that they feature basic differences. Since basic differences are held to be the realm of philosophy, so different paradigms are held to delineate different philosophical positions. By this reasoning, it would seem that organization studies are made substantially dependent on epistemology and ontology; that is, on metaphysics. What is beyond the scope of theory is recognized only in so far as it is a part of a different academic territory. On the other hand, what is beyond theory might be thought about as a number of other things – for example, ideology (as Clegg and Dunkerley), or as general culture, or as art, literature and science (as here). As a framework for the description and classification of ideas, this approach seems to exhibit very little feel for their organic properties, and the way that they relate to other bodies of knowledge and the general culture. Organization theory is a way of seeing that is part of a particular culture, a repertoire of motives and a context of evaluation relevant to a given time and place. Much of the writing produced since Burrell and Morgan shares a very similar lack of understanding of the way that knowledge of organizations must vary in content and emphasis over time and between different locations if it is to accurately describe and handle its subject.

References

Ackroyd, Stephen (1976) 'Sociological theory and the human relations school', *Sociology of Work and Occupations*, 3 (4): 379–410.

Ackroyd, Stephen and Hughes, John A. (1991) *Data Collection in Context*, second edition. London: Longmans.

Aldrich, Howard (1988) 'Paradigm warriors: Donaldson versus the critics of organisation theory', *Organisation Studies* 9 (1): 19–25.

Alvesson, Mats (1987) *Consensus, Control and Critique: Three Paradigms of Work Organisation Research*. Aldershot: Gower-Avebury.

Barnes, Barry (1974) *Scientific Knowledge and Sociological Theory*. London: Routledge.

Barnes, Barry (1982) *T.S. Kuhn and Social Change*. London: Macmillan Press.

Benson, J. Kenneth (1977a) 'Innovation and crisis in organisational analysis', *Sociological Quarterly*, 18 (1): 3–16.

Benson, J. Kenneth (1977b) 'Organizations: A dialectical view', *Administrative Science Quarterly*, 22 (1): 1–21.

Bittner, Egon (1965) 'The concept of organisation', *Social Research*, 32: 239–55.

Bouchiki, Hamid (1989) 'Vers une approche constructiviste des structures organisation-nelles', Cahiers du LAMSADE no. 95. Université de Paris Dauphin.

Brannigan, Augustine (1981) *The Social Basis of Scientific Discoveries*. London: Cambridge University Press.

Brown, Richard (1967) 'Research and consultancy in industrial enterprises', *Sociology*, 1 (1): 33–60.

Burrell, W. Gibson and Morgan, Gareth (1979) *Sociological Paradigms and Organisational Analysis: Elements of a Sociology of Corporate Life*. London: Heinemann.

Chanlat, Jean-François and Seguin, Francine (1989) *L'Analyse des organisations: Une anthologie sociologique* (Tome 1: *Les Théories de l'Organisation*). Paris: Editions Eska.

Clegg, Stewart (1979) *The Theory of Power and Organisations*. London: Routledge.

Clegg, Stewart (1988) 'The good, the bad and the ugly', *Organization Studies*, 9 (1): 7–12.

Clegg, Stewart and Dunkerley, David (1980) *Organisations, Class and Control*. London: Routledge.

Donaldson, Lex (1985) *In Defence of Organisation Theory: A Reply to the Critics*. London: Cambridge University Press.

Donaldson, Lex (1987) 'In successful defence of organisation theory: A routing of the critics', *Organisation Studies*, 9 (1): 28–32.

Donaldson, Lex (1989) 'Rethinking, redirecting or reiterating in organisational analysis: On reading Reed', Review article, *Australian Journal of Management*, 14 (2): 245–54.

Douglas, Mary (1986) *How Institutions Think*. London: Routledge.

Eldridge, John and Crombie, Anthony (1974) *A Sociology of Organisations*. London: George Allen and Unwin.

Elias, Norbert (1956) 'Problems of involvement and detachment', *British Journal of Sociology*, 7 (4): 226–52.

Harvey, Lee (1979) 'The use and abuse of Kuhnian paradigms in the sociology of knowledge', *Sociology*, 13 (1): 85–101.

Hinings, C. Robert (1988) 'Defending organisation theory: A British view from America', *Organization Studies*, 9 (1): 2–7.

Horton, Robin (1967) 'African traditional thought and Western science', *Africa*, 37 (3). Reprinted in M.F.D. Young (ed.), *Knowledge and Control*. London: Collier-Macmillan, 1971, pp. 208–66.

Hughes, John et al. (1989) *Working for Profit*. Brighton: Harvester.

Kuhn, Thomas S. (1962) *The Structure of Scientific Revolutions*. Chicago: University of Chicago Press.

Latour, Bruno (1987) *Science in Action*. Milton Keynes: Open University Press.

Latour, Bruno (1988) *The Pasteurization of France*. Boston: Harvard University Press.

Latour, Bruno and Woolgar, Steve (1979) *Laboratory Life: The Social Construction of Scientific Facts*. London: Sage.

Lepenies, Wolfgang (1988) *Between Literature and Science*. London: Cambridge University Press.

Lincoln, Yvonna (1985) *Organisational Theory and Enquiry: The Paradigm Revolution*. London: Sage.

Millar, Jean (1978) 'Contingency theory, values, change', *Human Relations*, 31 (10): 885–904.

Morgan, Gareth (1986) *Images of Organisation*. London: Sage Publications.

Morgan, Gareth (1989) *Creative Organisation Theory*. London: Sage Publications.

Mouzelis, Nicos (1967) *Organisation and Bureaucracy*. London: Routledge.

Mulkay, Michael (1979) *Science and the Sociology of Knowledge*. London: George Allen & Unwin.

Mulkay, Michael (1985) *The Word and the World: Explorations in the Form of Sociological Analysis*. London: George Allen & Unwin.

Perry, Nicholas (1977) 'A comparative analysis of "paradigm" proliferation', *British Journal of Sociology*, 28 (2): 38–50.

Perry, Nicholas (1979) 'Recovery and retrieval in organisational analysis', *Sociology*, 13 (3): 259–73.

Reed, Michael (1985) *Redirections in Organisational Analysis*. London: Tavistock.

Reed, Michael (1989) 'Deciphering Donaldson and defending organisation theory: a reply to Lex Donaldson's review of "Redirections in Organisational Analysis"', *Australian Journal of Management*, 14 (2): 255–60.

Rose, Michael (1979) *Industrial Behaviour*. London: Penguin.

Sacks, Harvey (1963) 'Sociological descriptions', *Berkeley Journal of Sociology*, 8 (1): 1–19.

Silverman, David (1970) *The Theory of Organisations*. London: Heinemann.

Silverman, David and Jones, J. (1976) *Organisational Work*. London: Macmillan.

Skinner, Quentin (1969) 'Meaning and understanding in the history of ideas', *History and Theory*, 8 (1): 3–53.

Whitley, Richard (1977) 'Organisational control and the problem of order', *Social Science Information*, 16 (2): 169–89.

Woolgar, Stephen (1980) 'Discovery: Logic and sequence in a scientific text', in K.D. Knorr, R. Krohn and R. Whitley (eds), *The Social Process of Scientific Investigation*. (Sociology of the Social Sciences Yearbook, Vol. 4.) Dordrecht: Reidel. pp. 239–68.

7

The Social Construction of Organizations and Markets: The Comparative Analysis of Business Recipes

Richard Whitley

The socially constructed nature of business enterprises as systems of coordination and control of economic activities seems self-evident to most social scientists in the same way that other social institutions and collectivities are socially constituted and variable. However, one corollary of this view, that the nature of firms – or economic actors (Whitley, 1987) – and successful ways of managing businesses in market economies vary significantly between societies is less widely accepted. While the socially constructed nature of social phenomena usually implies that their nature and operation depend on conventions and beliefs which often differ significantly between societies, many studies of business structures and practices continue to search for universal rules governing administrative structures and growth.

Some claim, for instance, that there are general relations between dimensions of organizational structure which hold for all successful businesses across all environments (for example, Hickson et al., 1974, 1979) and so are 'culture-free' (cf. Child, 1987). Others suggest that the patterns of growth and change found among successful large businesses in the USA by Chandler (1962, 1977) reflect general processes of economic development which occur in all industrialized societies, and so should be repeated in other countries, despite considerable evidence to the contrary (for example, Alford, 1976; Lane, 1989; Lévy-Leboyer, 1980). A third group, advocates of the 'new institutional economics', hypostatize a universal economic logic which determines the choice of institutional systems for organizing economic transactions, and therefore the existence of large managerial bureaucracies in different industries (for example, Daems, 1983; Williamson, 1985). All presume that inexorable market pressures generate identical, or very similar, forms of business organization and development across social contexts irrespective of institutional differences.

These assertions of a single economic logic governing the development of effective managerial structures and practices in all situations have, of course, been extensively criticized on both conceptual and empirical grounds (for example, Brossard and Maurice, 1976; Granovetter, 1985; Sorge, 1983). However, some of these criticisms have tended to assume an equally extreme position of cultural relativism, almost implying that since all business systems are social constructions, they are necessarily unique to different societies which, in turn, suggests they cannot be systematically compared (cf. Rose, 1985). While such an extreme culturally determinist view is unsustainable for many of the same reasons that render Winch's (1970) anthropological relativism incoherent (see Bhaskar, 1979: 170–9; Gellner, 1968), it does highlight the inadequacies of simple generalization of one pattern of business development in one society to all societies, just as reliance on the British industrial revolution as *the* model for industrialization has proved misplaced.

The differences between these views lie as much in the significance they attribute to the socially constructed nature of business organizations as in their acceptance or denial of its validity. While economic rationalists may accept that firms are complex social organizations whose constitution and activities reflect the conceptions and values of owners and/or their agents as well as employees, they consider competitive pressures to be so strong that efficient forms of business organization and 'rational' strategic choices quickly dominate all market economies whatever cultural and institutional variations may exist between them. Thus differences between owners' and managers' beliefs and preferences are essentially irrelevant to economic outcomes in this view because all competing firms are constrained to follow the logic of efficient market processes.

Conversely, cultural relativists regard differences in social conventions, rationalities and moral codes to be so important across societies as to generate highly distinctive forms of business organization and practice which are specific to their context and cannot be readily transferred. Because enterprises are socially constructed, in this view their actions and procedures reflect the beliefs of those in control so that efficient business practices are culturally variable and specific. What constitutes economic efficiency is here seen as being socially determined and contextual.

This contrast of perspectives raises a number of general conceptual issues in the analysis of economic relations and business structures which will now be discussed. They support the general conclusion that variations in economic agents' beliefs and rationalities do necessarily affect economic outcomes. However, the extent to which, and ways in which, dominant social institutions generate sharply distinct forms of business organization vary empirically and there is no overwhelming reason to presume that each 'culture' possesses a unique business system.

The Significance of the Social Construction of Business Systems

Considering first the view that there is a single dominant economic rationality which renders differences in beliefs and preferences essentially irrelevant to effective management structures and practices, this fails to take account of the variety of institutional environments which firms have to deal with and manage. These variations affect 'efficient' firms' structures and choices. Major differences in the financial systems of European countries, for example, affect relationships between banks and industrial companies and the management of financial risks to the extent that strategic priorities and the significance of financial skills differ considerably between major enterprises in these societies (Lane, 1989; Zysman, 1983). Thus 'efficient' firms in Britain have to adapt to the more active 'market for corporate control' (Lawriwsky, 1984) and separation of financial institutions from industry (Ingham, 1984) in ways that do not apply to firms on the European continent operating within credit-based financial systems. Successful forms of business organization develop interdependently with dominant social institutions and therefore differ significantly where these do. Because business environments vary in many important respects, so too do 'efficient' management structures and practices. This means that the contrast between technical and institutional sectors drawn by Meyer and Scott (1983: 140–1) in their analysis of organizational isomorphism is misleading since market efficiency is institutionally constructed (cf. Orru et al., 1988).

Second, the socially constructed nature of firms and markets implies that they are meaningful entities whose nature and operation vary according to differences in meaning systems and dominant rationalities. Thus, the 'rules of the game' in competitive markets can and do vary considerably between societal contexts as priorities and dominant conceptions of appropriate forms of economic competition within and between countries differ. Changes in these conceptions and priorities imply changes in market processes, so that what constitutes 'rational' economic action also alters, as when the post-war French state sharply changed its role in directing economic development and its attitudes towards international competition. Thus, as institutional views about economic phenomena differ and change, so too do market structures and imperatives. The socially constructed nature of business systems, then, implies that economic rationalities are culturally relative and variable.

Third, since market outcomes are the result of interdependent firms' actions, and since knowledge is always imperfect (Richardson, 1960), how major firms make decisions is both economically significant and a matter of judgements and beliefs. The pervasiveness of uncertainty and disequilibrium in market economies means that there is no way of knowing how to make 'rational' choices, so economic actors are forced to rely on their necessarily limited and idiosyncratic understanding of market processes. Differences in these understandings generate a variety of economic outcomes since firms' actions are interdependent and so economic efficiency and success can only be discerned *post factum* and are dependent on agents' rationalities. Thus, where dominant managerial beliefs and preferences change, so too will the results of particular strategies and actions. What constitutes a successful strategy and form of business organization varies, then, according to the context and cannot be reduced to a single logic which will 'work' in all circumstances.

Fourth, and relatedly, because markets, like all social systems, are essentially 'open', they do not generate stable conjunctions of events which are invariant over environmental changes. Open systems in this sense are those in which endogenous changes in the states of system components, and changes in the relations between these components and external phenomena, result in changes in the ways that systems behave (Bhaskar, 1979; Sayer, 1984). Since people, and collective social entities, learn and change their beliefs, assumptions and priorities as a result of both internal developments and external changes, social systems do not function as closed deterministic structures. As a result, decisions and practices which were successful in one situation may not be so effective in others, and managerial rationalities which 'worked' in one historical period may fail in later ones as participants learn and develop. Thus macro-economic policies which achieved the desired effect in one situation may generate different outcomes if major economic actors develop different views about their significance and implications, as in the use of interest rates to control inflation.

Together, these points suggest that the socially constructed nature of business systems has significant implications for the analysis of effective managerial structures and practices. In particular, variations in major economic agents' beliefs and rationalities affect economic outcomes and the nature of competitive efficiency. Just as the nature and development of scientific knowledge depend on the institutionalized conventions and practices of those who dominate the research system in our society (Bloor, 1976; Whitley, 1984), so too the establishment and success of particular forms of business organization depend on the ways in which controllers of economic resources understand and evaluate the world. The lack of any overriding and universally valid epistemological theory of scientific progress which could justify and explain scientists' judgements as necessarily 'rational' (Feyerabend, 1981) is echoed by the lack of any single economic logic which determines business success. The social construction of business structures and practices means that not only are they the product of collective beliefs, conventions and moral codes which vary between societies, but also the nature of economic success and ways of achieving it are dependent on dominant conceptions of economic practices and rationalities. Where these differ considerably, as they do between many European and East Asian countries, so too do dominant firms' goals and strategic choices (Bauer and Cohen, 1981; Kagono et al., 1985; Silin, 1976).

For example, many of the contrasts between Japanese and US large firms stem from the quite different logics – or rules of the game – that major economic actors follow in the two societies as a result of considerable differences in their institutional environments, particularly the role of the State (Johnson, 1982). In the recent past, the 'Japanese logic' seems to be more successful in many international markets, but this does not mean it always will be. Just as the historical success of the large, integrated and diversified US corporation through much of the twentieth century has been historically specific, so too is that of the Japanese 'specialized clan' (Clark, 1979). As other logics develop in different societal contexts the overall 'rules of the game' of international economic competition will alter, and there is no overriding reason to expect the currently successful Japanese form of business organization to continue to dominate indefinitely. Economic outcomes, like scientific ones, depend on the beliefs, priorities and actions of economic agents rather than some inexorable universal logic which inevitably leads to 'progress'. Thus, how particular kinds of economic actors come to control resources, and how they understand 'what is going on' (Taylor, 1985), affect business practices and economic outcomes to the extent that different groups of resource controllers following different logics and priorities generate different results. The socially constructed nature of economic action, then, implies that the way managers and owners think and act structures not only the organizations and resources they control, but also the nature of competitive processes and their outcomes. What is successful in one particular situation and context may not be in another, different, one and so particular 'recipes' for business success which are effective in one context are not necessarily valid across societies or over historical periods.

Once it is agreed that participants' beliefs and practices do have significant consequences for economic outcomes and the nature of economically successful business structures, a number of consequences follow. First, the processes by which different economic rationalities develop and become established in different societies are important influences on business behaviour and success. Second, the more these vary and remain distinctive, the more varied will successful forms of business organization be, and the less likely is it that any single pattern will dominate world markets. Third, the more varied and distinct are dominant business structures and practices in different societal contexts, the more difficult will it be to transfer successful techniques and strategies across these contexts. Fourth, as dominant economic rationalities develop and change, so too do market processes and the competitive 'rules of the game'. Successful business 'recipes' therefore may cease to be effective. Indeed, this decline in effectiveness of particular structures and practices may, in part, be the result of their earlier success as other economic actors learn from it and adopt new forms and logics to deal with it. Just as useful social theories and policy instruments can change the reality they purport to explain and influence, and thus alter the grounds of their validity and utility, so too effective ways of organizing and directing economic activities can generate new responses and rationalities which together so alter the system as a whole that they become ineffective (see Taylor, 1985).

These consequences in turn suggest that the study of organizations and business systems should focus more on how different ways of organizing economic activities become established and effective in different societal contexts than on searching for universally valid logics of economic action or general structural correlations. The lack of a single dominant logic governing economic outcomes in market systems means that the processes by which particular structures and practices become established and successful in particular societal contexts require analysis, as do the ways in which they change and develop. Once the existence of a universal economic rationality is denied and economic success understood as a contingent, changing phenomenon that varies according to context, it becomes important to explain differences in the relative success of different forms of business organization and sets of practices.

A major part of this analysis and explanation concerns the emergence of distinctive 'business recipes' in various institutional environments whose success is linked to particular features of dominant social institutions. These business recipes, or systems, are particular ways of organizing, controlling and directing business enterprises that become established as the dominant forms of business organization in different societies. They reflect successful patterns of business behaviour and understandings of how to achieve economic success that are reproduced and reinforced by crucial institutions. Whilst they vary in the degree to which they differ across institutional environments, and in their internal consistency and integration, the essential point is that business recipes institutionalize different economic rationalities which 'work' in particular circumstances.

In suggesting that the comparative analysis of the development, reproduction and change of business recipes is central to the study of business structures and practices, I am proposing that we should take the social construction of economic phenomena and relations seriously and follow its implications. Thus, acceptance of the economic significance of agents' rationalities – or ways of understanding, evaluating and acting in the world – requires examination of how such rationalities become established and dominant in different situations, especially between societies. Because they 'make a difference' to economic outcomes, and hence to effective managerial systems and practices, these rationalities are important phenomena whose operation and change it is crucial to understand. This is not to say that they constitute homogeneous national recipes which are culturally determined and immune to external influences. The extent to which distinctive business recipes are nationally homogeneous and stable depends on their institutional environments and the distinctive nature of dominant national institutions. It is to emphasize, though, that successful forms of business organization and practices reflect the circumstances in which they developed and cannot be simply transferred to qualitatively different environments. As meaningful social phenomena, business systems exhibit internal relationships with major social institutions such that if these latter change, so too do effective business practices. The comparative analysis of business recipes is therefore concerned with the plurality of effective business practices in different contexts, their establishment, development and change, as a key component of the social study of business systems in market economies.

This analysis is similar in certain respects to the study of organizational isomorphism developed in the 'institutional' school of organizational analysis (for example, Di Maggio and Powell, 1983; Meyer and Scott, 1983; Scott, 1987; Zucker, 1987). In this approach, organizations in the same sector of society are seen as adopting similar forms and practices as a result of institutionalized conventions and 'rules of the game'. Just as Stinchcombe (1965) suggested that organizations follow the dominant pattern established when an industry first developed, the institutionalists argue that schools, public television stations, hospitals and other organizations in the USA follow the pattern set by the most successful and legitimate organization in their particular field to demonstrate their correctness and modernity. This mimetic isomorphism is considered especially strong in fields where the standards of organizational success and effectiveness are ambiguous (Di Maggio and Powell, 1983), although Fligstein (1985) has discussed the spread of the multi-divisional corporate form in similar terms.

Most of the organizations studied by the institutionalists have been non-profit-making and there has been a tendency to regard isomorphism among privately owned businesses as primarily technical and competitive in nature rather than 'institutional' (Meyer and Rowan, 1977). This is despite the general assumption that powerful economic agents' beliefs and conceptions affect organization structures and practices (Scott, 1987). Indeed, some proponents of the institutionalist approach suggest that the search for institutional legitimacy and imitation of fashionable procedures necessarily lead to technical inefficiency, even though the nature of 'efficiency' is clearly institutionally dependent as argued above (cf. Meyer and Rowan, 1977; Zucker, 1987).

The comparative analysis of business structures and practices proposed here shares the institutionalists' view that integrated and strong institutional environments encourage isomorphism between organization structures and practices, so that differences between these environments lead to differences in organizational forms. Rather than drawing a distinction between technical and institutional isomorphism, though, it focuses on the ways that different institutional environments generate different kinds of technically efficient business recipes so that equally effective forms of business organization become similar within them but quite different between them. Social institutions, in this view, are key phenomena in the constitution of different competitive orders and should not be counterposed to market efficiency (cf. Orru et al., 1988).

The Nature of Business Recipes

In advocating a comparative analysis of successful ways of organizing economic activities, more than the cross-national study of micro-organizational phenomena is being proposed. In addition to this recognition of the national variability of many attitudinal and similar phenomena, it is important to be aware of the differences in what Richardson (1972) has called the 'organization of industry' between institutional contexts. These variations concern patterns of relations between firms and the extent to which they specialize in particular competences and activities. They thus focus on differences in market organization and the relations between markets and hierarchies in different contexts. As Imai and Itami (1984) have emphasized, there are considerable differences between Japanese and US firms in terms of both their internal structures and their interconnections in variously organized markets. These differences arise from the particular institutional environments in which successful firms developed.

Variations in market organization between institutional contexts have important implications for the nature of firms and their internal organization. Differences in the scope and intensity of connections between firms are related to differences in the sorts of activities they coordinate and their competitive strategies. The widespread use of 'relational contracting' between Japanese companies, and their common membership of inter-market business groups which exchange information and resources (Clark, 1979; Dore, 1986; Futatsugi, 1986), for example, enable them to specialize in particular activities and competitive capacities at lower risk levels than could firms in Anglo-Saxon societies (see Yoshino and Lifson, 1986: 37–50). The nature of firms as authoritative coordinators of economic activities, then, is interdependent with the ways in which they are organized as 'industries' and are embedded in reciprocal obligation networks which vary across institutional environments. These variations are also related to differences in authority structures and control systems as the example of Japanese employment practices and employer–employee commitment indicates (Clark, 1979: 221–2). Indeed, the dominant pattern of authoritative coordination and control in different business recipes is not, I suggest, fully comprehensible without considering how firms developed as particular economic decision-making units and their connections with business partners and competitors.

Distinctive business recipes, then, are particular arrangements of hierarchy–market relations which become institutionalized and relatively successful in particular contexts. They combine preferences for particular kinds of activities and skills to be coordinated authoritatively with differences in the discretion of managers from property rights holders and in the ways in which activities are coordinated, and also exhibit variations in the extent and manner in which activities are coordinated between economic actors. Thus the nature of firms as quasi-autonomous economic actors, their internal structures and their interdependences are all inter-related and differ significantly between institutional contexts.

The comparative study of business recipes therefore involves considera-tion of how 'firms' are constituted as relatively discrete economic actors in different market societies. While all market-based economic systems decentralize control over human and material resources to property rights owners and their agents, the nature of the collective entities that exercise that control, and how they do so, vary considerably, and so what a 'firm' is differs across societal contexts. In particular, it is clearly misleading to rely on purely legal definitions of firms' boundaries and activities if we are concerned to explore their role as economic decision-making units. Not only are French industrial groups often much more important than their constituent firms in making strategic choices (Bauer and Cohen, 1981), but among the expatriate Chinese it is clear that the key decision unit is the family business rather than the often numerous legally defined 'firms' controlled by family heads (Tam, 1990; Wong, 1985). These differences are important features of distinctive business recipes which are linked to the institutional environments in which they develop and emphasize the contextual nature of 'firms' as economic agents.

The variability of economic agents between societies and the different roles of legally defined firms mean that comparisons of business recipes cannot rely on purely formal means of identifying key units of economic action. Similarly, the importance of business groups and networks of rela-tionships between ostensibly independent firms in many countries, especially East Asian ones (Hamilton et al., 1990), raises questions about how economic agents are to be identified for comparative purposes. If business recipes vary in how they constitute firms as units of economic action, in other words, how are we to compare and contrast them in a systematic way? The critical point here, it should be noted, is not so much what 'firms' really are as how we are to conceive of the critical economic agents in market societies so that we can compare them and explain their differences. This obviously depends on our view of how firms and markets function.

Firms are important economic agents in market societies because they, or their controllers, exercise considerable discretion over the acquisition, use and disposition of human and material resources. They function as economic actors by integrating, coordinating and controlling resources through an authority system, and it is this authoritative direction of economic activities which is their central characteristic. Authority rela-tions provide the basis for continued and systematic coordination of activities and thus the integrated transformation of resources into produc-tive services (Penrose, 1980: 15–25; Whitley, 1987). It is through this system that firms 'add value' to resources and function as relatively separate units of economic decision-making. Although the degree of central direction of economic activities does, of course, vary, as does the primary basis of authority relations, it is this coordinated control of a varied set of resources which distinguishes firms as distinct economic agents from cooperative networks and *ad hoc* alliances. Thus, Taiwanese business groups consisting of informal networks between family firms based on kinship connections, joint ventures, financial assistance and so on, do not constitute the primary units of economic action in this view because they are better regarded as informal coalitions of partnerships than authoritatively integrated managerial hierarchies (Hamilton and Kao, 1990; Hamilton et al., 1990; Numazaki, 1987, 1989). Because each family business retains considerable freedom of action and remains the primary locus of authoritative decision-making and control in Taiwan, it is the family firm that functions as the dominant economic agent there, rather than the business group.

The importance of the highly personal, particularistic and diffuse ties between family firms in Taiwan, Hong Kong and other Chinese business communities, as well as the long-term alliances between Japanese companies (Futatsugi, 1986; Goto, 1982), demonstrate the variable nature of market relationships and the limited generality of the Anglo-Saxon model of firms and markets. It is particularly important to note here that the nature of inter-firm connections and market organization is closely linked to the nature of firms as economic actors in these societies and to key features of their 'internal' organization and management practices. Distinctive configurations of these interrelated characteristics have become established as separate business recipes in East Asian societies (Whitley, 1990). While not all societies institutionalize such different and integrated business recipes, variations in how firms are constituted are usually connected to differences in market organization, and in their authority structures and procedures, to form identifiable and distinct configurations. To illustrate these points, the major distinguishing characteristics of the dominant business recipes in Japan, South Korea, Taiwan and Hong Kong will now be summarized.

These characteristics can usefully be described under three broad headings derived from the major components of hierarchy–market configurations: the constitution of firms as economic actors, their interconnections in markets, and their internal systems of authoritative coordination and control. First, the nature of the firm as the unit of authoritative coordination of economic activities has two key features. The variety of the activities and skills being coordinated through authority hierarchies, and thus the extent to which firms specialize in their competitive competences and capabilities (see Richardson, 1972), differs considerably between East Asian societies. Relatedly, the dominant pattern of strategic choices and growth also varies in terms of firms' willingness to make discontinuous changes in the nature of the activities and resources they control.

The second area concerns market organization. This refers to the importance of long-term connections between firms and preferences for dealing with particular suppliers and customers, as opposed to engaging in impersonal, *ad hoc*, spot market contracting. It also incorporates the extent to which the activities of firms in different sectors are coordinated through alliances and membership of inter-market business groups or through State agencies. The third area focuses on the coordination and control systems of firms which can be divided into four major character-istics. Perhaps the most significant in East Asia is the importance of personal ownership and authority. Next, there are considerable differ-ences in the reliance placed on formal coordination and control systems. This, in turn, is related to the dominant managerial style in these firms and, in particular, to whether managers are closely involved in the work of the group and are responsible for maintaining high levels of group morale. Finally, the type and degree of mutual employer–employee commitment and loyalty clearly varies between these business recipes.

The particular configurations of hierarchy–market relations which have become established and successful in Japan, South Korea, Taiwan and Hong Kong since the Second World War are sufficiently homogeneous within these societies and distinctive between them to be characterized as separate business recipes (Hamilton and Biggart, 1988; Hamilton et al., 1990). In Japan the broad features of the large corporation, or *kaisha*, have been described by Abegglen and Stalk (1985) and Clark (1979) among many others, and it can be termed the specialized clan. In South Korea there is little doubt that the enormous family controlled conglomer-ates, or *chaebol*, dominate the economy (Amsden, 1989; Yoo and Lee, 1987). In Taiwan and Hong Kong, the primary unit of economic action in competitive markets is the Chinese family business (CFB), which is also an important form of business organization throughout south-east Asia (Redding, 1990; Silin, 1976).

Considering first the nature of firms as economic actors, the variety of economic activities coordinated through authority hierarchies in the Japanese *kaisha* and the CFB is much less than in the Korean *chaebol* (Amsden, 1989; Clark, 1979: 62–4; Cusumano, 1985: 186–93; Tam, 1990; Zeile, 1989). Japanese and Chinese businesses tend to restrict themselves to activities in which their specialized skills and knowledge provide distinctive capabilities and competitive advantages, and then rely on market contracting to coordinate complementary but dissimilar activities. While most of the Korean *chaebol* are vertically integrated, centrally controlling a variety of functions and activities through managerial hier-archies, Japanese and Chinese firms concentrate on specialized stages of production and are less managerially self-sufficient (Orru et al., 1988). When firms do extend their activities into new industries in Japan, they tend to separate them as distinct entities with their own access to financial resources and enterprise union as soon as they are successful (Clark, 1979: 60–2; Dore, 1986: 61–3).

Business specialization in Japan is reflected in relatively low rates of unrelated diversification and preferences for evolutionary growth strategies based on existing resources and capabilities rather than discontinuous ones (Kagono et al., 1985: 55–87; Kono, 1984: 78–80). The CFB combines growth through the expansion of current activities and capabilities with opportunistic diversification through partnerships and family controlled subsidiaries (Limlingan, 1986; Hamilton and Kao, 1990). The Korean *chaebol* have grown through vertical integration and State-directed diversification into heavy industry, as well as initiating successful moves into new industries such as construction and financial services (Amsden, 1989; Jones and Sakong, 1980). While both the Japanese and Chinese tendency to managerial specialization involves the risk of being committed to a declining industry and expertise, their responses to this risk differ. The former rely on high levels of employee commitment and flexibility, together with extensive sharing of risks with subcontractors and members of business groups. The Chinese, on the other hand, limit their commitment to a particular industry by remaining relatively small and relying on elaborate networks of mutual obligations with employees, suppliers and agents. These obligations are based on personal knowledge and reputations but remain limited and highly flexible (Tam, 1990).

Considerable differences also occur in the degree and type of market organization in these countries. High levels of business specialization in Japan, Taiwan and Hong Kong obviously imply high levels of dependence on purchasing agents, component suppliers and distributors, but the nature of these contractual linkages vary. They tend to be more stable and involve more extensive sharing of information and skills in Japan than in Taiwan and Hong Kong, reflecting higher levels of trust and, sometimes, reciprocal shareholdings. Generally, Japanese firms are embedded in extensive networks of 'relational contracting' (Dore, 1986: 77–83), while the CFB tend to be more opportunistic and less exclusively tied to particular business partners, though relying heavily on personal contacts and trust (Numazaki, 1986, 1989).

The extent of coordination of economic activities between sectors also varies between these three business recipes. Many large Japanese firms have long-term links with companies in other industries and with banks and insurance companies, which include mutual shareholdings, weekly or monthly 'presidents' club' meetings, the exchange of senior managerial personnel, and mutual support when under severe threats (Futatsugi, 1986; Goto, 1982; Hamilton et al., 1990; Miyazaki, 1980). These business groups are not as hierarchically structured or integrated as the pre-war *zaibatsu* and appear to function more as informal support groups, pooling information and expertise on an *ad hoc* basis (Dore, 1986: 79–80; Kiyonari and Nakamura, 1980). Korean *chaebol* are much less directly interconnected, but are liable to coordination by State agencies and political alliances (Kim, 1979). Taiwanese business groups are less significant and less institutionalized than Japanese ones (Hamilton and Kao, 1990; Hamilton et al., 1990). Inter-market linkages in the CFB are essentially family, or 'family type', connections and so are highly personal and more varied than those between members of Japanese business groups.

Turning now to consider the 'internal' authority structures of these firms, large Japanese enterprises manifest less centralization of decision-making and initiation of plans than Korean *chaebol* or the CFB (Kagono et al., 1985: 42–3; Liebenberg, 1982; Rohlen, 1974). This is linked to their less personal and more collective authority system which in turn is tied to their strong separation of ownership from control (Abegglen and Stalk, 1985: 177; Aoki, 1987; Dore, 1986: 67–72). In contrast, the association of personal authority with ownership is a key characteristic of *chaebol* and the CFB (Orru et al., 1988; Silin, 1976). Loyalties and obedience are focused more on the individual owner than on the collective enterprise in the latter two recipes. The importance of personal relations in Korea and Taiwan is highlighted by the extensive use of relatives and others with strong personal ties to the owner in senior management positions (Shin and Chin, 1989; Yoo and Lee, 1987).

Japanese companies also exhibit considerably greater formalization of procedures and rules (Pugh and Redding, 1985), though the existence of elaborate formal rules does not mean they always govern work activities (Lincoln et al., 1986; Rohlen, 1974). In general, they appear more formally 'bureaucratic' than their Korean and Chinese counterparts, where procedures and formal structures are often by-passed and ignored (Silin, 1976). Dominant images of managerial authority and appropriate ways of demonstrating managerial competence also differ in that Japanese managers are not expected to demonstrate omniscience and omnipotence, nor to be remote and aloof from subordinates (Clark, 1979; Rohlen, 1974; Smith and Misumi, 1989). Chinese owner-managers, on the other hand, are expected to reflect Confucian norms of those in authority and demonstrate their moral superiority by being reserved and dignified and by not revealing their emotions (Silin, 1976). While Japanese managers are responsible for group morale and facilitating group achievements, Korean and Chinese managers follow a more directive style with little or no attempt to explain decisions, let along justify them (Liebenberg, 1982; Redding and Richardson, 1986; Redding and Wong, 1986).

All these 'recipes' have different employment policies for different groups of workers, and reserve long-term commitments, seniority-linked reward systems and extensive bonuses for the core group of employees. However, the extent of such long-term commitment and employee loyalty does vary between Japan, Korea and the CFB, with higher labour turn-over being found in Korean companies than in Japan or Taiwan (Amsden, 1985; Michell, 1988) and loyalties being less 'emotional' and intense in large Taiwanese firms than in Japanese ones (Silin, 1976: 127–31). As might be expected, given the more personal nature of authority in Korean and Chinese businesses, long-term commitments and employment policies designed to elicit loyalty are less institutionalized in these firms than in successful Japanese ones and are more dependent on the

Table 7.1 *East Asian business recipes*

Characteristics	Japanese specialized clan	Korean *chaebol*	Chinese family business
Nature of firms			
Business specialization	High	Low	High within managerial hierarchies, medium to low across family business groups
Growth patterns	Evolutionary	Opportunistic, discontinuous	Volume expansion and opportunistic diversification
Market organization			
Relational contracting	High	Low	Medium
Inter-sector coordination	High, through business groups and State	Low, except through State	Medium, through personal alliances
Authority coordination			
Significance of personal authority and ownership	Low	High	High
Significance of formal procedures	High	Medium	Low
Managerial style	Facilitative	Directive	Didactic
Employee commitment	Emotional	Conditional	Conditional

personal choice of the owner. According to Clark (1979: 64–73), movement up the 'hierarchy of industry' in Japan is signalled by the adoption of such policies, partly to attract high-quality graduates and partly to advertise success. These differences between the three East Asian business recipes are summarized in Table 7.1.

Business Recipes and Institutional Environments

The comparative analysis of business recipes presumes that distinctive ways of organizing economic activities become established and effective because of major differences in key social institutions, such as the State, the financial system and the education and training system (Maurice et al., 1980, 1986). However, the distinctiveness and homogeneity of successful recipes clearly varies between societies, as does their institutional specificity. Those prevalent in East Asian countries, for instance, seem more different from each other and more homogeneous within each society than those apparent in Western European and North American nations, where variations between industries seem to be significant (Spender, 1989). Thus, authority relations and structures within firms differ considerably between Japan, Korea and Taiwan, while those in most large Western firms share a common reliance on legal–rational norms and bases of legitimacy. Similarly, the prevalence of capital market based financial systems and reliance on 'professional' modes of skill development and organization in Anglo-Saxon societies, means that dominant business recipes in Britain and the USA seem to share a preference for financial means of control of operations and subsidiaries, and accord the finance function higher status than many continental European firms (Granick, 1972; Horovitz, 1980; Lawrence, 1980). As a result, some features of particular recipes such as financial control techniques, may be readily transferred between particular contexts, such as Anglo-Saxon societies, while others require substantial modification and 'translation'.

The distinctiveness of business recipes, then, depends on the integrated and separate nature of the contexts in which they developed. The more that major social institutions, such as the political and financial systems, the organization of labour markets and educational institutions, form distinctive and cohesive configurations, the more dominant business recipes in those social systems will be different and separate. Where distinctive cultural systems and socialization patterns overlap with national boundaries, and State institutions are also distinctive and closely involved in economic development, we would expect successful firms to share major characteristics which differ significantly from those of dominant economic actors in different contexts.

Where, on the other hand, major social institutions are more differentiated and plural in a society, business recipes are likely to be more varied and not so sharply distinct from those elsewhere. Thus, the strong State commitment to the defence industries in Britain and the USA, in contrast to a more laissez-faire attitude to other ones, can be expected to affect attitudes to long-term investments as well as the composition of the dominant coalitions of firms across industries. Similarly, strong regional variations in the pattern of industrialization coupled with considerable local political and financial autonomy can generate quite distinct business recipes within a country, as in the case of Italy. Here, the industrial districts of north-east and central Italy have developed successful systems of subcontracting and highly decentralized production units, which contrast strongly with the predominance of large integrated businesses in north-west Italy (Bamford, 1987; Lazerson, 1988).

This contrast highlights the variable nature of the relationship between business recipes and national boundaries. Nation states with relatively homogeneous cultures and institutions generate more distinctive business recipes than do those characterized by greater homogeneity. While East Asian societies appear to have dominant business recipes that are quite dissimilar, for example, many south-east Asian nations are dominated by the recipe of the same ethnic minority, the Chinese family business (Lim-lingan, 1986; Redding, 1990; Yoshihara, 1988). These latter countries are often based on colonial boundaries that incorporate a variety of quite distinct cultures and different social institutions. Where political elites have tried to develop a business class drawn from the dominant ethnic group, as in Malaysia, they do not seem to have been successful in generating a viable alternative 'national' business recipe (Jesudason, 1989).

As well as major ethnic and cultural differences encouraging a variety of distinct business recipes within nation states, there are of course substantial differences between firm structures and connections across industries, especially in Western Europe and North America. Just as the national distinctiveness and coherence of business recipes depends on the integration and dissimilarity of national institutions, so too the variability of industry-based recipes depends on the differentiation of industrial contexts. However, since many important contextual institutions are common to all industries in each country, such as the financial and political systems, the extent to which industry recipes are sharply distinct and mutually exclusive is limited.

While, then, major differences in capital and energy intensity, in market structure and in the organization of transaction costs may well affect the nature of economic actors and their interrelations between different industries (Daems, 1983), they will not generate highly dissimilar business recipes. As Nishida (1990) has shown, different legal and political institutions in Hong Kong encouraged greater vertical integration among Chinese cotton spinners there than in Shanghai. Similarly, Limlingan (1986) has identified distinctive growth patterns and financial strategies in a number of industries dominated by Chinese family businesses in Asean. Industry differences here seem less crucial than institutional contexts, especially the significance of family identities and affiliations and of trust relations between business partners (Redding, 1990; Silin, 1976).

The relative importance of industry characteristics, as opposed to more general social institutions in a country, in generating distinctive business recipes depends, then, on the extent to which institutions are homogeneous across industries and dissimilar between societies. The more varied and differentiated are major social institutions – such as the financial, political and educational systems – the more likely economic actors will differ between industries in certain respects. Thus, societies in which occupational identities are important and distinct, and in which individual rights and duties are more significant than collective ones, are more likely to have a variety of overlapping business recipes than those with more collective and vertical commitments. Anglo-Saxon societies which share a common concern with 'professional' identities, market-based wage systems and commitments to individualism, then, generate greater variations between industries than many continental European and East Asian ones (Child et al., 1983; Dore, 1973; Lodge and Vogel, 1987).

The dependence of successful business recipes on dominant social institutions additionally implies, of course, that as the latter change so too will successful recipes. Clearly, if successful ways of organizing and controlling economic activities reflect the nature and operation of major contextual institutions, then as these alter so too will successful ways of dealing with them. Thus, if the 'globalization' of the financial services industry results in the standardization of financial systems on the Anglo-Saxon model – improbable as this may seem – then major Japanese firms are likely to change the ways in which they manage risk and make strategic choices. Similarly, if the British State implemented an education and training policy which resulted in 60 per cent of school leavers having certified practical skills, we would expect the employment practices of leading British companies to alter (see Lane, 1988; Maurice et al., 1980).

However, it is important to note that these influences are mutual in that established business practices and structures affect developments in their contexts as well as vice versa. The preference of large Japanese firms for recruiting the graduates of prestigious universities for managerial positions solely on the basis of their success in general competitive examinations, and concentrating on internal training of all staff rather than relying on externally certified skills, has inhibited the development of a public training system comparable to that in Germany (Clark, 1979; Dore, 1973; Maurice et al., 1986). Similarly, the extensive family, financial and other connections between banks, insurance companies and industrial firms in large French industrial groups (Bauer and Cohen, 1981) make it unlikely that Anglo-Saxon types of capital markets with short-term relations between financial institutions and firms will become established in France (see Encaoua and Jacquemin, 1982; Lévy-Leboyer, 1980). Thus, the development and change of dominant business recipes in a society is a two-way process and their success and growth affect related institutions just as they alter as a result of major contextual changes.

Turning now to consider briefly the major institutions which structure and enable different business recipes to develop and become established, we can distinguish between the more immediate and proximate institutions which affect business behaviour relatively directly and in the recent past from those more distant in origin and indirect in impact. In the former category I would place the sorts of phenomena that have been commonly cited as explanations for variations between managerial structures and practices in different countries such as the structure and policies of the State – developmental or regulatory (Johnson, 1982) – the nature of the financial system and its role in economic development (Ingham, 1984; Zysman, 1983), and the education and training system emphasized by the Aix group (Maurice et al., 1980, 1986; cf. Lane, 1988; Rose, 1985). Also included here, of course, are dominant patterns of labour market organization and, in particular, trades union structures and attitudes as well as more general and diffuse attitudes and beliefs about work, material values and authority relations.

The major institutions in the second category are those which developed during industrialization, and, where this was relatively recent, those which were important in pre-industrial periods and influenced the particular patterns of industrialization that occurred. In many countries the dominant political institutions and authority relations reflect those that emerged during or, arguably, that shaped the industrial process. Even

Table 7.2 *Major differences in the institutional contexts of East Asian business systems*

	Japan	Korea	Taiwan	Hong Kong
Departmentalist State	Yes	Yes	Yes	No
State coordination of strategies	Medium	High	Medium	Low
Integration of banks with industry	High	High	Medium	Medium
Differentiation of family authority	Considerable	Considerable	Low	Low
Primacy of family	Medium	High	High	High
Particularistic basis of trust and obligation	Medium	High	High	High
Recognition of reciprocity between superiors and subordinates	High	Low	Low	Low
Personal basis of authority	Medium	High	High	High

where earlier political systems have been discredited by the rise of militarism and defeat in war – as in Germany and Japan – key features of present State structures and policies as well as subordination principles stem from those current at the period of industrialization and, in some cases, earlier patterns of political and economic relationships.

Related significant institutions are family and kinship relations, identities and authority structures. The significance of family membership and prestige, for instance, varies greatly between cultures and has a considerable influence on conceptions of identity and the role of individual rights and duties as opposed to collective ones. Additionally important are historical patterns of trust and cooperation between kinship groups which continue to affect trust relations between exchange partners in recently industrialized societies (Redding, 1990; Silin, 1976). Finally, traditionally cosmologies and beliefs about the natural and social world often structure attitudes towards risk, planning horizons and preferences about specialization and formalization within authority structures, as Redding (1980; Redding and Wong, 1986) has shown in the case of the Chinese family business.

Considering the differences between the East Asian business recipes discussed earlier, the major variations in social institutions which help to explain them are listed in Table 7.2. In addition to important differences in the role of State agencies and banks, there are also significant contrasts in the organization of families, trust relations and vertical authority relations between Japan, South Korea, Taiwan and Hong Kong (Whitley, 1991). According to Pye (1985: 75–9), authority in Chinese families is more monolithic and patriarchal than in Korean and Japanese ones. While Japanese fathers feel able to admit to difficulties and involve other members of the family in deciding how to overcome them, Korean and Chinese fathers are commonly expected to be omnicompetent and lose their claim to authority if they admit uncertainty and call upon others for help. Similarly, emotional ties between parents, especially mothers, and children seem to be stronger in Japan. Although family identities and success are more significant in all these societies than in the West, the Japanese family is more outward facing and more willing to engage in cooperation across kinship boundaries than are Korean and Chinese ones. Family loyalties in Japan are also more easily transferred to larger collectives than elsewhere in East Asia (Clark, 1979: 38–41; Murayama, 1982), and trust between non-kin groups is easier to foster in Japan than in Korean or Chinese societies. In general, trust relations between Japanese are less particularistic and less derived from common ascriptive foundations, such as birthplace, school or university class, than between Korean and Chinese. Thus, Japanese obligation networks are often formed across ascriptive categories, whereas *guanxi* networks of mutual support amongst Chinese are usually tied to common background characteristics (Pye, 1985: 293–8; Wong, 1988).

Reciprocal commitments are also stronger between leaders and subordinates in Japanese society and vertical allegiances are more integrated (Pye, 1985: 287–90). Whereas loyalties in Korean and Chinese societies are primarily personal and focused on the family head, faction leader or head of the clan, they are more organized around particular collective entities in Japan which are, in turn, subordinate to larger ones. Thus reciprocity and recognition of mutual dependence between superiors and subordinates are here combined with strong beliefs in the common commitment to collective goals and the right of individuals to issue commands on the basis of their competence and subservience to common interests (Jacobs, 1985; Pye, 1985: 163–81; Redding and Wong, 1986). The role performance model of filial piety as the exemplary instance of obedience in Chinese society (Hamilton, 1984) limits the intensity of vertical loyalties and their mobilization for collective goals beyond the family unit.

Some of these institutional variations stem from the different political and economic systems of pre-industrial Japan, Korea and China and the organizations of agricultural production. In particular, the degree of political and economic pluralism was greater in Japan than in Korea or China, and power was based more on military success than on the presumption of moral worth as manifested through literary examinations (Jacobs, 1958; Pye, 1985). Both Japan and Korea had a hereditary aristocracy, though under the Confucian Yi dynasty in Korea it was relatively subservient to the ruler. This subservience was enhanced by the principle of equal inheritance of estates which ensured aristocratic dependence on royal favours (Jacobs, 1985: 205). Japanese villages seem to have been more cohesive communities than their Korean and Chinese counterparts, especially with regard to cooperation in agricultural production (Moore, 1966: 208; Smith, 1959: 50–2), and were more integrated into larger units of political authority with the village headman functioning as the key link between feudal lords and peasants. Collective responsibility for taxation and criminal law, together with the greater interdependence of households, limited open expression of conflicts between families in Japan and ensured that group solidarity was regarded as much more important than individual wishes (Smith, 1959: 60–2).

Conclusions

I have suggested in this chapter that the socially constructed nature of economic phenomena and business practices implies that there are a variety of forms of business organization which are effective and that no single economic logic can be regarded as uniquely 'rational'. The nature of successful managerial actions depends on key social institutions as well as how controllers of major economic resources conceive and evaluate realities and possibilities. Thus, different kinds of hierarchy–market relations develop and become established in different kinds of institutional environments, together with particular conceptions of how business should be structured and developed.

The more integrated and homogeneous are dominant social institutions in a society, the more they generate distinctive business recipes in which firms coordinate and direct certain kinds of economic activities through particular authority relations and manage risk through various quasi-market connections and networks. These business recipes also incorporate developmental strategies and ways of choosing priorities. They thus combine inter-firm and inter-sector modes of organizing economic activities with patterns of strategic choice and 'internal' authority structures. Their development, reproduction and change are central to processes of economic development and change, and their comparative analysis is a key component of the sociology of economic enterprises.

References

Abegglen, James C. and Stalk, George (1985) *Kaisha, The Japanese Corporation*. New York: Basic Books.

Alford, Bernard (1976) 'Strategy and structure in the UK tobacco industry', in L. Hannah (ed.), *Management Strategy and Business Development*. London: Macmillan.

Amsden, Alice H. (1985) 'The division of labour is limited by the rate of growth of the market: The Taiwan machine tool industry o the 1970s', *Cambridge Journal of Economics*, 9: 271–84.

Amsden, Alice H. (1989) *Asia's Next Giant*. Oxford: Oxford University Press.

Aoki, Masahiko (1987) 'The Japanese firm in transition', in K. Yamamura and Y. Yasuba (eds), *The Political Economy of Japan. I: The Domestic Transformation*. Stanford University Press.

Bamford, Julia (1987) 'The development of small firms, the traditional family and agrarian patterns in Italy', in R. Goffee and R. Scase (eds), *Entrepreneurship in Europe*. London: Croom Helm.

Bauer, M. and Cohen E. (1981) *Qui gouverne les groupes industriels?* Paris: Seuil.

Bhaskar, Roy (1979) *The Possibility of Naturalism*. Brighton: Harvester.

Bloor, David (1976) *Knowledge and Social Imagery*. London: Routledge & Kegan Paul.

Brossard, M. and Maurice, M. (1976) 'Is there a universal model of organisation structure?', *International Studies of Management and Organisation*, 6: 11–45.

Chandler, Alfred D. (1962) *Strategy and Structure*, Cambridge, MA: MIT Press.

Chandler, Alfred D. (1977) *The Visible Hand*. Cambridge, MA: Harvard University Press.

Child, John (1987) 'Culture, contingency and capitalism in the cross-national study of organisations', *Research in Organisational Behaviour*, 3: 305–56.

Child, J., Fores, M., Glover, I. and Lawrence, P. (1983) 'A price to pay? Professionalism in work organisation in Britain and West Germany', *Sociology*, 17: 63–78.

Clark, R., (1979) *The Japanese Company*. New Haven: Yale University Press.

Cusumano, Michael A. (1985) *The Japanese Automobile Industry: Technology and Management at Nissan and Toyota*. Cambridge MA: Harvard University Press.

Daems, H. (1983) 'The determinants of the hierarchical organisation of industry'. in A. Francis et al. (eds), *Power, Efficiency and Institutions*. London: Heinemann.

Di Maggio, Paul J. and Powell, Walter W. (1983) 'The iron cage revisited: Institutional isomorphism and collective rationality in organisational fields', *American Sociological Review*, 48: 147–60.

Dore, Ronald (1973) *British Factory – Japanese Factory*, London: Allen and Unwin.

Dore, Ronald (1986) *Flexible Rigidities*. Stanford University Press.

Encaoua, D. and Jacquemin, A. (1982) 'Organisational efficiency and monopoly power: The case of French industrial groups', *European Economic Review*, 19: 25–51.

Feyerabend, P.K. (1981) 'The methodology of scientific research programmes', in P.K. Feyerabend, *Problems of Empiricism: Philosophical Papers, Volume 2*. Cambridge: Cambridge University Press.

Fligstein, Neil (1985) 'The spread of the multidivisional form among large firms, 1919–1979', *American Sociological Review*, 50: 377–91.

Futatsugi, Yusaku (1986) *Japanese Enterprise Groups*. Kobe University, School of Business Administration.

Gellner, Ernest (1968) 'The new Idealism – cause and meaning in the social sciences', in Imre Lakatos and Alan Musgrave (eds), *Problems in the Philosophy of Science*. Amsterdam: North Holland.

Goto, A. (1982) 'Business groups in a market economy', *European Economic Review*, 19: 53–70.

Granick, David (1972) *Managerial Comparisons of Four Developed Countries*. Cambridge, MA: MIT Press.

Granovetter, Mark (1985) 'Economic action, social structure and embeddedness', *American Journal of Sociology*, 91: 481–510.

Hamilton, Gary (1984) 'Patriarchalism in imperial China and Western Europe', *Theory and Society*, 13: 393–426.

Hamilton, Gary and Biggart, N.W. (1988) 'Market, culture and authority: a comparative analysis of management and organisation in the Far East', *American Journal of Sociology*, 94 (supplement): 552–94.

Hamilton, Gary and Kao, C.S. (1990) 'The institutional foundation of Chinese business: The family firm in Taiwan', *Comparative Social Research*, 12: 95–112.

Hamilton, Gary, Zeile, William and Kim, W.J. (1990) 'The network structures of East Asian economies', in S. Clegg and G. Redding (eds), *Capitalism in Contrasting Cultures*. Berlin: de Gruyter.

Hickson, David, Hinings, C.R., McMillan, C.J. and Schwitter, J.P. (1974) 'The culture-free context of organisational structure: A tri-national comparison', *Sociology*, 8: 59–80.

Hickson, David, McMillan, C.J., Azumi, K. and Horvath, D. (1979) 'Grounds for comparative organisation theory: Quicksands or hard core?', in C.J. Lammers and D.J. Hickson (eds), *Organisations Alike and Unlike*, London: Routledge & Kegan Paul.

Horovitz, Jacques Henri (1980) *Top Management Control in Europe*. London: Macmillan.

Imai, K. and Itami, H. (1984) 'Interpretation of organisation and market. Japan's firm and market in comparison with the US', *International Journal of Industrial Organisation*, 2: 285–310.

Ingham, G. (1984) *Capitalism Divided? The City and Industry in British Social Development*. London: Macmillan.

Jacobs, Norman (1958) *The Origin of Modern Capitalism and Eastern Asia*. Hong Kong University Press.

Jacobs, Norman (1985) *The Korean Road to Modernization and Development*. Urbana: University of Illinois Press.

Jesudason, James V. (1989) *Ethnicity and the Economy: The State, Chinese Business and Multinationals in Malaysia*. Singapore: Oxford University Press.

Johnson, Chalmers (1982) *MITI and the Japanese Miracle*. Stanford University Press.

Jones, Leroy and Sakong, Il (1980) *Government, Business and Entrepreneurship in Economic Development: The Korean Case*. Harvard University Press.

Kagono, Tadao, Alonaka, Ikujiro, Sakakibara, Kiyonori and Okumara, Akihiro (1985) *Strategic vs. Evolutionary Management*. Amsterdam: North Holland.

Kim, Kyong-Dong (1979) *Man and Society in Korea's Economic Growth*. Seoul: Seoul National University Press.

Kiyonari, Tadao and Nakamura, Hideichiro (1980) 'The Establishment of the Big Business System', in K. Sato (ed.), *Industry and Business in Japan*. New York: M.E. Sharpe.

Kono, Toyohiro (1984) *Strategy and Structure of Japanese Enterprises*. London: Macmillan.

Lane, Christel (1988) 'Industrial change in Europe: The pursuit of flexible specialisation in Britain and West Germany', *Work, Employment and Society*, 2: 141–68.

Lane, Cristel (1989) *Management and Labour in Europe*. Aldershot, Hants: Edward Elgar.

Lawrence, Peter (1980) *Managers and Management in West Germany*. London: Croom-Helm.

Lawriwsky, Michael L. (1984) *Corporate Structure and Performance*. London: Croom-Helm.

Lazerson, M.H. (1988) 'Organizational growth of small firms: An outcome of markets and hierarchies', *American Sociological Review*, 53: 330–42.

Lévy-Leboyer, M. (1980) 'The large corporation in modern France', in A.D. Chandler and H. Daems (eds), *Managerial Hierarchies*, Cambridge, MA: Harvard University Press.

Liebenberg, R.D. (1982) ' "Japan Incorporated" and "The Korean Troops": A comparative analysis of Korean business organisations'. Unpublished MA Thesis, Dept of Asian Studies, University of Hawaii.

Limlingan, Victor S. (1986) *The Overseas Chinese in Asean: Business Strategies and Management Practices*. Pasig, Metro Manila: Vita Development Corporation.

Lincoln, J.R., Hanada, M. and McBride, K. (1986) 'Organisational structures in Japanese and US manufacturing', *Administrative Science Quarterly*, 31: 338–64.

Lodge, George C. and Vogel, Ezra F. (eds) (1987) *Ideology and National Competitiveness*. Boston, MA: Harvard Business School.

Maurice, Marc, Sorge, Arndt and Warner, Malcom (1980) 'Societal differences in organising manufacturing units', *Organisation Studies*, 1: 59–86.

Maurice, Marc, Sellier, François and Silvestre, Jean-Jacques (1986) *The Social Bases of Industrial Power*. MIT Press.

Meyer, John W. and Rowan, Brian (1977) 'Institutionalized organizations: Formal structure as myth and ceremony', *American Journal of Sociology*, 83: 440–63.

Meyer, John W. and Scott, Richard (1983) *Organisational Environments*. London: Sage.

Michell, Tony (1988) *From a Developing to a Newly Industrialized Country: The Republic of Korea, 1961–82*. Geneva: ILO.

Miyazaki, Yoshikazu (1980) 'Excessive competition and the formation of *keiretsu*', in K. Sato (ed.), *Industry and Business in Japan*, New York: M.E. Sharpe.

Moore, Barrington (1966) *Social Origins of Dictatorship and Democracy*. Boston: Beacon Press.

Murayama, Magoroh (1982) 'Mindscapes, workers and management in Japan and the USA', in Sang M. Lee and Gary Schwendiman (eds), *Japanese Management*. New York: Praeger.

Nishida, Judith (1990) 'The Japanese influence on the Shanghaiese textile industry and implications for Hong Kong', M. Phil. Thesis, University of Hong Kong.

Numazaki, Ichiro (1986) 'Networks of Taiwanese big business', *Modern China*, 12: 487–534.

Numazaki, Ichiro (1987) 'Enterprise groups in Taiwan', *Shoken Keizai*, December, 162: 15–23.

Numazaki, Ichiro (1989) 'The role of personal networks in the making of Taiwan's *Guanxiqiye* (related enterprises)'. Unpublished paper presented to the International Conference on Business Groups and Economic Development in East Asia held at the University of Hong Kong, 20–22 June.

Orru, M., Biggart, Nicole W. and Hamilton, Gary (1988) 'Organizational isomorphic in East Asia: Broadening the new institutionalism', Program in East Asian Culture and Development Research Working Paper Series no. 10, Institute of Governmental Affairs, University of California, Davis.

Penrose, E. (1980) *The Theory of the Growth of the Firm*. Oxford: Basil Blackwell.

Pugh, Derek S. and Redding, Gordon R. (1985) 'The formal and the informal: Japanese and Chinese organisation structures', in S.R. Clegg et al. (eds), *The Enterprise and Management in East Asia*. University of Hong Kong: Centre for Asian Studies.

Pye, Lucian W. (1985) *Asian Power and Politics: The cultural dimensions of authority*. Cambridge, MA: Harvard University Press.

Redding, Gordon (1980) 'Cognition as an aspect of Culture and its relation to management processes: An exploratory view of the Chinese case', *Journal of Management Studies*, 17: 127–48.

Redding, Gordon (1990) *The Spirit of Chinese Capitalism*. Berlin: de Gruyter.

Redding, Gordon R. and Richardson, S. (1986) 'Participative management and its varying relevance in Hong Kong and Singapore', *Asia Pacific Journal of Management*, 3: 76–98.

Redding, Gordon R. and Wong, Gilbert Y.Y. (1986) 'The psychology of Chinese organisational behaviour', in M. Bond (ed.), *The Psychology of the Chinese People*. Oxford University Press.

Richardson, George (1960) *Information and Investment*. Oxford: Oxford University Press.

Richardson, George (1972) 'The organisation of industry', *Economic Journal*, 82: 883–96.

Rohlen, Thomas P. (1974) *For Harmony and Strength: Japanese White-Collar Organisation in Anthropological Perspective*. Berkeley: University of California Press.

Rose, Michael (1985) 'Universalism, culturalism and the Aix group: Promise and problems of a social approach to economic institutions', *European Sociological Review*, 1: 65–83.

Sayer, A. (1984) *Method in Social Science*. London: Hutchinson.

Scott, Richard (1987) 'The adolescence of institutional theory', *Administrative Science Quarterly*, 33: 493–511.

Shin, E.H. and Chin, S.W. (1989) 'Social affinity among top managerial executives of large corporations in Korea', *Sociological Forum*, 4: 3–26.

Silin, R.H. (1976) *Leadership and Values. The Organization of Large Scale Taiwanese Enterprises*. Cambridge, MA: Harvard University Press.

Smith, Thomas C. (1959) *The Agrarian Origins of Modern Japan*. Stanford University Press.

Smith, Peter B. and Misumi, J. (1989) 'Japanese Management. A Sun Rising in the West?' in C.L. Cooper and I. Robertson (eds), *International Review of Industrial and Organizational Psychology*. New York: J. Wiley.

Sorge, Arndt (1983) 'Cultured Organisations', *International Studies of Management and Organisations*, 12: 106–38.

Spender, J.C. (1989) *Industrial Recipes*. Oxford: Basil Blackwell.

Stinchcombe, A. (1965) 'Social structure and organizations', in J.G. March (ed.), *Handbook of Organizations*. Chicago: Rand McNally.

Tam, Simon (1990) 'Centrifugal versus centripetal growth processes: Contrasting ideal types for conceptualising the developmental patterns of Chinese and Japanese firms', in

S. Clegg and G. Redding (eds), *Capitalism in Contrasting Cultures*. Berlin: de Gruyter.

Taylor, C. (1985) 'Social theory as practice', in C. Taylor, *Philosophical Essays*, Volume 2. Cambridge University Press.

Whitley, Richard D. (1984) *The Intellectual and Social Organisation of the Sciences*. Oxford: Oxford University Press.

Whitley, Richard D. (1987) 'Taking firms seriously as economic actors: Towards a sociology of firm behaviour', *Organisation Studies*, 8: 125–47.

Whitley, Richard D. (1990) 'East Asian enterprise structures and the comparative analysis of forms of business organisation', *Organisation Studies*, 11: 47–74.

Whitley, Richard D. (1991) 'The social construction of business systems in East Asia', *Organisation Studies*, 12: 1–28.

Williamson, Oliver E. (1985) *The Economic Institutions of Capitalism*. New York: Free Press.

Winch, Peter (1970) 'Understanding a primitive society', in Bryan Wilson (ed.), *Rationality*. Oxford: Basil Blackwell.

Wong, Siu-Lun (1985) 'The Chinese family firm: A model', *British Journal of Sociology*, 36: 58–72.

Wong, Siu-Lun (1988) 'The applicability of Asian family values to other sociocultural settings', in P.L. Berger and H.-H.M. Hsiao (eds), *In Search of an East Asian Development Model*. New Brunswick, NJ: Transaction Books.

Yoo, S. and Lee, S.M. (1987) 'Management style and practice in Korean *chaebols*', *California Management Review*, 29: 95–110.

Yoshihara, Kunio (1988) *The Rise of Ersatz Capitalism in South East Asia*. Singapore: Oxford University Press.

Yoshino, M.Y. and Lifson, Thomas B. (1986) *The Invisible Link: Japan's Sogo Shosha and the Organisation of Trade*. Cambridge, MA: MIT Press.

Zeile, William (1989) 'Industrial policy and organizational efficiency: The Korean chaebol examined', Institute of Governmental Affairs, University of California, Davis, Program in East Asian Culture and Development Research, Working Paper no. 30.

Zucker, Lynne, G. (1987) 'Institutional theories of organisation', *Annual Review of Sociology*, 13: 443–64.

Zysman, John (1983) *Governments, Markets and Growth: Financial Systems and the Politics of Industrial Change*. Ithaca: Cornell University Press.

8

Changing Organizational Forms:
From the Bottom Up

Mark Wardell

A commonly accepted hypothesis asserts that activities within organizations are shaped largely by external factors. Population, ecology, State regulation, culture, plus the ever-present product and labour markets, have been proposed as some of the more salient external factors. According to the typical scenario, top administrators mediate between activities within an organization and changes in external forces. In doing so, administrators forge policies that trickle down a hierarchy, ultimately influencing the workplaces where products are made or services rendered.[1] This scenario, often adopted by Marxists and non-Marxists as well, can be broadly characterized as a top-down approach. Overall, the approach explicitly portrays shop-floor activity and the organization of the workplace as being shaped almost entirely by the efforts of managers who respond to a problematic environment.

Recent arguments have questioned, to varying degrees, the taken-for-granted status of the top-down assertion. A few have proposed the possibility of a reversed influence between the workplace and management. Littler (1982), for instance, hints that workers may have the potential for autonomous activity. They have routinely resisted management directives, but, he concluded, they have never exerted systematic influence over the organization of the workplace. A more direct challenge to the central logic of the top-down approach has come from representatives of a dialectical standpoint (such as P.K. Edwards, 1986; Montgomery, 1987; Wardell, 1990). From a dialectical approach, understanding larger societal relations is not sufficient for understanding the activities in the workplace, or their effect on the larger organization. The workplace instead must be seen as an emerging frontier of organizations.

In this discussion, I elaborate two implications that follow from the notion of the workplace as an emergent frontier. First, I suggest that a practical autonomy grows out of the relation between the form of the organization in a workplace and the ongoing labour activity that takes place within it.[2] Secondly, I suggest that practical autonomy historically has prompted transformations of the capitalist workplace because it makes problematic the fulfillment of managerial objectives, resulting in a struggle to control the effort of labour. In short, contradictions emerge in the workplace wherever the economic interests of capitalists depend on the social contributions of labour for fulfillment. The succession of organizational forms in the capitalist workplace since the late 1800s, then, can be seen as adaptive responses by management to cope with the practical autonomy of labour.[3]

The Practical Autonomy of Labour

For Harry Braverman (1974), capitalistic forms of work, in contrast to the craft workshop, assault the basic integrity of being human. They degrade the quality of labour required from workers. Scientific management specifically, Braverman thought, contributed to transforming the workplace by aiding the separation of manual and mental production activity, thereby pre-empting labour from self-objectification in the labour process. But Braverman's work has attracted criticisms from Michael Burawoy (1985), among numerous others (including Littler, 1982; Wood, 1982: *passim*).

Regarding Braverman's emphasis on scientific management's influence in transforming the workplace, Burawoy (1985: 41–5) made three specific points. First, Taylor and other representatives of the scientific management movement attempted to gather and standardize knowledge about production, though they did not monopolize it. Instead, scientific management as a managerial practice may have contributed to a momentary undermining of capitalist controls. Second, Braverman failed to grasp the ideological component of the scientific management movement and its linkage to larger political–economic circumstances, such as the growing strength of craft unions and the ineffectiveness of traditional labour markets to regulate labour–capital relations within an emerging monopoly capitalism. Finally, Burawoy criticized Braverman for assuming that capitalists and managers acted in a unified manner, as if they possessed a common consciousness. Burawoy overall argued that Braverman exaggerated the practical effectiveness of scientific management, and perhaps of management generally, as tools of capital to alter and control the workplace.

For a second major criticism, Burawoy (1985: 23–4) charged that Braverman contrasted a romantic view of the craft worker with one of a scientifically managed worker. Braverman supposedly grounded his analysis in a conception of the ideal craft worker, an individual in possession of creative talents and in complete control of the product, process and distribution. Romanticizing the craft worker, Burawoy charged, stemmed from Braverman's adoption of a position within capitalism for his comparative analysis, and from which he could only assess 'variations within capitalism' (Burawoy, 1985: 24). Burawoy reasoned that this strategy fails to identify the essence of the organization of work within capitalism because it fails to incorporate an independent standpoint. Moreover, it fails to uncover the character of the labour–capital dynamic, since the process by which the mental aspects of production become severed from the manual aspects remains mysterious. Burawoy (1985: 56) maintained that Braverman in the end, like Max Weber's lament of the effects of the iron cage on individuals, 'mourns the eclipse of the bourgeois individual'.

For his part, Burawoy (1985: 29–35) contrasted the capitalistic labour process with that of the feudal era. He claimed that his analysis yielded the essence of the labour process within capitalism: the obscuring of the securing of surplus value. Otherwise stated, the essence of the capitalistic labour process involves the separation of the economic from the political moments of work, where the economics of production refer to regulation of the exchange-value of labour and the politics of production refer to the political and ideological regimes regulating the use-value of labour.

Burawoy's analysis can be summarized for present purposes by two broad generalizations. First, managers do not play an autonomous role in organizing the workplace. The practical activities of management are circumscribed by the same hegemonic processes of the State and the economy that impose on the labour process of the working class. Second, and most important, Burawoy portrays the effects of the economic and political apparatuses in a manner curiously similar to Durkheim's abstracted notions about the division of labour. The organization of the workplace links, but in no way provides a mediating social space between, labour and capital. The outcomes of workplace struggle at best reflect the larger division of labour in society because the various forms of workplace do not represent distinct moments of the labour–capital relation. Even 'the games workers play are not, as a rule, autonomously created in opposition to management . . . [rather they are] . . . strictly the production of a [repressive] society' (Burawoy, 1979: 80–1).

Burawoy seemingly did not distance himself from the more conventional top-down standpoints, even in his earlier efforts to understand the manufacturing of consent. To be sure, he has removed management from an overly active role in organizations and has moved labour into an active, but still minor, role. The net result appears to be a highly abstracted view of the organization and transformation of the workplace. The workplace is not problematic in Burawoy's scheme, since it reflects rather than mediates the class relations of society. This observation suggests a critical difference between Burawoy's and Braverman's standpoints.

Braverman's (1974: 4, 140) stated concern was to study the organization of the workplace, not the individual worker *per se*. But he explicitly opposed a Durkheimian analytical strategy because it requires that analyses begin with the global division of labour in society and presumes a downward influence towards the practical activity of individuals in the workplace. This strategy results either in ignoring various forms of the detailed division of labour or in viewing those forms as abnormal (Braverman, 1974: 74–5). Since Burawoy has concentrated entirely on the formal properties of class relations, at the expense of the ongoing processes that take place within capitalistic workplaces, he has overlooked the possibility that scientific management was a practical force in transforming the workplace, not merely an ideological factor (Montgomery, 1979: 91–112).[4] Braverman, by contrast, thought that analyses should begin with the detailed divisions of labour that organize capitalistic production, not that analyses necessarily should ignore the global division of labour within society. The latter is understood in terms of the former.

For example, Burawoy (1985: 31) concluded that the capitalistic labour process differed from that of the feudal era along several dimensions. Two dimensions are that workers within capitalism are dispossessed of the means of production, and that they are not able to set the means of production into motion on their own accord. For Braverman, though, workers are dispossessed from owning the means of production, not from access to the actual workings of the means of production. To the contrary, the detailed division of labour within capitalistic workplaces has one prevailing characteristic: the production process requires labour power from someone other than the owners of the enterprise (Braverman, 1974: chapter 1). Workers at minimum provide the practical human effort – the necessary hand work – that ultimately transforms raw material or bureaucratic rules into a productive act at the points of production. In addition, the practical knowledge about production required of labour – individually as well as collectively – enables labour to set the means of production into motion. Even in highly bureaucratized and technologically advanced capitalistic workplaces, labour power remains the first social prerequisite for production. The social dependency of capital on labour means that a social space necessarily exists between the formal control of labour and the outcomes generated in the production process, a space filled with the mental, physical and organizational contributions of labour.[5]

Analytically combining the detailed division of labour (the organization of the workplace) with the practical nature of production leads to inquiries about how the workplace mediates the social dependency of capital on labour power. These inquiries rest on the notion that organizations are the historical products of human construction. Within capitalist societies they are products of the class struggle taking place largely within social arenas at the points of production – at the bottom of organizations.[6]

In contrast to the top-down approaches where structure often dominates over consciousness and agency, a bottom-up approach rests on the ontological assumption that structure and agency are inextricably locked in an ongoing process (Hindess, 1982). This assumption does not deny the socio-economic dependency of class relations; it denies that the structural dependency determines the activities of actors. Nor does this assumption lead to the view that individuals are voluntaristic actors, or that in the case of workers, their consciousness emerges independent of their experiences at work. Rather, the consciousness of workers grows largely out of experiencing the workplace, including the form of organization that coordinates the detailed division of labour within it (P.K. Edwards, 1986).

In these experiences, workers form interests that help to orientate their activities within the workplace. In doing so, workers gain the potential to act in ways which undermine the legitimacy of capital to accrue value from production, as well as the right of management to manage. Thus, they can undermine the effectiveness of the accruing process itself, while generating concerns among the owners and managers alike for instituting changes in the workplace. The shape and transformation of the workplace, as a result, stem partly from the need to control the social contribution of labour in the production process. This need can never be satisfied because practical autonomy undermines even newly installed factory regimes. Still, workers do not uniformly represent that autonomy, as their efforts often cross purposes, but they are not necessarily less effective at undermining the interests and institutions of owners and managers (Castoriadis, 1976/77; R. Price, 1982). The following analysis is intended to show how the various struggles over labour's effort at the points of production have contributed to the shape, content, and transformation of the capitalist workplace.

Analysis

Production can be characterized by various dimensions, including the ownership of the means of production, plus the responsibility for the production process and the personnel involved in production. The workplace becomes organized in such a way that each dimension is delineated by numerous social arenas within which the exercise of discretion occurs. The arenas associated with the production process and with personnel will be of greatest interest in the following analysis. The former arenas include the speed of production, the amount of time workers spend on the job, the amount and type of labour power required, the design of the product including its quality, the market price of the product, and the quantity to be produced. For personnel, the specific arenas include hiring and firing, socializing of newcomers, disciplining people already in the workplace, setting the exchange rate for the social value of labour power, plus matters relating to the future, such as job security and promotion. In the following analysis, I concentrate on how these social arenas mediate labour–capital relations within the contractor and foreman forms of organization. If workers produce a practical autonomy from their experiences with the form of an organization, the relative importance of the various arenas, as issues in labour–capital relations, should vary from the contractor workplace to the foreman workplace.

I begin the analysis with a discussion of the ancient craft workplace. This part of the analysis meets one of Burawoy's criticisms of Braverman's work: namely, it establishes an external comparative reference point from which to discern the distinct and similar features of the contractor and foreman forms of organization. The analysis results in very broad characterizations drawn from the details of existing studies on each organizational form. Unfortunately, this approach ignores the obviously uneven and overlapping uses of particular forms across industries (Littler, 1982: 70–2).

The Craft Workplace A salient feature of the ancient craft workplace was the absence of any significant hierarchical arrangement. Workplaces generally were not organized along any type of status lines. For example, sculptors were considered stonecutters, and along with masons and quarrymen were considered equal to plasterers, in that all received the same basic wages prior to the Renaissance. Only after the Renaissance did sculptors become distinguished as artists (Gimpel, 1983).

Even the slave workers in early Greek and Roman workshops were considered equal to free workers in terms of the autonomous judgement they could exercise within the labour process (Burford, 1972: 51, 59, 91). Most slaves worked independently of their master, and slave wages were usually equal to those of free workers, occasionally even higher. In some cases slaves ultimately purchased their own freedom. Slaves and free workers alike began their careers as general labourers or as apprentices, knowing that with time and effort they would become craft workers, if not master craft workers with their own shop. This prospect of mobility lasted at least until the middle to late 1700s (Gimpel, 1983: 59, 152). If status differences characterized the general society, those differences were not obviously reproduced within the organization of the pre-modern workshop.

With respect to responsibility, here too ancient workshops seemed to lack a distinctive vertical hierarchy. Master craft workers usually worked side by side with other craft workers and apprentices in shops averaging four to eight workers. Other craft workers shared the responsibilities of socialization and supervision, but the arrangement of work still required that each craft worker or apprentice work independently at their separate jobs. The efforts of masters contributed to the overall productivity of the shop in the same way as the effort of any other craft worker. Effectively, the detailed division of labour in the craft workshop fostered a collective responsibility where the reputation of the shop most often superseded that of the individual.

George Sturt, for instance, noted that he knew little about the work or about the division of labour when he took over his father's wheelwright shop. But his ignorance had little effect on daily shop-floor operations. To the contrary, he said (1923: 68–9):

> [T]here was for the first months at any rate nobody to take command. Yet this seems not to have mattered. Waggons were constantly being 'taken down' for painting or mending, and then being lifted up again; and, as I remember no quarrel or disagreement over this work, I gladly believe that the workmen

themselves like to get it done efficiently and that their own friendly good temper taught them how to pull and lift together.

Collective responsibility existed in other settings too, many of which were more difficult to coordinate. Burford (1972: 62, 75–8) has offered several examples. One of these examples was the Greek stonemasons who fluted the six columns on the east front of the Erechtheion. Six separate groups of at least five to seven masons worked independently on each column. The specifications provided by the master builder assured that the columns were fluted uniformly, and the collegial structure within each group assured that the master builder did not have to oversee the independent groups.

Nor did the ancient craft workshop contain a rigidly defined division of labour. The tasks of ancient quarrymen, for example, were not simple. They were called upon routinely to cut rectangles or cylinders from the face so that the rough-cuts were within an inch or two of the final dimensions. Plus, they were known to rough out statues at the quarry, leaving the sculptor to add the finishing detail. Burford noted too that few unskilled labourers worked in these situations, suggesting the absence of a skill hierarchy. Burford concluded that 'even the merely competent' craft worker had to understand each stage of production and be able to perform well at the various tasks within the Greek workplace, and that 'no total division of labour, no absolute specialization' existed because the 'scale and nature of the workshop forbade it' (1972: 96–7).

Collective responsibility and the absence of differentiated skills inside the craft shop were supported by a collegial network broader than the workplace. Craft workers learned their trade over many years before acquiring the right to claim craft-worker status. Quite often the craft worker learned the trade within a family context, literally growing up in the workshop. Craft shops, though, typically were surrounded by other craft shops, making the neighborhood a craft community. Craft workers also organized themselves in terms of guilds and companies. Early guilds were dominated by masters charged with preserving the quality of craft products, as well as sanctioning individual craft workers for deviating from craft customs (Unwin, 1904; Bennett, 1970: 27; Gimpel, 1983). Thus, within the detailed division of labour in the craft workshop, the workers were collectively responsible for recruiting, socializing and disciplining their own kind, and managers, as a designated position, were not required at the points of production.

Discussion of wages and how wages were set are very scarce in studies of craft work prior to the 1800s (Burford, 1972: 135–44). The sparsity of information about wages might well indicate they were not a major issue. A similar lack of documentation exists regarding the determination of prices for products. Sturt (1923: 53) provided some insight about prices and profits:

Nobody asked for an estimate – indeed there was a fixed price for all the new work that was done. The only chance for me to make more profit would have been by lowering the quality of the output; and this the temper of the men made out of the question. But of profits I understood nothing. My great difficulty was to find out the customary price. The men didn't know. I worked out long lists of prices from old ledgers, as far as I could understand their technical terms.

As Sturt struggled to determine the customary price for a job – obviously a price not set in accord with principles of cost accounting – the 'steadiness of the men', he claimed, saved him and the shop. Respect for the tradition of the craft, along with collective responsibility for the quality of workmanship and material, brought customers back to the shop and enabled the shop to survive. The shop was economically solvent without being organizationally designed to maximize a return on investments.

The organization of most craft workplaces remained the same for centuries. Greek vases were made in the same way for over 700 years (Burford, 1972: 61). The organization of work associated with building the great French cathedrals and churches lasted at least 300 years (Gimpel, 1983). And the silk craft shops of Lyon were operated in 1830 the same as they had been for centuries (Unwin, 1904). Prior to 1700, conflict, to the degree any occurred, was primarily in the arenas of quality and design of the product. Burford (1972: 155) maintained that workers' revolts against administrators were noticeably absent from classical Greek and Roman societies. Not until the introduction of a more capitalistic form of organization did conflict begin to occur routinely and, then, in arenas other than quality of the product. In contrast to the ancient workshop, the early capitalistic workplaces brought the indirect influence of a third party into the labour process, and employment, wages, and responsibility for production increasingly became issues thereafter (Dobson, 1980: Appendix A; Hinton, 1973).

Capitalistic Workshops The emergence of the merchant class signalled the arrival of capitalism, on one level at least. Initially, merchants contented themselves by maintaining the detailed division of labour of the craft workshop and contracting with individual craft workers. Eventually, the contracting system became problematic and was replaced by the foreman system (Clawson, 1980). But it too was problematic, and subsequent changes altered this form of organization as well. I turn now to a discussion of both forms of workshop, paying attention to how each mediated the labour–capital relation, and specifically to how shop-floor activity created and maintained a social distance that undermined owners'/managers' intents for labour.

The Contracting System

A variety of industrial settings have been organized around contracting systems. Weaving, shoemaking, shipbuilding, mining, railroading, and car, ordnance and steel manufacturing are just a few. Inside contracting systems, where craft workers contract with a single merchant or entrepreneur, appeared as early as the 1400s, perhaps becoming the most dominant form of workplace between 1750 and 1900. In both the United States and Great Britain it quickly lost popularity following 1890.

An inside contracting system is characterized by decentralized responsibility. Contractors, much like master craft workers in 400 BC Greece, hired, trained and disciplined the labourers. They oversaw the production process, attending to the quality of the product, job safety and job security. They set the hours to be worked and the wages to be received by the labourers within their employ. Contractors also arranged with the merchants to provide output in accord with a predesignated payment formula, yet the exact rate was not necessarily fixed in advance. The 'capitalist . . . was freed from most of the technical problems associated with production, improvement of the manufacturing process, and labour supervision' (Buttrick, 1952: 207). Put somewhat differently, the detailed division of labour precluded capitalists and their managers from direct access to the daily operations of the means of production, the arenas in which the quantity and costs of production, in addition to the relations among the workers, were determined.

The silk weavers of Lyon, France, represented an early version of inside contractors. They typically contracted with a single merchant who provided the raw materials. The average weaver owned his loom and worked in his home assisted by family and a few journeymen, who may have lived in the contractor's home as well (Bezucha, 1979: 41). The master weavers and journeymen agreed by tradition that the latter would receive half of the contracted rate for the goods they wove. Moreover, the two groups were seldom at odds. They viewed themselves as locked together in a 'continual struggle' against arbitrary and exploitative treatment by the merchants (Bezucha, 1979: 50).

In contrast to the ancient craft workshop, where masters typically dealt directly with patrons, silk merchants intervened between the workshop and the consuming public. Merchants bargained on the principle of future economic gains from the product markets. Contractors, however, bargained on the basis of traditional craft criteria, expecting quality materials and fair rates in exchange for quality work. The merchants and the weavers routinely struggled over both. Poor threads and discounted rates, from the weaver's perspective, were attempts by the merchants to cheat the weavers.

Nevertheless, contractors, not merchants, oversaw the production process. Their practical and technical knowledge of the production process enabled them to anticipate the amount of labour power and raw material required to produce quality work, the rate of return from each piece, and importantly, the relationships among the workers, as well as between the worker and the production process. In conjunction with the requirements of the detailed division of labour, this knowledge effectively afforded contractors certain organizational advantages not available to the capitalists. To be sure, some contractors, especially the larger ones, took advantage of the owners and the journeymen (Clawson, 1980: 80). But the typical contractor employed only a few others, and a loyalty developed between contractors and journeymen, such as with the Lyon silk weavers (Bezucha, 1979) and the anthracite coal miners of Pennsylvania (Virtue, 1897). The loyalty and collective consciousness growing out of this workplace enabled contractors and their labourers to create an independence from capitalists which they fought to preserve through practices of exclusivity inside and outside of the shop (Buttrick, 1952; Hinton, 1973).

The loyalty contractors and labourers derived from their collegial division of labour became the focus of capitalists' attention. The Lyon silk merchants launched an unsuccessful campaign to win the journeymen away from the contractors, calling the contractors parasites. Companies in the United States steel industry took a slightly more direct route to break the contractor–labourer relationship. They established programs to train skilled workers and helpers, thereby avoiding the exclusivity of the apprenticeship system (Stone, 1974: 143–5). Textile, glass, coal, and railroad car companies introduced company towns, where threat of eviction was used to break the contractors' relation with labourers (Nelson, 1975: 90–5). But the managers of the Winchester Repeating Arms Company probably typified the most effective approach because they attacked the detailed division of labour itself. In about 1900 the Winchester managers removed from contractors the rights to hire and fire labourers; foremen were assigned these tasks. Contractors could choose only labourers from the labour pool assembled by the foremen. In the end, the foremen were precluded from the hiring process, which from 1903 was conducted entirely from the president's office (Buttrick, 1952: 217–18).

Loyalty was not the only advantage enjoyed by contractors and labourers. As long as they collectively maintained control over the production process, they could restrict production to maintain a preferred life style and to stabilize the product markets. In the mining industries, for example, miners were noted for working an average of less than six to eight hours per day (Archbald, 1922). Contract miners would take their gang to the face, prepare the face, and shoot the coal. Then they might leave the underground workplace, instructing their gang to load the coal and leave too. The miners frequently agreed to a weekly production rate, reflecting their knowledge about how much to produce in order for them and their mates to live comfortably. For decades prior to 1887, the Cornish copper miners, known as 'tributers', contracted by the yield not by the ton. Often they would share ore if one miner had a bad spot, hold ore back, or send rock to the outside with the copper in order to influence, as well as take advantage of, the market value of copper (L. Price, 1891). Similar practices were observed in the British coal industry (Goodrich, 1921; Dennis et al., 1956: 64–8).

The anthracite coal miners of Pennsylvania perhaps best illustrate the importance of output restriction. Miners contracted for a base rate per ton that could slide in accord with the market value of coal. The miners routinely tried to influence the market value by leaving the pits early, slowing production, and striking. From the 1860s to the early 1880s, they willfully, and often successfully, used these practices to control the market value of coal, and hence the value of their labour power (Wardell and Johnston, 1987). Mine owners in return short-weighed coal cars, used screens with small holes to separate the coal from the rock, or discounted entire cars of ore because of the rock content, and charged excessive prices at company stores. They also formed a monopoly of coal and railroad interests in hopes of combating the threat of labour. In some cases, owners began requiring contractors to work a specified number of hours each day, or to report at a specific time of day. Still, these were minor challenges to the organization of inside contracting and to the advantages it afforded contractors and labourers.

Despite inside contracting denying capitalists direct access to the arenas of production, it was economically efficient (L. Price, 1891; Marglin, 1974; Clawson, 1980; Bezucha, 1979). As Henry Brewer, executive for Winchester Repeating Firearms, explained:

> [T]o my surprise I found that in practically every instance where we changed from the contract to the non-contract system, the costs were increased. . . . However, in spite of the increased cost . . . we felt that the jobs were much better under the non-contract . . . because the Company had better control of the job. One of the difficulties which had arisen under the contract job was that the contractor would push that class of work on which he was making the largest profit and would hold back on the work on which the profit was low and it frequently became impossible for us to get the work which we needed the most to fill our orders. (Quoted by Williamson, 1952: 138)

The contracting system, then, was most efficient for contractors and their labourers, since capitalists could not be assured of the desired amounts of cooperation from labour at the points of production. While capitalists were freed from overhead costs and the burden of managing production, their interests were routinely undermined because contractors and labourers created advantages for themselves within the workplace.

John Duncan might well have represented the sentiment of most capitalists and managing engineers regarding the contract system. He noted that the inside contracting system at a Philadelphia plant had allowed contractors to build 'the perfect system . . . to retard work for the purpose of increasing the price' (1906: 305). Duncan's solution to this activity was to extend the contract system to all employees by instituting scientific management which included the functional foreman.[7] The foreman gave capital a formal representation at the points of production, and hence was an attempt to invade arenas in the workplace where production output was a contested issue between the shop floor and management.

The Foreman System

The foreman system was most popular in the United States from 1900 to 1945, and remained popular in Britain long after. Initially, foremen hired and fired labourers, and were former labourers or craft workers knowledgeable about the technical and practical aspects of production. In many cases, the foreman, like the contractor, worked alongside the members of his gang, establishing a loyalty and a collective responsibility for production and personnel (Walker, 1950: 73–81).

With the foreman system, however, capitalists and their top managers gained legitimate representation within the detailed division of labour for the first time. To that extent, a foreman differed significantly from a contractor. Unlike contractors, foremen could not negotiate contracts with management on the basis of output. The average foreman in the United States was paid a straight wage, sometimes with incentive bonuses. Seldom was overtime remunerated (Leiter, 1948). Basically, the opportunities were gone by which to generate an economic independence from owners, as the contractors and their labourers had done. Nor could the foremen be assured of their future. Their upward mobility could easily be reversed by a demotion, whereas craft workers and contractors never lost their status, though they might be fined or sanctioned by the guild or union.

Foremen occupied a contradictory nexus between capitalists' economic interests and labour's social contribution towards fulfilling those interests. They represented capitalists' interests on the shop floor, yet simultaneously were employees subject to the same uncertainties as any wage labourer. They were expected not simply to oversee the production process, but to assure that the work was done and that management directives were properly transmitted to labourers (Nelson, 1975: 43; Nichols and Beynon, 1977: chapter 4). Warner and Low (1947: 72) observed in a shoe factory that

> [t]he foremen were socially closer to the shoe operatives than any other group in the managerial hierarchy. Although a foreman's interest lay with management, he was more likely than his superiors to have a sympathetic understanding of the interests and needs of the workers.

To be sure, inequities across work units occurred as some foremen resorted to favouritism and intimidation (Jacoby, 1985), eliciting the scorn of workers (Cross, 1940). Still, many foremen, if not most, coalesced in some way with the rank and file (Littler, 1982: 93, 123; Lichtenstein, 1989). Frequently foremen would even conspire with labour to circumvent management directives (Mathewson, 1931: 30–53).

In instances where foremen were the watchful eyes of owners and managers, labourers learned to keep an eye open for them. C.N. Lauer (1903: 465) maintained that the 'smart' labourer 'puts as much energy into figuring out where and when he [the foreman] is likely to turn up again. In consequence his day's work is made up of a few spurts, and a tremendous amount of energy expended in figuring how to fool the "boss"'. Numerous other representatives of the modern management movement, such as Horace Arnold and Frederick Taylor, reported that rampant systematic soldiering was the main problem with the foreman system. But as Mathewson (1931) explained, restriction of production was widely practiced because the practices of modern management precluded labourers from contributing a full day's effort and receiving a full day's wage.

Not only output restriction but turnover rates increased dramatically during the 1890s and the early 1900s. Sumner Slichter conducted one of the earliest studies about turnover rates in the United States. In his 1913 study of 105 plants, ranging from automobiles and chemicals to furniture, meat packing, woodworking and watchmaking, he reported that the turnover rate for the sample approximated 100 per cent (Slichter, 1919: 22). And he estimated that between 1910 and 1913 the turnover rate for all establishments in the United States was at least 100 per cent (1919: 16). One estimate of turnover in the bituminous coal industry for 1920–1921 was approximated at 200 per cent (Central Pennsylvania Coal Operators' Association, 1923: 77, Table 23).[8]

The foreman system, however, did not deny all forms of shop-floor collective action among labourers. Even in assembly-line situations, many if not most of the workers remained part of gangs working at sub-assemblies or benches that fed into the final line (Lichtenstein, 1983). They learned, as a result, how to regulate their efforts, including by restriction, to influence the entire flow of the final assembly line. The practical understanding of the workplace included a collective awareness of the detailed division of labour, an awareness gained through the cooperation of fellow workers, and sometimes the foreman (Lichtenstein, 1989).

Nor did the foreman system discourage the construction of platforms external to the workplace from which labourers could gain some collective advantage in terms of job rules, job security and wages. Between 1890 and 1922, labourers in the United States organized and joined labour unions in unprecedented numbers. Between 1915 and 1920, union memberships in the United States gained 96 per cent (Wolman, 1924: 38, Table 4), and British union membership gained approximately 100 per cent for those years (Hyman, 1989: 231, Table 10.1).

In Britain, more so than in the United States, management adopted a conciliatory stance towards the new wave of unionism. Perhaps somewhat extreme, the North London Manufacturers' Association concluded in 1918, like a Birmingham employers' association shortly before, that the industrial system had radically changed and that as employers they were willing to recognize past errors and contemplate ' ''the surrender by Capital of its supposed right to dictate to Labour the conditions under which work shall be carried on''' (quoted by Cronin, 1982: 113).

The 1930s brought the birth of the Congress of Industrial Organizations in the United States and protracted strikes in the automobile industry, steel and coal. In a few industries, such as coalmining, foremen retained their union membership out of loyalty and to protect themselves in case of a demotion (Leiter, 1948). In 1941 the foremen too founded their own union, the Foremen's Association of America, which grew to 33 000 members with 152 chapters by early 1945 (Lichtenstein, 1989: 172). Over 100 000 foremen in the United States were represented by a formal collective bargaining organization in 1945. Foremen unions increasingly gained popularity in the United Kingdom as well, from coal mines to chemical plants (see, for example, Nichols and Beynon, 1977: 64). But in the practical decisions unionized foremen made, they were more likely to protect labour's interests than management's.

The foreman system, because of its hierarchical responsibility, coupled with more automated production processes, had opened new areas in which labourers designed ways to regulate their effort bargain. Management responded, though not uniformly, by installing various mechanisms to eliminate the exercise of discretion when it deviated from management objectives. The foremen's prerogatives to hire, fire and discipline personnel, for instance, had been largely replaced with personnel departments by 1945 in the United States (Jacoby, 1985). The American Management Association reported results from a survey in which 30 per cent of the foremen interviewed had lost to personnel departments the right to hire, whereas 67 per cent had to share that right with personnel departments. Only 10 per cent retained the sole right to discharge workers. Twenty-one per cent could discharge after consulting with a superior, but 57 per cent could only recommend a discharge, with the final authority being a supervisor or the personnel department. Less than 15 per cent of the foremen retained the right to set wage rates and make promotions without consultation, and less than 11 per cent retained the right to discipline (American Management Association, 1945).

Besides the introduction of personnel departments, capitalists and their managing engineers in the United States also sought ways to pay labour for the amount of labour power spent towards production. Over and above the introduction of standardized workdays, and the use of time cards and shop order cards, standard costing – a management accounting practice – was broadly adopted in the United States by 1920 as a tool for determining where labour had been less than 100 per cent efficient (Emerson, 1914: 155).[9] Also, engineers such as A. Hamilton Church introduced budgets, enabling each functional department to have a separate budget and giving management the means of holding each department accountable for the variance between the expected and actual costs of production. Budgets described managerial production goals in terms of a standard cost per unit. In turn, budgets became the foremen's objectives and the formula for setting labourers' pay. The net result of budgets and standard costs was the removal of any formal responsibility from foremen, unions and shop-floor workers for production goals and costs, in addition to wages paid to labour. The foremen remained responsible only for the amount of output, but without any effective means of accountability (R. Edwards, 1979: 119-20).

By the 1930s and 1940s the foreman system was clearly an unstable and inefficient form of workplace, at least from American management's perspective. Even those foremen who had never been unionized began joining or forming unions at a startling rate. Many of their concerns were the concerns of the average employee, such as wages, job security and, most importantly, autonomy to oversee production (Roethlisberger, 1945). Output was no longer the major issue for capitalists that it had been in the contractor system, but the cooperation of labourers at the points of production, including the foremen, had become increasingly problematic.

Reminiscent of the various attempts to eliminate the contractor system, the Ford Motor Company launched a campaign in 1945 to make foremen part of management in hopes of regulating the autonomy of labour. The campaign involved separate lockers and eating and parking facilities, plus a uniformed dress code coupled with name badges for foremen. Some British managers likewise sought to counteract any coalescence between foremen and labourers, though according to Littler (1982: 94), such efforts exacerbated the problems of winning the cooperation of labour. In the United States, passage of the Labor Management Relations Act in 1947 effectively closed the last chapter on the foreman system, after which foremen could no longer legally join a labour union, despite testimony to the US House of Representatives that the foremen – not the employers or their managements – had improved cooperation and efficiency in the workplace (Lichtenstein, 1989: 173). In retrospect, the problems associated with the cooperation of labour in the foreman system appear to have grown directly from the contradictions between the detailed division of labour and an emergent labour autonomy.

Summary and Conclusions

The main arenas of struggle in the foreman system were work rules, wages, discipline, job security and promotion. These arenas contrasted rather noticeably with those characteristic of the contracting system. There, the most volatile arenas were the quantity of output and its value, and the quality of materials as well as the socialization of workers. At least in terms of the arenas of quality and socialization, the contracting system was more similar to the pre-modern craft system than to the foreman system, since the exchange value of the output was not an issue prior to the institutionalization of capitalism.

Thus, from one perspective, studying the organizational forms of capitalistic workplaces, in comparison to the pre-modern workplace, has produced rather surprising results. If we assume that capitalistic relations of production had formed a hegemony over the workplace, as Burawoy has argued, the important arenas of struggle in the foreman's workshop should have resembled the important ones in the contractor's workshop. Moreover, the issues provoking conflict within the ancient craft workplace, theoretically speaking, should not have resembled the arenas of struggle in either of the two capitalistic forms of organization. From a dialectical perspective, however, the variance in the arenas of struggle between the two capitalistic workplaces is not so surprising. The differences minimally indicate something quite distinctive about each of the workplaces, and I suspect those differences would become even more pronounced when similar forms are systematically analyzed cross-nationally (see, for example, Herding, 1972; P.K. Edwards, forthcoming).

These differences can be understood on two levels. Capitalistic production processes require the cooperation of labour. This cooperation mandates that labourers have access to the means of production and have the practical knowledge to operate the means of production. But the detailed divisions of labour constituting the various capitalistic workplaces do not require the cooperation of labour in exactly the same ways. At one level, therefore, the practical activities of workers in a contractor situation should be quite different from those in a foreman situation.

At the level of interaction between practical efforts and the form of workplace organization, however, labourers construct their cooperation within the limits of the detailed division of labour. They do not simply react to or resist management directives. Nor are their responses necessarily consistent with a particular working-class agenda or with one another. Absenteeism and turnover represent quite different constructions from unionism or collective restriction. Nevertheless, individually and collectively, labourers offer their cooperation as modified by these different forms of practical autonomy, and their cooperation routinely tests, if not circumvents, the parameters of the workplace as specified by the rules of management. In the process, the objectives of capitalists and their managers are less than fully realized, while the legitimacy of their objectives and their methods are routinely challenged within the arenas of production. The dialectic between the social contributions of labour and the economic value generated in the labour process, in other words, makes problematic management's attempts to regulate the effort of labour.

The transition from inside contracting to the foreman system was launched in large measure because of the inability of management to control the actual labour process, not because the former was found economically inefficient. Yet, contrary to the intent of management, the foreman system, especially in the United States, augmented the struggles to control labour's effort at the points of production. Where the contractor system mediated the labour–capital relation by granting some legitimacy to labour autonomy, the foreman system mediated that relation quite differently, as labour became more directly accountable to surrogates of the owners and managers. Under these circumstances, the overall value of labour was in jeopardy of depreciation, for the foreman as well as for the workers, as was the collective responsibility customarily practiced on the shop floor. Paradoxically, the responses of both workers and foremen threatened the legitimacy of management's right to manage more than the contractor system had ever done, and in the United States at least, the State ultimately reinforced management's prerogatives over labour's. Thus, while the collective autonomy enjoyed in ancient craft workshops was systematically undermined by the successive organizational forms, each subsequent form still contained arenas within which workers could formulate and practice shop-floor agendas relatively independently of management's rules.

This conclusion is as germane to the work organizations of today as to those that existed prior to 1950. For example, several new management schemes were introduced in the United States following a long period (1940–1972) known as the union–management accord. During these thirty-odd years, organized labour fought for and secured some version of the right to collectively bargain at the industry level in most mass production industries. In return for that right, unions largely agreed to discipline labour and support technological changes within the workplace. From the mid-1960s to the mid-1970s, this so-called accord was eroded by an increasing number of rank-and-file wildcat strikes. The rank and file in large part called for a workplace democracy, much like they had sought prior to the turn of the twentieth century. Management responded by challenging union certification and by installing quality circles, flexible techniques, employee stock ownership plans (ESOPs) and the like. While such schemes undermined unionism in the United States, they did not necessarily undermine the practical autonomy generated by labour on the shop floor. Rather, they were intended to coopt that autonomy by making labour more responsible for certain daily activities on the shop floor; but these schemes have not resulted in greater workplace democracy, and conflict at work continues (Sirianni, 1984). The social contribution of labour and the value it generates, in effect, remain objects of struggle.

Labour's cooperation seems to have eluded, thus far, the rationalistic schemes management intended for the different capitalistic workplaces. For this reason, the efforts of modern management must be understood in large part as a response to the ongoing challenge of the practical autonomy created by labour at the points of production. Rather than view the external environment, such as markets or population density, as the only wellsprings which challenge management's plans, and hence take the workplace for granted, the perspective developed here suggests that the organization of organizations – when viewed from the bottom – must be seen as inherently problematic. In that sense, the workplaces of today are the emerging frontiers of organizations.

Notes

My thoughts for this chapter benefited greatly from discussions with Natalie Hunter, Robert Lophovsky, Bradley Nash, Heping Shi, and Anna Zajicek-Wagemann. Comments by J. Matthew Kessler, Thomas Steiger, Ian Taplin, Mike Hughes and Mike Reed were very helpful for preparing the final draft. I also appreciate the support of the Education Foundation and the College of Arts and Sciences at Virginia Polytechnic Institute and State University.

1 Lower and mid-range management, as well as technical and clerical staff assisting management, also work in organized settings to which much of the following discussion could be applied. The explicit focus, however, will be on those settings commonly discussed in labour process literature as the points of production.

2 Practical autonomy, as I use it here, means more than the exercise of choice by an individual worker. It refers to a collective awareness of the coordination of a work group in relation to a particular production process, and hence to a manipulation of the social contribution (or effort) workers make to the production process. As such, practical autonomy has both organizational and ideological dimensions which increase the social distance between labour and capital. David Montgomery's (1987: 13–16) discussion of functional autonomy, while limited to craft workers, comes closer to the meaning of practical autonomy than a definition which emphasizes the possession of a particular skill *per se* (see Soffer, 1960).

3 Increasingly, parallels are made between capitalistic and socialistic workshops. For the present, I accept these parallels. Thus, much of what I say here about the bottom-up approach to capitalistic workplaces could be applied to socialistic ones. See Miklos Haraszti (1977) for an excellent case study of a Hungarian workplace, and Touraine et al. (1983) for an analysis of Solidarity in Poland.

4 Burawoy's conclusion does not reflect those generated by specific investigations into the influence of Taylor and the scientific management movement (Hoxie, 1916; Nadworny, 1955; Epstein, 1978). And, if scientific management was not as pervasive as Braverman thought – though a debatable issue – scientific management was certainly a significant part of the trend toward systematic control (Litterer, 1963). See Richard Price (1982: 200) for a similar criticism of Burawoy's notions about the labour process.

5 The social dependency of capital on labour power has been discussed previously on numerous occasions. See, for example, Marx's (1977) discussion of the labour process, Braverman's (1974) 'Introduction' and chapter titled 'Labor and Labor Power', and Georg Lukács's (1980) *The Ontology of Labour*.

6 The bottom-up approach spans the academic boundaries of several disciplines, ultimately having its intellectual roots in the works of Karl Marx, Georg Lukács and Henri Lefebvre, as well as British Marxist historians such as E.P. Thompson and Eric Hobsbawm (see Kaye, 1984, for an in-depth study of the British Marxist historians).

7 Mechanization was another option for altering the detailed division of labour in the workplace (Warner and Low, 1947: 60; R. Edwards, 1979; Clawson, 1980).

8 Absenteeism too was a mechanism that increasingly became part of the workers' repertoire in the early 1920s, especially in defense industries (Lanfear, 1924: 279, Table XIX; 280, Table XX).

9 Management accounting did not become a prominent tool of British management until after 1950 (Loft, 1986), and one viable element in explaining this late development, compared to the United States, must be that the strength of rank-and-file democracy, or voluntarism, pre-empted British management from adopting such a centralizing scheme (Wardell and Weisenfeld, forthcoming).

References

American Management Association (1945) *The Development of Foremen in Management*. Research Report no. 7. New York.

Archbald, Hugh (1922) *The Four Hour Day in Coal*. New York: The H.W. Wilson Company.

Bennett, Eric (1970) *The Worshipful Company of Wheelwrights of the City of London, 1670–1870*. Newton Abbot: David & Charles.

Bezucha, Robert J. (1979) 'The "Preindustrial" worker movement: The *canuts* of Lyon', in Clive Emsley (ed.), *Conflict and Stability in Europe*. London: Croom Helm, pp. 37–64.

Braverman, Harry (1974) *Labor and Monopoly Capital*. New York: Monthly Review Press.

Burawoy, Michael (1979) *Manufaturing Consent: Changes in the Labor Process under Monopoly Capitalism*. Chicago: Chicago University Press.

Burawoy, Michael (1985) *The Politics of Production: Factory Regimes Under Capitalism and Socialism*. London: Verso.

Burford, Alison (1972) *Craftsmen in Greek and Roman Society*. Ithaca: Cornell University Press.

Buttrick, John (1952) 'The inside contract system', *The Journal of Economic History*, XII (summer): 205–21.

Castoriadis, Cornelius (1976/77) 'On the history of the workers' movement', *Telos* (winter): 3–42.

Central Pennsylvania Coal Operators' Association (1923) 'Report to the 1923 US Coal Commission', Altuna, Pennsylvania.

Clawson, Dan (1980) *Bureacuracy and the Labor Process: The Transformation of US Industry, 1860–1920*. New York: Monthly Review Press.

Cronin, James E. (1982) 'Coping with labour, 1918–1926', in James E. Cronin and Jonathan Schneer (eds), *Social Conflict and the Political Order in Modern Britain*. New Brunswick, NJ: Rutgers University Press, pp. 113–46.

Cross, Ira B., Jr. (1940) 'When foremen joined the CIO', *Personnel Journal* 18 (8): 274–83.

Dennis, Norman, Henriques, Fernando and Slaughter, Clifford (1956) *Coal is Our Life: An Analysis of a Yorkshire Mining Community*. London: Tavistock Publications.

Dobson, C.R. (1980) *Masters and Journeymen: A Prehistory of Industrial Relations, 1717–1800*. London: Croom Helm.

Duncan, John C. (1906) 'Methods of determining the efficiency of labor', *Journal of Accountancy* 1 (4): 301–9.

Edwards, P.K. (1986) *Conflict at Work: A Materialist Analysis of Workplace Relations*. Oxford: Basil Blackwell.

Edwards, P.K. (forthcoming) 'The struggle for control of the American workplace, 1920–1985', in John Davis (ed.), *Labour and Enterprise from the Eighteenth Century to the Present*. Oxford: Basil Blackwell.

Edwards, Richard (1979) *Contested Terrain: The Transformation of the Workplace in the Twentieth Century*. New York: Basic Books.

Emerson, Harrington (1914) *Efficiency as a Basis for Operation and Wages*, fourth edition. New York: The Engineering Magazine Co.

Epstein, Marc Jay (1978) *The Effect of Scientific Management on the Development of the Standard Cost System*. New York: Arono Press.

Gimpel, Jean (1983) *The Cathedral Builders*, translated by Teresa Waugh. New York: Harper Colophon Books.

Goodrich, Carter Lyman (1921) *The Frontier of Control: A Study in British Workshop Politics*. New York: Harcourt, Brace and Company.

Haraszti, Miklos (1977) *A Worker in a Worker's State: Piece-Rates in Hungary*, translated by Michael Wright. Harmondsworth: Penguin.

Herding, Richard (1972) *Job Control and Union Structure: A Study on Plant-Level Industrial Conflict in the United States with a Comparative Perspective on West Germany*. Rotterdam: Rotterdam University Press.

Hindess, Barry (1982) 'Power, interests and the outcomes of struggles', *Sociology*, 16 (4): 498–511.

Hinton, James (1973) *The First Shop Stewards' Movement*. London: George Allen & Unwin.

Hoxie, Robert Franklin (1916) *Scientific Management and Labor*. New York: D. Appelton.

Hyman, Richard (1989) *The Political Economy of Industrial Relations: Theory and Practice in a Cold Climate*. London: Macmillan.

Jacoby, Sanford M. (1985) *Employing Bureacracy: Managers, Unions, and the Transformation of Work in American Industry, 1900–1945*. New York: Columbia University Press.

Kaye, Harvey J. (1984) *The British Marxist Historians: An Introductory Analysis*. Cambridge: Polity Press.

Lanfear, V.W. (1924) 'Business fluctuation and the American labor movement, 1915–1922', *Studies in History, Economics and Public Law*, CX (2): 201–325. New York: Columbia University.

Lauer, C.N. (1903) 'The importance of cost-keeping to the manufacturer', *The American Academy of Political and Social Sciences* (November): 459–69.

Leiter, Dave Robert (1948) *The Foreman in Industrial Relations*. Columbia University Studies in the Social Sciences, 542. New York: Columbia University Press.

Lichtenstein, Nelson (1983) 'Conflict over workers' control: The automobile industry in World War II', in Michael H. Frisch and Daniel J. Walkowitz (eds), *Working-Class America: Essays on Labor, Community, and American Society*. Urbana, IL: University of Illinois Press, pp. 284–311.

Lichtenstein, Nelson (1989) '"The man in the middle": A social history of automobile industry foremen', in Nelson Lichtenstein and Stephen Meyer (eds), *On the Line: Essays in the History of Auto Work*. Urbana, IL: University of Illinois Press, pp. 153–89.

Litterer, Joseph A. (1963) 'Systematic management: Design for organizational recoupling in American manufacturing firms', *Business History Review*, 37: 369–91.

Littler, Craig R. (1982) *The Development of the Labour Process in Capitalist Societies: A Comparative Study of the Transformation of Work Organization in Britain, Japan and the USA*. London: Heinemann Educational Books.

Loft, Ann (1986) 'Towards a critical understanding of accounting: The case of cost accounting in the UK', *Accounting, Organizations and Society*, 11: 137–69.

Lukács, Georg (1980) *The Ontology of Social Being: Labour*, translated by David Fernbach. London: The Merlin Press.

Marglin, Stephen A. (1974) 'What do bosses do? The origins and functions of hierarchy in capitalist production', *Review of Radical Political Economics*, VI (2): 60–112.

Marx, Karl (1977) *Capital*, vol. I, translated by Ben Fowkes. New York: Vintage.

Mathewson, Stanley (1931) *Restriction of Output Among Unorganized Workers*. New York: Viking Press.

Montgomery, David (1979) *Workers' Control in America: Studies in the History of Work, Technology, and Labor Struggles*. Cambridge: Cambridge University Press.

Montgomery, David (1987) *The Fall of the House of Labor: The Workplace, the State, and American Labor Activism, 1865–1925*. Cambridge: Cambridge University Press.

Nadworny, Milton J. (1955) *Scientific Management and the Unions 1900–1932: A Historical Analysis*. Cambridge, MA: Harvard University Press.

Nelson, Daniel (1975) *Managers and Workers: Origins of the New Factory System in the United States, 1880–1920*. Madison: University of Wisconsin Press.

Nichols, Theo, and Beynon, Huw (1977) *Living With Capitalism: Class Relations and the Modern Factory*. London: Routledge & Kegan Paul.

Price, Langford L. (1891) *'West Barbary' or Notes on the System of Work and Wages in the Cornish Mines*. London: Oxford University Press.

Price, Richard (1982) 'Rethinking labour history: The importance of work', in James E. Cronin and Jonathan Schneer (eds), *Social Conflict and the Political Order in Modern Britain*. New Brunswick, NJ: Rutgers University Press, pp. 179–214.

Roethlisberger, Fritz J. (1945) 'The foreman: Master and victim of double talk', *Harvard Business Review*, 23 (3): 283–98.

Sirianni, Carmen (1984) 'Participation, opportunity, and equality: Toward a pluralist organizational model', in Frank Fischer and Carmen Sirianni (eds), *Critical Studies in Organization and Bureaucracy*. Philadelphia: Temple University Press, pp. 482–503.

Slichter, Sumner H. (1919) *The Turnover of Factory Labor*. New York: D. Appelton and Company.

Soffer, Benson (1960) 'A theory of trade union development: The role of the "autonomous workman"', *Labour History*, 1 (spring): 141–63.

Stone, Katherine (1974) 'The origins of job structures in the steel industry', *Review of Radical Political Economics*, 6: 113–73.

Sturt, George (1923) *The Wheelwright's Shop*. Cambridge: Cambridge University Press.

Touraine, Alan, Dubet, F., Wieviorka, M. and Strzelecki, J. (1983) *Solidarity, The Analysis of a Social Movement: Poland 1980–1981*. Cambridge: Cambridge University Press.

Unwin, George (1904) *Industrial Organization in the Sixteenth and Seventeenth Centuries*. London: Frank Cass and Company.

Virtue, George O. (1897) 'The anthracite mine laborers', *Bulletin of the Department of Labor*, 13: 728–74. Washington, DC: US Government Printing Office.

Walker, Charles R. (1950) *Steeltown: An Industrial Case History of the Conflict Between Progress and Security*. New York: Russell & Russell.

Wardell, Mark (1990) 'Labour and labour process', in David Knights and Hugh Willmott (eds), *Labour Process Theories*. London: Macmillan, pp. 153–76.

Wardell, Mark, and Johnston, Robert L. (1987) 'Class struggle and industrial transformation: The US anthracite industry, 1820–1902', *Theory and Society*, 16 (6): 781–808.

Wardell, Mark and Weisenfeld, Leslie (forthcoming) 'Management accounting and the workplace in the United States and Great Britain', *Accounting, Organizations and Society*.

Warner, W. Lloyd and Low, J.O. (1947) *The Social System of the Modern Factory. The Strike: A Social Analysis*. New Haven: Yale University Press.

Williamson, Harold F. (1952) *Winchester, The Gun that Won the West*. New York: A.S. Barnes and Company.

Wolman, Leo (1924) *The Growth of American Trade Unions, 1880–1923*. New York: National Bureau of Economic Research.

Wood, Stephen (ed.) (1982) *The Degradation of Work? Skill, Deskilling and the Labour Process*. London: Hutchinson.

9

Back to the Future: Time and Organization

Gibson Burrell

The 'management of change' has become a very popular option on the curriculum of Western business schools. The content of such courses varies enormously, ranging from those with an emphasis on technological change to those which see demography as the major driving force of organizational life, yet they appear to share much in common at the meta-theoretical level. For example, there appears to be much unspoken support for Heraclitus's contention that 'no man steps in the same river twice' and a wide acceptance of terms such as 'flux', 'chaos' and 'turbulent environment' as being meaningful descriptions of organizational life in the 1980s. The work of Tofler in particular is *de rigueur* for many such courses. Given that the whole notion of 'change' relies heavily upon a conception of temporality, it is remarkable that the philosophy of time has been a neglected issue in almost all such syllabuses. To my mind, this demonstrates an unhealthy aversion to self-reflexivity which needs remedying.

In a somewhat dated paper by Herminio Martins (1974) one still finds a sophisticated approach to the whole issue of time and theory in the social sciences. He recognized as his major problem the lack of temporality within functionalism at that moment in social science and sought to analyse this weakness. To do so, he made a distinction between thematic temporalism and substantive temporalism. The former refers to the issues of time, change and history being taken as serious objects of study, or themes in which we should get embroiled; and the latter refers to the issues of becoming, process and change being viewed as the essential features of social life which explain social phenomena. In other words, these issues of time are seen as the *explanandum* and the *explanans* of the social world respectively. Martins claims that these are meta-theoretical issues which lie beyond normal theory yet must be seen as providing a context in which all theories have to be placed. He argues that many sociological schools of thought *could* deal with temporality if provoked into doing so, but many have not bothered. In the 1970s, therefore, the levels of thematic and substantive temporalism in social science were quite low.

Recently, however, the rise of postmodernism has convinced many writers that time had been considered by functionalist social science, at least to some extent, whereas space had not. In David Harvey's magisterial survey on *The Condition of Postmodernity* (1989) one finds a worry that social theories 'typically privilege time over space in their formulations' (Harvey 1989: 205). For him, Becoming and progress rather than Being in one's place are *the* focus of modernity. Giddens, of course, had made this point earlier, most notably in *A Contemporary Critique of Historical Materialism* (1981), where social systems were seen as constituted by time–space relations. Giddens discusses Heidegger and G.H. Mead on the philosophy of time and maintains there are three intersecting planes of temporality: the continuous flow of day-to-day life (the *durée* of activity), the life cycle of the organism (*Dasein*), and the *longue durée* of institutional time and the development of social institutions. Giddens seeks to consider all three types – a task he claims that others before him have avoided – and relate them to space. In Harvey's recent work, there is a complete part devoted to the experience of space and time in which he uses Gurvitch (1964) and goes on to claim the contemporary sense of time–space transformation is leading many to a postmodern anguish.

To use Martins' terminology, both Giddens and Harvey, despite their concern for space in relation to time, evidence high levels of both thematic and substantive temporalism in their work. But what of organizational analysis in the 1980s? The management of change material clearly should deal with such issues but the level of sophistication one encounters is worrying low.

Peter Clark is one notable exception to this generalized criticism of those organizational analysts who teach the management of change. He argues (1990: 139) that:

> there has been a strong assumption that organisations could be designed and could be changed in the planned directions desired by management. Simplistic yet elegant prescriptions overpowered a concern for description and explanation. Few disputed the postulate of fast, direct change.

This assumption is characteristic of much of the writing on the management of change and is in Clark's view unwarranted. His paper on 'chronological codes and organisational analysis, argues for a recognition of the existence of heterogeneous codes alongside those which assume a singular, unitary time. By recognizing a plurality of chronological codes, organization studies might be in a better position to analyse corporate change and gain an international perspective on culturally different organizational forms. Clark opines (1990: 143) that:

> organisation sciences as a whole are still utilising the theory and philosophy of a singular unitary, objective time against which all events can be periodised and ordered. Consequently, research programmes have so far failed to address the issue of a technological and organisational process located in plural chronological codes.

By using Gurvitch's well known work (Gurvitch, 1964) on temporality, Clark constructs an elaborate taxonomy though, somewhat ironically, we are referred back to an earlier piece of his through which to better understand the present work. His focus is on those chronological codes possessed by large corporations as well as organizational analysts, and Clark claims that there are lessons to be learnt from the differences which exist between Japanese and British organizations and how change is managed therein. Fortunately, Clark's work at the University of Aston has influenced a younger generation of writers who have come to see time as being of central importance.

For example, in Paul Blyton et al., *Time, Work and Organization* (1989), we have a set of essays which concentrate upon the role of 'linear' time in industrial organizations where the clock has become dominant and chronarchy well entrenched. The authors claim that the book represents a multidisciplinary approach to the study of work and organization, drawing upon separate but related fields of study such as sociology, psychology, economics, organization theory and industrial relations. The authors develop arguments around the rise of chronarchy, the commodification of time, and the inherent tendencies towards rigidity, precision, punctuality, calculability, standardization, bureaucratization, invariance and routineness within organizational forms based upon clock time. And since linear time is the conception which pervades most of our thinking, there are good reasons to believe that the philosophy of time should become an issue in areas other than the management of change.

In addition to linear concepts of time, many writers have recognized the legitimacy of cyclical perspectives on temporality. According to Clark, cyclical *and* linear viewpoints are both homogeneous codes because they allow for 'objectivity', measurability, stability and atomistic ordering (Clark, 1990: 147). Both cyclicality and linearity take highly regular events as the frame of reference so that, for example, it is easy to point to a tradition which existed long before the invention of the clock and linear datings, to a time where many societies bowed down before 'the myth of the eternal return'. The rise and setting of the sun, the phases of the moon, the seasons and the tides, were all of such significance to many pre-industrial societies that it is easy to imagine how *cyclical* approaches to time should come to be widely accepted by humans seeking to understand nature and their place within it. Where such views of time become established there is little room for conceptions based on linearity. Even the 'stages' in individual human life leading inexorably from birth to death are not perceived as linked by a train of logic which demands a line to be drawn. The concept of 'individual' itself is not too strong, so that individual 'passages' are not well marked in those societal value systems which take much more of a holistic perspective. The concept of the life cycle raises the issue of birth–death and rebirth for the human grouping *in toto*, whilst, for the individual, reincarnation is held out to be a real possibility.

Whilst Clark sees these two ancient traditions both as part of an homogeneous code, others see them as fundamentally opposed perspectives which need contrasting and comparison (see, for example, Blyton et al., 1989). If we were to use each viewpoint in turn and analyse changes within organizations, there is little doubt that we would end up with very different analyses. To begin with, the metaphors of 'the line' and the 'eternal return' will govern to some extent the conclusions which we reach, and these are not trivial. For example, if we analyse linear versions of time they are often associated with notions of progress, where what is contemporary and fashionable is claimed to represent a 'higher' level of development (as well as a newer one) than that which has preceded it. This assumption of unilinear progress rests heavily upon an optimistic view of the Enlightenment and a belief that the rationalistic management of change is possible. Two exemplars drawn from modernist work will suffice – Bronowski's *The Ascent of Man* (1971) and Elias's *The Civilizing Process* (1979–82), which have in common a commitment to the onward and upward development of the human race. But such a personal commitment from both authors is based in politics and the extreme experience of the Holocaust in each case. Both Bronowski and Elias lost parents in Auschwitz and large numbers of other relatives and friends to the gas chambers in the Second World War. Their commitment to a belief in progress is almost astounding, given such deep contact with forces of this kind. Yet their view of the Ascent of Man and of the Civilizing Process contain hardly any discussions of regress, perturbations or descent. To all intents and purposes, the grand historical sweep Bronowski and Elias identify is unilinear. The death camps, for all their impact on the last chapter of Bronowski or on the dedication of Elias's book, become subsumed in one upward sweep towards less social violence and more control of nature. Such views need explanation and part of the story may be the particular response of German Jewry to Nazism in the post-war period.

More general explanations are possible, however. Camille Paglia's recent work (1990) arrestingly offers one way of looking at this type of linearity as a reflection of male anatomy and the rule of the penis. She writes 'Man is sexually compartmentalized. Genitally he is condemned to a perpetual pattern of linearity, focus, aim, directedness. Without aim, urination and ejaculation end in infantile soiling of self or surroundings'. In her view, art springs from anatomy. Perhaps a case could be made for the crude historicisms of many who believe unabashedly in progress, as having a similar basis. But it is worth remembering that all those with penises may not be historicist, and there are many historicists who do not find the absence of a penis any great loss – just the opposite.

In any event, contrast this linearly based optimism with the sense of foreboding that would come from a belief that the Holocaust was a cyclical phenomenon to be repeated through history as each new pogrom replaced the old. Whilst Clark may be right that cyclicality and linearity have something in common, there are very crucial differences between them.

Such has been the antithetical tension between these two versions of chronology that several writers have attempted to create a 'third synthetic conception' which marries the insights of both. Filipcove and Filipec, two Czech sociologists, call this third view 'spiral time'. Disappointingly, their discussion is not too helpful (Filipcove and Filipec, 1986). They argue that this version of a chronological code might be represented pictorially as a coiled serpent, which is a typical Hindu representation of cosmic eras. The snake, in biting its tail, represents the partial intervention and clash in repetitive, synchronous segments of two different traditions (Filipcove and Filipec, 1986: 20). In their views of time, it may be perhaps that ancient cultures were more sophisticated than we are today. For example, Minoan society upon the island of Crete developed a culture in which there was an aversion to the straight line. The labyrinth was the architectural reflection of this abhorrence, in which the primary room decoration is the spiral. The Minoans had an ethics of geometry (Lachterman, 1989) which reflected a belief in 'life after life' where the 'sleeping' dead were buried in the foetal position. Arguably, this shape is not unlike the coiled snake and its potent symbolism for another civilization.

However, how one would illuminate a course on the management of change solely with a picture of a body in the foetal position or the coiled serpent is not immediately apparent, but the articulation of spiral time as a notion appears to me to be worth attempting. At least it breaks free from linear and cyclical patterns with the assumption of the march of progress in the former and that of overarching repetitive stability in the latter. This chapter, then, will follow through each of these three conceptualizations of time, drawing out their relevance for organizational forms.

Within organization theory dominated still by the Modernist project, it is clear that the unilinear progression of organizational forms has been assumed by many Western writers. 'Unilinear' because forms are seen as following in sequence, with the origins of the now fashionable mode being visible in the previously fashionable way of organizing. The antecedents of the present are seen in what is the immediate past. 'Progression' because what is contemporary and fashionable is often seen to represent a 'higher' level of development as well as a newer level. New forms are often seen to be superior to the old, for have they not developed out of the old and out of the attempts of good men (rarely are women mentioned) to ameliorate the shortcomings and weaknesses therein recognized? The most recent reflection of such an assumption of unilinear progression is in Arthur Francis' piece 'The structure of organizations', where approaches to organization theory 'are discussed in rough date order' (Francis, 1989: 60).

Typically, the progress of organizational forms is seen in this evolutionary way, with its origins in the guild system, through entrepreneurial subcontracting, to the bureaucratic pyramids identified by Weber and erected by Ford. Once here, the progress to Sloanism and the 'M' form is usually charted; these gave way in the 1970s to the Matrix form of organization and are now being jostled by the flexible firm for fashionable recognition.

The forms identified here are those typically isolated for analysis, but consideration of the differences within each category, the relevance of the category, and its significance for the other categories recognized is rarely well developed. Obviously, each organizational form contains within it a heterogeneity of elements. Consider, for example, the guild system, often identified as an early form of organization of the labour process within Europe, and its supposed relevance for later organizational forms. Guilds were supposedly internally homogeneous, orientated to the total end-product, hierarchically organized, and possessed a low division of labour and simple technology. Social relations within the guild were not based upon production but upon its 'cultural milieu' and an 'occupational community'. Such a characterization has some utility but it does not reflect the internal dynamics of many guilds where journeymen felt excluded, the great heterogeneity between guilds in one society, and the differences between one European society and another.

Similarly, entrepreneurial subcontracting contained a vast array of differing attempts to solve issues of cost, profit, control, quality and output. Characterized as a simple form of class structure with entrepreneur and worker, capital and labour, linked together in a 'voluntary' way, and quite distinctive from the guild system's caste-like nature, the putting-out system is often seen as a *transition* phase between guild system and factory system. Work was home-based so it was not until the development of geographically separate places of work, with their own architecture, specifically designed to be places to work and not in which to live a full rounded set of activities, that a revolutionary form of new social relations developed.

The factory system is often characterized as reaching its apogee in Highland Park or the Fiat plant in Turin. Here the geographical expression of vertical integration, hierarchy, mass production is made visible for all to see. But how are these plants related to the putting-out system and the guilds, particularly since the example of Fordism is derived from a non-European society? We would do well to remember Clegg and Dunkerley's (1980: 49) warning:

> In the first place, the three systems did not develop in the simple chronological sequence suggested. There was, of course, overlapping between them – at times between all three. The emergence was neither temporally nor spatially unilinear. They were both temporally and spatially disarticulated.

Nor are things any clearer when we consider 'later' developments. The 'M' form, matrix and flexible firm are all categories which contain certain key features, but on close examination the overlap between them is in some places quite extensive. Moreover it is not at all clear how well developed these categories are in the organizational form articulated by theorists when we come to survey organizational reality.

Nevertheless, such progressions continue to be made.

The very potted and brief historical 'explanations' of such a progression evolve perhaps around the role of the 'market(s)' and changes within it (or them) (Williamson, 1975), or around technological development and its costs, or around motivational techniques required to secure the services of skilled personnel, or around growth in organizational size driven on by competitive pressures (Chandler, 1977), or around the impetus to gain enhanced control over the workforce by organizational superordinates (Marglin, 1974). The issue of managerial choice versus structural determination need not concern us at this precise point but, clearly, explanations differ about the extent to which management leads or is driven by changes in fashions in organizational forms. The rise of the notion of the flexible firm, perhaps the latest in most current unilinear progressions (Lash and Urry, 1987; Francis, 1989), has raised this issue yet again (Atkinson, 1984; Pollert, 1987; Hyman, 1990).

More importantly, perhaps, the issue of unilinear progression can be seen in a markedly different light, depending upon the degree of difference which supposedly exists between the 'old' and the 'new'. For some, the development of 'new' organizational forms always involves a 'rupture' with the 'old'. As Martins (1974) has shown, rupturism is a well developed and respectable approach to social scientific thinking, with such terms as 'epistemological break', 'paradigm shift', 'caesurism', 'gestalt switch', 'conversion experience' and so on, all reflecting the place of the rupture with the past in our conceptualizations. Chandler, for example, in his very influential work on 'the visible hand' (1977), attempts to demonstrate the *genesis* of managerialism around 1840. He attempts to show that prior to this date management as we understand it today did not exist. Similarly Pollard in *The Genesis of Modern Management* (1965) is concerned to demonstrate that before 1830 in Britain, there was no managerial class nor managerial science nor managerial technology. Thus, for Pollard and Chandler, the rise of management hierarchies and the organizational forms consequent upon this represent a fundamental break with what went before. Like Giddens (1981), they appear to believe that the managerial efforts supposedly necessary to create the hydraulic works within societies of an oriental despotic nature (Wittfogel, 1961) are merely exceptional, untypical and isolated examples which can be therefore excluded. Kaplan, however, builds up our understanding of the genesis of management accounting by using Chandler, but rejects any notion of rupturism in seeing developments within accounting as natural and predictable – in other words as evolutionary. In this view (Kaplan, 1984), there are evolving organizational forms and emerging industries but no hint of the dramatically new suddenly appearing without historical precedent.

Similarly, the thesis of the disorganization of capitalism which is currently enjoying the centre of debate is seen by many to be a rupture or 'institutional paradigm shift' (Offe, 1985; Lash and Urry, 1987). As *Marxism Today* has it, there is a crucial movement from Modern Times to New Times (*Marxism Today*: October 1988, June 1989). These types of view supposedly signify a sharp epistemological, theoretical and ideological break with evolutionary theories of social development.

One example of a view that is heavily rupturist and dependent upon a unilinear conception of time (time's arrow as it is sometimes called), is Lash and Urry's articulation in *The End of Organized Capitalism* of the rise of new forms of organization, or as they somewhat disconcertedly call it, 'disorganization'. Since 'all that is solid has melted into air', what we are witnessing are new forms of societal and indeed global organization of key importance. These changes, of course, are expressed in terms of what has gone before within organized capitalism and can only be understood as developments coming out of that prior set of structural arrangements. Thus the industrial city declines in size and dominance to be replaced by smaller towns and semi-rural areas. It is here we should seek the networker and her electronic cottage. Thus the nation state declines in saliency, capital deconcentrates in national markets; thus there is a decline in class-based politics, and the large bureaucracies give way to flexible forms of organization. What is happening could and can only be perceived in terms of what has gone immediately before.

Geoff Mulgan (1988) has used engineering theory to describe this modern form of organizing society. The period up to the 1960s and beyond contains *strong power controls*, which use large amounts of energy relative to the processes they control. Bureaucracy is the classic form of a strong power control where control consumes a lot of time and energy. Structured as a pyramid, the organization, whether it is State Department, trade union, corporation or hospital, depends on vertical lines of authority and accountability. Communication is mainly vertical, authority is derived from position not knowledge, and formal rules govern behaviour. Based on the nineteenth-century army (particularly that of Prussia), the archetypal organization of organizational society is based on a pyramid.

For Lash and Urry and for Mulgan, the shift to flexible firms is of key, indeed epochal, importance. Mulgan argues that *weak power controls* are now in the ascendancy at the cost of the bureaucratic firm. These are decentralized without a single point of leadership; communication is horizontal, structures are cellular (*The Economist*, 1989) rather than pyramidical. Units control and regulate themselves. They thrive on fluidity, change and the creative use of chaos (Peters, 1987). Energy is directed outwards rather than towards the internal sustenance of a fixed structure.

Whilst such examples of 'epochal thinking' cover the whole range of social, economic and political phenomena, a key part of this debate concerns flexible specialization where there has been some agreement reached that an old industrial order has been eclipsed and that the Fordist mode of regulation has undergone a crisis. The notion that the 1980s represented an historical disjuncture and that post-Fordist economies and politics are now much more important than those based upon mass production, mass consumption, centralized regulation of the market, welfare provision and trade union involvement, is part of a rupturist scenario. In this perspective, 'post-Fordism' becomes a cipher for fundamental shifts from one era to another based upon 'production paradigms'.

It is possible, however, to see the elements of post-Fordism (when they are laid out for our perusal) as part instead of neo-Fordist attempts to develop new forms of labour control and ways of ensuring capital reproduction. Here, what is occurring is seen, not so much as part of a fundamental paradigm shift, but as a significant redrawing of managerial strategies. In other words, 'neo-Fordism' is a (nebulous, imprecise) term used by those of an evolutionary bent in considering change in organizational forms, whereas 'post-Fordism' suggests much more of a rupturist orientation to the same evidence. Hyman (1990) has given some consideration to the issue of flexibility and is highly sensitized to concerns of revolutionary versus evolutionary perspectives being brought to bear on empirical events. He argues in *Plus ça change*? (Hyman, 1990) that the 1980s can be plausibly identified as a major turning-point in production relations because it was then that the post-war economic order succumbed to crisis and an attack developed upon the post-war settlement. Thus only 'Against the background of a conception of historical disjuncture, the flexibility debate can become more comprehensible' (Hyman, 1990: 23). Hyman is not a fully-fledged rupturist by any means, and the questioning title of the article bears testimony to his ambivalence; but given the self-defined choice between continuity and change, stability and flux, precursor and novelty, he errs on the side of the latter.

But his very sophistication highlights the problems associated with a *unilinear* conception of time. Balancing carefully between revolutionary and evolutionary perspectives on history is possible as Hyman shows in the following passage (1990: 2):

> Plus ça change, plus c'est la même chose . . . If history is a continuous process of transition, it provides no absolute turning points: even revolutionary change involves major elements of continuity: proclaimed novelties mimic obscure precursors. Does this mean, though, that the search for discontinuities – for a basis for historical periodization – is futile? Surely not: but what is essential is that our historical generalizations (which like all generalizations are bound to oversimplify) should be sensitive to the significance of both flux and stability, and to the inter-relationship between the two.

But is even this approach to temporality enough? What if history, and the passage of time which marks its subject matter, are cyclical not unilinear. The concepts used by Hyman of transition, precursor, novelties and even change itself are built upon domain assumptions of unilinearity and newness. Put crudely, the unrolling before us of the carpet of time, which has never been seen until it enters each living generation's field of vision, is a metaphor of immense persuasion and has dominated much of Western thinking. Nevertheless, it is a limiting vision and excludes the possibility of history repeating itself. In the same way as we are subjected to the influence of many cultural assumptions and beliefs, we are easy prey for *chronarchy* in our approaches to change. Where history is seen as an onward march, an unfolding before us of the new in linear ways, we will tend to find the domination of *chronos* with its atomized uniform sequential perspective on the passage of time.

But what would a cyclical approach to organizational forms actually look like? Are there pieces of work upon which we could, if we wished, begin to build our refuge from chronarchy? A number of sources suggest themselves immediately. Take Fox's *History and Heritage* (1985), for example. In his final chapter he states that 'The nineteenth-century links with middle-class groups which helped the unions to wage these political struggles *"carried echoes of seventeenth-century experience"*' (emphasis added). In the same way as the Levellers represented certain artisanal groups (as well as tenant farmers) and tried to critique the ruling class, the chartered companies, powerful oppressive landlords, and oligarchical domination in its many forms, by seeking to build upon ancient rights possessed by the Anglo-Saxons (Brailsford, 1976), some 200 years later *their* programme struck chords with radical movements. As Sabine (1963: 478) argues, the Levellers gave expression 'With remarkable distinctness, [to] the modes of thought and argument which were to characterise revolutionary liberalism in the 18th and early 19th centuries'. In Fox's and Sabine's approaches, we get clear examples of forms of subordinate organization, ideology and programme which recur in history in what is essentially a cyclical way.

One might also wish to look to the libraries of work on Kondratieff and the so-called 'long waves' which he identified. The influence of this type of thinking on the work of Gordon, Edwards and Reich (1982), and on Friedman (1977), is clear. The contrast between these somewhat cyclical and linear modes is brought into stark relief in *The Nature of Work* by Paul Thompson, where he discusses Andy Friedman's notions of direct control and responsible autonomy. Thompson reveals his view of history as chronological when he says: 'In some ways Friedman does not present a historical analysis *in that a schema of stages of development in forms of control is absent*' (emphasis added). Anything which smacks of cyclicality and avoids stages of development is therefore not seen to be 'history'.

There is also a degree of cyclical thinking in Piore and Sabel's work *The Second Industrial Divide* (1984). Far from asserting the eradication of craft skills, these become the basis for new work organization practices. Far from the pessimism of Braverman and the deskilling thesis, Piore and Sabel's work bears a 'family resemblance' to the optimism in research associated with the technological determinism of post-industrial society theories. Forms of advanced manufacture allow a *return* to craft-based small-batch manufacture where operators *regain* control within small, decentralized organizations more typical of a previous era. Building upon evidence from the Third Italy of Emilia–Romagna, neo-Fordism is seen to be giving way to 'new' production concepts more reminiscent of pre-Fordist times. Here then we are *Back to the Future* (Cooke, 1990), where Cooley's *Architect or Bee* (1987) portrays a world ahead which is based on what has gone before.

Such a view inevitably raises questions about romanticizing the past and the intrinsic worth of much of the bucolic imagery found in cyclical perspectives. For example, a key problem with Piore and Sabel's discussion of the Third Italy in the Second Industrial Divide is the rural idyll it presents smack in the face of the subordination of local small-scale producers to multinational corporations within the region. Similarly, Cooley's *Architect or Bee* reflects many of the political forces underlying the move towards deskilling, and concentrates on the efficiency benefits of human-centred technology outside of hierarchical concerns.

Parallel views have been developed by anarchists and libertarian socialists when imagineering their utopian societies to be based on pre-industrialism. Despite the fact that the heyday of anarchism was from around 1880 until the First World War, and that some feel it has been assigned to the scrapheap of history, there are issues and concepts developed in that period to which those concerned to organize differently return time and time again. More importantly, perhaps anarchist practice, with its emphasis on egalitarianism, mutual aid, self-management, decentralization, spontaneity, and delegated not representative membership, has never disappeared. Such forces merely enjoy cyclical periods of prominence and then obscurity. As Tom Cahill (1989: 235) argues, 'The recent upsurge of co-operatives is one part of the "new social movements" which are themselves anarchism in its latest practical manifestation'. It has been said that anarchists have no theory of history, and if by this we mean one based on chronarchy this is probably correct. Ursula Le Guin articulates this rather well in the penultimate page of *The Dispossessed* (1974: 318):

> 'My race is very old', Ketho said. 'We have been civilised for a thousand millennia. We have histories of hundreds of those millennia. We have tried everything. Anarchism, with the rest. But *I* have not tried it. They said there is nothing new under any sun. But if each life is not new, each single life, then why are we born?'

The tension in this passage between human individuality and race, between a life span and millennia, between experienced organizational forms and novel ones, serves to highlight the reasons why many anarchists might reject chronarchy and the conventionally perceived need for histories. Their rationale is as old as humanity itself. Moreover, the passage quoted represents a balance between cyclicality and unilinearity which might be fruitfully compared to Hyman's position presented earlier.

At the University of Warwick, the issue of the cyclicality of organizational forms has exercised members of a recently formed research grouping known as CAOS (Centre for Alternative Organizational Studies). In searching for alternatives to bureaucratic hierarchy, the group has begun to assemble material on historical examples of non-bureaucratic structures. In this search, we have raided the literature on voluntary organizations, cooperatives, communes, anarchism and so on (Lindenfield and Rothschild-Whitt, 1982; Brown and Hosking, 1986), and have been struck by how much real alternatives have been 'hidden from history'. Unilinear approaches have neglected the great significance of alternative modes of organization in the past which, for many people, represented superior forms to those which supposedly triumphed in the onward trek of history. Clearly, for a proportion of North Italians at one point in time Gramsci and the worker councils represented something more desirable than Olivetti and Fiat's offerings (Clegg and Dunkerley, 1980; Adler, 1977). Similarly, before the First World War in Britain, Syndicalism represented a real alternative to industrial capitalism and its forms of work organization at that time. It is more than a shame that these well developed theories and practices of previous ages should now be ignored. They are, believes CAOS, a tremendous repository of ideas, methods and practical experience which may offer insights to the future. Within human existence, some of it recorded, a plethora of attempts at organizing have been made. Simply because they do not appear to have succeeded in previous circumstances does not mean they will be useless for the future. Thus CAOS's first task is to build up a picture of the range and variety of organizational forms which have been attempted and to categorize these on some theoretical basis. Clearly, a commitment to chronarchy is eschewed by CAOS's membership. If we forget the experiences, thinking and views of those who inhabited different organizational worlds, then we have turned our back on a great resource for the future.

Of course this view of history as cyclicality would be seen as problematical by many. For example, Clark (1990: 149) would claim that such a view was representative of an *homogeneous* code because it allows for atomistic ordering, objectivity, measurability and stability by taking highly regular events as its frame of reference. What role does cyclicality allow for heterogeneous codes of chronology? Second, the trouble with cyclical views of work organization and the organizational forms associated with it is that 'eternal return' is a myth. The language we have seen used in the literature upon which we might seek to draw reveals this clearly, for Fox speaks of 'echoes' and 'of striking chords', Thompson of 'family resemblance' and so on. It would be foolish to think, perhaps, that every form of organization will find expression in a later period and in turn that it is an expression of a previous form, recognizable as a reflection of its own antecedent and its own descendant. Britain under

Thatcherism in 1982 appeared to many to have appalling similarities with Britain in 1932, but we know that it was also very different.

Should we then throw out any hopes of cyclicality and return to the suzerainty of chronarchy? Is it not possible to move away from simple 'linear' and 'cyclical' versions of time, where the metaphors of the line and 'the myth of the eternal return' vie with each other as antonyms?

By considering the issue of heterogeneous time codes alongside the replacement of linearity and cyclicality by a conceptualization of spiral time, we begin to see the basic points which might mark out an alternative approach to understanding change in organizational forms. As noted above, Clark's comments on heterogeneous codes can create some confusion. They are 'socially constructed and intersubjectively known trajectories of events which have been selected and labelled because they are anticipated to unfold in a more or less sequential manner in the future' (Clark, 1990: 143). In this they are identical to homogeneous codes. Apparently they *differ* from the latter because they do not take highly regular events within a single time concept as their frame of reference. But if we take the definitionally shared issues of 'unfolding sequentially in an anticipatory way' then surely there is little significant difference between homogeneous and heterogeneous codes?

To my mind, what is needed before we begin any analysis of plural chronological codes as used by managers is an understanding of the fundamental undecidability of past, present and future which would be in keeping with postmodern critiques of assumptions of a unity in history. Philip Dick, in a recently republished novel *The Man in a High Castle* (1974), raises some of these issues by relating the I Ching to the possibility of parallel universes in which multiple histories have taken place. His example of a world in which Japan and Nazi Germany have won the Second World War and as a consequence the USA has been politically divided down the Rockies brings home the multiplicity of possible histories within which we might live. Such possibilities resonate well with postmodern concerns.

Related to the undecidability of the chronological is the attempt which many make to escape from chronarchy. Absenteeism, 'going over the wall', sabotage and so on are conceivable as 'escape attempts' (Cohen and Taylor, 1971), in which escape can take the form of accessing alternative reality, enclaving a free area of activity, or momentary slips through the fabric. Although they are expressed primarily in spatial terms, each strategy can be seen as a way of escaping from the paramount chronological code operant within dominant reality. Whilst it would be naive to deny that such behaviours are often predictable and organized, equally there is an element of uncertainty and unpredictability in the spontaneous actions of those who reject time discipline (Thompson, 1989). Time is made uncertain by human intervention, for by collective action we can shift the temporal fabric.

Also, *chronos* needs to be compared and contrasted to *kiros* – those intense periods of lived experience in which *chronos* as the regular, atomized passage of time is suspended and made inoperative. The sex act is one form of human behaviour in which *kiros* often nudges aside the dominance of *chronos* and where a momentary slip through the fabric becomes possible. In a sense, the pleasure principle is diametrically opposed to the chronarchy of the reality principle, and it should not surprise us that for many human beings their body has become the vehicle of escape from the present. But building upon such postmodern concerns within the culture of narcissism (Lasch, 1979), a number of authors (such as Clegg, 1990; Cooper, this volume) have begun to ask what organization might look like in an age of 'postmodernism'. Of course, the term itself is often suggestive of a rupture with a previous era and can be equated with the 'death of Reason' in an epochal sense. Some writers, such as Wellmer (1985) and Cooke (1990), reject the discontinuity thesis and maintain that postmodernism is but the latest version of modernism; but Lyotard (1985) is clear on adopting a caesurist conceptualization of these new developments. Lyotard is keen to develop the notions of undecidability and paralogy in which everything is questioned through abnormal discourse and methodological anarchy; and through respecting a suspicion of suspicion (Rorty, 1989). But, unfortunately (and this may be because he is a kind of anarchistic sceptic), there is no set of guiding principles developed by Lyotard on what culture or organization under postmodernism would be like. Over and beyond a 'free play' of a community of scholars who suspect all and trust nothing, there is very little in the way of guidance offered. As Power has persuasively argued, Lyotard's work may not be well received by organization theorists because of his tendency to conflate levels of analysis (Power, 1990: 119), and drawing out conclusions is not at all easy. According to Power, Lyotard's conception of social organization produces a vision of an 'irreducible plurality of language games' in which there is a danger that all talk of organization in any sense is outlawed (Power, 1990: 122–3).

The danger here is that 'one flies in ever-decreasing circles'. But if one was to ride upon a spiral, is that not likely to be a similar experience?

For those of us concerned to understand postmodernism and particularly its anarchistic leanings, there is a worry that a descent into complete relativism and particularism may be just around the corner. Balancing the seductiveness of Lyotard's advocacy of paralogy is a feeling that all talk under full postmodern conditions about postmodernism would lead to the tower of Babel in which only personal language games were possible. If Harvey is correct, and there are good reasons to believe he is, when he says the present postmodern epoch is characterized by 'Fiction, fragmentation, collage and eclecticism all suffused with a sense of ephemerality and chaos' (Harvey, 1989: 98), he engenders in many readers a sense of pessimism. The meta-narratives, of which Lyotard is so critical, perform a key function in our disciplines; indeed they provide discipline by de-emphasizing personal language games and stressing commonality. If one gives up the search for narratives, then in a very real sense one gives up the search for academic understanding. Of course, this does not mean that only one narrative is possible – far from it. But it does mean that stories will attract monoglot listeners and readers in sufficient groupings to make discourse and idea exchanges possible.

Thus, in order to avoid the pessimistic regress into these features and private language games in an era of undecidability, it is perhaps necessary to hang on to some basic modernist notions of unity and narrative – particularly if we seek to understand organizational forms. So here let us return to the spiral concept of time as an escape from a fully developed postmodernism. Let us use its geometry as a meta-narrative.

Lachterman's work *The Ethics of Geometry* is interesting here because it attempts to demonstrate the links between mathematics, geometry and philosophy. He argues that geometry and how it is practised and how it is perceived have changed over the millennia and that a fundamental difference exists between ancient and modern understandings. In other words, the way in which we perceive geometric shapes depends upon the *ethos* of mathematics pertaining at any one time and our basic ontological assumptions. Accepting the contextual nature of this, it might be argued that a spiral conception of time has a number of advantages. It seems to allow for the possibility of heterogeneous temporal codes as well as homogeneous ones; it synthesizes the insights of cyclical and linear versions of time; it allows for the concept of contradiction and gives it a place in analysis; and it has a fundamental undecidability locked within it which resonates with a rudimentary but contemporary postmodern understanding of the world.

Metaphorically, the anti-linear representation of late Minoan art, particularly in the form of the Phaistos Disk, stands up for such a spiral conception. This clay tablet has etched upon it hieroglyphic writing, which no one has yet deciphered, in a spiral form. Whether it should be read from the centre to the periphery or vice versa is not at all clear. The signs depict human figures, animals and various tools, and despite many attempts to decipher it there is no generally accepted version of what it represents. For example, is it a hymn, a set of accounts, or a story? Its essential undecidability, spiral nature and the human quest for its 'true' message invest it, for me, with much metaphorical significance. The Disk represents a patent rejection of linearity in writing and its spiralling form is highly unusual. Its attractiveness comes from its 'difference' and its unwillingness to offer up easy truths. If writing is a machine for the suppression of time, there has been an obvious mechanical breakdown. The spiral has not (yet) rendered itself and the past up to the present. It is to these concerns that we turn in the concluding section.

Conclusions

I have argued that the 'management of change' topic as it is now taught on many postgraduate courses has suffered from a neglect of self-reflexive analyses of issues of substantive and thematic temporalism and of *how* these are to be addressed. *Why* they should be addressed is locked into the topic itself and whilst the whole notion is certainly open to critique in and of itself, for present purposes we may as well let it stand. Theories of time, put simply, are often informed by elementary geometry. Our sense of space informs our sense of time in this way as in so many others. Time may be conceived to be a straight line, or circular or spiral in form, and human events and artefacts which necessarily take place in time come to take a form and shape which reflect this temporal shape. In other words, organizational forms may be thought to be progressive, linear, thoroughly new and innovative *or* repetitive, cyclical and historically rooted *or* both *or* neither.

Within spiral time, perhaps, progress and reversals would be common occurrences acting in one direction at one moment and in another at the next. If one shares a commitment to the complex notion of *contradiction* (Jay, 1985), with its oversimplified expression as the interpenetration of opposites, then surely spiral conceptions of temporality fit in with 'contradiction' much better than linear or cyclical version of this dimension? How can we hope to progress analyses in which contradiction plays some sort of role if we see history as unilinear and 'staged' or as repetitive and pre-seen? Our view of time needs to reflect the complexity of the real world and its multiple histories. The modernist project (Cooper and Burrell, 1988), where one history, one truth, one progress are worshipped in one rationality, will have to be rejected. But this does not imply that *all* narratives will have to be eschewed. Many questions need to be asked in relation to the development of stories (in the plural) concerning the history or organization forms, and many sources will need to be utilized. As we know, many organizational forms are hidden from history. Surveys of the survival rates of organizations over a 100-year period indicate that 99.5 per cent will disappear from view and within this population many forms exist sooner rather than later. For example, whilst the relevance of anarchist forms for the twenty-first century can be easily argued, one has to explain why this form went into decline.

Goodway (1989) has recently argued that 'anarchism seems currently to be in the process of removing itself from its consignment to the scrap heap of history' and that 'anarchist theory has never been more relevant, that anarchist practice is necessary and that, therefore, the history of anarchism must be seriously and appropriately studied' (Goodway 1989: 2). And what is true of anarchism is also true of the cooperative movement. Cornforth et al. argue that, without ideological or practical support, producer cooperatives almost completely stopped being formed and 'by the time the ''new wave'' of worker cooperation began in the

1970s, less than thirty co-partnerships remained, and most of these have now ceased trading' (Cornforth et al., 1988: 17). Had one viewed organizational forms in the UK in the late 1970s, then there would have been very few examples of anarchist or cooperative types. It is easy to see the contradictions which blight such organizational forms and which may continue to impact upon them, but to analyse these forces properly one must possess a 'serious and appropriate approach to historical study'. One must keep one eye on the past, therefore, but the other on the future.

Anarchists and cooperative advocates of the 1990s may well face new challenges. For example, 'the challenge over the next decade will be to develop new relationships, structures and procedures, both within and between cooperatives, that enable them to grow and meet new commercial opportunities without undermining democratic control . . . there are some guidelines that can be followed, but frequently cooperatives will be charting new waters' (Cornforth et al., 1988: 103). And in this spatial metaphor of covering old ground but charting new waters at one and the same time, there is something of what we need to begin to understand. It suggests organizational analysts should be historiographers and field researchers; we should talk to those at the leading edge of practice and read those dead authors whose ideas now carry little weight; we should be simultaneously archaeologists and genealogists of knowledge (Foucault, 1984); we should be philosophically aware yet eager futurologists. In other words, we must be bearers of contradiction in our professional lives as well as our private lives.

Of course, if we are to be actively Janus headed, constantly peering back into the future, and forward into the past, we must beware of choking ourselves to death. But *this* conclusion assumes we can stand outside the spiral of time and observe its twists and turns through our own neck movements and cerebration. Much more likely is the situation where we ride the spiral, perceiving it as a straight line of life and career, subject to chronarchy, and where we can manage change, more or less effectively. Typically then, we are riders rather than observers and that makes life (and death) so much more complicated. But *this* conclusion assumes the primacy of the individual and her/his privileged position as actor. It assumes time is perceived from a fixed spatial position – namely wherever the individual actor happens to be. Timothy Mo (1988) tells us that in the language known as Mandarin there is no past tense. Thus, for Mandarin speakers history is part of the present and alive humans are part of their ancestors. Because the self is seen to play a much smaller role in the scheme of things in mainland China than it does in the West, it is much easier there to 'decentre the subject' and escape from a view of time which is person-bound. Access to the spiral of time comes through one's collective ancestors, of whom the individual is an indivisible component within this world view. But in the 'management of change' and courses which cover the topic in British business schools, one is dealing with students whose sense of individuality has been finely honed and whose regard for the past, since they were not part of it, is not high. So raising issues of time and history and individuality and their interconnectedness is not at all easy in such a context. Common sense is a powerful block to such reflexive thinking. Nevertheless, to raise such issues is a challenge to which some might wish to respond.

References

Adler, F. (1977) 'Factory councils, Gramsci and the industrialists', *Telos*, 31: 67–90.

Arthur, M. et al. (1989) *The Handbook of Careers*. Cambridge University Press.

Atkinson, A.B. (1984) 'Manpower strategies for flexible organization', *Personnel Management*, August: 28–31.

Berman, M. (1983) *All that is Solid Melts into Air*. Polity.

Blyton, P. et al. (1989) *Time, Work and Organization*. Routledge.

Brailsford, H.N. (1976) *The Levellers*. Spokesman.

Bronowski, J. (1971) *The Ascent of Man*. BBC.

Brown, M. and Hosking, D. (1986) 'Distributed leadership', *Human Relations*, 1: 65–79.

Cahill, T. (1989) 'Cooperatives and anarchism: A contemporary perspective', in D. Goodway (ed.), *For Anarchism*. Routledge, pp. 235–58.

Chandler, A.D. (1962) *Strategy and Structure*. MIT Press.

Chandler, A.D. (1977) *The Visible Hand*. Harvard University Press.

Clark, P. (1990) 'Chronological codes and organisational analysis', in J. Hassard and E.D. Pym (eds), *The Theory and Philosophy of Organizations*. Routledge.

Clark, P. and Starkey, K. (1988) *Organisation Transitions and Innovation – Design*. Pinter/ESRC.

Clegg, S. (1990) *Modern Organizations*. Sage.

Clegg, S. and Dunkerley, D. (1980) *Organisation, Class and Control*. Routledge.

Cohen, P. and Taylor, L. (1971) *Escape Attempts*. Penguin.

Cooke, P. (1990) *Back to the Future*. Unwin Hyman.

Cooley, M. (1987) *Architect or Bee*. Hogarth.

Cooper, R. and Burrell, G. (1988) 'Modernism, postmodernism and organizational analysis', *Organization Studies*, 9 (1): 91–112.

Cornforth, C. et al. (1988) *Developing Successful Worker Cooperatives*. Sage.

Dick, P. (1974) *The Man in a High Castle*. Penguin.

The Economist (1989) *How to choose and use a management consultant*. Special Report no. 183.

Elias, N. (1979–82) *The Civilizing Process*. 2 vols. Basil Blackwell.

Filipcove, B. and Filipec, J. (1986) 'Society and concepts of time', *International Social Sciences Journal*, 107: 19–32.

Foucault, M. (1984) *The Foucault Reader*, edited by P. Rabinow. Penguin.

Fox, A. (1985) *History and Heritage*. George Allen & Unwin.

Francis, A. (1989) 'The structure of organizations', in K. Sisson (ed.), *Personnel Management in Britain*. Basil Blackwell, pp. 55–77.

Friedman, A. (1977) *Industry and Labour*. Macmillan.

Gherardi, S. and Strati, A. (1988) 'The temporal dimension in organization studies', *Organization Studies*, 9 (2): 149–64.

Giddens, A. (1981) *A Contemporary Critique of Historical Materialism*. Macmillan.

Goodway, D. (ed.) (1989) *For Anarchism*. Routledge.

Gordon, R., Edwards, R. and Reich, M. (1982) *Segmented Work: Divided Workers*. Cambridge University Press.

Gurvitch, G. (1964) *The Spectrum of Social Time*. Reidel.

Harvey, D. (1989) *The Condition of Postmodernity*. Basil Blackwell.

Hyman, R. (1990) *Plus ça change?* Warwick University Paper in Industrial Relations.

Jay, M. (1985) *Marxism and Totality*. Polity.

Kaplan, R. (1984) 'The evolution of management accounting', *Accounting Review*, 59 (3): 390–418.

Lachterman, D.R. (1989) *The Ethics of Geometry: A Genealogy of Modernity*. Routledge.

Lasch, C. (1979) *The Culture of Narcissism*. Penguin

Lash, S. and Urry, J. (1987) *The End of Organized Capitalism*. Polity.

Le Guin, U. (1974) *The Dispossessed*. Penguin.

Lindenfield, F. and Rothschild-Whitt, J. (1982) *Workplace, Democracy and Social Change*. Porter Sargent.

Lyotard, J. (1985) *The Postmodern Condition*. Manchester University Press.

Marglin, S. (1974) 'What do bosses do?' *Review of Radical Political Economics*, 6: 60–112.

Martins, H. (1974) 'Time and theory in sociology', in J. Rex (ed.), *Approaches to Sociology*. Routledge, pp. 246–94.

Mo, T. (1988) *An Insular Possession*. Penguin.

Mulgan, G. (1988) 'Strong and weak power controls', *Marxism Today*.

Offe, C. (1985) *Disorganized Capitalism*. Oxford University Press.

Paglia, C. (1990) *Sexual Personae: Art and Decadence from Nefertiti to Emily Dickinson*. Yale University Press.

Peters, T. (1987) *Thriving on Chaos*. Macmillan.

Piore, M. and Sabel, C. (1984) *The Second Industrial Divide*. Basic Books.

Pollard, S. (1965) *The Genesis of Modern Management*. Edward Arnold.

Pollert, A. (1987) *The Flexible Firm?* Warwick University Paper in Industrial Relations.

Power, M. (1990) 'Modernism, postmodernism and organisation', in J. Hassard and E.D. Pym (eds) *The Theory and Philosophy of Organizations*. Routledge, pp. 109–24.

Rorty, R. (1989) *Contingency, Irony and Solidarity*. Cambridge University Press.

Sabine, G.H. (1963) *A History of Political Theory*. Harrap.

Thompson, P. (1989) *The Nature of Work* (2nd edn). Macmillan.

Wellmer, A. (1985) 'On the dialectic of modernism and postmodernism', *Praxis International*, 4 (4): 337.

Williamson, O. (1975) *Markets and Hierarchies*. Free Press.

Wittfogel, K. (1961) *Oriental Despotism*. Yale University Press.

10

The Transformation in Work: Post-Fordism Revisited

Alan Whitaker

This chapter takes as its point of departure recent changes in the world of work. That significant changes have occurred in the 1970s and 1980s seems to be uncontested. From a variety of standpoints, commentators would probably agree with Pahl's view (1988: 4) that 'we are living through a period of change that is qualitatively and quantitatively different from that typical of most of the twentieth century'. However, whilst the pace and variety of change may be common ground, its nature has been the subject of considerable controversy and debate.

Without disputing that significant and sometimes dramatic changes have taken place, there arise two important and related questions. The first is whether we are in fact witnessing a fundamental transformation in institutional structures (and in the character and organization of work). The second, and perhaps more important, is how the changes which are underway are to be interpreted or theorized. This chapter seeks to address both of these issues. In so doing it draws upon recent British experience, particularly that centring on the notions of 'flexibility' and the 'flexible firm'. However, British experience, though instructive, is only one small part of the changes which are ongoing. The 'flexibility' debate has an important international dimension, and in its different guises has served as a focus for research, analysis and assessment of developments affecting the labour process, industrial organization, employment structures and the restructuring of economies. If the 'flexible firm' model is perhaps best regarded as a British construct (Hyman, 1991; Bagguley, 1991), other interpretations of 'flexibilization' are much more ambitious in scope, claiming to identify the end of the old industrial order as Western capitalism passes over 'another historical divide akin to that of fifty to sixty years ago, that we are witnessing a transition to a new order or phase of socio-economic development' (Martin, 1988: 202).

As will be seen, the approach taken here is more temperate and is cautious of extravagant claims, such as that what has occurred or is occurring amounts to a 'fundamental transformation' in the world of work (Leadbeater and Lloyd, 1987). The view that we are entering a new 'post-Fordist' phase of development, which has attracted considerable attention of late, albeit from different perspectives (for example, Piore and Sabel, 1984; Murray, 1988; Scott, 1988; Harvey, 1989), remains to be substantiated.

The Changing World of Work: The International Context

As was observed above, few would deny that since the early 1970s both the pace and direction of change have shifted markedly. In one commentator's words 'there has been a sea-change in the surface appearance of capitalism' (Harvey 1989: 189). A number of elements can be identified as having contributed to this and as having combined over this period to form a potent mixture, affecting the context, character and conceptualization of work. (For overviews and analyses of these features see, for example, Harvey, 1989; Thrift, 1988; Hyman, 1991).

If a particular focus of this chapter is the changes which have been occurring in the organization of production and work in Britain, it is appreciated that these can only be understood by placing them within a broader context of socio-economic and political changes at the international level. As Massey (1984: 136) has observed, 'contrasting sections of British capital have been reorganising themselves into new spatial structures, each of which forms the basis for new kinds of geographical differentiation, and which together are an important element in the changing intranational spatial division of labour'. However, equally important for an assessment of British experience is the evidence of an increasing internationalization of markets, production and labour, amounting to a significant restructuring of transnational capital (Purcell et al., 1986; Hyman and Streeck, 1988; Tailby and Whitston, 1989), and reinforcing the core and periphery divisions between countries.

It has been argued (Martin, 1988: 216) that what we are seeing is the outcome of a variety of 'intersecting forces or processes' which have combined and, from within and without, which are producing the breakup of the social, economic and political structures of the post-war period. Martin's remarks are directed at British experience, but his analysis is echoed by others attempting a broader perspective on international restructuring (for example, Harvey, 1989; Lash and Urry, 1987). Amongst the more important of these forces are, firstly, the massive deindustrialization of the manufacturing base; secondly, the wave of technological innovation based upon micro-electronics and information processing. This is seen as both generating new industries and services and transforming the operation of existing areas. Another process regarded as crucial is the acelerating growth of the service sector, with much of this in finance and related areas. A fourth relates to political developments and involves the 'reorientation and reconfiguration of government policy and state intervention away from the Keynesian social democratic model'. Finally, there is the intensification of pressures on Britain's overall economic performance, competitiveness and position within the international economy and division of labour as a consequence of changes in the global economy, particularly expanding overseas competition. Martin rightly recognizes that these 'destabilizing disturbances' are not purely exogenous but are very much a consequence of the tensions and contradictions inherent within the post-war framework itself: 'its organizational characteristics and its latent and emergent rigidities' (1988: 216).

British Experience

The outcomes of these processes have been reviewed and discussed at considerable length elsewhere (Handy, 1984; Leadbeater and Lloyd, 1987; Purcell et al., 1986; Massey and Allen, 1988; Martin and Rowthorn, 1986; Green, 1989). Here, only a brief sketch of some of the more important features will be provided.

As I have already remarked, the 1970s and 1980s have witnessed significant structural changes in the British economy. The manufacturing sector has borne the brunt of these, resulting in major alterations to its size and importance within the economy. This change has a number of different dimensions. There has been a massive reduction in the numbers employed within manufacturing, with a loss of approximately three million jobs since 1971, some 36 per cent of manufacturing employment (Martin, 1988), leading one commentator to call it a collapse (Beynon, 1983). The causes of this contraction are not our concern here, but notwithstanding a recognition of the deep-seated nature of the decline (Gamble, 1981), most analysts seem to accept that it is part and parcel of a process of 'deindustrialization' of the British economy (Blackaby, 1978). Accompanying this there has occurred a changing geography of production, which has seen a decline in the traditional 'heartlands' of manufacturing and the emergence of new areas of work (Massey, 1984; Bassett, 1986; Leadbeater and Lloyd, 1987). Recent research has demonstrated that small towns and rural areas have gained manufacturing capacity and employment at the expense of large industrial conurbations (Fothergill et al., 1986). Dispersal has also taken other forms, as organizations have sought to come to terms with the need for economic restructuring. Thus, since the 1970s there has been an overall reduction in the average size of workplaces, as employment in large firms has fallen, coupled with a growth in small firm employment. However, it is also the case that large manufacturing firms, through a process of decentralization, have increased the number of plants they operate, whilst reducing the numbers employed in each plant (Shutt and Whittington, 1987). Further, the search for productive efficiency and competitiveness has meant an acceleration in the internationalization of production. Reinforcing the trend away from manufacturing in this country has been the preference of major British manufacturing companies to meet demand for their goods from foreign-based rather than UK subsidiaries (Martin, 1986). For example, a study by *Labour Research* (May 1987) indicated that in 1986 the 40 largest UK-owned manufacturing companies in the UK employed 290 000 fewer people worldwide than they had done some 7 years before (1979). This represented a reduction of some 12 per cent. However, it was not spread evenly across their whole operations, but was made up of 415 000 jobs lost in the UK, offset by 125 000 gained overseas. One can readily acknowledge that the geographical dispersal of production is a long-established feature of capitalism. Nevertheless, it has been remarked that the 1980s have seen a qualitative and quantitative change in the decentralizing process which is leading to the decline of the 'mass collective' worker (Murray, 1983).

Alongside the restructuring of the workplace there have occurred important, related changes in the composition of the workforce and in the employment base. The key features of the latter are, first, the decline of manufacturing employment coupled with the continuing expansion of the service sector (industries and occupations). Since the mid-1960s the number of jobs in the service sector has risen by over 3 million, so that by the mid-1980s it accounted for 65 per cent of total employment (Allen, 1988: 97). Perhaps more significant is the fact that this renewed expansion of service activity is in the private sector, particularly in the business, financial, research and development, and professional services areas. As Martin argues (1988: 220), this can be traced to three developments: an increasing preference by manufacturing companies to externalize services previously provided in-house, the national and international boom in financial trading and money markets, and the spread of new computerized methods of data handling and information processing.

Second, there has occurred the re-emergence and persistence of mass long-term unemployment and recurrent short-term unemployment. However, concealed within such macro level shifts are other significant aspects of labour market restructuring – for example, changes in the proportion of male and female employment as the latter's participation grows (Hakim, 1987), and the growth of part-time work (Robinson, 1985), of temporary workers (Casey, 1988) and the self-employed (Hakim, 1988). For some, these changes are taken as evidence of greater flexibility of labour utilization, especially within internal labour markets (Atkinson, 1984; Atkinson and Meager, 1986; Atkinson and Gregory, 1986), as firms divide their labour into 'core' and peripheral groups. This point will be taken up again below in my discussion of the concept of the 'flexible firm'. For others, the fragmentation of the workplace, which is occurring in manufacturing but which also is increasingly prominent in the service sector, has broader social and political implications. In particular, it creates social polarization and tensions as labour markets are divided between elites in the core and a growing peripheral mass of unemployed, underemployed and casual workers (Leadbeater, 1987). It is also recognized as having had tremendous implications for trade unionism (Bassett, 1988; Massey and Miles, 1984). One should also note in passing that such restructuring can, in any case, only be properly explained by taking into account gender and the sexual division of labour (Walby, 1988; Purcell et al., 1986; Dex, 1988).

If the above represent some of the more macro level structural changes, at the organizational level the picture is equally complex and variegated. It can be said that the 1980s has been a decade of quantum organizational change, much of it focusing on the pursuit of flexibility. As Streeck (1987: 285) has perceptively observed, the strategic problem corporate managers have had to face is 'to find ways of managing an unprecedented degree of economic uncertainty, deriving from a need for a continuous rapid adjustment to a market environment that seems to have become permanently more turbulent than in the past'. The outcome has been a search for organizational flexibility, but not just with respect to systems of employment. Attempts to effect these are 'inseparable from the simultaneous search of enterprises for higher flexibility of product ranges, technology, capital equipment, methods of finance relationships with suppliers etc.' (1987: 290). In this regard recent British experience clearly connects with other aspects of the flexibility debate underway in many other countries. Not surprisingly, perhaps, flexibility in labour markets has attracted a good deal of attention elsewhere (Boyer, 1988; *Labour and Society*, 1987), but other issues such as flexible manufacturing systems (Jones and Scott, 1987), new production concepts (Dankbaar, 1988), and flexible specialization (Piore and Sabel, 1984; Hyman 1988), are also significant. These debates are far from resolved (Wood, 1989).

Towards the Flexible Firm?

Elsewhere, with a colleague, I have argued that within manufacturing two sorts of interest in flexibility can be distinguished: 'investment led' flexibility in which it is sought primarily in terms of the use of new manufacturing technologies and, secondly, 'labour led' flexibility, in which emphasis is placed on variable uses of labour, often as a substitute for more adequate levels of capital investment (Ackroyd and Whitaker, 1990). Whilst one can recognize that firms can and do pursue a variety of flexibility strategies, the former, which centres on what has been termed the 'technostructure of flexibility' (Morris, 1988) is, arguably, less significant in Britain. It is the latter with its focus on the 'division of labour, its organization and ownership', both internally and externally, which has been more prominent.

Externally, the use of production subcontracting in particular has allowed organizations greater flexibility, and its use appears to be increasing (Morris, 1988). Shutt and Whittington (1987) have argued that it is one of a range of strategic responses operated by large firms which allow them to displace market fluctuations and uncertainty on to small firms. Other types of fragmentation strategy include the decentralization of production into smaller units with formal ownership responsibilities retained by the large firm (mentioned earlier), and devolution, whereby ownership responsibilities are transferred to smaller firms but the parent company generates a guaranteed revenue through licensing or franchising agreements. Whether these strategies are used individually or in combination, they are responses to increased innovation risk, demand risk and the difficulties of controlling the labour process. Fragmentation of operations, however, does not necessarily imply fragmentation of control.

Internally, it has been argued, labour markets and employment practices are in the process of being restructured at an unprecedented pace and in ways which have significant implications for the conduct and pattern of industrial relations. Changes are taking place in the ways labour is 'contracted, skilled and paid' (Brown, 1986). One influential interpretation of such developments is that organizations are dividing their workforces into core and peripheral groups in order to achieve different kinds of flexibility (Atkinson, 1985; Atkinson and Gregory, 1986). Thus a new (flexible) model of the firm may be emerging, as 'novel and unorthodox' forms of labour deployment are introduced which establish a 'significant break with the conventional, unitary and hierarchical labour markets which dominate UK manpower . . . These innovations are intended to secure greater flexibility from the workforce, in terms of its responsiveness both to the level of economic activity (numerical flexibility) and to the nature of that activity (functional flexibility)' (Atkinson, 1985: 3). The latter is provided by core groups of workers who acquire and use a variety of skills to carry out different tasks (managers and other 'professionals', and multi-skilled craft workers). A central feature of such employees is that their skills are not readily available in the wider labour market. Efforts are therefore made and incentives provided (financial rewards, security of employment and better working conditions) to retain their services.

Clustering around the core are a number of peripheral groups: full-time workers who are hired to fill specific jobs, usually of a semi-skilled kind. They experience weaker job security and other inferior conditions of employment, but provide the necessary numerical flexibility. Next come part-time and temporary workers, performing similar tasks to the first peripheral group but employed on a contract basis which acts to supplement numerical flexibility when needed. The use of both these groups can be adjusted relatively easily and rapidly as market conditions dictate. Finally, there is a group of external workers who provide numerical flexibility through subcontracting, outsourcing and self-employment.

The concept of the flexible firm has been heavily criticized on a variety of counts. Pollert (1987, 1988) has trenchantly exposed its weaknesses on empirical, methodological, conceptual and policy grounds. Likewise MacInnes (1987, 1988) has observed that flexibility itself is a 'contradictory and controversial concept which is limited in its potential application' (1987: 113–24). Certainly, it is the case that there are difficulties in assessing the available evidence for the extent of flexibility and the emergence of the 'flexible firm', not least of which is that different theorists have subsumed a range of different developments within it (Allen, 1988: 185). Moreover, there are good grounds for questioning the originality of Atkinson's model in that employers have always sought enhanced labour flexibility and employment practices. Nor is the idea of core and periphery novel. Rather it can be seen as a reformulation of ideas drawn from dual labour market theory (Pollert, 1987). Questions can also be raised about the connections between flexible labour markets and other types of flexibility involving management practices, product markets and labour processes. As yet, the scenario of flexible specialization, with all this is said to entail, appears a limited one.

Turning to the empirical evidence for the emergence of the flexible firm, it has to be said that it is somewhat thin. This is not to say that changes are not occurring, but simply to observe that the extent of deliberate management intent is questionable. Certainly, the evidence from authoritative surveys (for example, Millward and Stevens, 1986) does not provide support. There appears to be little use by firms of groups in the peripheral workforce in the early 1980s. The general conclusion was one of continuity and stability rather than upheavals in workplace industrial relations. Changes have taken place, but they do not amount to an employers' offensive against labour and trade unions, seeking to intensify and reorganize work, to eliminate restrictive practices, and to attack trade unions.

Similarly, other surveys would appear to call into question how far the changes which have been taking place in patterns of employment reflect a widespread and coherent strategy of numerical flexibility. Thus Marginson and his colleagues (Marginson et al., 1988; Marginson, 1989) conclude that examples of subcontracting of mainstream activities amongst large companies are few; where subcontracting does occur it tends to be in service activities such as cleaning, maintenance and catering. Whilst recognizing that changes have occurred, they comment that they are not 'sufficient to justify' the extensive claims for the emergence of flexible firms. Further, 'they doubt how far there are coherent policies on peripheral employment and how far any plans developed at higher levels are turning into thoroughgoing appraisals of employment structure on the ground' (Marginson et al., 1988: 95).

If one turns to functional flexibility, once again the evidence is not clear cut or easy to interpret. On the one hand, it does seem that there has been a great deal of change in working practices in recent years: demarcation lines between jobs have drastically blurred and multi-skilling of craft workers is becoming more widespread. Surveys of manufacturing plants bear out this picture (Edwards, 1987), as does the more representative workplace industrial relations survey (Daniel, 1987). However, such changes do not in themselves mean that labour is being utilized more flexibly. Rather, they may indicate the introduction of new machinery without major alterations in job content.

In sum, then, the flexible firm thesis appears to be difficult to substantiate in practice. Changes in the external labour market (which have occurred) cannot simply be taken as confirmation of an argument centring on the restructuring of firms' internal labour markets. To the extent that numerical flexibility exists, it is probably attributable to sectoral shifts in the structure of the economy which, in turn, requires a consideration of the significance of gender (Walby, 1989). As regards functional flexibility, the view (Batstone, 1988) that the changes we have experienced are not qualitatively different from those introduced in the past (or likely to be more effective) seems difficult to ignore.

However, it is, perhaps, worth noting that for advocates of the flexible firm concept what is important at this juncture is the 'combination of long-term changes with the more recession-based changes that leads to both a sharper cutting edge and a degree of permanence to the flexibility offensive' (Atkinson and Gregory, 1986: 15). In this sense, flexible labour strategies make up just one of the dimensions of a more general restructuring of work. Seen in this way, they may be regarded as one of the factors contributing to a 'flexibilization of the basis of economic growth', and the transition to a more flexible regime of accumulation. It is to this and other explanatory frameworks that I now turn.

Theorizing Work Restructuring: Disorganized Capitalism or Flexible Accumulation?

One can distinguish various attempts to theorize the current period of change underway in Britain and other advanced capitalist countries. For example, explanation has been sought by some in terms of Kondratieff long waves of economic development (Mandel, 1980; Freeman, 1984). Specifically the 1970s and early 1980s represent the trough of the down-swing phase, a period of 'creative destruction' which prepares the way for a new wave. The restructuring which has ensued from the downturn provides the foundation for a new long-wave upswing whose momentum will be provided by new microelectronic technologies and related innovations.

In this section, however, attention will be paid to two theories which have been attracting a good deal of attention recently. Both seek to address what has been called the transition from Fordism to post-Fordism and, as will be seen, both clearly connect with the kinds of changes outlined in the first part of this chapter – in particular, notions of increased flexibility.

Disorganized Capitalism

The notion that contemporary changes in Western industrial capitalist economies can best be interpreted as a move into an era of disorganized capitalism has been advanced most comprehensively by Lash and Urry (1987), and in a less ambitious formulation by Offe (1985). The latter, in using the term, seeks to provide a heuristic perspective, commenting that 'to speak of "disorganized capitalism" is not to propose an elaborate and coherent counter model against that of "organised capitalism"'. Rather, he is attempting to answer whether Western democracies are best viewed as highly disorganized systems of social power and authority and, if so, what the symptoms, consequences and remedies might be.

It is the work of Lash and Urry which forms the focus for discussion here. Their thesis is ambitious and wide-ranging in scope, attempting, as it does, to theorize the history of industrial capitalism. For them, 'disorganization' is not simply a 'shift into a sort of high-entropy disorder; disorganization is instead a fairly systematic process of dis-aggregation and restructuration' (1987: 8). The 'disorganizing dynamic' they seek to establish encompasses processes as diverse as deindustrializa-tion, spatial restructuring, patterns of industrial relations, and political and cultural changes.

Very briefly, Lash and Urry contend that a broad set of interrelated changes have been taking place within North America and Western Europe. Drawing upon and amplifying Kocka's work, they argue that organized capitalism was characterized by a number of interconnected features: the increasing dominance of large, national, economic and social institutions; increasing concentration, centralization and bureaucratization of industrial and financial capital; a rising rate of capital concentration; an increase in the average size of workplaces; banks, industry and the State were working together; residential and plant locations tended to be found in large urban centres; collective bargaining took place more and more on a national scale; the industrial male working class reached its largest size; and politics and culture reflected the confrontation of nationally organized social classes in which the capital–labour relationship and class inequality played a dominant role (Urry, 1988: 30; Lash and Urry, 1987: 3–4).

They acknowledge that national differences are important. Thus the pace, scale and timing of organization varied from country to country, depending upon the point in history at which it began to industrialize, the survival of pre-capitalist organizations into the capitalist period, and the size of the country. If the example of Germany is regarded as the closest approximation of organized capitalism, with high levels of organization at the 'top' (such as the concentration of industry) and 'bottom' (such as national trade unions, working-class parties and the welfare state), the British 'Makler' ('middleman') economy provides a stark contrast, being characterized by an absence of horizontal and vertical integration, of diversification and modern managerial structures in the key organized capitalist sectors. This was the decisive feature. At the same time, it was organized at the bottom earlier than it was at the top, and earlier than in other sectors.

For various reasons, they argue that the period between the mid 1960s and early 1980s has seen the onset of disorganized capitalism as many of the developments underpinning organized capitalism have gone into reverse. For Lash and Urry (1987: 300–1; Urry, 1988: 30–1), this is the outcome of three parallel and interdependent processes. First, the impact of various internationalizing processes from above: 'globalization' of economic, social and political relationships is taking place. Especially important here are the emergence of new forms of economic organization, the decline of organized relationships between industrial and financial capital, the declining distinctiveness of companies producing fixed products for given national markets, and the development of global communication technologies. Also important are new international state structures and broader cultural changes.

Secondly, a variety of 'decentralizing' processes have undermined societies from below. It has meant the dislocation of many of the central structures and processes of key industries, classes and cities. Thus there has been a decentralization of population and industry; manufacturing facilities have become smaller and have increasingly been dispersed into small towns and rural settings and to the Third World; a population shift has occurred, with small towns and rural localities gaining at the expense of large cities; established occupational communities are breaking up and regional distinctiveness is disappearing. Further, within the workforce, divisions are increasingly apparent and the attractions of mass organizations such as trade unions are in decline.

Thirdly, such societies are being transformed from within by the growth in size and effectiveness of the service (middle) class. This has been significant in the 'generation of a more diverse, pluralistic and politically contrasted civil society' (Urry, 1988: 31).

Lash and Urry's focus on the processes of organization and disorganization clearly offers a range of insights into developments in contemporary capitalism. It identifies a series of interrelated, structural changes which have gained in momentum and significance since the 1970s. At the same time it has a number of important weaknesses.

To begin with, their characterization of organized capitalism can be called into question on empirical grounds. In what is in many respects a sympathetic critique, Cooke (1988a) has made the point that the features they associate with the 'organized' period of capitalism (for example, capital concentration and centralization) were neither a 'ubiquitous tendency' nor necessarily permanent. 'The criticism . . . is not that there are no common features . . . to be found across some sectors and many advanced economies from the 1880s to the 1960s but that the universality of these features is overstated. The organization of capital, the relationship between finance and industrial capital, their relationship to the state and to labour varied over time and space, both internationally and interregionally' (Cooke, 1988a: 234–5).

A second and, perhaps, more significant difficulty is whether what is occurring should be conceptualized as 'disorganization'. The problem may, of course, lie in what seems to be a general inclination of much recent writing to adopt 'binary histories' as a way of making sense of the sheer variety and pace of change. As Sayer (1989: 666) rightly remarks, 'inevitably we risk ending up with overburdened dualisms and overly

elastic concepts'. The implication is that the 'organization–disorganization' dichotomy is too simple, and obscures too many separate and
complex processes. In essence it is perhaps being asked to explain more
than it can. Interestingly, Sayer goes on to point out that a significant
omission from Lash and Urry's comparative work is Japan, remarking
that 'it is ironic that the main challenger to the industrial hegemony of
the (Western) countries they examine comes from a country whose capital
(though not its labour) is organized with a vengeance' (1989: 670).
Reflecting on the post-Fordist debate more generally, his comment that 'it
is simply not adequate to ignore Japan in discussing epochal changes in
western capitalism' is apposite and telling. Nevertheless, the question of
whether capitalism really is becoming disorganized (less organized?)
merits further consideration here. As will become clear, there appears
considerable substance in the view that what we may be witnessing, in
fact, is the more or less successful – albeit uneven – reorganization of
capital. Moreover, in the changes which have been occurring the role of
multinational capital has been crucial – as Lash and Urry would certainly
agree, though for them this is central to the 'genesis of disorganization'.

Certainly, the evidence marshalled by Thrift (1988), assessing the
changing world economic order, points to a conclusion of reorganization
and reintegration rather than a 'process of disorganization'. The features
associated with the increasing internationalization of capital are, he
concludes, resulting in the world economy becoming 'more integrated
than ever before. There are new links between the multinational corporations, banks and countries, and the old links have been strengthened'
(1988: 41).

Others would appear to endorse this conclusion (Cooke, 1988a; Harvey,
1989). Once again there is no disagreement that important changes in
economic, social and political life are taking place. However, whilst
accepting that the environment in which world finance capital operates is
more turbulent and uncertain, Cooke observes that by the 1980s finance
capital had re-equipped, especially through the application of new
technology, to speed up the rate at which trading information could be
acquired, and its capacity to 'read the market' is now vastly enhanced.
Likewise, in the industrial sphere a similar argument can be made in that
global corporations, particularly the largest, have weathered the recession
well and have demonstrated the capacity to 'restructure functionally and
over space and are penetrating ever deeper into the under-capitalized
world, including the state socialist countries as market places or production platforms' (1988a: 235). More will be said later on the role of
multinationals in the widespread restructuring which has occurred, but it
seems doubtful whether the latter can meaningfully be interpreted as
'disorganization'. For Cooke the force of his criticisms points to the
'partial nature' of Lash and Urry's interpretation 'rather than its
erroneousness'. This, however, seems surprisingly generous, particularly
given his observation in a later paper (1988b: 285) that 'if . . . capitalism

operates as a system the structures of which may change or be adjusted, then for it to cease being organized it would have to cease *per se*, or be transcended by chaos or by another system. Since neither of these alternatives has happened, then the system and with it its organising principles remain in place, albeit altered'.

The significance of these and other (Kelly, 1988; Reed, 1991) criticisms are clear. It is surely to call into question the view that we are moving into an 'era of disorganized capitalism'. As Harvey (1989: 159) perceptively notes, 'what is most interesting about the current situation is the way capitalism is becoming ever more tightly organized *through* dispersal, geographical mobility, and flexible responses in labour markets, labour processes and consumer markets, all accompanied by hefty doses of institutional, product and technological innovation'.

Flexible Accumulation

The second recent important attempt to theorize the restructuring processes which have characterized Britain and other advanced capitalist countries to be considered here is that in terms of a transition from one regime of accumulation to another. Different labels have been used to describe what is happening, reflecting different strands of theorizing. The debate has been multi-faceted and complex but, at considerable risk of oversimplification, one can perhaps distinguish two lines of explanation. Both have important points of similarity but at the same time one should recognize substantial differences within each as well as between them (for an overview of these see Wood, 1989, and Meegan, 1988). What unites them is the common assumption that crucial to understanding the shift from boom to recession and stagnation in the 1970s and 1980s is the rise and fall of a particular form or regime of economic organization and regulation. In essence, the argument is that the post-war Fordist paradigm is being replaced by an emergent post-Fordist regime of 'flexible accumulation'.

This new regime has been labelled 'neo-Fordism' by those associated with the so-called 'Regulation School' (Aglietta, 1982; Palloix, 1976), and 'post-Fordism' by theorists associated with the so-called flexible specialization debate (for example, Piore and Sabel, 1984). For others such as Harvey (1989) and Scott (1988) the preferred term is 'flexible accumulation'.

The characteristics of Fordism are well known and need not be repeated here (Sabel, 1982; Marsden et al., 1985; Murray, 1988). Its beginnings can be traced back to the early part of the twentieth century, but it was not until the post-1945 period that it is regarded as becoming fully developed, albeit to different extents and taking different forms in different countries. However, by the early 1970s this structure of accumulation and regulation was beginning to experience acute internal and external difficulties. It has been said there occurred a 'fracturing of the foundations of predictability upon which Fordism was based' (Murray, 1988: 9). Amongst these difficulties were the tensions arising from the technical and social rigidities of mass production, growing problems of labour militancy and worker morale, and the rising costs of production acting to slow down productivity growth and erode competitiveness. It is out of the breakdown of Fordism that a new regime of accumulation is emerging, and despite the basic differences in underlying conceptualization (Meegan, 1988) both schools of thought exhibit similarities in what they see as happening, particularly as regards the significant role of new production technologies. As Martin describes it (1988: 211–12),

> Its hallmark . . . is flexibility: of production technologies, labour processes, products, labour markets and patterns of consumption. Within production, the focus of innovation is flexible specialization and flexible integration, and on small batch processing and product customizing – what some have called internal economies of scope – shifts facilitated by the development of an array of computer-aided and computer-controlled design, tooling, machine and stock handling systems, and the 'electronicization' of office machinery and information processing. This flexibilization of production, and the new forms of 'soft automation' on which it is based, are being paralleled by the de-rigidification and redrawing of skill boundaries and work practices, by new systems of labour utilization, management and organization, all of which carry major implications for the operation of labour markets.

He goes on to note that such activities are not confined to manufacturing but are also affecting service industries.

The flexible accumulation thesis in its various forms has also attracted a good deal of criticism. Some critics, focusing on Piore and Sabel's framework, have questioned the extent to which the Fordist model became the dominant form of social and economic organization. In a review and critique of *The Second Industrial Divide*, Williams et al. (1987: 421–3) argue that 'Ford's innovation of the assembly line factory had a limited field of application and Ford did not provide a strategic model which his successors imitated . . . for that reason alone the concept of Fordism is seriously misleading' and should 'be rejected because it elides too many differences and establishes an uninformative stereotype. Furthermore any notion of a generic modern system of mass production should be treated with great caution because there are many different ways of organising production, even in the assembly industries'.

A related line of criticism has centred on the evidence of a move towards a 'flexibly specialized tomorrow'. As Meegan (1988: 171) points out with regard to the UK, at present the evidence is 'fragmentary, but what there is does caution against an uncritical acceptance of some of the claims of its proponents'. Others have, likewise, cast doubt upon both its spread and the more exaggerated accounts of its potential (Jones, 1988; Williams et al., 1987; Hyman, 1988). Linked to this is the question of changing consumption patterns and whether markets are indeed saturated and fragmented in the manner suggested by flexible specialization theorists.

If growing differentiation in consumer tastes and demand are to be satisfied, more flexible production systems are required, necessitating a shift away from Fordist mass production. Again, Williams et al. (1987: 426–7) remark on the relative lack of evidence to support this view and conclude that 'markets may be breaking up but not in a way which is really threatening . . . Piore and Sabel . . . crucially fail to draw the distinction between simple product differentiation and market fragmentation which has quite different consequences'.

In a sense, what the above criticisms raise is, perhaps, the important question of the value of conceptualizing change in terms of 'national regimes of accumulation', whether these be Fordist, neo-Fordist or post-Fordist. As Massey (1988: 80) observes in respect of Fordism, 'the characteristics . . . seem sometimes more an amalgam of features of different societies . . . than a precise analysis of any one society'. Clearly the 'elasticity' of such broad concepts allows a wide range of developments to be included, but in the process may serve to stretch them to a point where they hinder rather than assist explanation. In an important, detailed paper examining changes in 'old industrial regions' (discussed in more detail below), Hudson (1989) questions whether ideas about a transition from Fordism to flexible accumulation provide a satisfactory framework for understanding the changes in the conditions of labour markets, production and consumption found in these regions. He cautions against 'oversimplified theoretical interpretations' and comments that the concept of '"flexible mode of accumulation" may conflate different tendencies in capitalist restructuring strategies' (1989: 20). It is with these points in mind that we move to some concluding remarks.

Conclusions

What emerges from the previous section is, firstly, that the 'disorganizaton' thesis advocated by Lash and Urry and, in a more limited fashion, Offe, has serious weaknesses. Whilst their broad historical sweep offers much as a description of important changes underway in the five countries they examine, its analytical and explanatory value for understanding contemporary developments is more limited. Certainly, when recent economic and organizational changes are considered carefully the simple conclusion that what we are seeing is better characterized as new forms of reorganization is hard to avoid.

At the same time, it can be noted that much of the critical thrust against the 'disorganization' thesis has come from scholars sympathetic to the profound nature of the changes, but who prefer to conceptualize this in different terms, namely that of a historical transition to a new flexible regime of accumulation (see, for example, Harvey, 1989; Cooke, 1988a, 1988b; and Thrift, 1988). However, what has been argued here is that there are also significant difficulties with the notion that some such fundamental shift is occurring. As Sayer (1989: 666) trenchantly remarks, the literature on post-Fordism is 'confused in its arguments, long on speculation and hype, and based on selected examples whose limited sectoral, spatial and temporal range is rarely acknowledged'. Likewise, Amin and Robins (1990: 8) are highly critical of certain of the more optimistic transformational scenarios advanced by theorists such as Piore and Sabel, and Scott and Storper: 'Thus although important changes are certainly happening, there are real problems in suggesting that they represent a fundamental break with the past and the dawning of a wholly new era of accumulation' (see also Costello et al., 1989).

In fairness, it can be said that many of those arguing for a transition to a new regime of accumulation are sensitive to the uncertainty and complexity of the present as well as the past, and appreciate only too well that the old 'regime' (if such it can be characterized) has far from disappeared, and the new is a long way off ascendancy. Thus Harvey (1989: 189–97) raises the important question of 'flexible accumulation – solid transformation or temporary fix?' (see also Cooke, 1990, and Scott, 1988).

Nevertheless, I would concur with Lovering (1990a: 170) that the concept of flexible accumulation should not be seen as a 'theoretical master key which can unlock all the secrets of the new economic order'. Accepting this, however, means that we are still left with the question of how contemporary economic and organizational restructuring can best be interpreted. To address this requires that more precise questions be asked about the nature of current restructuring in employment and work so as to take account of the complex and contradictory nature of the trends which are emerging. Doing this also means one can confront and hopefully avoid the tendency to polarize debate and discussion along the lines of 'everything or nothing' has changed (Elger, 1990). Moreover, when such questions are asked, what emerges is the key role played by multinational corporations in the reordering and reshaping which has taken place (a feature recognized by all the scholars considered in this chapter). In the remainder of this section I want to explore this crucial dimension further.

Although one needs to be sensitive to the difficulties involved in assuming that one group of actors has primacy in the restructuring process, especially at the international or world-economy level (Thrift, 1988: 7), the contention here is that multinational corporations are the most powerful agents involved in contemporary economic restructuring. They are the 'real shakers and shapers of the world economy' (Amin and Robins, 1990: 26; see also Dicken, 1986). Whilst it may not yet be the case that they have achieved 'new global structures of control and coordination' (Gordon, 1988: 25), a brief review of some key organizational developments reveals their centrality in what has been taking place. At the same time, the view taken here is that such innovative changes are not to be regarded as being part and parcel of a 'disorganizing dynamic' or a shift towards a new regime of flexible accumulation. Rather, they are better characterized as 'defensive' responses to the economic crisis of the 1970s and 1980s. In this sense they perhaps represent a further extension of existing Fordist structures.

If economic turbulence and uncertainty has become a permanent feature for the foreseeable future, then one can begin to grasp why flexibility in all its varied forms has become 'a value in itself – a permanent property of economic organizations that is sought almost for its own sake in a situation in which adaptation seems to consist above all in increasing the general capacity to adapt' (Streeck, 1987: 290).

Whilst the restructuring choices are not unlimited and can, in fact, be constrained in various ways, multinationals, in particular, have engaged in a variety of novel, innovative initiatives to enhance their capacity to adapt and be more flexible. As Cooke (1990: 143) puts it, they have sought to 'reorganise in ways surprising to those who expect normal company behaviour to be ruggedly competitive'. What he identifies are organizational strategies being adopted by large corporations. Some are directed at internal relationships within the firm which aim to encourage 'internal competition' and seek to 'de-rigidify' organizational systems. Others are externally oriented and are attempts to rearrange relationships with other firms. These can result in what are termed 'strategic alliances' with other large corporations (forms of precompetitive partnerships found in joint ventures and similar cooperative agreements). It can also mean that relationships with smaller firms change, as larger corporations subcontract production outwards from within formerly vertically integrated systems of production. In his view, what we are seeing is the emergence of networking, cooperative relations: 'the adoption by many corporations and smaller firms of the techniques of flexible integration' (Cooke, 1988b: 281). However, although a new emphasis upon cooperation may be evident this does not signal the 'demise of competition'.

Others, less sympathetic to the post-Fordist perspective of Cooke, would still accept that organizations have actively sought to achieve flexibility and adaptability by utilizing a 'repertoire of restructuring forms' (Massey and Meegan, 1982), often on an international scale, to reassert control and restore profitability. These have included, for example, rises in the level of foreign direct investment, especially through mergers, takeovers, physical relocation, multiple sourcing, parallel production, multinational coproduction, the international fragmentation and subcontracting of the production process, 'hollowing-out', collaborative ventures involving joint research and development, technology transfers, licensing agreements and many more. The list is a long but by no means exhaustive one (for additions and discussion, see the initiatives reviewed in Harvey, 1989; Dicken, 1986; many of the contributions in Scott and Storper, 1986; Amin and Robins, 1990; and Gordon, 1988).

In assessing these, two points are worth noting. The first is that implementation of such strategies by large multinationals should not be taken as implying a fragmentation of capital and control. The second, and more important, is that what one sees in this blurring of corporate boundaries across territory and ownership is flexibility of industrial organization on a global as opposed to a local scale. In the words of Amin and Robins (1990: 28),

> contemporary experimentations in the corporate economy tend to support the view that decentralised production, where it is occurring, is actually part of, rather than separate from, a wider deepening and extension of oligopolistic competition and control, now being realised through the development of a globally networked economy bestraddled and overseen by a relatively contained number of giant corporations.

Adding weight to this interpretation is the work of Hudson (1989) referred to earlier. His paper is wide-ranging, detailed, and repays careful reading. In it he seeks to engage with the debate regarding a transition to a new regime of accumulation, more specifically the work of Harvey, Storper, and Scott. Evidence is drawn from the USA, UK and Western Europe, focusing on recent changes in the labour markets, labour processes and the organization of production in what are termed '"old" industrial regions' (OIRs) – 'Those areas that formed the cradles of industrial capitalism and are situated where capitalist production grew rapidly in the 19th century around industries such as coalmining, chemicals, iron and steel and related metal processing. From an early stage they were organized in large oligopolistic conglomerates and were tied into international markets' (1989: 6).

His review suggests several conclusions relevant to our discussion here. The first is that the changes taking place in these regions do not represent some kind of structural transition from one regime of accumulation to another (Fordist to post-Fordist), and, in any case, he notes, 'Fordism' has never established more than a tenuous hold in many of these regions (see also Williams et al., 1987). Rather, he argues, the 'related changes in production and in consumption are most appropriately interpreted as being part of strategies by capital to preserve old modes of accumulation in a political climate very different from the welfare state Keynesianism of the 1960s (Hudson, 1989: 24).

Secondly, in both the 'traditional' pre-Fordist industries still located in these regions and in the Fordist branch plants of the 'new' industries, the changes which have been taking place – for example, 'flexibilization' of employment, working practices and so on – the common link is a reassertion of managerial control over labour and the labour process in order to improve productivity and enhance competitiveness.

> Changed labour market conditions and a backdrop of very high unemployment in the OIRs, allow the relationship between capital and labour to be redefined, and allow management to recover or, for the first time, impose authority and control over labour in a variety of ways that depend upon particular technical conditions of production in an industry, and upon the specifications of local labour markets (for example, in terms of culture and politics, as well as the skill composition of the workforce, and so on). (Hudson, 1989: 24)

For Hudson, what is occurring is best understood as a 'selective reworking' which reproduces, in modified form, pre-Fordist and Fordist methods of production, rather than a fundamental transformation (though the fact that these processes are still working themselves through means that the latter cannot be excluded).

It is noteworthy also that his account brings out the role of multi-national corporations in such regions: investing in new plant and seeking to establish new work practices and employment conditions in ways which are not simply responses to modified technologies and labour processes, but which clearly aim to encourage flexibility and adaptability. Thus, speaking particularly of Japanese corporations in the 1980s, he remarks that 'it is not so much that they have introduced new practices (although they have) but rather that they have intensified existing ones and combined them in novel ways'. However, he goes on, 'this does not repre-sent a transition from Fordism to flexible production but rather represents one element in corporate strategies to preserve Fordist production' (1989: 12).

Hudson's analysis and his focus on 'selective reworking' connects well with other recent research which highlights what has been termed the 'remaking' of management–labour relationships (Morgan and Sayer, 1985). Moreover, in so doing it once again points to the importance of multinational (particularly Japanese) firms as the key 'bearers' of new organizational forms, and prime movers in the restructuring of work and work relationships. Although Morgan and Sayer's study was a limited one, of new electronics plants in South Wales, the practices they identify are confirmed by other recent commentaries and analysis. (See, for exam-ple, Elger's (1990) detailed assessment of technical innovation and work reorganization in British manufacturing; also Bassett (1986). Wood (1986) is useful on the US automobile industry. For accounts and analysis of certain Japanese companies operating in the United Kingdom, see Wickens, 1987, and Crowther and Garrahan, 1988, on Nissan; Trevor, 1988, on Toshiba; and Oliver and Wilkinson, 1988.)

Whilst the advantages and opportunities that so-called 'greenfield' sites offer to firms seeking to relocate their operations have long been acknowledged, as Morgan and Sayer rightly point out, 'workers of particular qualities are not just born waiting to be hired; they have to be made, both in the workplace and the community' (1985: 381). Crucial to the successful resolution of this issue is the 'mobilization of consent' (cf. Burawoy's (1979) study of how consent within the workplace is 'manufac-tured'). In their study, the main innovations were in recruitment and selection procedures which were more rigorous and tailored to the specific needs of particular firms. There was an emphasis on flexible working practices and simplified pay structures (often focusing much more on individual performance) to support them. Finally, managerial control was achieved and reinforced especially when it came to collective relationships with unions. In various ways unions might be circumvented or bypassed by management, or found their freedom of action 'constrained' as a consequence of concluding 'strike-free' agreements.

An important aspect of their analysis, however, is its recognition of how management seeks to generate and sustain consensual labour relations rather than continually to have to assert and reassert control. In this, the development of behavioural skills (alongside the technical) amongst the workforce is vital. The focus, then, is upon what has been called 'attitudinal restructuring' (Wood, 1986), based upon the encouragement of self-discipline, cooperativeness and responsibility for some decisions. Through mechanisms such as quality circles, firms sought to tap, in a more extensive manner, the knowledge and skill of the workforce.

It is not being suggested here that all multinational corporations follow the same strategies. At both macro and micro levels, different initiatives and strategic changes can be identified and, indeed, as the work of Cooke and others demonstrates, individual companies may utilize a number of different strategies depending upon the precise circumstances in which they find themselves. This is hardly surprising given the contradictory and divergent nature of much of the restructuring.

At the same time, to argue that what has occurred in recent years represents a fundamental change from the past or the transition to a new era of accumulation is to stretch the available evidence beyond what it will bear. To quote Amin and Robins again on the present situation (1990: 27), 'rather than some fundamental shift from centralisation, concentration, and integration towards a new historical era of decentralisation, dissemination and disintegration, what we are seeing in the present period are organisational developments that are in significant ways an extension of Fordist structures. What is at work is not corporate fragmentation, but, in fact, more effective corporate integration' (see also Lovering, 1990b).

Finally, it should perhaps be reiterated that to argue for the existence and significance of deep-seated continuities with the past is not to deny that dramatic change has occurred. Rather, it is simply to recognize that there is, at present, little certainty as to its character. If our understanding of the present period of change is to deepen it may well be that there is a need for the debate to be 'recast' (Wood, 1989: 28–30), but in ways which allow 'a clearer specification and differentiation of concepts', which question the use of stereotypes from the past as benchmarks (for example, Fordism), and which specify both the level of abstraction and level of aggregation with which we are working.

At present we are faced with a situation whereby

> Too many theories predicting a major transformation of work seem to jump too readily from the production system to the basic structures of economies or even capitalism, or vice versa. It ought to be possible to admit of the importance of flexibility without assuming that this involves a fundamental change in the mode of regulation, or alternatively of changes in the economy or political institutions without assuming a transformation of labour processes or

consumption patterns such as the end of mass production. (Wood, 1989: 30):

At the moment, whether the focus is the labour process or industrial organization, it is difficult to discern any kind of substantial, qualitative shift in production relations, notwithstanding elements of novelty and innovation (Thompson, 1989: 229). It is a conclusion which holds even firmer at the macroeconomic and international levels. Given the increased 'tendencies towards internationalism and the global integration of local and national economies' (Amin and Robins, 1990: 26) which seem to be taking place, the verdict as to whether there has occurred a transformation in work must be 'not proven'.

References

Ackroyd, S. and Whitaker, A. (1990) 'Manufacturing decline and the organisation of manufacture in Britain', in P. Stewart et al. (eds), *Restructuring for Economic Flexibility*. Avebury.

Aglietta, M. (1982) *A Theory of Capitalist Regulation* (revised edition): New Left Books.

Allen, J. (1988) 'Fragmented firms, disorganized labour?', in J. Allen and D. Massey (eds), *Restructuring Britain. The Economy in Question*. Open University/Sage.

Amin, A. and Robins, K. (1990) 'The re-emergence of regional economies? The mythical geography of flexible accumulation', *Environment and Planning D: Society and Space*, 8: 7–34.

Atkinson, J. (1984) 'Manpower strategies for flexible organisations', *Personnel Management*, August.

Atkinson, J. (1985) 'The changing corporation', in D. Clutterbuck (ed.), *New Patterns of Work*. Gower.

Atkinson, J. and Gregory, D. (1986) 'A flexible future', *Marxism Today*, April.

Atkinson, J. and Meager, N. (1986) 'Is "flexibility" just a flash in the pan?' *Personnel Management*, September.

Bagguley, P. (1991) 'Post-Fordism and enterprise culture: Flexibility, autonomy and changes in economic organisation', in R. Keat and N. Abercrombie (eds), *Enterprise Culture*. Routledge.

Bassett, P. (1986) *Strike-Free: New Industrial Relations in Britain*. Macmillan.

Bassett, P. (1988) 'Non-unionism's growing ranks', *Personnel Management*, March.

Batstone, E. (1988) *The Reform of Workplace Industrial Relations: Theory, Myth and Evidence*. Oxford University Press.

Beynon, H. (1983) 'False hopes and real dilemmas: The politics of the collapse in British Manufacturing', *Critique*, 16.

Blackaby, F. (ed.) (1978) *Deindustrialisation*. Heinemann/NIESR.

Boyer, R. (ed.) (1988) *The Search for Labour Market Flexibility*. Clarendon Press.

Brown, W. (1986) 'The changing role of trade unions in the management of labour', *British Journal of Industrial Relations*, 24 (2): 161–6.

Burawoy, M. (1979) *Manufacturing Consent*. University of Chicago Press.

Casey, B. (1988) *Temporary Employment: Practice and Policy in Britain*. PSI/Anglo-German Foundation.

Cooke, P. (1988a) 'Spatial development processes: Organized or disorganized?', in D. Massey and J. Allen, *Uneven Re-Development: Cities and Regions in Transition*. Hodder and Stoughton.

Cooke, P. (1988b) 'Flexible integration, scope economies and strategic alliances: Social and spatial mediations'. *Environment and Planning D: Society and Space*, 6: 281–300.

Cooke, P. (1990) *Back to the Future: Modernity, Postmodernity and Locality*. Unwin Hyman.

Costello, N., Michie, J. and Milne, S. (1989) *Beyond the Casino Economy*. Verso.

Crowther, S. and Garrahan, P. (1988) 'Invitation to Sunderland: Corporate power and the local economy', *Industrial Relations Journal*, 19 (1).

Daniel, W. (1987) *Workplace Industrial Relations and Technical Change*. Frances Pinter.

Dankbaar, B. (1988) 'New production concepts, management strategies and the quality of work', *Work, Employment and Society*, 2 (1): 25–50.

Dex, S. (1988) 'Gender and the labour market', in D. Gallie (ed.), *Employment in Britain*. Basil Blackwell, pp. 281–309.

Dicken, P. (1986) *Global Shift: Industrial Change in a Turbulent World*. Harper and Row.

Edwards, P.K. (1987) *Managing the Factory*. Basil Blackwell.

Elger, T. (1990) 'Technical innovation and work reorganisation in British manufacturing in the 1980s: Continuity, intensification or transformation?', *Work Employment and Society*, Special Issue (May): 67–101.

Fothergill, S., Gudgin, G., Kitson, M. and Monk, S. (1986) 'The deindustrialisation of the city', in R. Martin and R. Rowthorn, *The Geography of Deindustrialisation*. Macmillan.

Freeman, C. (ed.) (1984) *Long Waves in the World Economy*. Frances Pinter.

Gallie, D. (ed.) (1988) *Employment in Britain*. Basil Blackwell.

Gamble, A. (1981) *Britain in Decline*. Macmillan.

Gordon, D.M. (1988) 'The global economy: New edifice or crumbling foundations?', *New Left Review*, 168: 24–64.

Green, F. (ed.) (1989) *The Restructuring of the UK Economy*. Harvester (Wheatsheaf).

Hakim, C. (1987) 'Trends in the flexible workforce', *Employment Gazette*, 95 (11): 549–60.

Hakim, C. (1988) 'Self-employment in Britain: A review of recent trends and current issues', *Work, Employment and Society*, 2 (4): 421–50.

Handy, C. (1984) *The Future of Work*. Basil Blackwell.

Harvey, D. (1989) *The Condition of Postmodernity*. Basil Blackwell.

Hudson, R. (1989) 'Labour market changes and new forms of work in old industrial regions: Maybe flexibility for some but not flexible accumulation', *Environment and Planning D: Society and Space*, 7: 5–30.

Hyman, R. (1988) 'Flexible specialisation: Miracle or myth?', in R. Hyman and W. Streeck (eds), *New Technology and Industrial Relations*. Basil Blackwell.

Hyman, R. (1991) 'Plus ça change? The theory of production and the production of theory', in A. Pollert (ed.), *Farewell to Flexibility*. Basil Blackwell.

Hyman, R. and Streeck, W. (eds) (1988) *New Technology and Industrial Relations*. Basil Blackwell.

Jones, B. (1988) 'Work and flexible automation in Britain: A review of developments and possibilities', *Work, Employment and Society*, 2 (4): 451–6.

Jones, B. and Scott, P. (1987) 'Flexible manufacturing systems in Britain and the USA?', *New Technology, Work and Employment*, 2 (1): 27–36.

Kelly, J. (1988) *Trade Unions and Socialist Politics*. Verso.

Labour Research (1987) 'UK firms seek rosier climes', May: 13–14.

Labour and Society (1987) Issue on Labour Market Flexibility, 12 (1), January.

Lane, C. (1989) *Management and Labour in Europe*. Edward Elgar.

Lash, S. and Urry, J. (1987) *The End of Organized Capitalism*. Polity Press.

Leadbeater, C. (1987) 'In the land of the dispossessed', *Marxism Today*, April: 18–25.

Leadbeater, C. and Lloyd, J. (1987) *In Search of Work*. Penguin.

Lovering, J. (1990a) 'Fordism's unknown successor: A comment on Scott's theory of flexible accumulation and the re-emergence of regional economies', *International Journal of Urban and Regional Research*, 14 (1): 159–74.

Lovering, J. (1990b) 'A perfunctory sort of post-Fordism: Economic restructuring and labour market segmentation in Britain in the 1980's', *Work, Employment and Society*. special issue, May: 9–28.

MacInnes, J. (1987) *Thatcherism at Work*. Open University Press.

MacInnes, J. (1988) 'The question of flexibility', *Personnel Review*, 17 (3): 12–15.

Mandel, E. (1980) *Long Waves of Capitalist Development*. Cambridge University Press.

Marginson, P. (1989) 'Employment flexibility in large companies: Change and continuity', *Industrial Relations Journal*, 20 (2): 101–9.

Marginson, P. et al. (1988) *Beyond the Workplace*. Basil Blackwell.

Marsden, D., Morris, T., Willman, P. and Wood, S. (1985) *The Car Industry: Labour Relations and Industrial Adjustment*. Tavistock Publications.

Martin, R. (1986) 'Thatcherism and Britain's industrial landscape', in Martin, R. and Rowthorn, R. (eds), *The Geography of De-industrialisation*. Macmillan.

Martin, R. (1988) 'Industrial capitalism in transition: The contemporary reorganisation of the British space economy', in D. Massey and J. Allen (eds), *Uneven Re-development: Cities and Regions in Transition* Open University/Hodder & Stoughton.

Martin, R. and Rowthorn, R. (eds) (1986) *The Geography of De-industrialisation*. Macmillan.

Massey, D. (1984) *Spatial Divisions of Labour*. Macmillan.

Massey, D. (1988) 'What's happening to UK manufacturing?', in J. Allen and D. Massey (eds), *The Economy in Question*. Sage.

Massey, D. and Allen, J (eds) (1988) *Uneven Re-development: Cities and Regions in Transition*. Open University/Hodder & Stoughton.

Massey, D. and Meegan, R. (1982) *The Anatomy of Job Loss*. Methuen.

Massey, D. and Miles, N. (1984) 'Mapping out the unions', *Marxism Today*, May: 19–22.

Meegan, R. (1988) 'A crisis of mass production?', in J. Allen and D. Massey (eds), *The Economy in Question*. Sage.

Millward, N. and Stevens, M. (1986) *British Workplace Industrial Relations 1980–84. The DE/ESRC/PSI/ACAS Surveys*. Gower.

Millward, N. and Stevens, M. (1988) 'Union density in the regions', *Employment Gazette*, May. HMSO.

Morgan, K. and Sayer, A. (1985) 'A "modern" industry in a "mature" region', *International Journal of Urban and Regional Research*, 9 (3): 383–403.

Morris, J.L. (1988) 'New technologies, flexible work practices and regional sociospatial differentiation: Some observations from the United Kingdom'. *Environment and Planning D: Society and Space*, 6: 301–19.

Moulaert, F. and Swyngedown, E.A. (1989) 'Survey 15: A regulation approach to the geography of flexible production systems', *Environment and Planning D: Society and Space*, 7: 327–45.

Murray, F. (1983) 'The decentralisation of production and the decline of the mass collective worker', *Capital and Class*, 19 (spring).

Murray, R. (1988) 'Life after Henry (Ford)', *Marxism Today*, October: 8–13.

Offe, C. (1985) *Disorganised Capitalism*. Polity Press.

Oliver, N. and Wilkinson, B. (1988) *The Japanization of British Industry*. Basil Blackwell.

Pahl, R.E. (ed.) (1988) *On Work: Historical, Comparative and Theoretical Approaches*. Basil Blackwell.

Palloix, C. (1976) 'The labour process: From Fordism to Neo-Fordism', *The Labour Process and Class Strategies, Stage 1*. Conference of Socialist Economists.

Piore, M.J. (1986) 'Perspectives on labour market flexibility', *Industrial Relations*, 25 (2): 146–66.

Piore, M.J. and Sabel, C.F. (1984) *The Second Industrial Divide: Prospects for Prosperity*. Basic Books.

Pollert, A. (1987) 'The flexible firm: A model in search of reality (or a policy in search of a practice?)', *Warwick Papers in Industrial Relations*, 19.

Pollert, A. (1988) 'The flexible firm: Fixation or fact?' *Work Employment and Society*, 2 (3): 281–315.

Pollert, A. (ed.) (1991) *Farewell to Flexibility*? Basil Blackwell.

Purcell, K. et al. (eds) (1986) *The Changing Experience of Employment*. Macmillan

Reed, M. (1991) 'The end of organised society: A theme in search of a theory?' in P. Blyton and J. Morris (eds), *A Flexible Future?* de Gruyter.

Robinson, O. (1985) 'The changing labour market: The phenomenon of part-time employment in Britain', *National Westminster Bank Quarterly Review*, November: 19–29.

Rubery, J. (1988) 'Employers and the labour market', in D. Gallie (ed.), *Employment in Britain*. Basil Blackwell, pp. 251–80.

Sabel, C.F. (1982) *Work and Politics: The Division of Labour in Industry*. Cambridge University Press.

Sayer, A. (1989) 'Post-Fordism in question', *International Journal of Urban and Regional Research*, 13, (4): 666–95.

Scott, A.J. (1988) 'Flexible production systems and regional development: The rise of new industrial spaces in North America and Europe', *International Journal of Urban and Regional Research* 12 (2): 171–86.

Scott, A.J. and Storper, M. (1986) *Production, Work, Territory: The Geographical Anatomy of Industrial Capitalism*. Allen & Unwin.

Shutt, J. and Whittington, R. (1987) 'Fragmentation strategies and the rise of small units: Cases from the North West', *Regional Studies*, 21 (1): 13–23.

Smith, C. (1989) 'Flexible specialisation, automation and mass production', *Work, Employment and Society*, 3 (2): 203–20.

Streeck, W. (1987) 'The uncertainties of management in the management of uncertainty: employers, labor relations and industrial adjustment in the 1980s', *Work, Employment and Society*, 1 (3): 281–308.

Tailby, S. and Whitston, C. (eds) (1989) *Manufacturing Change, Industrial Relations and Restructuring*. Basil Blackwell.

Thompson, P. (1989) *The Nature of Work* (second edition). Macmillan.

Thrift, N. (1988) 'The geography of international economic disorder', in D. Massey and J. Allen (eds), *Uneven Re-Development: Cities and Regions in Transition*. Hodder & Stoughton.

Trevor, M. (1988) *Toshiba's New British Company*. Policy Studies Institute.

Urry, J. (1988) 'Disorganised capitalism', *Marxism Today*, October: 30–3.

Walby, S. (ed.) (1988) *Gender Segregation at Work*. Open University Press.

Walby, S. (1989) 'Flexibility and the changing sexual division of labour', in Wood, S. (ed.), *The Transformation of Work?* Unwin Hyman.

Wickens, P. (1987) *The Road to Nissan*. Macmillan.

Williams, K., Cutler, T., Williams, J. and Haslem, C. (1987) 'The end of mass production?', *Economy and Society*, 16 (3): 403–39.

Wood, S. (1986) 'The cooperative labour strategy in the US auto industry', *Economic and Industrial Democracy*, 7 (4): 415–48.

Wood, S. (ed.) (1989) *The Transformation of Work?* Unwin Hyman.

11

Organization Theory in the Postmodern Era

Kenneth J. Gergen

Why do we find it so congenial to speak of organizations as structures but not as clouds, systems but not songs, weak or strong but not tender or passionate? Is it because organizations physically resemble one but not the other, that we somehow discern through the clamorous hurly burly something that is structural, but not cloudlike, systemic rather than rhapsodic, strong but not tender? What kind of 'structure' could we have in mind that the continuous movements of eyeballs, arms, legs, words, papers, and so on should bear a physical resemblance? And are those who think they observe structure simply blind to systemic 'process', and those who spy 'strength' insensitive to obvious signals of 'tenderness'? No, there is little sense to be made of the assumption that organization theories are read off the world as it is, inductively derived from our experiential immersion in a world of continuous flux.

A far more promising alternative for understanding the intelligibility of organizations is to be found in the discursive context. For our theories of organizations are, first and foremost, forms of language. They are guided by existing rules of grammar, and constructed out of the pool of nouns and verbs, the metaphors, the narrative plots, and the like found within the linguistic context. In this sense, theories of the organization do not exist apart from or independent of the surrounding intelligibilities of the culture. As theorists we must 'make sense', and if we are to make sense within our own culture, we have no recourse but to obey the culture's rules of intelligibility. We thus borrow and steal from the cultural ways of talking about organizational life, for if we do not rely on our cultural surrounds we cannot serve as their insightful informants. This does not mean that we are simply redundant, speaking back to the culture what it already knows. Yes, the cultural intelligibilities must necessarily guide or inform our ways of speaking. However, as a profession we then act upon these intelligibilities – expanding and elaborating on the dominant metaphors, synthesizing, purifying, explicating, elaborating, and following their implicature into the realm of the as yet unspoken. So when we do our work well, the culture does indeed learn anew from our sayings.

This image of inter-discourses – in this case the cultural and the professional – provides a prelude to the major concerns I wish to address in this chapter. For I believe that organization theory of the present century has drawn its chief sustenance from two cultural leitmotifs, or hegemonic bodies of discourse. In the first case our theories have been enriched and informed by romanticist discourse of the nineteenth century, and in the second, by the modernist understanding of the person dominant within the twentieth century. However, in my view the gains to be acquired through continued intercourse with these traditions are diminishing. Already, romanticist discourse is largely displaced by modernist understandings. And at present the intellectual and cultural *Zeitgeist* is substantially undermining the rhetorical force of modernism. As many believe, we are entering a period of postmodernism. And as we do so, new formulations are invited, formulations that are essential to the intellectual, political and practical significance of organization theory.

In what follows I shall first take a brief scan of the influence of romanticism and modernism on traditional and current accounts of the organization. I shall then outline what I believe to be critical ingredients of the postmodern turn within the intellectual sphere. Finally, I shall offer a preliminary scaffold for a postmodern theory of power and efficacy in the organization.

Romantic Dimensions of Organizational Life

Any intelligible theory of organizational life must be coherent with prevailing conceptions of the human being. The theorist cannot make sense about persons in relationship without relying on a forestructure of understandings concerning the nature of human functioning more generally. Yet, cultural conceptions of human functioning are hardly cumulative; they are subject to vast upheavals and decay across time. In this context, let us consider the romanticist discourse largely reaching its ascendancy within the nineteenth century. For, not only is there a coherence in this discourse across many sectors of Western culture – an array of interrelated and commonly held assumptions – but in many respects this emerging view of human functioning is both distinct in quality and profound in implication. Here I am not only speaking of the verbally articulate – of poets, novelists and philosophers, from Goethe, Hölderlin, in the early phases, through Byron, Keats, Shelley, and Wordsworth somewhere toward the center, to Nietzsche, Rimbaud and Edgar Allen Poe toward the latter phase. I am also including as purveyors of the romantic idiom artists (from Casper David Friedrich to the Pre-Raphaelites and symbolists), composers (from Beethoven and Brahms to Chopin and Rachmaninov), and architects (including both Victorian and Art Nouveau).

In my view the chief contribution of the romanticists to the prevailing concept of the person was their rhetorical creation of *the deep interior*. That is, what was truly significant about the individual, that which rendered persons uniquely identifiable as persons, is the existence of a repository of capacities or characteristics lying deeply within human consciousness. These capacities and characteristics are not given immediately to conscious rationality – simply there for the passing glance of any errant philistine. To understand them, to express them, and to appreciate them – either in oneself or others – requires special sophistication, an introspective sensitivity, a willingness to be wrenched from the contented perch of the ordinary. Among the chief constituents of the deep interior was the human soul, a concept resuscitated from medieval texts, and which served to give the individual inherent worth – a value above and beyond that assigned to marketplace commodities. To the deep interior was also allocated a powerful and mysterious energic force. For many this force was wondrous – nothing short of pure love – and its expression (both in committed love and friendship) furnished life its fundamental meaning. And, because of the power of this force, one might also experience grief (at the loss of the loved one) and a sense of longing or remorse so profound that suicide was its most appropriate mode of expression. For others, particularly the late romanticists, this force was also endowed with evil potential – possibly leading to madness. In addition to these constituents of the deep interior, romanticists located entities such as inspiration, creativity, and genius along with the power of will and the capacity for moral sensibility. The resources at a depth were rich indeed.

For many romanticists, the deep interior was also rooted in nature. No, it was not crassly biological nature – material, brute-like, there for medical inspection. Rather, in the great chain of being, which linked God at the uppermost, with the kingdom of animals and plants toward the lower spectrum, the deep interior was of God, but at the same time, endowed with natural forces. It was natural in that it was God-given, and not a product of human artifice. And it was natural in that it was at home within and vulnerable to the surrounding forces of worldly nature. Genius, inspiration, creativity, will power and moral sensibility were not, then, products of simple training and instruction. They were inherent gifts within the natural order.

Today the romanticist perspective is sustained largely by the arts, literature, religion, and the mass media. They urge people to find 'meaning in life', to 'give all to love', to achieve moral worth, to know oneself, and to express one's deepest impulses. And romanticism also furnishes a significant rhetorical legacy for theories of the organization. Let me cite only a few perspectives that owe their power or appeal largely to the romanticist language of the deep interior:

Work emanating from the Tavistock Institute (including Bion, Jacques, Menzies and Bridger) along with other psychoanalytically based theories of the organization (for example, Zaleznick) in which unconscious dynamics furnish the explanatory fulcrum.

Theoretical work inspired by Jung's theory of archetypical bases of action (for example, Denhardt, Mitroff).

Theory and research presuming fundamental human needs, including human resource management and human potential perspectives (for example, Mayo, Maslow, McGregor).

Positions emphasizing the personal resources essential for successful leadership (for example, Fiedler, Hollander).

That aspect of Japanese management theory, as made intelligible in the West, emphasizing organizational commitment, and bonds between organizations and their members which transcend market exigencies.

Inquiries into executive appreciation that emphasize the workers' needs for positive regard and the significance of empathy and dialogue to organizational success (for example, Cooperider and Srivastva).

It is essential to note at this point that by viewing these accounts as forms of language, not in themselves derived from what is the case, achieving their impact through rhetorical artifice, my aim is not at all derogatory. In my view the value of organization theory does not lie in its accuracy, how well it matches or reflects the way things are. (In what way can words be matched against visual images, sounds, and the like?) Theory cannot be evaluated by its capacity to predict, for words in themselves are simply sounds or markings, lifeless and inert; words in themselves do not predict. Rather, theory gains its importance from the activities which it enables, which essentially means, by the way in which it figures in ongoing patterns of relationship. Thus, by drawing sustenance from the romanticist vocabulary, organization theorists hammer out intelligibilities that resonate with a significant part of the cultural vernacular. In this sense, they find an eagerly appreciative audience. Further, when such intelligibilities are inserted into organizational life, old practices seem wrong-headed, and new forms of organizational life are invited. It is not that the new practices are superior in some sense of 'truer' or more 'fundamental'. Rather, the new practices often enable people to live out their cultural meaning systems in ways that seem congenial or 'more fully expressive'.

From Romantic to Modernist Conceptions of the Organization

To be sure, romanticist vocabulary of understanding is still very much alive in Western culture; many would say that without it life ceases to have meaning. However, it is also a vocabulary in remission. In the intellectual world most particularly, romanticist voices largely speak from the margins. The chief replacement for the romanticist world-view is the modernist. There are as many reasons for the flourishing of modernism in the present century as there are pitfalls to overall characterization of the era. The interested scholar may wish to consult relevant works by Bradbury and McFarlane (1976), Berman (1982), Frisby (1985), and

Habermas (1981). However, in very brief form, I would characterize modernism as:

1 *A revival of Enlightenment beliefs in the powers of reason and observation*, linked importantly to Darwinistic views of species survival. Through observation we record the character of the world, and through reason we can develop and test theories about the world. As our theories become progressively more accurate and predictive, so do our potentials for survival increase.
2 *A search for fundamentals or essentials.* Sustained by powers of reason and observation, we may lay bare the secrets of the universe, whether it be atomic particles, chemical elements, economic behavior, architectural form, or musical tonality.
3 *A faith in progress and universal design.* Because of the obvious gains in knowledge or understanding of fundamentals, we can be assured of a steadily improving future. As we succeed in mastering fundamental knowledge of energy, biological systems, psychological mechanisms, social structures and the like, we can move toward utopian societies. Knowledge of essentials is also universal knowledge, and thus we may have faith in rationally derived, large-scale designs for society.
4 *Absorption in the machine metaphor.* There are many reasons: the enormous social consequences of the industrial revolution, the efficiency of lifestyles increasingly engendered by the machine, and the Enlightenment presumption prevailing in science (and thus rational) of the world as 'one great machine'. In any case, the existing confluence of images and ideas gave rise to a prevailing metaphor of understanding: the machine. That is, whatever the essentials – from atoms to architecture – the model theoretical picture stresses the systematic (typically causal) relationships between or among basic elements. Thus, like any good machine, if one understands its internal functioning, and has control over the inputs, one can depend on a reliable product.

These various presumptions remain vital throughout contemporary culture, and they have left an indelible mark on theories of organization from early in the century to the present. Not only have modernist beliefs granted the scholar an honorable niche (grounded expertise in a given domain of inquiry), but they have promised the scholarly community that with the assiduous application of research technology, fundamental progress can be attained in our understanding of organizational life. Such views, along with the associated metaphor of the machine, are variously represented in:

Scientific management theory along with time and motion methodology. General systems theory in its various modifications and extensions, including contemporary contingency theory (for example, Lawrence and Lorsch).
Exchange theories (for example, Homans), along with related investigations

of equity and bargaining and expectancy value analyses of individual behavior.

Cybernetic theory, in which organizations approximate sophisticated mechanical automata.

Trait methodology, which presumes the stability of individual patterns of behavior and the possibility of selecting individuals to fit different positions (for example Fiedler).

Cognitive theories of individual behavior (see Ilgen and Klein's 1989 review).

Theories of industrial society based on rational laws of economic organization and development.

The Postmodern Transformation

To be sure, romantic and modernist discourses are hardly moribund. They have many champions and charges, and a great deal of research and organizational planning is carried out within their purview. And so it should be. However, for many these voices have lost their sense of lived validity. For many, they seem more akin to formalisms or to ideological mystifications. There is a yearning for alternatives. In my view, this sense of unease can largely be traced to what many see as the postmodern turn in intellectual and cultural life more generally. As in the preceding, I must be mercilessly brief in accounting for major contours and rationales. But for present purposes, let me summarize the postmodern turn in the following way.

For modernists there were essentials to be discovered through reason and observation, and to be reflected in language. The relationship of language to the essential was thus one of master to slave. The essentials of the universe (atoms, neurons, economies, and so on) served as masters, fixed and foremost, and the language was to be their servant – flexibly bending to the contours of the essential. The creditable language was thus one which depicts or maps the essentials as they truly are. I shan't review here all the many counter-currents that came to challenge this view. Among the initially prominent were certainly Wittgenstein's (1963) writings on language games, Quine's (1960) critique of the word–object link, Kuhn's (1970) account of paradigm incommensurability, Garfinkel's (1967) ethnomethodology, critical school challenges (Habermas, 1975) to interest-free knowledge, Nelson Goodman's (1978) views on world construction, and various discussions (for example, Pepper, 1972; Burke, 1968; White, 1978) of the metaphoric and rhetorical basis of knowledge. And of more recent vintage, one should have to mention feminist critiques (Harding, 1986; Keller, 1985) of the androcentric biases underlying seemingly neutral science, Foucault's (1978) analysis of the relationship of knowledge to power and control, inquiries in the sociology of knowledge (Latour, 1987; Knorr-Cetina, 1981; Barnes, 1974), social constructionist accounts (Gergen and Davis, 1985; Harré, 1986) of taken-for-granted knowledge, communicationist accounts of the negotiation of meaning (Pearce and Cronen, 1980), inquiries into the discursive basis of ordinary understanding (Billig, 1987; Potter and Wetherall, 1987), and to be sure, the many semiotic (Barthes, 1964) and deconstructionist (Derrida, 1974; DeMan, 1979) analyses of literary and philosophic works.

All of these movements across the disciplines conspire to reverse the modernist view of language as picturing the essentials of reality. Collectively they achieve a counter-intelligibility drawing heavily from three related arguments.

The Replacement of the Real by the Representational

For the modernist, language was simply a tool for the logical representation of the essential or the real. However, as the impossibility of a picture theory of language became increasingly clear, one might justifiably ask about other sources of representation (such as description and explanation). As demonstrated in these various lines of inquiry, one can make a compelling case that knowledge, as a body of discourse, is governed, influenced or constrained by ideological or valuational interests, by social processes, and by the rules or conventions of language formation itself. However, as attention is increasingly addressed to the forces governing representation – other than reality itself – reality becomes subject to erasure. That is, if what we call 'the real' is governed by the ideology of the caller, attempts to inform society of what is 'actually the case' must be regarded with suspicion. A genuine interest in discovering the nature of things in themselves seems both naive and misleading.

In this context, all the modernist attempts to determine through empirical investigation – through sensitive measuring devices, experimental variations and sophisticated statistical procedures – the actual nature of organizations become suspect. The entire empirical apparatus is a handmaiden to the traditional assumption that language is a pawn to nature; it presumes that with sufficiently rigorous research, we can eventually 'straighten the language out', rectify it with reality. Yet, as postmodern consciousness sets in, the empirical process is redefined. Rather than correcting the language of understanding, primary research is typically justificatory. It proceeds on the basis of assumptions, or discourses, already shared within the scientific sub-community, and generates evidence that is interpreted within this restricted discursive domain. Because it commences with theoretical views already intact, whatever data are produced by the research will inevitably be named or defined within this theoretical spectrum. In this sense the theoretical perspective is self-fulfilling; all that exists does so by virtue of theoretical definition. Research results do not stand as separate and independent vindicators of position; they are essentially reification devices for positions already embraced.

Representation as a Communal Artifact

Within the postmodern view, language loses its role as functionary in the realm of reality. However, for many contributors to this colloquy language is not thereby set free. Rather, it acquires a new master, and this master is the community. Language gains its meaning and significance through its placement within social interchange. Words fail to make sense (they remain nonsense) until there is at least one other person to give assent to their meaningfulness. Sense-making is thus a collective manifestation, or in John Shotter's (1980) terms, a *joint action* – requiring the coordinated participation of two or more persons. This view is favored by Wittgenstein's views of language games and meaning; it is implied by Kuhn's (1970) work on the history of paradigm shifts; it is articulated most clearly within certain sectors of the sociology of knowledge (Latour, 1987), discourse analysis (Billig, 1987) and social constructionism (Gergen, 1985). Further, the social basis of appropriate, just, or 'correct' description is congenial with feminist and critical school analyses of ideological bias, as well as postmodern literary theory (see especially Fish, 1980).

It is important to note in this regard that for many contributors to the postmodern turn, these developments have meant an abandonment of psychological explanation. This falling away from mental explanation is, first of all, an obvious conclusion to the replacement of reality by representation. That is, psychological events (motives, traits, rational decision processes) have traditionally been viewed as among the essential realities that scientists should seek to elucidate. However, as one becomes aware that representations of these realities cannot be dictated by their essence, then their essential nature becomes dubitable. Is not the very concept of 'essence' a move within the game of language? Or more directly, if we cannot move beyond the realm of representation, is the concept of mental events essential to our understanding?

However, by placing language in the hands of the community, the second major move in postmodernism, the mind is subjected to double jeopardy. For the traditional account of language held that it was a product of the individual mind, a conduit by which internal thought made its way into the public sphere. Yet, if mind is not something we can know about (in the sense of representation), then why must we posit a reasoning mind behind the sounds and markings that make up language? As Derrida has phrased it, we fall heir to a *logocentric* bias, in which we presume an internal, reasoning agent. There are no grounds on which to justify such a view, and as Richard Rorty (1979) argues it is a view that leads to enormous philosophic confusion. Thus, to place language into relational space, an achievement of coordinated action, we need make no mention of knowing minds or reasoning powers. Language is not thus a means by which I overcome my Cartesian isolation. I do not express myself in relationships through language; relationships express themselves through me.

Ironic Self-Reflection

As Lawson (1985) has proposed, self-reflexivity, or critical suspicion of one's own suppositions, is a prevailing theme within many sectors of postmodernism. The chief reason for this self-critical attitude should be clear from the preceding. For, as it becomes painfully clear, all those propositions removing representation from the grip of reality are themselves representations. They treat as a putative reality both language and a world independent of this language. As a result, they fall heir to their own critical assessment. Or, in terms of the traditional argument against skepticism: how can an argument negating the concept of truth itself be true? Postmodernists have reacted to this irony in a variety of ways. Derrida engages in elliptical, intentionally ambiguous, and often self-negating practices, essentially deconstructing his own writings. French feminists such as Julia Kristeva (1980) see the Western metaphysics of language as itself androcentric, and attempt to escape through developing alternative forms of expression (nonsense within the traditional conventions, but as they believe, sensible within a primordial semiotic). Action researchers in a variety of disciplines attempt to escape the responsibilities of representing their subjects (as objects) by allowing the subjects to speak for themselves, to control their own voice as represented in the professional literature. Others propose that the scholar should play the fool or the dandy, or more provocatively, go piss in public (Sloterdijk, 1987).

If there is one theme that unites most of those confronting the postmodern irony, it is a certain sense of ludic humility. The view of knowledge-making as a transcendent pursuit, removed from the trivial enthrallments of daily life, pristinely rational, and transparently virtuous, becomes so much puffery. We should view these bodies of language we call knowledge in a lighter vein – as ways of putting things, some pretty and others petty – but in no sense calling for ultimate commitments, condemnations, or profound consequences. We should rather be more playful with our sayings. We who utter them are giving voice neither to reality as it is nor to internal possessions (insights, reasons, intentions). Rather we are engaging in public pastimes, rituals, or lifeforms and for such enterprises there are no vindicating foundations.

Let us briefly reconsider traditional organizational inquiry in this light, for one must be cautious regarding the distribution of levity in this case. For the greater part of the twentieth century the major approach to organizational study has been modernist, mixing both romanticist and modernist metaphors of human functioning, but in general attempting to lay bare the essentials. Or, in Lyotard's (1984) terms, organizational theorists have participated in the grand modernist narrative of progress. It is a story we repeat to ourselves in order to justify what we do, one that says that with a combination of rigorous rationality and methodology we can move ever closer to knowledge of the object (and thus toward rational decisions regarding its welfare). It is the seriousness of this grand narrative that postmodernists would challenge, for not only is it mystifying, but it generates zero-sum conflicts and suppresses a multitude of alternative voices. Rather than founders of 'the last word' (where in the beginning was the word of God), we should perhaps view ourselves as balloon craftsmen – setting aloft vehicles for public amusement.

And yet, this metaphor for the theorist is incomplete. For there is a more serious side to the enterprise that follows from the earlier treatment of language and social interdependence. As we find, languages of understanding are interlaced with what else we do; they are insinuated into our daily activities in such a way that without the languages the patterns of activity would be transformed or collapse. (Remove all talk of God, and what is left of religious ceremonies; abandon all talk of profit and loss and what happens to economic enterprise; abandon the language of emotions and the love affair ceases to be a love affair.) It is in this sense that theories of organization are most fully subject to critique and to credit. They are subject to critique if and when we feel the theories lend themselves to repugnant patterns of social life. (Here consider Barry Schwartz's volume *The Battle for Human Nature* (1986), in which behavior theory and economic rationality theory are condemned for the sanctimonious selfishness they help to foster.) They are subject to credit, as well, for such theories may contribute to activities of positive consequence for organizations and society more generally. We shall return to this latter point shortly.

Toward Postmodern Theories of the Organization

Organization theory has hardly been immune to these various developments within the intellectual world. Indeed, the organizational community has made an active and important contribution to many of the issues at stake. Argyris' (1980) critique of inner contradictions of rigorous research, ideological critiques of organizational realities (see, for example, Salaman and Thompson, 1981), and critiques of the empiricist philosophy of science in the organizational context (Bhagat, 1983), were all important conceptual steps toward the postmodern. More focused work on paradoxical group processes (Smith and Berg, 1987), cooperative group inquiry (Reason, 1988), the social construction of leadership (Dachler, forthcoming; Srivastva and Barrett, 1988), and on action research (see, for example, Pasmore and Friedlander, 1982), moves importantly in the postmodern direction. Morgan's (1986) treatment of existing organizational theories as literary metaphors adopts a postmodern stance. As cybernetic systems theory has moved through its second-order phase, questioning the epistemological foundations of empiricism, and generating a keen appreciation of self-reflexive processes (see Steier, 1991) it has made a strong contribution to postmodernism in organizational theory. The corpus of work on organizations as cultural systems creating and generating symbolic realities (see summaries by Morgan, 1986; and by

Schein, 1990), is both congenial with and makes a significant contribution to postmodern views of representation and reality. Reed's (1985) 'social practice framework' does much to orchestrate and develop many of these themes along postmodern lines. Further, theories of emerging hetero-geneity, disorganization and information dependency in contemporary society (Lash and Urry, 1987; Piore and Sabel, 1984) all suggest that postmodern shifts in organization theory and practices may be essential to the continuing viability of organizations.

Yet, moving toward fully developed theory within the postmodern context is not an easy task. It is difficult, for one, to generate theories where there is no existing forestructure of intelligibility to be extended and elaborated. And the postmodern turn does remove the luster from tradi-tional argots of understanding; that is, romanticist and modernist. So, if we do not base theories on conceptions of rationality, motivation, emotion and the like, where do we turn? Of equal importance, how can we take the process of theory construction seriously? If we cannot offer truth, objective accounts removed from our own valuational biases, then on what grounds can any new formulations be justified? If there are no foundations for theoretical formulations, and these are only linguistic constructions, then why play the fool – whose serious words turn to mere posturing in the hands of the deconstructionist critic?

As I have tried to indicate throughout this chapter, and most succinctly in my cautions about theoretical playfulness, the theorist is not rendered voiceless by postmodern argumentation. To be sure, there is little reason to suppose that theories are pictures, and that the concept of truth is more than hand waving. Yet, we are moved to silence only if persuaded by the modernist presumption that objective truth is the only game in town. If the function of theories is *not* derived from their truth value, but from their pragmatic implications, then the theoretical voice is restored to significance. And the potential of theoretical work is far greater than that assigned to it under modernist conditions. For under modernism, the proper theory should be fortified with years of research, and its applica-tion undertaken by yet another culture (the practitioners). In the postmodern context, the primary ingredient of theory is not its data base but its intelligibility, and the very communication of this intelligibility already establishes grounds for its utility. Theory and practice are inseparable.

The postmodern theorist confronts, then, the following condition: There is no language of understanding placed beyond the boundaries of potential. That is, the postmodern need not fear the resuscitation of romanticist language, nor abhor all that is modernist. All such formula-tions enable or abet certain patterns of action, or solve certain kinds of problems. Nor should these forms of discourse be viewed as our only sources of theoretical intelligibility. Not only does Western culture have a long and richly laminated history of conceptualization, but we are continuously in the process of absorbing other cultural intelligibilities into our own. Like the postmodern architect, we should feel free to draw from the entire repository of potentials within human history.

At the same time, we must pause before partaking, to ask more critically into the potentials of such work. We must inquire not only into the kinds of cultural patterns served or discredited by given theoretical positions, but also into the potential for theories to offer new alternatives and options to the culture (both organizational and otherwise). Elsewhere I have spoken of a *generative* criterion for evaluating theory; that is, evaluating a theory in terms of its challenge to the taken-for-granted and its simultaneous capacity to open new departures for action (Gergen, 1982). It is in this latter respect that I find myself currently drawn to bodies of postmodern writings themselves. For in my view, these writings furnish a new and exciting forestructure for theorizing about the organization. We may fruitfully extend, elaborate, and transform this argot of understanding in ways that open new options for action within the organization. It is to this latter possibility that the remainder of the present chapter is devoted.

Power, Signification and Organizational Efficacy

The concept of power has been of enormous significance to the traditional understanding of organizational life (see Clegg's 1989 review). At the same time, conceptions of power have typically been wedded to the existing conventions of understanding within the culture. Thus, from the romanticist perspective, power is often equated with personal capabilities: drive, determination, intelligence, inspiration, insight, charisma, and the like. With modernism, power is often associated with machine functioning. Thus, depending on the structure of the organizational machine, those occupying certain positions will possess more power than others. Power, on this account, is less a matter of personal depth than one's function within the structure. With Foucault's writings (1978, 1979) playing a pivotal role, however, we find these traditional views no longer viable within the postmodern sphere. And, while Foucault's work is richly suggestive, it does not fully articulate an alternative view of power. In this regard, I have viewed with keen interest the work of Robert Cooper and Gibson Burrell (1988) on postmodern organization analysis. They too have been drawn by the possibilities of elaborating postmodern discourse into a theory of organizational life. I would like to use two of the central concerns in their 1988 paper as the beginning point of the present offering. These concerns are, first, the indeterminacy of meaning and, second, the resulting tension between forces for organization and disorganization. I wish, however, to extend these concerns to lay out the conceptual scaffolding for a theory of organizational power and efficacy. For purposes of clarity, the arguments will be developed around five emblematic themes.

Indeterminate Rationalities

Let us begin with a simple focus on the organizational manager. For the most part managerial functions are essentially discursive; they are carried out by means of language. Further, it is incumbent on the manager to make sense within the confines of the organization. Thus, the typical manager will draw from the repository of wise, perspicacious or 'true' sayings within the particular subculture of the firm to generate intelligibility. Or to put it another way, he or she manages the available language conventions to achieve a sense of rationality as defined within the organization.

The postmodern drama begins, however, with the realization that the 'rational sayings' available to the individual are of indeterminate meaning. Derrida's (1974) concept of *différance* is most applicable here for, as Derrida proposes, the meaning of any word or phrase is derived from a process of *deferral* to other words or phrases that *differ* from itself (with the single concept, *différance*, representing the simultaneous and conflated processes). Thus, for example, a bit of corporate rationality embodied in the words 'Let's be logical about this; the bottom line would be the closing of the Portsmouth division' does not carry with it a transparent meaning. Rather, its meaning depends on what we make of words like 'logical' 'bottom line' 'closing' and the like. These meanings require that we defer to still other words. What does the speaker mean by the term 'logical' for example? To answer we must defer to other words, like 'rational' 'systematic', or 'coherent'.

But the plot now thickens, for at the outset it is clear that there are multiple meanings for such terms as 'logical', 'bottom line' and the like. Or, as it is said, they are *polysymous*; they have been used in many contexts, and thus bear 'the trace' (in Derrida's terms) of many other terms. For example, 'logical' can also mean 'right thinking', 'conventional', or 'superior'. Which of these does the speaker really intend? Yet, again, convolutions of complexity; for, as we find, each term employed for clarifying the initial statement is itself opaque until the process of *différance* is again set in motion. 'Right thinking' can also mean 'morally correct', 'conventional' can also mean 'banal', and so on. And in turn, these terms bear the traces of numerous others in an ever-expanding network of significations. What seemed on the surface to be a simple, straightforward piece of wise advice, on closer inspection can mean virtually anything.

Cooper and Burrell (1988) are particularly concerned with the ironic self-negation underlying this spread of signification. Drawing importantly from Derrida's works, they see the possibility (if not the theoretical necessity) for every saying to imply its contradiction. To affirm something is to set in motion a chain of signification that simultaneously confirms its negation. (In simplest terms, for example, the exhortation 'Let's be logical about this . . .' is to make reference to the possibility of irrationality, which possibility is affirmed by the nature of the exhortation itself . . . which is not logically grounded.)

Social Supplementarity

Because of the fundamental undecidability of language meaning, it is often said by deconstruction theorists that signifiers are 'free floating'. Their meaning is never fixed, always in motion, ever demurring. Yet, while this is so in principle, in practice signifiers do not float freely. The advice 'Let's be logical . . .' does not, in practice, simply mean anything including its negation. Its definition is circumscribed or contained, and this containment is to be located within the social milieu. The speaker signifies, but a supplement is required to determine its meaning: it is the listener who supplies the supplement. More concretely, this is to say that managers themselves are never rational; their sayings are never wise or realistic. Their rationality, wisdom or objectivity is dependent on their colleagues, for it is their colleagues who supply the interpretations of the sayings. Rationality is pre-eminently a product of social collaboration.

It is important to emphasize at this point that such products are both transient and local. Both speakers and listeners are, in the first instance, free to resignify at any time. Managers may reframe their sayings over time; colleagues may reinterpret. Rationalities are never written in stone. Further, as a given saying proliferates across different social settings, its meanings may undergo further change. Each attempt to decode the original is yet another encoding. And these encodings are open-ended, undecidable until constrained by listeners. A manager's words, then, are like authorless texts; once the words are set in motion, the manager ceases to control their meaning. They are possessions of the community.

Power as Social Coordination

As this analysis makes clear, traditional conceptions of power as inhering either in individuals or in organizational flow charts must be abandoned. It is not individual actors who, either by dint of personal style or office location, possess power. Actors do not control the fate of their expressions; we are empowered only through the actions of others. Let us reconsider the problem of power, then, from a postmodern perspective. In particular, let us begin by defining power roughly as the *capacity to achieve specified ends*. If we do so, then we find at least two components essential for the existence of power. First, it is necessary to *articulate criteria for the achievement of power*. (For many people, for example, the power of a corporation is defined in terms of its capital assets.) The achievement of this initial component is inherently social, requiring co-ordinated agreements among participants. In effect, there is a mutual agreement regarding the containment of the signifiers. As a second component of power, a range of *activities must be coordinated* around the achievement of these locally defined ends. Such activities will include both discourse and other forms of action. This is to say that participants must generate constraints over the free play of signifiers, and confine their activities to those which fit the language so constrained. (We may agree, for example, that 'bottom line' is a financial tally – gains minus losses – and that activities called 'investment' and 'market evaluation' are important to achieving a satisfactory bottom line.) In effect, then, power is inherently a matter of social interdependence, and it is achieved through the social coordination of actions around specified definitions.

Power as Self-Destructive

As social units achieve power, so do they simultaneously architect its undoing. This is chiefly so because the achievement of coordination within a group erects a barrier between it and adjoining communities of signification. Not only are its own signifiers prevented from escaping, or playing into the surrounding languages, but the languages of the surrounding milieu fail to enter the coordinated unit. In this sense the unit fails to achieve the kinds of supplementarity in meaning that would enable its self-contained definitions to be honored from without, and it fails to supplement the meanings of others in ways that would invite reciprocation and further coordination. To illustrate: within organizations divisions of marketing, personnel, planning, production and the like each attempt to achieve power of functioning. In doing so, each develops local definitions of the real and the good and coordinates its actions around these definitions. However, as power of functioning is achieved within each group, signification is solidified – as it must be for reliable coordination of actions among persons. And, as local criteria of the real and the good are solidified, so do members of these divisions become insulated against the realities of the adjoining divisions. Their languages seem progressively alien, unreal, possibly erroneous or foolish. And their own reality becomes rarefied and opaque within the adjoining worlds. In effect, as each unit becomes increasingly powerful within itself, so is the organization as a whole disenabled – with the ultimate end being the destruction of all.

Much the same situation holds in terms of the relationship of an organization to its broader social surrounds. With attention given to a common language – where all definitions of means and ends are shared – participants may coordinate themselves to achieve an efficient and effective organization. Conflict, misunderstandings, ambiguities, and the like are all minimized, and power is maximized. Yet, if their internal view of 'efficient production' is seen as a 'local sweatshop' from without, their 'effective disposal system' is defined from without as 'industrial pollution', their 'reasonable policy of equal employment' is regarded as 'racist', their 'effective computerization' is perceived as 'hopelessly out of date' and their 'innovative line of merchandise' is described as 'derivative', then the organization slowly perishes. Its local realities fail to penetrate the public arena, and the public array of signifiers fail to enter the internal system.

Heteroglossia and the Recovery of Efficacy

What we find is that as organizations strive to achieve power of operation, so must they coordinate themselves within. Such an achievement requires the arresting of meaning, the containment of signifiers. At the same time, this achievement carries with it an ultimate cost, which is the very negation of the power originally sought. Required, then, are means for sustaining organizational efficacy, for creating a dynamic tension between empowerment and disempowerment. Cooper and Burrell (1988) are again drawn to this possibility in their emphasis (following Lyotard) on the balance of consensus and dissensus. For them, full consensus within an organization robs it of its vitality, for that which makes consensus possible, namely dissensus, is negated. Organizational vitality thus depends on restoring the process of *differance*. My own argument rests less on principled issues of linguistic antinomy than on more practical considerations of language and social coordination. However, the resulting conclusion is much the same: to restore efficacy the signifiers must be set free. The result will threaten the power base of the organization as constituted; at the same time it will set in motion a process by which power will be reconstituted – but now within a broader social network.

To explicate, it is useful to draw again from the domain of literary theory. Specifically, the Russian literary theorist Mikahil Bakhtin (1981) has introduced the term *heteroglossia*, referring at least in one of its uses to the fact that the languages of any culture thrive on polyglot. Thus, as we speak English we are borrowing as well from the French, German, Norse, Spanish, Italian, and so on. And we are, as well, falling back on linguistic forms from previous cultural periods, and from a mixture of subcultures. Essentially, there are no thoroughbred languages, and the very capacities of the language for flexibility and multiple usage depend on this fact. In this case let us reconstitute Bakhtin's concept of heteroglossia as a dimension. That is, we can view organizations (or their sub-units) as varying in the degree to which they incorporate the discursive forms of surrounding cultures (or other organizational units). Following the argument that the constitution of power is ultimately self-destructive, it follows that organizations acting to increase internal heteroglossia, up to a point, are those most capable of surviving in postmodern society. That is, an active emphasis must be placed on (1) sharing organizational realities across sub-units within a firm, (2) exporting organizational realities into the outside culture, and (3) enabling external realities to enter freely into organizational life.

On a practical level such a conclusion leads in a variety of different directions. Attention is invited to ways in which members of various organizational sub-units can shift from one locale to another within the firm, incorporating diverse viewpoints, values, and modes of action. Such shifting should be undertaken in such a way that consensus within any unit is constantly contested. The emphasis is removed from developing and implementing strong and rational leadership, the voice of which attempts to dominate decision-making throughout the firm. Centrality is displaced by heterogeneity and an *ad hoc*ing through the complexities of an ever shifting sea of meaning and action. Rationality becomes situated, expendable or defeasible as context and contingency are altered. Means must also be sought for pressing the localized realities of the organization into the public sphere. As they are shared within the surrounding cultures, they will be transformed. They will meet with resistance, alternative interpretations, metaphoric replacements, gouging and distortion. However, in the process the organizational realities are married to the realities of the surrounding culture. Although not in its own terms, the organization becomes intelligible to the social surrounds.

Finally, means must be sought for opening the organizational doors to alien realities. For example, minority voices, voices of dissensus within the organization, must be invited to speak out; and, although unsettling the fluid operation of the organization, their messages must be made intelligible, absorbed and integrated. Organizational members should also be encouraged in alternative pursuits – to master alternative argots, from various fields of study, politics, sports, the arts, foreign cultures, specialty clubs, and the like. Instead of detracting from the time devoted to organizational ends, and engendering 'peculiar' points of view, such extraneous pursuits will enrich the realm of signification within. Minority hiring should not be viewed as an obligation so much as an opportunity for expanding the discursive (and practical) capacities of the organization. And organizations might wisely invite criticism – from various political, intellectual and moral corners – not with an intent to improve their defensive skills, but to understand and incorporate alternative realities. Again, constant challenges to the smooth coordination of internal realities are essential to organizational vitality. Or, more bluntly, if everything is running smoothly the organization is in trouble.

The result of this constant challenge to naturally occurring tendencies toward consensus will be, from the present standpoint, the prevention of hegemonic tendencies of various sub-units (including high-level management) within the firm and the more complete integration of the organization into the surrounding environment. In the first instance, this will mean a more fully developed integration of the internal segments of the organization. In the second, it will mean that the organization and the surrounding culture will come to form a more thoroughly symbiotic relationship. The tendency to view the organization as an autonomous, self-contained system will recede, and instead, the organization's outcomes will become inseparable from those of the broader community. The misleading distinction between *inside* and *outside* the organization will blur. Ultimately we may be able to see the end of the Hobbesian view of cultural life, along with the demise of the free market as a zero-sum game. For as organizations join with their surrounding cultures for purposes of mutual empowerment, and the circle of interdependence is ever widened, we may become aware of the world as a total system.

References

Argyris, C. (1980) *Inner Contradictions of Rigorous Research*. NY: Academic Press.

Bakhtin, M. (1981) *The Dialogic Imagination: Four Essays by M.M. Bakhtin* (trans. M. Holquist). Austin, TX: University of Texas Press.

Barnes, B. (1974) *Scientific Knowledge and Sociological Theory*. London: Routledge & Kegan Paul.

Barthes, R. (1964) *Elements of Semiology*. London: Jonathan Cape.

Berman, M. (1982) *All that is Solid Melts into Air*. NY: Simon & Schuster.

Bhagat, R. (1983) 'Intellectual performance and utilization in a two-paradigm administrative and organizational science: A philosophy of science-based assessment', in R.H. Kilmann and K. Thomas and associates (eds), *Producing Useful Knowledge for Organizations*. NY: Praeger.

Billig, M. (1987) *Arguing and Thinking*. London: Cambridge University Press.

Bion, W.R. (1959) *Experience in Groups*. NY: Basic Books.

Bradbury, M. and McFarlane, J. (1976) *Modernism, 1890–1930*. Harmondsworth: Penguin.

Burke, K. (1968) *Language as Symbolic Action*. Berkeley: University of California Press.

Clegg, S. (1989) *Frameworks of Power*. London: Sage.

Cooper, R. and Burrell, G. (1988) 'Modernism, post modernism, and organizational analysis: An introduction', *Organizational Studies*, 91–112.

Cooperider, D.L. and Srivastva, S. (1987) 'Appreciative inquiry into organization life', *Research in Organizational Change and Development*, 1: 129–69.

Dachler, H.P. (forthcoming) 'Constraints on the emergence of new vistas in leadership and management research: An epistemological overview', Saint Gall Graduate School of Economics, Law, Business and Public Administration. Switzerland.

DeMan, P. (1979) 'Shelley disfigured', in H. Bloom, P. DeMan, J. Derrida, G. Hartman and J.H. Miller (eds), *Deconstruction and Criticism*. NY: Continuum.

Denhardt, R.B. (1981) *In the Shadow of Organization*. Lawrence, KA: Regents Press.

Derrida, J. (1974) *Of Grammatology*. Baltimore: Johns Hopkins University Press.

Fiedler, F., Chemers, M. and Mahan, L. (1976) *Improving Leadership Effectiveness: The Leader Match Concept*. NY: John Wiley & Sons.

Fish, S. (1980) *Is there a Text in this Class? The Authority of Interpretive Communities*. Cambridge, MA: Harvard University Press.

Foucault, M. (1978) *The History of Sexuality*. NY: Random House.

Foucault, M. (1979) *Discipline and Punish*. NY: Vintage.

Frisby, D. (1985) *Fragments of Modernity*. Oxford: Polity.

Garfinkel, H. (1967) *Studies in Ethnomethodology*. Englewood Cliffs, NJ: Prentice-Hall.

Gergen, K.J. (1982) *Toward the Transformation in Social Knowledge*. NY: Springer-Verlag.

Gergen, K.J. (1985) 'Social pragmatics and the origin of psychological discourse', in K.J. Gergen and K.E. Davis (eds), *The Social Construction of the Person*. NY: Springer-Verlag.

Gergen, K.J. and Davis, K.E. (eds) (1985) *The Social Construction of the Person*. NY: Springer-Verlag.

Goodman, N. (1978) *Ways of Worldmaking*. NY: Hackett.

Habermas, J. (1975) *Legitimation Crisis*. Boston, MA: Beacon Press.

Habermas, J. (1981) 'Modernity versus postmodernity', *New German Critique*, 22: 3–14.

Harding, S. (1986) *The Science Question in Feminism*. Ithaca, NY: Cornell University Press.

Harré, R. (1986) 'The social constructionist viewpoint', in R. Harré (ed.), *The Social Construction of Emotion*. Oxford: Basil Blackwell.

Hollander, E. (1958) 'Competence, status and idiosyncrasy credit', *Psychological Review*, 65: 117–27.

Homans, G.C. (1974) *Social Behavior in its Elementary Forms*. NY: Harcourt Brace Jovanovich.

Ilgen, D. and Klein, H. (1989) 'Organizational behavior', in M. Rosenzweig and L. Porter (eds), *Annual Review of Psychology*, 40: 327–52.

Jacques, E. (1955) 'Social systems as a defence against persecutory and depressive anxiety', in M. Klein (ed.), *New Directions in Psycho-analysis*. London: Tavistock.

Keller, E.F. (1985) *Reflections on Gender and Science*. New Haven: Yale University Press.

Knorr-Cetina, K.D. (1981) *The Manufacture of Knowledge*. Oxford: Pergamon.

Kristeva, J. (1977) *Polylogue*. Paris: Seuil.

Kristeva, J. (1980) *Desire in Language: A Semiotic Approach to Literature and Art*. NY: Columbia University Press.

Kuhn, T.S. (1970) *The Structure of Scientific Revolutions* (second revised edition). Chicago, IL: University of Chicago Press.

Lash, S. and Urry, J. (1987) *The End of Organized Capitalism*. Cambridge: Polity Press.

Latour, B. (1987) *Science in Action*. Cambridge, MA: Harvard University Press.

Lawrence, P. and Lorsch, J. (1967) *Organization and Environment*. Cambridge, MA: Harvard Graduate School of Business Administration.

Lawson, H. (1985) *Reflexivity, the Post Modern Predicament*. London: Hutchinson.

Lyotard, J.F. (1984) *The Post Modern Condition: A Report on Knowledge*. Minneapolis: University of Minnesota Press.

McGregor, D. (1960) *The Human Side of Enterprise*. NY: McGraw-Hill.

Maslow, A.H. (1961) 'Peak experiences as acute identity experiences', *American Journal of Psychoanalysis*, 21: 254–60.

Mayo, E. (1933) *The Human Problems of an Industrial Civilization*. NY: Macmillan.

Menzies, I. (1960) 'A case study in the functioning of social systems as a defence against anxiety', *Human Relations*, 13: 95–121.

Mitroff, I. (1984) *Stakeholders of the Mind*. San Francisco: Jossey-Bass.

Morgan, G. (1986) *Images of Organization*. London: Sage.

Pasmore, W. and Friedlander, F. (1982) 'An action research program for increasing employee involvement in problem solving', *Administrative Science Quarterly*, 27: 343–62.

Pearce, W.B. and Cronen, V.E. (1980) *Communication, Action and Meaning*. NY: Praeger.

Pepper, S. (1972) *World Hypotheses*. Berkeley: University of California Press.

Piore, M.J. and Sabel, C.F. (1984) *The Second Industrial Divide: Possibilities for Prosperity*. NY: Basic Books.

Potter, J. and Wetherall, M. (1987) *Discourse and Social Psychology*. Beverly Hills: Sage.

Quine, W.V.O. (1960) *Word and Object*. Cambridge, MA: MIT Press.

Reason, P. (1988) *Human Inquiry in Action*. London: Sage.

Reed, M. (1985) *Re-directions in Organizational Analysis*. London: Tavistock Publications.

Rorty, R. (1979) *Philosophy and the Mirror of Nature*. Princeton: Princeton University Press.

Salaman, G. and Thompson, K. (1981) *Control and Ideology in Organizations*. Cambridge, MA: MIT Press.

Schein, E.H. (1990) 'Organizational culture', *American Psychologist*, 45: 109–19.

Schwartz, B. (1986) *The Battle for Human Nature*. NY: Norton.

Shotter, J. (1980) 'Action, joint action and intentionality', in M. Brenner (ed.), *The Structure of Action*. Oxford: Basil Blackwell.

Sloterdijk, P. (1987) *Critique of Cynical Reason*. Minneapolis: University of Minnesota Press.

Smith, K. and Berg, D. (1987) 'A paradoxical conception of group dynamics', *Human Relations*, 40: 633–58.

Srivastva, S. and Barrett, F.J. (1988) 'The transforming nature of metaphors in group development: A study in group theory', *Human Relations*, 41: 31–64.

Steier, F. (ed.) (1991) *Research and Reflexivity*. London: Sage.

White, H. (1978) *Tropics of Discourse*. Baltimore: Johns Hopkins University Press.

Wittgenstein, L. (1963) *Philosophical Investigations* G. Anscombe. NY: Macmillan.

Zaleznick, A. (1970) 'Power and politics in organizational life', *Harvard Business Review*, 48: 47–60.

12

Re-writing Gender into Organizational Theorizing: Directions from Feminist Perspectives

Marta B. Calás and Linda Smircich

By the time you get to this chapter you may feel there is little more to be said toward 'rethinking organization'. The previous chapters have already pointed to at least two areas of concern in academic circles: world conditions are changing and our theories lag behind; and more generally, theorizing itself is now seen as a problematic activity. Similar to other authors in this book we address both concerns, but from a different point of departure and perhaps with a different 'destination' in mind.

With our title 'Re-writing Gender into Organizational Theorizing' we mean to suggest that gender has been written into organizational theorizing in incomplete and inadequate ways and that organizational analysis has understood gender very narrowly. We would like to alter that understanding.

A few years ago this may have been our only objective. That is, our earlier concerns were with how gender had been mis- or under-represented in organization theory, and we were concerned with correcting the record. Today, under the inspiration of feminist poststructuralist theory, we mean to suggest more with our title. We want to explore how the idea of 'gender' can be a strategy through which we can question what *has been represented* as organization theory. And further, we want to begin to discuss how that questioning may lead to a different way of writing 'organization'.

The ideas for this chapter are drawn from feminist theory, and the history of feminist theorizing has influenced how we have organized it. But despite the phrase 'feminist theory' there is no single feminist *theory*. Rather, feminist theory covers the scholarly terrain, from the biological sciences to the social sciences to literature and philosophy. Diverse theoretical perspectives are joined together under the name 'feminist' because of their shared concern with gender relations and gender arrangements, and because of their concern for social change.

Since the early 1970s there has been an explosion of production of feminist scholarship in various disciplines. However, with a few exceptions (such as Alvesson and Billing, nd; Balsamo, 1985; Calás and Smircich, 1989; Donelson et al., 1985; Grant, 1988; Hearn and Parkin, 1987;

Hearn et al., 1989; Jacobson and Jacques, 1989; Marshall, 1984, 1989; Martin, 1990; Mills, 1988), this discussion has been going on *outside* the borders of organization theory. One point to emphasize at the start of our chapter is that feminist theorists would recognize that we are saying little that is new. The only thing new is its location – in a conversation about reshaping organizational theorizing. Another caveat, we are writing from the standpoint of women academics in a school of management in the United States, and so our location orients us in particular ways. Others, located differently, may understand these ideas differently.

Our purpose is to summarize some of the important aspects of feminist literature and use them to help us rethink our field. Our purpose is not to argue that feminist theory is 'good' and that organization theory is 'bad', or that feminist theory should replace organization theory. Instead we wish to call attention to areas of intersection. It is our opinion, however, that while feminist theory won't replace organization theory, an encounter of organizational theory with feminist theorizing may render organization theory as we know it unrecognizable.

In the rest of the chapter we look very briefly from the vantage point of the history of feminist theorizing at the ways organization theory has considered gender. Then we begin to investigate how we may write gender differently. Our discussion is organized around three important activities in the history of feminist 'knowing' that we label: 're-vising' 're-flecting' and 're-writing'. After explaining these we discuss their implications for organizational theorizing. We do not intend to propose some possibly utopian views about feminine organizing and managing. Rather, we want to pose what we see as more immediate questions: How is organization theorizing (male) gendered and with what consequences? And how may organizational theorizing be rewritten through 'gender'?

What is Feminist Theorizing?

There is variety in feminist scholarship, yet it is all addressed to the subject of gender (for example, A. Ferguson, 1989). 'The single most important advance in feminist theory is that the existence of gender relations has been problematized. Gender can no longer be treated as a simple, natural fact' (Flax, 1987: 627).

At least two distinct issues are at the root of feminist theorizing: a particular form of gender relations – patriarchy – (male dominance), is fully assumed; and changes from this form of domination are sought. These are minimum conditions in the development of feminist theoretical positions; but they are ascribable to a wide range of social and political viewpoints, and to an even wider range of issues from the personal to the institutional to society at large.

Early feminist theorizing distinguished between 'sex' (biologically based) and 'gender' (a social construction) (Oakeley, 1972). On a TV talk show recently this was explained simply as 'sex is between your legs and gender is between your ears'. While apparently helpful at first for opening a theoretical space to explore gender as a socially constructed category, feminist theorists realized this distinction could not be maintained for very long. Doing so obscures how humans live – in *both* a physical, material body and a socially, historically constituted ideational space. To oppose biological sex against socially constructed gender accepts the idea of a separate non-culturally mediated body. It maintains the idea that biology (the body) is separate from culture (the mind).

Later feminist theorizing does not accept this distinction. Instead its focus is on gender *relations*. It is through gender relations that 'men' and 'women', two categories of persons, are created and their bodies connected to culture. From this perspective, both men and women are 'prisoners of gender', although in different ways (Flax, 1987; Scott, 1986).

How Has Gender Been Written into Organizational Theorizing?

For the moment, the analytical distinction between sex and gender *is* helpful for understanding the situation in organizational theorizing. This is because organizational theorizing has been explicitly and primarily concerned with sex and not gender.

The organizational literature that supposedly considers gender has been labelled the 'women-in-management' literature. It is relatively recent, coinciding with the second wave of the women's liberation movement and associated civil rights legislation in the 1960s and 1970s which brought more women into previously male-dominated professions. The 'women in management' label reveals that gender is important to organizational theorizing only because the biological entities – women – suddenly arrived into management, changing the nature of the situation. Prior to the entrance of women there is (apparently) no 'gender' in *man*agement.

But, as we will argue later, gender *has* been present all along, even if ignored or repressed (Hearn et al., 1989). However, most organizational theorizing treats issues of gender as collapsed into the category of sex: a biologically determined variable easily measured. And further, sex is reduced to the category 'women'. This approach to sex/gender helps maintain organizational theorizing's traditional premises.

For example, Calás and Jacques (1988) found that the women in management literature represented issues and theories identical to traditional micro organizational behavior research. And Jacobson and Jacques (1989) noticed that it appeared as if only women were gendered. The implicit formula underlying the literature is gender = sex = women = problem. And 'solving the problem' has been mostly equivalent to 'masculinizing' the defective as a normalizing practice. Producing this literature required no 're-thinking'. Instead a concept – 'women' – was grafted onto the pre-existing structures of questioning. The same pattern was seen in the USA in our professional organization, the Academy of

Management, when a new Women in Management division was established; and it too was added onto the pre-existing structure.

What is missing is recognition of the wider operation of gender relations – how women are denied a normal presence in organization theory and how the male presence becomes the standard on the basis of that denial. Thus in spite of the pervasiveness of gender relations as a social issue in the USA, and of sex and gender in the workplace as dominant structural principles, organization theory has succeeded in 'taming' sex and ignoring 'gender' in its discourses of knowledge. But has it?

Writing Gender Differently: Three Activities in Feminist
Theorizing with Relevance for Organizational Theorizing

In organizational analysis gender has been mostly another variable in an otherwise (presumably) neutral constellation of empiricist works. But there are other ways to consider gender, and feminist theories and theorizing offer powerful insights for understanding its dynamics. In our view the major 'new direction' that feminist theorizing offers to organizational analysis is that it raises the problem of the 'genderedness' of knowledge. It means asking the question: *How is organization theorizing (male) gendered, and with what consequences*?

We have organized our discussion around three epistemological activities from the history of feminist 'knowing': the *'activity of re-vising'*, the *'activity of re-flecting'*, and the *'activity of re-writing'*. These three activities seem to be, from our standpoint, necessary steps for formulating more appropriate conceptualizations for today's world, but only recently have they been conceived as distinct *and* necessary. Taken together, they comprise more fully formed theoretical positions than they would separately, even if – as we will discuss – paradoxically so. In conjunction they can provide a very strong basis for re-examining any traditional disciplinary body of knowledge. Thus, inspired by these activities, we raise some questions and issues that may help us reconceptualize organizational theorizing.

Revising the Record: How Patriarchy Shows Up in Knowledge

Feminist scholars have been re-examining and re-vising the production of knowledge in their disciplines. Early work called attention to exclusionary institutional arrangements. But then attention shifted from equity issues to examination of the consequences of women's absence as knowledge producers. They questioned the extent to which the historical under-representation of women as scholars skewed the choice of research problems and biased the design of research and the interpretation of results.

At the same time, universities in the USA established Women's Studies programs and departments in response to the women's movement. These provided the context for much of the feminist scholarship done since the 1970s. Faculty members teaching Women's Studies courses usually hold positions in a disciplinary department and split their time between units. This structure has contributed to the multidisciplinary character of much feminist scholarship.

Below we sketch very briefly the epistemological questioning feminist scholars addressed to their disciplines. For purposes of illustration we consider feminist writing in history, psychology, anthropology, and literature. Our review shows that feminist theorizing has problematized 'knowing' as an already (male) gendered sphere of action. It traces changing concerns, paraphrasing Sandra Harding, 'from the woman question in knowledge' to 'the knowledge question in feminism' (Harding, 1986). Furthermore, the review provides us with a list of questions, summarized in Table 12.1, showing new directions for organization theorists deriving from the activity of re-vising.

Examples of Re-vising Activities

History   What is now referred to as the 'new history' in the USA had its roots in the black civil rights movement and the women's liberation movement. Historical research inspired by these social and political currents offered redefinitions of the American past and pointed out that what has been written as history over the last several hundred years is the history of white men (Degler, 1981; Bernstein, 1988).

For instance, historians researching women's experiences of the settlement of the American frontier by examining documents previously ignored by historians (diaries and letters written by women) found the women's side of the story was quite different. Rather than an heroic adventure, to women, western movement represented tremendous loss and suffering (Faragher and Stansell, 1975). Other accounts of women and slavery (Davis, 1972), women and the industrial revolution (Dublin, 1979), women and the US reform movements of the nineteenth and early twentieth centuries (Freedman, 1981), demonstrated that women were also active agents and not merely victims carried along by the forces of history/men.

Women's history, then, aims to re-write history as herstory, a narrative of women's experiences, and in so doing it fits a new subject – women – into received historical categories (Scott, 1987). These writings offer a more complex picture of history, in effect serving to complete and correct the historical record.

At the same time the very idea of what history is – with its focus on military, political and legal activity – came to be questioned. New topics of investigation such as child bearing, child rearing, prostitution and birth control became legitimate historical subjects (Degler, 1981; Gordon, 1977).

Psychology   Feminist re-vising of knowledge in psychology has also been
wide ranging, looking at who the research subjects were (and were not),
what research questions were investigated (and which were not), and how
results were interpreted, in order to assess the extent of male bias. Some
investigated the one-sidedness of data-gathering (Meyer, 1988); for example, a series of experiments on interpersonal attraction from the late 1960s
to mid-1970s all measured conditions under which men felt attracted
towards women, but not vice versa. Even when the research was done by
women (for example, Walster) it was concerned with assessing the male's
reactions; females were only stimuli.

   A well known example of the one-sidedness of data-gathering is
Gilligan's revision of Kohlberg's research on moral development. Typical
of much research practice, Kohlberg called his a theory of moral development, not a theory of moral development of white, privileged males –
although they formed his sample (Minnich, 1986). When Gilligan did her
study of moral development based on a sample of males *and* females, she
derived two *different* systems of thinking rather than a single general
model. Gilligan characterized these different patterns as moralities of
rights and moralities of care. Gilligan's arguments about women's
'different voice' have generated a lot of debate. She is accused of sustaining a stereotypical view of women and of being guilty of the same universalizing tendencies that characterized Kohlberg's work. Nevertheless, her
work was significant because it called attention to the gendered nature of
standards that were supposedly neutral.

   The imagery of women's 'different voice' was picked up by other
researchers who examined 'women's ways of knowing' (for example,
Belenky et al., 1986). Similar to the work of historians of women, these
writings documented 'women's experience' and asserted it as valid
knowledge in its own right. This research showed how certain values,
more common to male socialization, had come to be accepted as the standard for human beings. It demonstrated that the presupposition involved
in scientific research – that there are generalizable standards for all
humankind – was problematic.

   Feminist re-analysis of psychological research shows also how gender,
politics, and social conditions interweave with the workings of science.
Consider, for example, Witkin's (1940s–70s) research on perception,
which elaborated the psychological construct 'field dependence-
independence'. Witkin concluded that 'as a general rule' women are more
field dependent than men. But is this a neutral description of empirical
reality?

   Haaken (1988) noted that the name of a construct suggests embedded
social assumptions. 'Dependence' has negative connotations in a society
that values autonomy and independence. To Witkin, field independence
represented the higher form of development; he compared field
dependence to childlike behavior and an 'arrest' in development toward
emotional maturity.

But, as Haaken argued, it is entirely possible to have interpreted field dependence in a positive way. That is, the 'inability to separate a stimulus from its embedded context' could mean greater sensitivity to contextual elements in matters of judgement and decision-making. Haaken's analysis detailed how Witkin's findings were consistent with and reproduced prevailing stereotypes of women during the post-war shift in ideas about essential differences between the sexes.

Other researchers questioned the meanings of psychological research on sex differences altogether (Weisstein, 1971; Sadker and Frazier in DuBois et al., 1987; Hochschild, 1973), suggesting that supposed sex differences had their origins in researchers' prejudices about women and in the social institutions in which sexism is sustained.

Anthropology   The period 1972–1976 was characterized by many critiques of male bias in anthropology and by a heightened interest in women's roles (Lamphere, 1987). A well known example is Sally (Linton) Slocum's 'Woman the gatherer: Male bias in anthropology' (1975). Slocum's analysis maintains that the image of 'man the hunter' as the critical factor in human evolution ignored the cooperative activities of women. Traditional anthropological theory maintained that males' hunting activities were the important site for the development of the crucial social skills of cooperation and communication and tool making. In this societal portrait, women wait at home for men to return with dinner; left behind with the children, they contribute little to human evolution. Slocum formulated a theory of evolution that included women's activities in gathering, child bearing, and child rearing. She argued that women's gathering and child raising activities also required complex communication, sharing, cooperation, and tool and container making. Her analysis presented a counter-argument that women's gathering activities rather than men's big-game hunting were the key factor in human evolution. Her work demonstrated that it matters who is doing the interpreting.

In another critique of a male perspective on culture, Annette Weiner (1976) revised Malinowski's picture of the Trobrianders. Weiner believed that Malinowski did not give enough importance to women's roles in the exchanges so central to Trobriand life (Shapiro, 1981). She focused on the symbolic dimensions of exchange and argued that Trobriand men and women understood their exchange activities in terms of their beliefs about the complementary roles of women and men in reproduction. Weiner makes the case that Trobriand society values femaleness in a way that Malinowski (and with him male anthropology and male Western society) did not, and so did not see (Shapiro, 1981).

Many writers documented that in various societies the work women did, no matter what it was, was valued less than the work men did. There was variation in culture, but sexual asymmetry (women's subordination) seemed universal. Some anthropologists attempted to explain it (Rosaldo and Lamphere, 1974; Lamphere, 1987). Others challenged this thesis, claiming that the Eskimo and Hopi had egalitarian societies, characterized by separate, but equal, division of labor. Debates continue over how to characterize societies, as do debates over whether sexual asymmetry is universal. Today, however, the trend in anthropology is writing that deals with the particular and the local rather than the general and the universal.

Literature Feminist criticism of literature reassessed the texts that make up the literary canon, the generally accepted 'great books', and reassessed literary theories. Early feminist criticism exposed misogyny in literary practice, including stereotypical images of women in literature as saints or monsters and the exclusion of women from literary history (Showalter, 1985). When the literary canon was re-examined in light of the women's movement its male bias became apparent.

Where were the women authors on the lists of great books used for courses in English and Western civilization? What values guided the choices of masterpieces; which works were the ones that dealt with 'universal' themes? Immediately, similar to what was happening in history, scholars worked to recover the 'lost' or ignored writings of women. This excavation work led to the discovery that women writers had a literature of their own and that its artistic importance and historical and thematic coherence had been invisible under patriarchal values (Showalter, 1985: 6).

In a short time there was an outpouring of scholarship documenting women's literary history as well as developing the notion of a female aesthetic. The idea of a female aesthetic, incorporating the concept of a women's culture and a women's way of writing, paralleled the 'different voice' perspective in psychology. And similarly, it was the subject of controversy. To what extent can one speak of 'women's style', when lesbians and women of color had very different lives and expressive concerns? In the 1970s and 1980s literary studies saw increasing differentiation among types of readers and writers (women, lesbian, gay, people of color, for example). The change of attention, evident in anthropology, from the universal and general to the particular and local was taking place in literary studies as well. The emphasis on differences encouraged even more far reaching questioning about the conceptual grounds of literary criticism and the social practices of reading and writing that have been based entirely on male literary experiences (Showalter, 1985).

Re-vising: Implications for Organizational Theorizing

Based on the activities of re-vising, how would we re-write gender into organizational theorizing? What kinds of questioning would it lead us to ask in organizational theorizing? Table 12.1 summarizes possible new directions for organizational theorizing coming from feminist questioning of related disciplines. Following through with this agenda will enable organizational scholars to study the extent to which organizational theorizing is male gendered. As you read through them, consider to what extent these questions and concerns have made their way into organizational theorizing. And what would be the consequences of answering them?

Table 12.1   *Re-vising organizational theorizing: Directions from feminist revisions of knowledge*

Completing/Correcting the Record
Implies recovering 'lost' women, accounting for women's absence and exclusion, both as subject of inquiry and author of knowledge.
Implies adding in women's contributions and women's experiences.

Assessing Gender Bias in Current Knowledge
Implies retracing the conceptual history of our field to assess the consequences of the under-representation of women.
Implies re-reading our important texts with different eyes. Is there misogyny/sexism in the great books?
Implies systematically retracing the pattern of questioning in multiple streams of research, such as motivation, leadership, career development, organizational life cycle, culture, effectiveness, population ecology, job design, and so on, to assess whose viewpoints are solicited in the research and whose viewpoints are absent?
Implies assessing the extent to which the concepts through which we produce knowledge are male gendered.
Implies reconsidering the underlying values that guide the interpretation of data.

Making the 'New' Organizational Theorizing
Implies that the narratives of organizational theorizing will be more diverse.
Implies that other topics, of more concern to women, will be written into organizational theorizing.
Implies re-thinking the grounds for judging what is true, good, beautiful in organizational theorizing.

Re-writing gender from the perspective of feminist re-vising takes at least two moves: recognizing that gender no longer equals women – therefore *the implicitly male gendered organizational theorizing practices get noticed* – and recognizing that the implicitly male gendered organizational theorizing has kept women's voices silent – therefore *women's voices begin to be written into organizational theorizing.*

In our judgement these moves are just beginning in organizational theorizing. The women's voice/women's experience perspective is beginning to be heard regarding organizational practices (for example, Marshall, 1984; Grant, 1988). Others are noticing the male genderedness of organizational theorizing (for example, Hearn and Burrell, 1989), or questioning the values that are represented in the choice of research questions and the modes of analysis (Calás and Smircich, 1989). However, it is our observation that few researchers discuss this issue. Dachler (1988: 283–4) is an exception in voicing these concerns in relation to leadership research.

> [When] mostly male researchers choose certain issues as important to describe in a primarily male leadership and management population, a choice is made regarding what is 'worthy' or 'interesting' or 'profitable' or 'status enhancing' to be described in the leadership and management world . . . Clearly the kind of leadership traits we choose to investigate, and the methods we use to measure them, tell a story about how we as intelligent and knowledgeable researchers see the subjects we are investigating.

A few years ago we would have stopped our chapter about here. We would have been calling for writing that demonstrates how male bias operates in our field, for work that corrects the record by adding the perspectives from women's voices, and for work that introduces and develops new topics of more concern to women. In fact, this is similar to what one of us did (Smircich, 1985) several years ago. But such a stopping place today would mean not taking part in the changing discourse of feminism. Although feminist theorizing in various disciplines offers blueprints for rethinking the organizational, the later profusion of feminist theorizing has generated additional, more wide ranging, questions that imply even more from us than revising knowledge.

Re-flections on 'Doing the Disciplines': Looking back at Re-vising

At first, feminist inquiry started out to add women in. In this sense, organizational analysis with its 'women-in-management' research paralleled feminist theory. But then feminist inquiry took different turns that organizational analysis has barely begun to consider. The 'women's voice/women's experience' or '(her)story' approaches went further than including women into traditional formulations, to more assertive stances about women's differences as a valid form of representing human experience. The writing moved from noticing the absence of women's accounts to seeing women as agents, to documenting their separate forms of action/writing, to questioning the traditions of the disciplines in which this acting and writing is taking place. It is clear that feminist scholarship represents both a sophisticated area of inquiry and a growth industry in academic publishing. But has it been successful?

From a conventional perspective many would raise an eyebrow to this question. Aren't 'Women's Studies' programs, and their acceptance and legitimation in academic circles, a clear measure of success? What more do women want?

However, in feminist circles there are second thoughts about the meanings of this 'success'. These concerns emerge from the *strong political awareness* underlying feminist epistemological positions, and from their mistrust of any definition of success which does not consider the complex consequences stemming from any one 'gain'.

Recent writings are repeatedly calling attention to feminist 'theoretical unrest'. As feminist scholars engaged in revisionist approaches to their disciplines, rather than a coherent 'feminist perspective', their efforts created fragmented feminist theorizing. They reproduced the plurality of disciplines and the plurality of approaches (such as liberal, socialist, Marxist, Freudian, Object Relations, and so on) rather than any unified feminist perspective. This theoretical variety has become problematic, especially when it is followed by the question 'which account is the best account?' (Jaggar and Rothenberg, 1984; Glazer, 1987; A. Ferguson, 1989). But the way the questioning has been posed in 'feminisms' is different from typical epistemological concerns about 'attaining good knowledge'. 'Which account is the best account?' has to be answered with regard to the consequences of the many accounts of feminism(s).

Knowledge on Knowing

The proliferation of feminist epistemological approaches accompanied by reflexivity over the multiplicity of theoretical accounts has returned feminism(s) to philosophy of science. The question, however, has changed from 'What is feminist epistemology?' or 'What is the distinctive character of feminist knowledge?' to 'What is the meaning of epistemological and multiplicity in feminism?'

This 'return to philosophy' raises questions beyond issues of the legitimacy of women's privileged claims to knowledge and the 'crisis' associated with these claims (for example, K. Gergen, 1988). That is, while there is clear awareness of the current problematics posed by knowledge claims based on diverse epistemological tenets and diverse women's experiences – including diverse women's experiences *in theorizing as an activity* – feminist scholars are addressing these issues, at the same time, with regard to their political implications.

Their reflections focus on the following. First, despite existing claims about 'women's ways of knowing', most 'feminist epistemologies' are revised versions of traditional non-feminist epistemological approaches. In that sense the revisions may result only in critiques and distortions, by reversal, of the original theoretical claims while not creating any more adequate theoretical ground. And beyond the issue of epistemological adequacy, 'the very fact that we borrow from these theories', says Sandra Harding (1987: 248), 'often has the unfortunate consequence of diverting our energies into endless disputes with the nonfeminist defenders of these theories: we end up speaking not to other women but to patriarchs'.

Second, even when some traditional epistemological positions provide tenable approaches for feminism, others have consequences which reinforce patriarchal arrangements. For example, feminist empiricism ends up at odds with the traditional model of positivist science when the tenets of neutrality and value-free knowledge are contested by feminist criticism, and when the feminist approach is labelled 'bad science'. Re-vising the record has been particularly difficult in those disciplines that hold on – non-reflexively – to the values of positivist science and empiricism.

Feminist re-visions appear to have more impact in literature, history and
anthropology than in psychology and sociology (Stacey and Thorne, 1985;
Acker, 1987; Smith, 1979). Some feminist scholars still believe that there
is no possible immediate resolution to this impasse in a world where scientific claims are *the* model of knowledge (for example, Harding, 1986,
1987). Others, however, consider the feminist critique of empiricism and
of traditional epistemology in general, as part of a current critique of
knowledge in which feminism should be involved (for example, Hawkesworth, 1989).

Third, the two previous issues become more politically relevant with the
question 'Which women do theory?' As acknowledged by many (for
example, Harding, 1987; Shotter and Logan, 1988; Spelman, 1988;
Collins, 1989) the realization of the diversity of women's experiences,
compounded by race and class, for example – and the difficulties in
legitimizing these 'Others'' knowledge – makes the political nature of
'knowing' and knowledge claims even more salient. This problem extends
beyond the particulars of any feminist theory – whether relevant or not
to 'all women' – to the more general problem of the ways in which the
practices of 'doing knowledge' are structured. This situation, thus, gives
way to another strand in the 'activity of reflecting'.

The Structure of the Women's Place in the Academy

While the content of feminist knowledge has captured a lot of attention
in academic circles and publications, what are the consequences of
creating this knowledge within the structures of the academy? Thus, as
part of feminist epistemology there is also the emerging reflexivity of
sociology of knowledge (Morawski, 1988). There are several areas of
immediate interest. For example, in moving from 'women' to 'gender'
what happens to the political agenda which stood behind the creation of
Women's Studies in the first place? And does widening the scope of questioning – from the problems of women to the problems of gender – in
effect depoliticize feminist inquiry?

The task of going beyond women's studies has often taken the path of
'mainstreaming' women's issues into the traditional curriculum of the
disciplines. Ideally, bringing feminism into the traditional curriculum
means, at the same time, exposing the invisible paradigms that rule what
is taught and how it is taught, and their relation to the ideologies of the
dominant groups in society (see, for example, Andersen, 1987; Reinharz,
1985; Schuster and Van Dyne, 1985). While integrating feminist theory
into the disciplines has been attainable in various cases, it seems that the
critical force of this integration has more often than not failed (see, for
example, Aiken et al., 1987; Glazer, 1987).

Similarly, the social structure of science has been resistant to the critical
impetus brought about by feminist theorizing (for example, Hubbard,
1988; Andersen, 1987; Keller, 1983, 1985; Harding and Hintikka, 1983).

The social construction of science has been explicitly addressed in feminist writings with questions such as 'Which women are excluded from science?' 'How is science taught?' 'What are the scientific research questions that, as feminists, we need to ask?' 'How is difference studied in scientific institutions?' and 'How is the exclusion of women from science related to the way science is thought and done?' (Andersen, 1987). But it seems that little has changed in the practice of science as a result of feminist perspectives.

Images of scientific work as integration of hand, brain and heart (Rose, 1987), or spinning and quilt-making (Rose, 1986), or craft-structured inquiry (Harding, 1987), or non-hierarchical science (Bleier, 1984), have had little impact in traditional scientific approaches. As many now recognize, this situation cannot be understood without recourse to the accorded prestige of the scientific enterprise in the university and society, and to the related emphasis on 'being scientific' which seems required of many disciplines outside the natural sciences (see, for example, Stacey and Thorne, 1985).

Still, other reflections pertain to the specific conditions of academic women as outsiders and marginal even when in tenured positions (see, for example, Aisenberg and Harrington, 1988). This is, indeed, a remark on the pervasiveness of patriarchal arrangements in the university despite many years of feminist theorizing. Patriarchy at 'the site of knowledge' becomes even more present when the possibility of *Men in Feminism* is considered (Jardine and Smith, 1987). It shows the distinct possibility of another privileged space for male academics when they speak 'from the woman's position' (see, for example, Heath, 1987).

Thus, is it even possible to come out of this paradox? Isn't 'doing knowledge' part and parcel of the reproduction of patriarchal conditions of power/knowledge? Explorations of these questions have brought feminism and postmodernism face to face, and into 'the activity of re-writing'. But before we get into that activity we consider some implications of 'the activity of re-flecting' for organizational theorizing.

Re-flecting: Implications for Organizational Theorizing

From the theoretical debates in feminist theorizing some might infer that epistemology in feminism(s) is facing the same unrest which now plagues organizational theorizing. Are we to choose between paradigmatic pluralism or shall we engage in paradigm wars? Such an inference, however, loses sight of the political awareness which defines feminist theories every step of the way. Have we, organizational theorists, been willing to ask how has paradigmatic pluralism changed the ways we do academic life? How many of us are trying to re-evaluate forms of teaching, modes of engagement with the subject matter, research, consulting, relationships with students and colleagues, out of accepting paradigm plurality? We know that some are. But it seems that the only consistent result of at least ten years' worth of paradigmatic pluralism in organization theorizing is additional opportunities for creating 2 x 2 models – or similarly discrete models based on binary logic – to explain, one more time, the meaning(s) of paradigmatic pluralism (for example, Rao and Pasmore, 1989). Otherwise, effort has been spent in controlling pluralism by legislating theoretical or semantic agreements (for example, Webster and Starbuck, 1988; Bacharach 1989; Whetten, 1989), or by subsuming multiplicity into 'higher order constructs' (for example, Poole and Van de Ven, 1989; Osigweh, 1989). These are never-ending (phal)logocentric tasks under the guiding 'gaze' of patriarchy.

Feminism's re-flections, on the other hand, notice epistemological multiplicity and question, first, the depoliticization and neutralization that pluralism and relativism, as much as any totalizing approach, may bring to feminist epistemologies. At the same time, feminism's reflections focus on the institutional norms, on the modes of existence brought about by the knowledge-making enterprise.

To embrace feminist re-visions means also to embrace a reflexivity that constantly assesses the relationship between 'knowledge' and 'the ways of doing knowledge'. The assessment evaluates approaches to knowledge as they reproduce or change existing gender relations and patriarchal models. That is, to move back and forth between 'saying' and 'doing' is a necessary activity for feminist epistemology.

Thus, adopting a feminist stance in organizational theorizing means more than just adding 'a feminist paradigm' to the existing multiplicity. It would mean more than engaging in a revisionary activity regarding exclusions and limitations embedded in content matters. Rather, it would mean embracing the political consequences of having recognized exclusions and limitations under feminist tenets. What would come to the fore would be the gendered principles sustaining the traditional knowledge-making enterprise, including the gendered principles embedded in current paradigmatic pluralism in organization theorizing. This current paradigmatic pluralism is only capable of 'talking about' pluralism, while the knowledge-making enterprise remains untouched.

In summary, the consequences of feminist reflexivity over epistemological issues in organizational theorizing would also imply political engagement over the limits of 'knowledge-making'. It would imply questioning the gendered nature of traditional epistemologies and institutional arrangements, and of the interests they have been serving under the guise of 'knowledge'.

Re-writing Gender Relations

And so we arrive at the space for which the rest of the chapter was the occasion, as if we were waiting to send what was sent already. From the beginning we were re-writing gender relations in organization theorizing. We were doing so *as if it were* others' writings; we were doing so *as* 'talking about re-vising' – showing oppositions and reversing them *as if* they were another's; we were doing so *as if* we were 'talking about re-flecting' – creating an undecidable present/future in a 'we must re-flect'. And so we arrive at the 'trap' of the text. Where do feminism(s) stand (lie?) in postmodernity?

The relationship between feminist epistemology and postmodernism/post-structuralism is an ambiguous one. For example, one can think of the three 'feminist activities' in this paper as feminism's historical impulse towards deconstruction (reversal, undecidability, dissolution). As observed in some writings (for example, Scott, 1988) it is difficult to conceive of the postmodern space without considering that it shares a self-conscious critical and historical relationship with late-twentieth-century feminism. What kind of relationship is it? Before we review some feminist commentaries about this issue, let us acknowledge that the mere attempt to articulate postmodernism is a way to stay out of it. But isn't this also the case with feminism(s) today? Is it possible, then, to define other than a casual intersection between these elusive entities?

As in the previous sections of this chapter, we are focusing on the arguments 'making the rounds' in US academic settings. We are aware of non-American 'post-structuralist feminist' works and their influence in most of the American writings, but we have chosen not to mention them. We are explicitly creating in this writing the elements of our own location, of our own academic setting, and of the conditions under which we perform. And this text, neither inside nor outside of these conditions, should be taken likewise as a performance.

With these caveats in mind, we review some of the intersections and digressions ongoing between feminism(s) and postmodernism.

Postmodernism(s): Have critiqued totalizing theories of 'knowledge', 'justice', or 'beauty'. Consider these ideas rooted in the *modernist* pursuit of transcendent reason, able to separate itself from the body, and from historical time and place.

Feminism(s): Have enacted and supported the postmodernist critiques. They are consistent with feminist concerns regarding the masculine logic embedded in the notions of 'objectivity' and 'reason'. The critiques also provide a basis for avoiding the construction of 'feminist' theoretical accounts which generalize to all women the experiences of Western, white, middle-class women. Explicit discussions of the relationships between feminism(s) and postmodernism include views of feminist theory as possible correction for the androcentrism and political naivety of postmodernism. Conversely, postmodernism would correct essentialist tendencies in feminism by replacing the unitary notions of 'woman' and 'feminine gender identity' with plural and complex conceptions of social identity, treating gender as one relevant strand among others (Fraser and Nicholson, 1988).

Some are skeptical. They see these critiques as a masculine reaction to the principles of the Enlightenment where, after all, only men participated. They question whether it may be too early for feminism to embrace positions against epistemology which would weaken feminist theories (for example, DiStefano, 1990). Others question the alternatives provided by postmodernist positions such as Lyotard's (1984), because on negating privilege to any meta-narrative while accepting the need to adjudicate knowledge claims one may end up privileging some domain of knowledge over others through a hidden criterion. Such would be an unfortunate occurrence if feminist theories had been discounted as just another meta-narrative (see, for example, Benhabib, 1984).

Postmodernism(s): Question the norms of neutrality and objectivity of the academy and its ruling values of universalism and the authority of science. Regarding methods of inquiry, there is a suspicion of generalizations which transcend time, culture, and region.

Feminism(s): Feminist scholarship emerged and gained legitimacy precisely by countering the ruling values of the academy, and by demonstrating how gender had influenced those values. Arguing that all scholarship reflected the perspectives of its creator, feminism promoted a view of the academy where narrowness of knowledge could only be avoided by the inclusion of a multitude of points of views, even if contradictory to one another (for example, Nicholson, 1990).

On the other hand, there are serious concerns regarding the consequences of postmodern relativism for feminism. Harding's (1987) feminist empiricism and standpoint theories are presented as ways to leave intact traditional understandings of the cumulative nature of scientific research and as a way to adjudicate knowledge claims while supporting feminist principles. A particular concern refers to the fate of 'theory' under postmodernism. If the relatively unified notion of 'woman' as theoretical construct has to be abandoned, 'feminist theorizing' may end up being nothing more than a nominalist ontology tied to an individualistic politics. Thus, feminism(s) worry about maintaining theoretical power without totalization (for example, Hartsock, 1987).

Postmodernism(s): Promote celebration of difference. Promotion of human experience(s) and the notion of 'self' as multiple, disjointed, and transient rather than unified, centered, and immutable.

Feminism(s): Recent feminist critiques of 'women's experience', which try to identify the 'ultimate factor' in women's oppression, point at the contradiction of a unitary perspective in feminism. The ideal of inclusiveness claimed by feminism is negated as that *one* 'ultimate factor' would not represent the experience(s) of all women. As expressed by Flax (1987: 633–4), postmodernism helps us see that 'reality can have *a* structure only from the falsely universalizing perspective of the dominant group', which may include privileged women. Thus, on promoting the partiality, ambiguity, and ambivalence of a postmodern 'feminism' she prefers to focus on 'gender relations', which include men and women involved in one of many forms of social domination. A postmodern view of these relations would also deconstruct their assumed stability and order.

Other views are not so comfortable with postmodernist critiques of 'experience' and 'self'. Bordo (1990) focuses on the *body* as both materiality and metaphor to insist that human bodies are limited in their mobility and flexibility and, therefore, situated somewhere and bounded. Theory, representing these limitations, is equivalent to the finite capabilities of human understanding. Bordo considers gender and the bodies of women as a theoretical stopping point which feminism(s) should not lose. Still, on this point it is difficult to find strong disagreements between feminism and postmodernism. As illustrated by Bordo's concerns, the disagreements are mostly expressed within the discourse of post-structuralism rather than outside of it. For example, Alcoff (1988: 435) while openly opposing postmodernism proposes the concept of 'positionality' which calls for a fluid identity of women, where 'being a "woman" is to take up a position within a moving historical context and to be able to choose what we make of this position and how we alter this context'.

Postmodernism(s): View political engagement as temporary alliances, discursive formations, negation of categorization, openness and indetermination.

Feminism(s): Perhaps this is the most difficult postmodern issue for feminism. Some support is found among those who consider postmodernism a viewpoint for current times, justified only by the conditions of the time. Particularly notable is Haraway's (1985) metaphor of Cyborgs as entities which, like the mixed values of the present, violate previous dominant categories. She sees the possibility of a postmodern politics for feminism which rests on a conscious negation of identification with fixed criteria. As such, feminist 'otherness' and 'difference' are paradoxical identities in their multiplicity and contradictions. Regarding the politics of discourse, Scott (1988) supports the power of deconstruction as a form of political engagement for feminism. In deconstructing 'equality-versus-difference' she demonstrates that in a world made up by discursive strategies perhaps the best political tool is a discursive strategy.

However, many are ambivalent about the actual possibilities in these forms of political engagement. For example, Hawkesworth (1989) commends the ways in which post-structuralism has helped our understanding of power/knowledge constellations but she considers that 'rape, domestic violence, sexual harassment . . . are not fictions or figurations that admit of the free play of signification' 1989: 555). Her approach is to maintain a strategic position in the space between world and text while furthering the feminist agenda against patriarchy.

Repeatedly, then, these evaluations maintain the tension between feminism and postmodernism in ambivalent and partial acceptance of the tenets of postmodernism(s) (for example, Haraway 1985; Flax, 1987; Weedon, 1987; Diamond and Quinby, 1988; Kauffman, 1989; Harding, 1990; Nicholson, 1990), while maintaining a critical distance from them. It is clear that for feminism(s) the quarrel with postmodernism(s) is not around a naive hope for the promises of the Enlightenment or around faith in logocentric understandings. Rather, it is a quarrel around *the consequences* of completely abandoning the modern principles when *the powerful* may still be performing and oppressing under these principles. At the same time, the quarrel includes suspicion that the only possible postmodern space may be patriarchal.

Because of postmodern feminism(s)' strong awareness of conditions of domination it is possible for them to maintain a flexible relationship between the traditional 'women's experience' re-visionist approaches – more inspired by a modern sensibility – and the newer 'post-structuralist– feminist' re-writings (for example, Flax, 1990; Kathy Ferguson, forthcoming). 'Post-structuralist feminism' exposes the apparently unimpeachable structures of truth and knowledge in society, and helps to debunk mythical social constructions which silence and oppress many of society's members. 'Women's experiences' construct new possible views. Together they stand in constant tension, since the 'post' position prevents 'women's experiences' from establishing themselves as 'the last word'. They need each other for creating the space which brings society, *constantly*, toward a more just state. But this is a never-ending task given the partiality, ambiguity, and complexity of any understanding in the postmodern. Thus, isn't this doubleness already a postmodern sensibility? And, more importantly, can any of us choose to live or not in the postmodern hyperspace now? Isn't any 'feminism' now necessarily postmodern?

Re-writing Organizational Knowledge

It is impossible to illustrate the contribution of 'postmodern feminism(s)' for organizational theorizing through a commentary. Re-writing *cannot be* a theoretical account (the modern 'talking about') of 'what *might be* re-writing' – even though it may be so if the 'theoretical' commentary is an indefinite deferral of saying 'what might be'. More typically, 're-writing' would be an activity where we can show the politics of a text by calling attention to the strategies of 'truth-making', while leaving the 'original' text under 'erasure' – that is, recognizing that the genre (in this case 'organization theory') must be defined under these strategies, but its 'truth' can still be doubted. At the same time, texts are the primary sites of our political engagement in the academy – they determine our 'location' through the institutional conditions of 'publish or perish' and the consequences of where and how we 'get published'. Our texts are the sites for re-writing.

The postmodern feminist political 'depoliticization' (deconstruction, re-writing) of the text is particularly compelling if one assumes that textual constructions in Western (modern) academic disciplines proceed under a rhetoric of gender relations, subordinating 'the feminine' under 'the masculine'. While this rhetoric is explicit in literature about gender in organizations (such as 'women-in-management'), it is even more interesting to notice its (metaphysical) presence in non-explicitly gendered organizational accounts. Thus, we engage now in some re-writing of 'organization theory' under premises (guise) of 'postmodern feminism'. In our example, gender is not part of the content but, as we will illustrate, it is none the less a very gendered text.

The example comes from a recent article by Karl Weick (Weick, 1989), and this choice, we believe, makes our points stronger. First, the article's topic is theory construction in organizational studies, thus it addresses 'the origin' of our concerns in this chapter. Second, the author is a widely known and admired organization theorist. Third, his ideas and approaches are different from 'the mainstream' in the field, favoring theoretical innovation and eclectic views. Fourth, we enjoy, quote, and support Weick's approaches, and we respect his scholarship. Fifth, we are personally aware of Weick's concern with possible 'sexism' in his work, and of his recent interest in feminist theorizing. For all these reasons, we hope that our re-writings of his words are not seen as an opportunity to engage in an adversarial academic 'game' but as a way to show the inescapable patriarchal (modern) condition of *published* organization theorizing.

Weick:

'Much as theorists may resist the notion, most theory construction depends on conjectures, preserved in well-crafted sentences, that are tested in substitute environments by people who have a stake in the outcome of the test and may be tempted to bias that outcome.'

Calás and Smircich's 're-writings':

Establishes an opposition between theorists and people as a problem. [Theorist = Mind represented in well-crafted sentences, Mind as the origin of knowledge and language as transparent representation of Mind] [People = Body/the flesh, subject to temptation]
Theorists [Mind] may resist, but they/it still suffer from the bias of the People/[Body's] temptation. The opposition of thinker/doer (theorist/people) follows the mind/body Cartesian split and promotes as problematic – devalues – the concrete body

versus the ideal mind. Adam/Eve, male/female, culture/nature, superior/subordinate can easily substitute the opposition theorist/people.

'This is the drama that lies behind trial and error thinking, and it lies close to the surface in much theory construction. However, it is a manageable drama.'

The rhetorical strategy poses as dramatic the previously staged theorist/people opposition. But the danger that lies behind trial and error (the serpent?) can be resolved in the patriarchal dream of transcendence (it is manageable). Thus the drama is heroic not tragic; there can be a return to the site of the 'original sin' which can be overcome in the Promised Land. So the text proceeds:

'The choice is not whether to do mental testing. Instead, the choice is how well this less than ideal procedure can be used to improve the quality of theoretical thinking.'

To arrive in the Promised Land (of knowledge) there is no alternative but to do mental testing ('shed the body'). Purifying oneself (of temptation), one can sacrifice pleasure of the flesh to achieve quality of thought.

'To do better theory, theorists have to "think better". That empty platitude takes on more substance when better thinking is interpreted to mean a more informed and deliberate use of a simulated evolutionary system' (1989: 529; end of text).

And the problem is solved. In the Hegelian progress of Reason, mind and nature overcome their duality, or immature stage, into progressively higher levels of consciousness. The immature stage, however, remains as a memory in the wilderness of animal consciousness which has been superseded. [It allowed the first paragraph to be written.] This recognition of 'having superseded' constitutes, by allowing a comparison, the continuous presence of immature stages in relationship to more advanced ones. Thus, if one reads the Hegelian logic in Weick's paragraphs, the first three paragraphs enacted the stage for 'superseding' in this last one. And as it happened, in his writing Hegel related femininity to lesser stages in the advance of Reason (see, for example, Lloyd, 1984). So it is, after all, Hegel's promised Absolute Knowledge – in a logic 'transcending femininity' and ignoring its own genderedness – which fulfills the Promised Land of the text. 'Simulated evolutionary system' (a higher stage of consciousness) overcomes the mind/body, culture/nature, masculine/feminine splits (since now 'the thinker' can simulate evolution [a technological feat?] and 'think better'. Paradoxically, this paragraph, then, closes the signification of this article [giving 'substance to emptiness' as a way to fulfill the promised progress] by keeping 'open' the possibility of 'better' organization theory.

It is important for us to reiterate that we are not criticizing Weick's intentions in this article, nor are we stating that his language is purposely anti-feminine. We are writing, instead, over his text – as a generic organization theory text – to show how 'the organization theory discourse' is sustained, and made possible, by traces of previous discourses of 'knowledge' and 'reason'. We should acknowledge that a feminist post-structuralist reading of these discourses does not differ significantly from other forms of deconstruction. Re-marking the male genderedness of philosophical discourse in general has often been a concern of deconstruction (for example, Derrida, 1978, 1986; Irigaray, 1985). Our readings here are a way to foreground the limit that 'woman' (the signifier) defines for theoretical discourse (the discourse of 'knowledge' and 'reason') which we all have inherited in what we call disciplines.

Thus we are also writing to argue the *inescapable* condition in which *we* all are, as we cannot avoid this discourse if we want to speak 'organization theory'. At the same time, our writing (re-writings) in this space, calling attention to organization theory's discursive formations through 'feminist theories', is a form of theorizing but is it organization theory? And since we cannot answer one way or the other to that question, we will have to leave it for you, the reader, to make the decision.

Concluding Comments

To summarize this chapter, in re-writing/deconstructing taken-for-granted discourses in organizational theory, our approach first used 're-vising from women's experiences' to notice the absence of women's values and concerns in organizational discourses. Then 'feminist re-flections' helped us consider the political consequences of what we were doing. Who will benefit, who will perish under the structures of domination which control our discourses? Finally, it moved toward 'postmodern feminism' to help us notice how the signs 'woman' and 'feminine' function as general limits in our discourses and institutions, and how they can be deployed to create textual undecidability. In general, feminist re-writing allows us to understand how *normal* organization theorizing can be regarded as normal in so far as we don't question the gender orientation that sustains that 'normality'.

As we close our chapter we want to avow the ambivalence with which we have produced it. We supposed we should have been happy. We were invited to attend a conference, be amongst people whose work we respect, and to write a chapter for this volume. But we're skeptical. After all, although this book is staged for the purposes of re-thinking organizational analysis and pointing to new directions for research, its form is also one for promoting the School of Management at the University of Lancaster, for enhancing the careers of all who participate, and for making a product for Sage. And so it helps to sustain the circumstances it is supposedly re-thinking. Such are the conditions under which we all work and write and speak, and the most we can do at this moment is to call attention to them.

And as we write these lines with the obligatory disclaimer 'You are welcomed to re-write the text we have just "re-written" because ours is not "the last word"', we realize that we have written as women can write in a writing that is already gendered. Thus, it seems we have come to occupy 'the women's position' which was written for us before we came into this text. We were asked to fill the space on women and organizations for the conference and the book and so we did.

And now you can return to the beginning of this text and read it all as 're-writing organization theory'.

Note

An earlier version of this chapter was presented at the conference on 'Re-Thinking Organization' held at the University of Lancaster on 6–8 September 1989.

References

Acker, J. (1987) 'Hierarchies and jobs: Notes for a theory of gendered organizations. Paper presented at the American Sociological Association Annual Meeting, Chicago, IL, August.

Aiken, S.H., Anderson, K., Dinnerstein, M., Lensink, J. and MacCorquodale, P. (1987) 'Trying transformations: Curriculum integration and the problems of resistance'. *Signs*, 12 (2): 255–75.

Aisenberg, N. and Harrington, M. (1988) *Women of Academe*. Amherst, MA: The University of Massachusetts Press.

Alcoff, L. (1988) 'Cultural feminism versus post-structuralism: The identity crisis in feminist theory', *Signs*, 13 (3): 405–36.

Alvesson, M. and Billing, Y.D. (nd) 'Gender and organization: Towards a differentiated understanding'. Unpublished manuscript, University of Stockholm.

Andersen, M.L. (1987) 'Changing the curriculum in higher education', *Signs*, 12 (2): 222–54.

Bacharach, S.B. (1989) 'Organizational theories: Some criteria for evaluation', *Academy of Management Review*, 14 (4): 496–515.

Balsamo, A. (1985) 'Beyond female as a variable: Constructing a feminist perspective on organizational analysis'. Paper presented at the conference 'Critical Perspectives in Organizational Analysis'. Baruch College, September.

Belenky, M.F., Clinchy, B.M., Goldberger, N.R. and Tarule, J.M. (1986) *Women's Ways of Knowing*. New York: Basic Books.

Benhabib, S. (1984) 'Epistemologies of postmodernism: A rejoinder to Jean-François Lyotard', *New German Critique*, 33: 103–26.

Bernstein, R. (1988) 'History convention reflects change from traditional to gender studies', *New York Times*, 9 January.

Bleier, R. (1984) *Science and Gender*. Oxford: Pergamon.

Bordo, S. (1990) 'Feminism, postmodernism, and gender-scepticism', in L.J. Nicholson (ed.), *Feminism/Postmodernism*. New York: Routledge, pp. 133–56.

Burrell, G. (1984) 'Sex and organizational analysis', *Organization Studies*, 5 (2): 97–118.

Calás, M.B. and Jacques, R. (1988) 'Diversity or conformity?: Research by women on women in organizations'. Paper presented at the Seventh International Conference on Women and Organizations, Long Beach, CA.

Calás, M.B. and Smircich, L. (1989) 'Using the F word: Feminist perspectives and the social consequences of organizational research', Academy of Management *Best Papers Proceedings*, Washington, DC, pp. 355–9.

Collins, P.H. (1989) 'The social construction of black feminist thought', *Signs*, 14 (4): 745–73.

Dachler, H.P. (1988) 'Constraints on the emergence of new vistas in leadership and management research: An epistemological overview', in J.G. Hunt, B.R. Baliga, H.P. Dachler and C.A. Schriesheim (eds), *Emerging Leadership Vistas*. Lexington, MA: Lexington Books, pp. 261–85.

Davis, A. (1972) 'Reflections on the black woman's role in the community of slaves', *Massachusetts Review*, 13: 81–100.

Degler, C. (1981) 'What the women's movement has done to American history', in E. Langland and W. Gove (eds), *A Feminist Perspective in the Academy: The Difference it Makes*. Chicago: The University of Chicago Press, pp. 67–85.

Derrida, J. (1978) *Spurs*. Chicago: University of Chicago Press.

Derrida, J. (1986) *Glas*. Lincoln: University of Nebraska Press.

Diamond, A. and Edwards, L.R. (1988) *The Autonomy of Experience*. Amherst, MA: The University of Massachusetts Press.

Diamond, I. and Quinby, I. (1988) *Feminism and Foucault*. Boston: Northeastern University Press.

DiStefano, C. (1990) 'Dilemmas of difference: Feminism, modernity, and postmodernism', in L.J. Nicholson (ed.) *Feminism/Postmodernism*. New York: Routledge, pp. 63–82.

Donelson, E., Van Sell, M. and Goehle, D. (1985) 'Gender biases in management research: Implications for theory and practice'. Paper presented at the Fourth Annual International Conference on Women and Organizations, San Diego, CA.

Dublin, T. (1979) *Women at Work: The Transformation of Work and Community in Lowell, Massachusetts, 1826–1860*. New York: Columbia University Press.

DuBois, E.C., Kelly, G.P., Kennedy, E.L., Korsmeyer, C.W. and Robinson, L.S. (1987) *Feminist Scholarship: Kindling in the Groves of Academe*. Urbana, IL: University of Illinois Press.

Faragher, J. and Stansell, C. (1975) 'Women and their families on the overland trail 1842–1867', *Feminist Studies*, 2: 160.

Farnham, C. (ed.) (1987) *The Impact of Feminist Research in the Academy*. Bloomington: Indiana University Press.

Ferguson, A. (1989) *Blood at the Root: Motherhood, Sexuality and Male Dominance*. London: Pandora.

Ferguson, K.E. (1984) *The Feminist Case Against Bureaucracy*. Philadelphia: Temple University Press.

Ferguson, K.E. (forthcoming) *Reversal and its Discontents: The Man Question*. Manuscript in preparation.

Flax, J. (1987) 'Postmodernism and gender relations in feminist theory', *Signs*, 12 (4): 621–43.

Flax, J. (1990) *Thinking Fragments: Psychoanalysis, Feminism and Postmodernism in the Contemporary West*. Berkeley: University of California Press.

Fraser, N. and Nicolson, L.J. (1988) 'Social criticism without philosophy: An encounter between feminism and postmodernism' in L.J. Nicholson (ed.), *Feminism/Postmodernism*. New York: Routledge, pp. 19–38.

Frazier, N. and Sadker, M. (1973) *Sexism in School and Society*. New York: Harper & Row.

Freedman, E.B. (1981) *Their Sisters' Keepers: Women's Prison Reform in America, 1830–1920*. Ann Arbor, MI: University of Michigan Press.

Freedman, S.M. and Phillips, J.M., (1988) 'The changing nature of research on women at work', *Journal of Management*, 14 (2): 231–51.

Gergen, K.J. (1988) 'Feminist critique of science and the challenge of social epistemology', in M.M. Gergen (ed.), *Feminist Thought and the Structure of Knowledge*. New York: New York University Press, pp. 27–48.

Gilligan, C. (1977) 'In a different voice: Women's conceptions of self and morality', *Harvard Educational Review*, 47: 481–517.

Glazer, N.Y. (1987) 'Questioning eclectic practice in curriculum change', *Signs*, 12 (2): 293–304.

Gordon, L. (1977) *Woman's Body, Woman's Rights: A Social History of Birth Control in America*. New York: Gron Publishers.

Grant, J. (1988) 'Women as managers: What they can offer to organizations', *Organizational Dynamics*, Summer: 56–63.

Haaken, J. (1988) 'Field dependence research: a historical analysis of a psychological construct', *Signs*, 13 (2): 311–30.

Haraway, D. (1985) 'A manifesto for Cyborgs: Science, technology, and socialist feminism in the 1980s', *Socialist Review*, 15 (80): 65–107.

Harding, S. (1986) *The Science Question in Feminism*. Ithaca, NY: Cornell University Press.

Harding, S. (1987) 'Conclusion: Epistemological questions', in S. Harding (ed.), *Feminism and Methodology*, Bloomington, IN: Indiana University Press, pp. 181–90.

Harding, S. (1990) 'Feminism, science, and the anti-Enlightenment critiques', in L.J. Nicholson (ed.), *Feminism/Postmodernism*. New York: Routledge, pp. 83–106.

Harding, S. and Hintikka, M.B. (eds) (1983) *Discovering Reality: Feminist Perspectives on Epistemology, Metaphysics, Methodology, and Philosophy of Science*. Dordrecht, Holland: Reidel.

Hartsock, N. (1987) 'Foucault on power: A theory for women?', in M. Leijenaar (ed.), *The Gender of Power: A Symposium*. Leiden: Vakgroep Vrouwenstudies/Vena.

Hawkesworth, M.E. (1989) 'Knowers, knowing, known: Feminist theory and claims of truth', *Signs*, 14 (3): 533–57.

Hearn, J. and Burrell, G. (1989) 'The sexuality of organization', in J. Hearn, D.L. Sheppard, P. Tancred-Sheriff and G. Burrell (eds), *The Sexuality of Organization*. London: Sage, pp. 1–28.

Hearn, J. and Parkin, W. (1987) *'Sex' at 'Work': The Power and Paradox of Organization Sexuality*. New York: St. Martin's Press.

Hearn, J., Sheppard, D.L., Tancred-Sheriff, P. and Burrell, G. (1989) *The Sexuality of Organization*. London: Sage.

Heath, S. (1987) 'Men and feminist theory', in A. Jardine and P. Smith (eds), *Men in Feminism*. London: Methuen, pp. 41–6.

Hochschild, A. (1973) 'A review of sex role research', in J. Huber (ed.), *Changing Women in a Changing Society*. Chicago: University of Chicago Press, pp. 249–67.

Hubbard, R. (1988) 'Some thoughts about the masculinity of the natural sciences', in M.M. Gergen (ed.), *Feminist Thought and the Structure of Knowledge*. New York: New York University Press, pp. 1–15.

Irigaray, L. (1985) *This Sex which Is Not One*. Ithaca: Cornell University Press.

Jacobson, S.W. and Jacques, R. (1989) 'Feminism(s) and organization studies: Possible contributions to theory from women's experiences'. Unpublished manuscript, University of Massachusetts, School of Management.

Jaggar, A.M. and Rothenberg, P.S. (1984) *Feminist Frameworks: Alternative Theoretical Accounts of the Relations Between Women and Men*. New York: McGraw-Hill.

Jardine, A. and Smith, P. (1987) (eds) *Men in Feminism*. London: Methuen.

Kauffman, L. (ed.) (1989) *Feminism and Institutions: Dialogues on Feminist Theory*. Oxford: Basil Blackwell.

Keller, E.F. (1983) 'Gender and science', in S. Harding and M.B. Hintikka (eds), *Discovering Reality: Feminist Perspectives on Epistemology, Metaphysics and Philosophy of Science*. Dordrecht, Holland: Reidel, pp. 187–205.

Keller, E.F. (1985) *Reflections on Gender and Science*. New Haven, CT: Yale University Press.

Kelly-Gadol, J. (1977) 'Did women have a Renaissance?', in R. Bridenthal and C. Koonz (eds), *Becoming Visible: Women in European History*. Boston: Houghton Mifflin, pp. 137–64.

Lamphere, L. (1987) 'Feminism and anthropology: The struggle to reshape our thinking about gender', in C. Farnham (ed.), *The Impact of Feminist Research in the Academy*. Bloomington: Indiana University Press, pp. 11–33.

Lloyd, G. (1984) *The Man of Reason: 'Male' and 'Female' in Western Philosophy* Minneapolis: University of Minnesota Press.

Lugones, M.C. and Spelman, E.V. (1983) 'Have we got a theory for you! Feminist theory, cultural imperialism and the demand for "The Woman's Voice"', *Women's Studies International Forum*, 9 (6): 573–81.

Lyotard, J.F. (1984) *The Postmodern Condition*. Minneapolis: University of Minnesota Press.

Marshall, Judi (1984) *Women Managers: Travellers in a Male World*. Chichester, UK: Wiley.

Marshall, Judi (1989) 'Re-visioning career concepts: a feminist invitation', in M.B. Arthur, D.T. Hall and B.S. Lawrence (eds.), *Handbook of Career Theory*. Cambridge, UK: Cambridge University Press, pp. 275–91.

Martin, J. (1990) 'Deconstructing organizational taboos: The suppression of gender conflict in organizations', *Organization Science*, 1: 1–21.

Meyer, J. (1988) 'Feminist thought and social psychology', in M.M. Gergen (ed.), *Feminist Thought and the Structure of Knowledge*. New York: New York University Press, pp. 105–23.

Mills, A.J. (1988) 'Organization, gender and culture', *Organization Studies*, 9 (3): 351–69.

Minnich, E.K. (1986) 'Conceptual errors across the curriculum: Towards a transformation of the tradition'. A publication from the Research Clearing House and Curriculum Integration Project, Center for Research on Women, Memphis State University.

Morawski, J.G. (1988) 'Impasse in feminist thought?', in M.M. Gergen (ed.), *Feminist Thought and the Structure of Knowledge*. New York: New York University Press, pp. 182–94.

Nicholson, L.J. (ed.) (1990) *Feminism/Postmodernism*. New York: Routledge.

Oakeley, A. (1972) *Sex, Gender and Society*. London: Temple Smith.

Osigweh, C.A.B. (1989) 'Concept fallibility in organization science', *Academy of Management Review*, 14 (4): 579–94.

Poole, M.S. and Van de Ven, A.H. (1989) 'Using paradox to build management and organization theories', *Academy of Management Review*, 14 (4): 562–78.

Rao, M.V.H. and Pasmore, W.A. (1989) 'Knowledge and interest in organization studies: A conflict of interpretations', *Organization Studies*, 10 (2): 225–39.

Reinharz, S. (1985) 'Feminist distrust: Problems of context in sociological work', in D.N. Berg and K.K. Smith (eds), *Exploring Clinical Methods for Social Research*. Newbury Park, CA: Sage.

Rosaldo, M. and Lamphere, L. (eds) (1974) *Women, Culture and Society*. Stanford, CA: Stanford University Press.

Rose, H. (1986) 'Women's work: Women's knowledge', in J. Mitchell and A. Oakley (eds), *What is Feminism: A Re-examination*. New York: Pantheon, pp. 161–83.

Rose, H. (1987) 'Hand, brain, and heart: A feminist epistemology for the Natural Sciences', in S. Harding and J.F. O'Barr (eds), *Sex and Scientific Inquiry*. Chicago: The University of Chicago Press.

Schuster, M. and Van Dyne, S. (eds) (1985) *Women's Place in the Academy: Transforming the Liberal Arts Curriculum*. Totowa, NJ: Rowman and Allanheld.

Scott, J.W. (1986) 'Gender: A useful category of historical analysis', *American Historical Review*, 91 (December): 1053–75.

Scott, J.W. (1987) 'Women's history and the rewriting of history', in C. Farnham (ed.), *The Impact of Feminist Research in the Academy*. Bloomington: Indiana University Press, pp. 34–50.

Scott, J.W. (1988) 'Deconstructing equality-versus-difference: Or, the uses of poststructuralist theory for feminism', *Feminist Studies*, 14 (1): 33–50.

Shapiro, J. (1981) 'Anthropology and the study of gender', in E. Langland and W. Gove (eds), *A Feminist Perspective in the Academy: The Difference it Makes*. Chicago: Chicago University Press, pp. 110–29.

Shotter, J. and Logan, J. (1988) 'The pervasiveness of patriarchy: On finding a different voice', in M.M. Gergen (ed.), *Feminist Thought and the Structure of Knowledge*. New York: New York University Press, pp. 69–86.

Showalter, E. (1985) *The New Feminist Criticism*. New York: Pantheon.

Slocum, S.L. (1975) 'Woman the gatherer: Male bias in anthropology', in Rayna R. Reiter (ed.), *Toward an Anthropology of Women*. New York: Monthly Review Press.

Smircich, L. (1985) 'Toward a woman centered organization theory'. Paper presented at the Academy of Management national meeting, San Diego, CA.

Smith, D.E. (1979) 'A sociology for women', in J.A. Sherman and E.T. Beck (eds), *The Prism of Sex*. Madison: The University of Wisconsin Press, pp. 135–87.

Spelman, E.V. (1988) *Inessential Woman*. Boston, MA: Beacon Press.

Stacey, J. and Thorne, B. (1985) 'The missing feminist revolution in sociology', *Social Problems*, 32: 301–16.

Webster, J. and Starbuck, W.H. (1988) 'Theory building in industrial and organizational psychology', in C.L. Cooper and I.T. Robertson (eds), *International Review of Industrial and Organizational Psychology*, 3.

Weedon, C. (1987) *Feminist Practice and Poststructuralist Theory*. Oxford: Basil Blackwell.

Weick, K.E. (1989) 'Theory construction as disciplined imagination', *Academy of Management Review*, 14 (4): 516–31.

Weiner, A. (1976) *Women of Value, Men of Renown*. Austin: University of Texas Press.

Weisstein, N. (1971) 'Psychology constructs the female', in M.H. Garsk (ed.), *Roles Women Play: Readings Toward Women's Liberation*. Belmont, CA: Brooks/Cole, pp. 68–83.

Westkott, M. (1979) 'Feminist criticism of the social sciences', *Harvard Educational Review*, 49 (4): 422–30.

Whetten, D.A. (1989) 'What constitutes a theoretical contribution?' *Academy of Management Review*, 14 (4): 490–5.

13

Formal Organization as Representation: Remote Control, Displacement and Abbreviation

Robert Cooper

In recent years, organizations have come to be seen as organizers of information. An early stimulus to this way of thinking was Simon's (1955) famous criticism of the theory of rational choice: that the latter imputes to the rational actor exaggerated capacities for processing information. In reality, human rationality is severely bounded. Formal organization was seen as an instrument for solving problems specifically deriving from bounded rationality. Williamson's (1975) theory of transaction costs is one attempt to explain bounded rationality in terms of the supply of information and its effects on the organization of the market. Two factors are salient: the cost or difficulty of acquiring necessary information about the market, and the number of firms in it. If information is freely available and firms are numerous, then, because transaction costs are low, the profit advantage goes to the individual who is self-employed. On the other hand, where information is costly and where there are few firms, transaction costs become too high and it therefore pays the individual to take employment with a big firm that can control information and thus reduce transaction costs.

Extending Williamson's analysis, Schotter (1981) has reworked the relationship between rationality and organizations in the language of information theory. Information is no longer a commodity that is more or less available; it is now that which has surprise value. If an event can be predicted or is already known, it carries little or no information. Information increases with unpredictability. Schotter views organizational structures as forms of informational complexity. Past experience becomes sedimented in an organization's structures where it functions as a guide to future events. The more completely organizational structures encode information, the less unpredictability or uncertainty there is likely to be.

Williamson and Schotter both underline the boundedness of individual rationality and then go on to say that by constructing organizations, individuals extend the limits of their capacities for processing information. For Williamson, organizations augment bounded rationality by controlling the flow of information, so reducing transaction costs for individual actors. For Schotter, organizations augment the limits of rationality by encoding as much information as possible in their structures and rules. But both Williamson and Schotter overlook a fundamental and mandatory act in the processing of information: representation. Information theory begins with the construction of a representation (pattern, picture, model) of some aspect of the world (MacKay, 1969). The representation must exist before we can go on to think about information in the Williamson–Schotter sense. When Williamson, for example, talks about the effects of information on the organization of the market he is really talking about *changes* in a representational construct of that market. The representation comes first; information is that which augments or reduces the power of the representation. On this analysis, organizations are not merely organizers of information; they also construct the forms in which information appears.

This insight has been taken up by Zuboff (1988) in a study of the effects of information technology in various commercial and manufacturing organizations. Zuboff distinguishes two functions of information technology: it *informates* as well as *automates*.

The automating function of technology refers to the machine's appropriation of human skills and effort; its informating function is its power to translate activities, events and objects into visible information. In manufacturing, for example, microprocessors enable robots, programmable logic controllers and sensors 'to translate the three-dimensional production process into digitized data. These data are then made available within a two-dimensional space, typically on the screen of a video display terminal or on a computer printout, in the form of electronic symbols, numbers, letters, and graphics' (Zuboff, 1988: 10). Informating is in effect a process of representation. The function of representation is to translate difficult or intransigent material into a form that facilitates control. As Zuboff shows, information technology does precisely that: it absorbs and substitutes for the debriefed, implicit knowledge and skills of workers and managers; it impersonalizes the authorship of the system and so makes control less vulnerable to criticism; it makes information transparent and 'instant'; when information is uncoupled from its action context and represented symbolically, events can be manipulated and combined in new ways, so enabling greater control. In short, information technology encapsulates a general function of all formal organization: the need to make transparent what is opaque, to make present what is remote, and to manipulate what is resistant. It is not just a question of information or symbolization but of technologies which enable us to represent information and symbols in a convenient form. This is how the Voyager II spacecraft can bring the planet Neptune on to the computer screens of the Houston space centre, how geologists can probe the depths of the earth for minerals and oil, and how medical doctors can see inside the human body by means of X-ray tomograms. All rely on specific technologies of representation.

In Zuboff's analysis, three specific features of the informating process can be singled out as having special relevance for understanding the role of representation and its technologies in organizations: (1) symbols and electronic devices substitute for direct human involvement with the raw material and thus abstract thought from action: 'Absorption, immediacy, and organic responsiveness are superseded by distance, coolness, and remoteness' (1988: 75); (2) organizational activity becomes less a structure of discrete acts coordinated in space and time and more a series of displacements or transformations along informational networks: 'The electronic text exists independently of space and time. . . The contents of the electronic text can infuse an entire organization, instead of being bundled in discrete objects, like books or pieces of paper' (1988: 179–80); (3) information technology abbreviates complexity: a three-dimensional world is reduced to a two-dimensional representation on a terminal screen which can be read instantly. These three themes – remote control, displacement, abbreviation – are by no means unique to information technology; they are simply hyperbolized there. They define all techniques of representation, however ordinary and unobtrusive. Ironically, their constitutive ordinariness has led to their neglect in organizational analysis.

These features of representation help us to understand the relationship between bounded rationality and organizations as organizers of information. Unfortunately, the literature on bounded rationality gives the impression that rationality is a cognitive process which takes place 'in the brain' and that its boundedness is a function of the limited capacity of the human mind:

> The capacity of the human mind for formulating and solving complex problems is very small compared with the size of the problems whose solution is required for objectively rational behaviour in the real world – or even for a reasonable approximation to such objective rationality. (Simon, 1957: 198)

When we view the question of bounded rationality in terms of techniques of representation, both rationality and boundedness take on a wholly different meaning. To illustrate the difference, let's take two simple examples of human technology: chair and glove (Scarry, 1985). Both chair and glove represent (that is, replace or stand in place of) specific aspects of the body in its dealings with the world. The chair represents the general shape of the human skeleton and compensates for the body's tendency to tiredness. Likewise, the glove (let's say an industrial glove) represents the hand; while the natural hand is frail (for example, it can be easily burnt), the industrial glove is robust and refractory. Whereas the body and its parts are limited by a natural fragility, it is precisely these limiting conditions that enable and promote the process of representation. In these examples, we see that human 'rationality' is not characteristically cognitive but is intrinsic to the general field of action of the body and its parts, and that boundedness, far from being a restriction, is a required stimulus for representation. As representations, techniques and artefacts are *embodied* (note, not just 'enacted'[1]) processes that remedy and compensate for the body's deficiencies and, at the same time, extend, magnify and make more durable its power. In short, representations embody a principle of economy which turns losses into gains.

It is this principle of economy which makes the logic of representation more fundamental to the understanding and analysis of organizations than the traditionally more limited concept of information. This is an economy of convenience in which the affairs of the world are made pliable, wieldable and therefore amenable to human use through technologies of representation. It turns a boundary or limit from a privation into a profit.[2] Remote control, displacement and abbreviation are the mechanisms by which representation realizes this economy of mental and physical motion. In the case of remote control, such economy is made possible by substituting symbols and other prosthetic devices for direct involvement of the human body and its senses. Administrators and managers, for example, do not work directly on the environment but on models, maps, numbers and formulae which represent that environment; in this way, they can control complex and heterogeneous activities at a distance and in the relative convenience of a centralized work station. Events that are remote (that is, distant and heterogeneous) in space and time can be instantly collated in paper form on the desk of a central controller. This has the paradoxical effect of bringing remote events near while, at the same time, keeping them at a remove through the intervention of representations. In other words, the power of representation to control an event remotely is a form of displacement in which representation is always a substitution for or re-presentation of the event and never the event itself.

Remote control underlines the economy of convenience intrinsic to representation: one may not be able to move the mountain itself but it is easy to move a model or map of it. This mobility of representation helps us to understand why paperwork of all kinds is so essential to organizations: mobility is central to control. Representation displaces the intractable and obdurate; it denies the idea of fixed location and emphasizes movement. Displacement, therefore, means mobile and non-localizable associations. It therefore becomes inappropriate to talk, for example, about the organization and its environment since this gives the impression of distinct domains separated in space and time. In terms of displacement, organizing activity is the transformation of boundary relationships which are themselves continually shifting. Again, the concept of the boundary comes into its own. The organization's inside and outside are correlative: 'No inside is conceivable . . . without the complicity of an outside on which it relies. Complicity mixed with antagonism . . . No outside would be conceivable without an inside fending it off, resisting it, "reacting" to it' (Starobinski, 1975: 342). In this way, inside and outside, organization and environment, continually displace each other. But neither remote control nor displacement are thinkable without abbreviation. Abbreviation makes possible the economy of convenience that underlies representation.

It simplifies the complex, makes the big into the small, converts the delayed into the instantaneous. It works according to a principle of condensation in which as much as is needed is condensed into as little as is needed so as to enable ease and accuracy of perception and action. Through abbreviation, representations are made compact, versatile and permutable. The development of the computer in recent years perhaps best exemplifies the abbreviation process: 'The power of ten cubic meters of 1965-vintage computer can now be held in the palm of the hand. Thanks to telephone hook-up, the mini-computer presently affords us access to millions of data' (Bertin, 1983: x). In these examples, representation combines with electronics to provide increasingly powerful means of 'abbreviating' the world.

This schematic characterization of the components of representation – remote control, displacement, abbreviation – clearly needs amplifying within the organizational context and it is to this that we now turn, with two specific objectives in view: (1) to illustrate the operation of the three components in terms of concrete examples; and (2) to show how they can augment more conventional dimensions of organizational analysis, such as formalization and centralization.

Remote Control: The Case of the Portuguese East Indies Company

We illustrate the workings of remote control with the story of how the Portuguese created and extended the organization of their East Indies Company at the end of the fifteenth century (Law, 1986). The basic question is how the Portuguese were able to set up a large organization based on *control at a distance*. The main technology in this story is the ship. The medieval European sailing vessel's range and endurance were limited and its carrying capacity small; it was also unable to cope well with adverse weather conditions and it was not very effective in navigating out of sight of land or without regular soundings. Clearly, such vessels could not deal with the challenge of controlling the Indies spice markets which the Portuguese were keen to exploit. What was required was a ship (with associated technology) that was both mobile and durable enough to match the uncertainties and rigours of long-distance sailing in unknown territories. The development by the Portuguese of new vessels that were more mobile and more durable placed them in a better position to control not only the sea and weather (for example, new types of sail enabled the extraction of more power from the wind), but more discipline was required of everyone involved – seamen, masters, merchants, envoys – in order to comply with the greater demands of the new technology. All this was realized through the development of more powerful technologies of representation.

As we have seen, representation is really a reversal process in which a disadvantage is turned into an advantage – for example, chair and glove embody this power. This is essentially how the Portuguese extracted compliance from the heterogeneous elements – social, technological, natural – that constituted the maritime organization of their East Indies Company. In the larger context, this meant that some centre in Lisbon could dominate activities on the other side of the world. But the success of this enterprise was built on the patient accumulation of many small technical advances arranged in an interlocking series. Each small advance was a triumph of remote control. Long-distance control became possible through a sequence of short-distance achievements of remote control, all of which embodied the following steps: (1) the substitution of a symbol or technical device for direct human involvement; which led to (2) the curious effect of bringing the remote – that which is cut off by a limit or boundary – near, while at the same time keeping it at a remove.

Among the major technical advances of remote control developed by the Portuguese were new forms of sail and new navigational devices. Natural forces such as winds and sea currents became prevalent dangers as soon as the Portuguese left the relative safety of European waters for the uncertainties of the African and eastern seas. The technical task facing the Portuguese was how to represent these natural forces in their own maritime organization and thereby turn potential hazards into benefits. This was a case of extracting compliance from the natural forces by incorporating them into the ship's sociotechnical organization so that these forces would augment rather than hinder the voyage. In the case of the winds, smaller sails at bow and stern made the vessel more manoeuvrable; smaller sails needed fewer crew, which further increased the ship's mobility and durability since less crew meant less sickness and mortality, common problems on such long voyages. By means of increased geographical knowledge and improved navigational competence, ocean currents were also harnessed.

The navigational advances of the Portuguese were even more dramatic. In 1484 King John II of Portugal set up a prototypal research and development group and charged it with the task of developing a system for navigating outside European waters. The system developed by the group, the *Regimento do Astrolabio et do Quadrante*, 'not only fulfilled the expectations of the king but it also laid the foundations of modern astronomical navigation' (Law, 1986: 248). The *Regimento* was essentially a comprehensive representation of the new navigational contexts being charted at that time by the Portuguese vessels; it modelled not only the seas and land but also the heavens. It used written or printed inscriptions based on the positions of the North Star, the Sun and its declinations, and so on. In short, the new system represented the wider world and the heavens in models, tables, rules, and their possible permutations; it reproduced a complex astronomical and geographical framework in a portable and manipulable system, as Law (1986: 252) illustrates:

Consider one case, that of the table of solar declination. This represented the distillation . . . of many years of astronomical expertise, of correspondence, of argument and of innovation . . . this created a kind of surrogate astronomer. It was not necessary to take along the inventors and designers of the new system. Their force, and the work of their predecessors, was being borrowed, converted into a highly transportable and indefinitely reproducible form, and being put to work on every ship. The production of tables of solar declination for the purpose of navigation may thus be seen as a way of reducing the relevant aspects of a weighty astronomical tradition to a form that, in the context of the vessel, was more mobile and durable than the original. It seems . . . to have been a way of capitalising on generations of astronomical work by converting this into a nicely simplified black box that might be carried anywhere within the Portuguese system of long-distance control and which would contribute to this when posed the right questions.

Here we have all the elements of remote control: build a reduced model of the original, bring the distant to the here-and-now, make a visual representation of that which defies physical contact. The solar table not only represents the sun's declinations but it also represents the work of countless predecessors, which remains ever present in the sociotechnical organization of the Portuguese vessels. Both the heavens and history may be distant but they are nevertheless actively present in the remote control capacities of representation. Remote control in this case borrows power from astronomical, geographical, natural and historical sources. By incorporating significant features of the environment into representational forms, by appropriating environmental powers through models, data and instruments and turning them back on their sources, remote control ensures independence from external forces, freedom of mental and physical motion and, ultimately, secures a position from which it is able to dominate the world and not be dominated by it.

Displacement: Louis Pasteur and the Management of Microbes

As we have just seen, the whole Portuguese enterprise was built on many small technical advances arranged in an interlocking series. Viewed in this way, the total organization of the Portuguese East Indies Company is best understood as a sociotechnical network of displacements or translations; for example, the appropriation of the powers of wind and sea currents by the various technologies of representation on board ship are really displacements or borrowings of power and energy from one point to another. Organizing thus becomes a network of mobile and non-localizable associations instead of the static distinction between organization and environment. Organizing, as we have noted, is the transformation of boundary relationships which are themselves continually shifting. It is this theme of organizing as displacement or transformation that we now turn to in a brief discussion of the work of the microbiologist Louis Pasteur on the development of an antidote to the anthrax bacillus (Latour, 1983, 1988).

In the early 1880s, Pasteur's laboratory, situated in the Ecole Normale

Supérieure in Paris, turned its attention to finding a preventive to the disease anthrax, which at that period was proving excessively damaging for the French cattle industry. The variable and unpredictable nature of the disease made it difficult to study, especially in terms of one single cause. This made the disease unamenable to traditional laboratory investigation. Pasteur's laboratory and French cattle, at this point, are worlds apart. But, in order to get nearer the source of the disease and to simulate its own milieu more accurately, Pasteur takes his 'laboratory' to a farm in the French countryside. Pasteur is now out in the 'field' and so confuses the usual distinction between the laboratory and the outside world. He and his colleagues learn from the veterinarians' and the farmers' knowledge of the anthrax bacillus and how it affects the cattle. After a period, Pasteur returns to his main laboratory in Paris and takes with him a significant part of the field, the cultivated bacillus. Back in the laboratory, he is able to grow the bacillus in isolation and in large quantities. The bacillus, formerly invisible because of its microscopic size and its admixing with millions of other organisms, now becomes visible and therefore amenable to investigation. The cause of the anthrax disease can now be *seen* at the Ecole Normale Supérieure, while back at the farm it remains invisibly lethal. This is a major displacement, but bigger ones are to come. Pasteur is now able at will to simulate anthrax outbreaks in his laboratory by inoculating animals with the anthrax culture he has specially created. This makes it possible to chart and record – that is, represent – all the important features of the controlled simulation. Pasteur scales down the problem and reduces it to its essentials: his animals die from being inoculated with anthrax microbes and from no other cause. The nature of this displacement is obvious: by representing the disease on a small scale (a form of remote control), by isolating its cause and developing an effective vaccine, Pasteur and his colleagues increase their own power while reducing the power of the microbes. Still weak in relation to the microbes, the veterinarians and the farmers are forced to go to Pasteur in order to become strong, so further enhancing the power of his laboratory.

But it was still necessary to make a further displacement: to return the anthrax (now in the form of a vaccine) to the farm in order to demonstrate its effectiveness, otherwise it would simply remain a micro level achievement under the artificial conditions of the laboratory. The next step, therefore, was to organize a field trial on a larger scale. This displacement is also a representation since Pasteur has to re-present relevant features of his laboratory in the French countryside in order to ensure that his experimental work can be repeated effectively. Veterinarians and farmers then see that, provided they reproduce certain basic laboratory practices such as disinfection, inoculation technique, timing and recording, they too can practise Pasteur's power. Through its portable knowledge and techniques, the laboratory is simulated or represented in every French farm. The displacements, when added up, describe a reversal: first, the power of the invisible microbe that decimates the population of cattle on the farms of France; second, the overturning and incorporation of the microbes' power in the laboratory vaccine; third, the return of the domesticated microbe as vaccine to the farms where, supported by appropriate laboratory practices, it serves to neutralize the population of 'wild' microbes.

Pasteur's displacements begin to make us see the artificiality and limitations of thinking in terms of discrete terms such as laboratory and agriculture, organization and environment, since they also displace the traditional static distinction between 'inside' and 'outside'. As we have noted, inside and outside are not separate places; they refer to a correlative structure in which 'complicity is mixed with antagonism . . . . No outside would be conceivable without an inside fending it off, resisting it, "reacting" to it' (Starobinski, 1975: 342). Pasteur reproduces inside his laboratory 'an event that seems to be happening only outside – the first move – and then . . . extend[s] outside to all farms what seems to be happening only inside laboratories. As in some topological theorem, the inside and the outside world can reverse into one another very easily' (Latour, 1983: 154). This is what we meant earlier when we described displacement as a series of mobile and non-localizable associations. It is difficult to think of associations as having insides and outsides; for example, the inner spaces of the human body – mouth, stomach, and so on – are really pockets of externality folded in. Organization as an active process of displacement or transformation denies and defies such categories as inside and outside; it is more like a process that travels along sociotechnical networks. This is what Pasteur discovered when he first tried to extend the anthrax vaccine to the farms of France: the vaccine would only work on the farms if the necessary laboratory conditions were set up beforehand.

The displacement of the inside–outside problem also has consequences for Simon's (1957) idea of bounded rationality, discussed earlier, and its suggestion that rationality is somehow located 'in the brain'. The argument from displacement denies the existence of special cognitive or personal qualities intrinsic to individuals or organizations. Pasteur is not necessarily more rational or more cognitively gifted than the veterinarians and farmers he comes to help. Pasteur's advantage is that he has a laboratory and the others don't. In the laboratory, Pasteur works on small-scale representations of large outside problems which are then made easy to control; during the experimental period he is insulated from the outside world, so that the mistakes he makes do not go beyond the laboratory walls and are therefore hidden from public view. Each mistake is carefully recorded and cumulatively built on until 'certainty' is gained. It is not Pasteur's cognitive, social or psychological dispositions nor even his unbounded rationality that make him more 'certain' than the veterinarian or farmer, but the special sociotechnical organization of the laboratory which enables Pasteur to reverse the power of the microbes and to extend this capacity by re-presenting it in farms throughout France. By this means, the farmers of France become Pasteur's representatives.

Abbreviation: The Economy of Representation and the Birth of Modern Administration

Neither remote control nor displacement are thinkable without abbreviation. To achieve remote control, the Portuguese abbreviated the magnitude of the heavens to a set of tables and a clutch of astronomical techniques. Pasteur abbreviated France's anthrax epizootic to a single bacillus and a micro level representation of the larger farm context. Abbreviation is intrinsic to the economy of convenience and control that representation embodies.

Behind every act of representation lies the urge to minimize effort; the economy of convenience works according to a principle of least effort (Zipf, 1949). Representation reproduces the events and objects of the world in a curtailed and miniaturized form so that they can be more easily engaged by mind and body. Representation in its abbreviation mode is a tactics of micropractices; it displaces the molar for the molecular. Abbreviation economizes space and time in two ways: by close packing and by the reduction of size and mass (Zipf, 1949). By arranging the elements of representations – tools, techniques, symbols, models – as closely together as possible, close packing reduces the amount of time and effort involved in manipulating them. For example, information in a computer database is more closely packed than the equivalent information in a printed book or written record and thus can be more easily retrieved. The principle of close packing is important because it implies the abbreviation of size and mass: the smaller in size and mass the elements are, the closer together they can be packed. The miniaturization of computer parts, especially the silicon chip, illustrates the significant advantages of abbreviating size and mass to facilitate close packing.

The degree to which technologies of representation contributed to the historical development of the practical disciplines of administration and management is not widely appreciated. One aspect of this development was the tendency from the seventeenth century onwards to think in terms of the economy of convenience – instant information, knowledge 'at a glance', was what administrators demanded. In effect, this required a radical restructuring of the administrative and governmental process towards strategies of abbreviation. These strategies were directed mainly to the sense of vision – for good reasons. It is known that vision is the most efficient of the sensory systems: it can take in a far wider range of information in a much shorter span of time (Bertin, 1983). For this reason, optic-friendly technologies of representation began to emerge systematically with the increasing complexity and range of administrative problems that accompanied the population explosion in Europe in the eighteenth century.[3]

Foucault (1979) tells us that the arts of administration and government in the modern sense arose out of the demographic expansion of the eighteenth century. Before this period, government was conceived on the model of the family and governors and administrators, like good fathers, viewed their roles in terms of the management of the household where the common welfare of all was uppermost. The word 'oeconomy' in this context was limited to the benign control 'of the head of a family over his household and his goods' (Foucault, 1979: 10). With the population increases of the eighteenth century, the interpretation of government, administration and 'oeconomy' underwent radical change. From now on, one managed a large amorphous mass whose sheer magnitude kept it at a distance, and which one could only understand in terms of statistical representations – statistics being 'the science of the State' – of population density, rates of birth and death, epidemics, cycles of scarcity, and so on. Government and administration no longer dwelt on citizens as members of a large 'family' but on the 'complex unit constituted by men and things' (1979: 11) – men in their relation to resources, to territory, means of subsistence, work, accidents, death. In short, the management of social–economic systems began to take shape in men's minds. A new metaphor takes the place of the family in the minds of the administrative theorists of the time – that of the ship. What does it mean to govern or manage a ship?

> It clearly means to take charge of the sailors, but also of the boat and its cargo; to take care of the ship means also to reckon with the winds, rocks and tempests, and consists in that activity of setting in relation with one another the sailors who are to be taken care of with the cargo which is to be brought safely to port, and with all these events such as winds, rocks and tempests, etc. This is what characterizes the government of a ship. (Foucault, 1979: 11)

The family is no longer the model of good government; it is now the ship as a sociotechnical metaphor that forces itself on the attention of administrators. Whereas the members of the family have to be *cared for*, the ship has to be *managed*. And this of course is exactly the problem encountered on a smaller scale by the Portuguese East Indies Company three centuries before. For the new art of administration and for the Portuguese, it is the same question of how to extract maximum productive compliance from all elements – people, technical devices, printed documents – of the 'ship'. Just as the Portuguese were forced to develop more effective technologies to represent and control the distant heavens and the refractory natural forces of sea and weather, so the new breed of administrators were forced to develop more effective ways of representing and thus controlling the new urban masses of the eighteenth century. Almost by definition, a human mass defies formal knowledge and representation. Any mob or mass, simply because it lacks classification and resists calculation, is 'already seditious' (Miller, 1987: 17). In this sense, the masses were remote; their sheer numbers also made them physically unmanageable. Before they could be organized and managed, the masses had to be re-presented in the form of remote control, displacement and abbreviation. No one understood this better than Jeremy Bentham (1748–1832), the utilitarian and father of administrative theory.

Bentham's extensive writings on various aspects of government, administration and management are marked throughout by a combative concern to tame the mass and its aberrations: the mass 'evades taxonomies, makes enumerations indeterminable. Instead of regulated relationships, confusion reigns, fomenting unrest, excluding reflection; change is constant in a mob, giving rise to impressions as varied as they are striking' (Miller, 1987: 17). Bentham's answer was to divide and rule: the spatial and temporal division of workers at their benches, pupils at school, prisoners in their cells, enabled classification and counting, the rudiments of representation. The next major step of control was the abbreviation of the physical disposition of organizational incumbents in their architectural contexts in the form of written records. 'Books must be kept. "Bookkeeping" is a science . . . Chronological entries will be made daily, methodological entries – products, population tables, stock inventories, health records, moral conduct records, requests, punishments (with a black cover), rewards (with a red cover) . . .' (Miller, 1987: 19). By this 'methodization' (Bentham's term), large numbers of people distributed over a large area can be represented in the small space of a book and inspected 'at first glance'. Bentham had begun to systematize a principle that is fundamental to modern cybernetics and information technology: representation is not the reproduction of *things* or *meanings* but their organization in space and time and this is why representation (as Bentham so clearly saw) deals with factors such as 'ordering, listing, display, hierarchy of arrangement, edge and margin, sectioning, spacing, contrasts . . .' (McArthur 1986: 23). Just as a series of numbers is distributed over a page in, say, an accounts book, so people and things are distributed in space and time. This correspondence between the world 'out there' and techniques of representation is essential to the construction of management 'at first glance'; in Bentham's eyes, all factories, schools and prisons are materialized classifications, lists, hierarchies, and statistics. Through representation, the big and the small become interchangeable.

The principle of abbreviation is 'much condensed into little'. It is the fulcrum of Bentham's theory of management. Bentham brought it to perfection in his architectural concept of the Panopticon, 'the polyvalent apparatus of surveillance, the universal optical machine of human groupings' (Miller, 1987: 3). The Panopticon was a circular building with a central tower from which continuous surveillance could be unilaterally exercised by one inspector on many inmates individually housed in perimeter cells. In effect, it was a technological eye which capitalized on the natural efficiency of the visual sense. The function of the Panopticon was part of Bentham's economy of division: what can be divided, kept separate yet closely packed in physical space, can be more easily transferred to the smaller space of the record book. The purpose of the Panopticon was not only to guarantee managerial control and the efficiency of working but to facilitate the abbreviated representation of the physical world in classes, numbers, and names; to enable administrators to see more clearly and more quickly: 'To procure for a small number, or even for a single individual, the instantaneous view of a great multitude' (Foucault, 1977: 216).

The whole idea of the Panoptic principle was to connect abbreviated representations – models, signs, summaries, and the like – with a many-layered imbrication of social, political, architectural and other factors in a kind of *semio-technical hierarchy* where the simplest term could represent the most complex series, where the most intricate details of institutional behaviour could be orchestrated to respond to the briefest command, the most peremptory signal.[4] Today, this programme is being dramatically advanced by means of information technology. Zuboff (1988) shows how the informating function of information technology reveals the organization as the managing of 'electronic texts' (that is, representations) in which the major aspects of the organization's work (behavioural, technical, and so on) can be centrally summarized as real-time data on terminal screens; and in which Bentham's criterion of 'at-a-glance' management becomes doubly instantaneous because organizational processes are re-presented as they actually happen.

Re-presenting Organization: Formalization and Centralization Transfigured

Institutional approaches to information view it either as a commodity (for example, Williamson, 1975) or as an event that has surprise value (for example, Schotter, 1981). When information is placed in the context of representation, it takes on a different meaning. Representation is the more fundamental concept simply because information must first be represented in some way. 'By a representation is meant any structure (pattern, picture, model) whether abstract or concrete, of which the features purport to symbolize or correspond in some sense with those of some other structure' (MacKay, 1969: 161). Information is that which contributes to the efficiency of a representation: 'Information may be defined in the most general sense as *that which adds to a representation*' (MacKay, 1969: 163). Information thus provides *advantage* or *gain*. This is the same as saying that representations embody a principle of economy which turns losses into gains, as argued earlier. As we also noted, the principle of economy revolves around the concept of boundary or limit. The boundary is simultaneously a constraint and an advantage, where complicity is mixed with antagonism (Starobinski, 1975); it is a site of struggle. Representation and information are therefore always preoccupied with the struggle for representational and informational gain, since this is what enhances power and control. We saw this struggle in the case of the Portuguese navigators who incorporated the external powers of nature and the heavens into a range of shipboard technologies of representation, in Pasteur's successful attempt to displace the anthrax microbe's power through various techniques of laboratory representation, and in the efforts of the early administrative theorists to represent complex organizations in the abbreviated techniques of statistics, optical models and the like.

At this point it is appropriate to ask how the representational view of organizing relates to more traditional approaches to the analysis of organizations. It is certainly possible to suggest points of contact with Weber's (1947) characterization of bureaucracy: the reliance on written documents, the cultivation of 'depersonalization', and the 'concentration of the means of administration' all clearly imply remote control and abbreviation. But Weber was more interested in developing a general picture of bureaucratic organization as a political–economic structure than in understanding the pragmatic and mundane logic that lies behind the techniques he identified. More recent analyses of organizations have summarized much of Weber's account of bureaucracy in the organizational dimensions of *formalization* and *centralization* (see, for example, Hall, 1987). Formalization is traditionally defined in terms of rules and procedures that are written down in official documents – that is, formalized. Centralization is the degree to which power and decision-making are located within one individual or group in the organization. Again we see in these definitions only tenuous echoes of representation. The active logic of the representation process is of course lost here. The reason for this would seem to be the prior assumption that there is a 'natural' entity called '*the* organization' which, like bounded rationality, is already constituted for us, and it is this spontaneously supposed structure that requires detailed definition. The definitions of formalization and centralization follow from this supposition. The argument from representation makes no such assumption; instead, it poses the more fundamental question of how representation processes serve to construct organizations. Again, representation comes first. Let's see how this reversal of the question helps us to get closer to the formalization–centralization issue in organizations.

Conventional definitions of formalization and centralization can be reduced to two basic ideas: *objectification* and *control*. The function of formalization is the objectification of structures so as to make them appear external to the subjectivities of the participating actors (Scott, 1987). Centralization (which is also controlization) is the control of events in space and time; it realizes this control by incorporating the power of external objects and events into its own structures (usually called *centres*). It is exactly these functions that representation makes possible: technologies of representation convert the inaccessible, unknown and private into the accessible, known and public; they convert the deferred and faraway into the instantaneous and immediate; and their portability or mobility makes them easy to manipulate and control. Viewed in this way, formalization and centralization are less like static structures and more like active conversion processes.

Formalization makes structures clear, visible, transparent; its aim is to make the 'organization' *seeable*. Bentham saw this as the first problem of administration: to give written substance to the complex matrix of interacting factors that was otherwise impossible to see. For Bentham, the first step was to re-present the multi-dimensional world of administrative events, objects and people in two-dimensional paper forms – 'bookkeeping'. Hence, the initial step of dividing organizational incumbents in architectural and administrative space in order to apply classes, numbers, names, job descriptions, incentive schemes, which served as the content of the written representations. As we have seen, this is the logic of remote control, which reduces what is distant and resistant to what is near, clear and controllable; at the same time, the significance of representation through remote control is that it takes precedence over the event it represents. This means, for example, that we no longer see a 'picture of the organization' but the organization grasped as a formalized picture. Transparency and visibility in two-dimensional media become significant factors in management by formalization. As Zuboff shows, these factors become exaggerated with the introduction of information technology: 'In each of the organizations I studied, information technology had textualized [that is, formalized – R.C.] not only the content of work but also the task-related behaviours of the men and women who engaged with the data interface' (1988: 319). In a telecommunications company, 'Computerization meant that the work itself . . . had become transparent. The [new system] meant that the workers' behaviour was now almost as visible as their work. Gone were the bins filled with paper "trouble tickets"; gone were the ledger books and files. All the information was "at your fingertips" in a moment' (1988: 331). The computer made formalization instantaneous and certain: 'I can know everything in an instant'; 'Now we have it in black and white' (1988: 331).

Zuboff's (1988) case studies also show how the computer is able to centralize the textualized work structures through the instant collation and integration of information on terminal screens and printouts. The computer becomes a mechanized centre which is not only continuously registering and displaying (that is, formalizing) system behaviour but is also able to condense data from many sources and focus it at one point. This, of course, is the conventional definition of a centre. But the concept of a centre (and the centralization processes that go with it) has another and less obvious aspect: it displaces power from its peripheral sources in order to augment its own power. This enables the centre to dominate its world and not be dominated by it. The computer only becomes a centre when the systems designer appropriates the skills and knowledge that reside in people and books and then, as Zuboff (1988) shows, uses this appropriated power to dominate the very sources it borrows from. This is what happened with the Portuguese navigators and their techniques of representation when they borrowed the powers of such distant factors as the heavens, the winds and currents of the Atlantic Ocean and turned these powers against their sources; the Portuguese vessels became centres able to dominate an environment which formerly dominated them. Ultimately, of course, the Portuguese vessels became subcentres of the main centre of the Portuguese East Indies Company in Lisbon which not only dominated in turn the vessels, the heavens, the winds and ocean currents but also the spice industry of the East Indies. A site becomes a centre to the extent that it incorporates relevant features of its periphery and makes those features work for it.

In addition to the appropriation of space, the centre ideally has to appropriate time. The power of the computer is that it can collate and integrate complex data from various sources in real time. A centre is powerful to the degree it can predict or know in advance. It is easy to show that prediction is a result of efficient technologies of representation. When Pasteur announced the field demonstration of his anthrax vaccine, he was in effect making a prediction that all the vaccinated animals would live and all the non-vaccinated animals would die. Of course, Pasteur had already successfully performed this prediction in his laboratory; its successful extension to the farm required, as we saw, the transformation of the farm into the laboratory. The prediction was fulfilled but it was really a *retrodiction* that relied both on prior work and on physically extending this prior work to the farm in the form of specific laboratory techniques. In other words, Pasteur's prediction would not have worked outside the specific practices *previously* developed in the laboratory. When Pasteur demonstrated that he could 'predict' the outcome of the field trial, his laboratory became a centre for interested farmers and the agriculture business.

Conventional organizational analysis typically views its field in terms of separate categories, which are assumed to inhabit insulated and singular spaces. The traditional division between organization and environment is an example of this mode of analysis. Formalization and centralization are also traditionally understood in this way. Formalization creates a set of structures which occupy an objective space separate from the subjective space of individuals. Centralization creates singular and specific locations of authority in the organization. Simon's (1957) concept of bounded rationality is a further example of an insulated and singularized space: the 'rationality' is located *within* the limited cognitive capacities of individual decision makers. Serres (1982) has called this mode of thinking 'Euclidean': it casts everything into single spaces, displacements without change of state, disconnected morphologies.

> Euclidean space was chosen in our work-oriented cultures because it is the space of work – of the mason, the surveyor, or the architect . . . My body lives in as many spaces as the society, the group, or the collectivity have formed: the

Euclidean house, the street and its network, the open and closed garden, the church or the enclosed spaces of the sacred, the school and its spatial varieties containing fixed points, and the complex ensemble of flow-charts, those of language, of the factory, of the family, of the political party, and so forth. Consequently, my body is not plunged into one space but into the intersection or the junctions of this multiplicity. (1982: 44–5)

Serres goes on to argue that a topology of movement is required which recognizes that human actions occur not *in* spaces but *between* them. As we have seen, this is exactly what the logic of representation offers. It works on the boundaries or intersections of the inside and the outside, between here and there, this and that. It displaces space (and time) through remote control and abbreviation; it traverses a mobile space of non-localizable relationships.

If we look back at our examples of representation in action, we get a good idea of how this new topology works. Since it is not a space of singularities but of intersections or interactions, it always works in terms of *folds* or *doubles* – for example, the complicity–antagonism fold of the inside–outside relationship. The Portuguese navigators were able to displace the Atlantic winds when they saw their sails as folds in which an *inside* (the protective sociotechnical system of the vessel) was doubled with an *outside* (threatening winds). This simple example of the topology of the fold also shows that the inside is an interiorization of the outside, a kind of doubling of the outside. Pasteur's laboratory became a fold of the infected farm, his anthrax vaccine doubled the anthrax bacillus.

Formalization is also a topological fold: its objectivity is the double of its subjectivity, just as Bentham's institutional formalizations were mirror images of the wayward and intransigent behaviour of the eighteenth-century masses. The centre, too, is a fold; it doubles itself around a periphery whose power it borrows and simulates. Representation also shows that the inside is always a doubling *of* the outside, that the inside is always an inversion of the outside, and never the other way round. In remote control, representation displaces the outside of the remote and 'beyond' into the inside of the near and familiar. In abbreviation, it displaces the outside of the dispersed and macroscopic into the inside of the compact and manageable. Representation displaces the outside inside. In contrast, bounded rationality, as a singularity, must always be an inner resource which acts on an outer problem; it is allied to intentions and goals which are also presumed to be integral to the organizational decision-making apparatus directed from the 'inside' of the individual. For representation, however, intentions and goals are themselves displacements in the topological folds of organizational space.

Finally, representation enables us to see formal organization and information in a new light. Information is no longer commodity or surprise. Representation shows it to consist of a spatial and temporal fold where an inside of familiar and manageable forms is constructed, re-presented, from an outside of resistant and retroactive non-forms or forces.

Representation becomes the conversion of force or power into information. Conventional organizational analysis is still generated in a Euclidean space that prevents it from understanding the outside of its object.[5] Representation offers a way out of this conceptual impediment.

Notes

1 See Weick (1979) on 'enactment' and organizing.
2 O'Hara (1988) uses the oxymoron 'enabling constraints' to describe this phenomenon.
3 Foucault (1977) analyses a range of vision-oriented administrative technologies that were constructed or perfected during this period; for example, hierarchical observation, normalizing judgement, the examination, the Panopticon.
4 Again, Foucault (1977: Part 3, Chapter 1) provides some details of this technique; for example, the association between 'signalization' and the 'precise system of command'.
5 These final comments (as well as a borrowed turn of phrase) rely heavily on Deleuze (1986) who has analysed the fold and the inside–outside relationship in some detail.

References

Bertin, J. (1983) *Semiology of Graphics: Diagrams, Networks, Maps*. Madison, Wisconsin: University of Wisconsin Press.
Deleuze, G. (1986) *Foucault*. Minneapolis, MN: University of Minnesota Press.
Foucault, M. (1977) *Discipline and Punish: The Birth of the Prison*. London: Allen Lane.
Foucault, M. (1979) 'Governmentality', *Ideology and Consciousness*, 6: 5–21.
Hall, R.H. (1987) *Organizations: Structure and Process*. Englewood Cliffs, NJ: Prentice-Hall.
Latour, B. (1983) 'Give me a laboratory and I will raise the world', in Kn. Knorr-Cetina and M. Mulkay (eds), *Science Observed: Perspectives on the Social Study of Science*. London: Sage Publications.
Latour, B. (1988) *The Pasteurization of France*. Cambridge, MA: Harvard University Press.
Law, J. (1986) 'On the methods of long-distance control: Vessels, navigation and the Portuguese route to India', in J. Law (ed.), *Power, Action and Belief: A New Sociology of Knowledge*? London: Routledge & Kegan Paul.
McArthur, T. (1986) *Worlds of Reference: Lexicography, Learning and Language from the Clay Tablet to the Computer*. Cambridge: Cambridge University Press.
MacKay, D.M. (1969) *Information, Mechanism and Meaning*. Cambridge, MA: MIT Press.
Miller, J.-A. (1987) 'Jeremy Bentham's Panoptic device', *October*, 41: 3–29.
O'Hara, D.T. (1988) 'What was Foucault?', in J. Arac (ed.), *After Foucault: Humanistic Knowledge, Postmodern Challenges*. New Brunswick: Rutgers University Press.
Scarry, E. (1985) *The Body in Pain: The Making and Unmaking of the World*. New York: Oxford University Press.
Schotter, A. (1981) *The Economic Theory of Social Institutions*. Cambridge: Cambridge University Press.
Scott, W.R. (1987) *Organizations: Rational, Natural and Open Systems*. Englewood Cliffs, NJ: Prentice-Hall.
Serres, M. (1982) *Hermes: Literature, Science, Philosophy*. Baltimore: The Johns Hopkins University Press.
Simon, H.A. (1955) 'A behavioral model of rational choice', *Quarterly Journal of Economics*, 69: 99–118.
Simon, H.A. (1957) *Models of Man*. New York: Wiley.
Starobinski, J. (1975) 'The inside and the outside', *The Hudson Review*, 28: 333–51.

Weber, M. (1947) *The Theory of Social and Economic Organization*. Glencoe, IL: Free Press.

Weick, K. (1979) *The Social Psychology of Organizing*. Reading, MA: Addison-Wesley.

Williamson, O.E. (1975) *Markets and Hierarchies: Analysis and Anti-Trust Implications*. New York: Free Press.

Zipf, G.K. (1949) *Human Behavior and the Principle of Least Effort*. Reading, MA: Addison-Wesley.

Zuboff, S. (1988) *In the Age of the Smart Machine: The Future of Work and Power*. New York: Basic Books.

14

Formative Contexts and Activity Systems: Postmodern Approaches to the Management of Change

Frank Blackler

Lecturing in 1917, Freud suggested that his theory of the unconscious had delivered the 'third blow' to human narcissism. The first blow to human vanity had, Freud suggested, been Copernicus's revelation that the earth was not the centre of the universe. The second was Darwin's discovery that human beings were descended from animals. The third, he argued, was his own realization that the ego is not master in its own house. It is undoubtedly true that these shifts in thinking about human beings' relationship to physical, biological and psychological realities have been profound, but since Freud wrote, a fourth revolution in our understanding of its situation has occurred that is at least as significant as these three. It concerns the nature of social life and is the recognition that, whatever our everyday assumptions about their propriety or good sense, social systems are arbitrary. Social order is not God-given, social traditions have no inevitability, social regularities do not result from immutable natural laws. Societies are man-made and social institutions result from the actions of those who participate within them.

Recognition of the arbitrary bases of social systems is not attributable to any single writer. Doubtless, the efforts of many social scientists have played their part but the key factor in making the point obvious has been the extraordinary range of social, economic, political and technological developments which have transformed societies during the twentieth century. Through them, human beings' own role in determining their cultural forms has been exposed as never before.

While the point that social life is an artefact can be simply stated, its recognition does not immediately solve any problems. Questions about how social structures constrain or liberate their members, about why changes to social systems are difficult to engineer, or about what alternative social forms are possible, remain to be answered. What an appreciation of the point does is to help to (re-)formulate questions about the ways in which social order is created and sustained, how social changes are possible and how they may be managed. This chapter is concerned with such matters and their relevance to organizational changes. An adequate treatment of the various theoretical, practical and moral issues that they raise can only be undertaken by theory that is both interdisciplinary and action-oriented. The development of such theory is not easy, but in recent years researchers working in different areas of the social sciences have, independently, developed similar approaches to the problem. The article outlines the key notions associated with two of these: Unger's theory of formative contexts and Engestrom's notion of activity systems. The suggestion is that, applied to organizational analysis, these approaches are complementary and provide the basis of a new approach to the planning of change.

The chapter is divided into six sections: a review of the changing nature of organization change; a discussion of the requirements of a theory of disjunctive organizational change; a presentation of the theory of formative context; an overview of its relevance to organization theory and analysis; a review of weaknesses associated with the approach, and a presentation of complementary approaches derived from activity theory; and summary and conclusions.

The Changing Nature of Organization Change

In the current context of international changes Britain appears to be a relatively stable society. Yet to those of us who live there, the extent of changes affecting the country is much in evidence. Changes in work organizations have occurred or are occurring, for example, because of the shifts in world economy, newly emerging relations with Europe, changes in the structure of the UK economy, an ideology of the enterprise culture, new approaches to public sector management, the enactment of new labour laws, the introduction of new technologies, demographic changes, and changing attitudes to the environment. This list is a long one, though other examples could be added. The pattern of such developments has not been coherent, and different sectors have been affected differently. None the less, such changes raise considerable problems of management and policy making. Collectively they have involved major shifts in priorities, and new patterns of resource utilization, vested interests, organizational structures and relations between government and companies.

Ever since Marx, it has been recognized that capitalist societies are societies of change and what is happening in the UK is by no means untypical of events in other countries. What does seem unusual, though, is the rate and extent of changes currently affecting the developed world. Changing attitudes on this point amongst social scientists are well illustrated by a comparison between two books on change, one published over a quarter of a century ago, the other very recently. In 1964, introducing their collection of readings on social change, Etzioni and Etzioni were able to comment on the stability of modern social democracies:

we do not wish to imply that a perfect balance has been achieved, making for permanent stability. But in the near future, modern societies seem comparatively stable and – barring a major nuclear disaster – unlikely to change rapidly on a large scale.

Compare this to the manner in which Lash and Urry concluded their 1987 study of change in modern societies.

the world of 'disorganised capitalism' is one in which the 'fixed, fast-frozen' relations of organised capitalism have been swept away. Societies are being transformed from above, below and from within. All that is solid about organised capitalism, class, industry, cities, collectivity, nation state, even the world, melts into air.

Lash and Urry's analysis of 'disorganized capitalism' has been reflected, of course, in other accounts of developments in Western societies. 'Post-industrialism', 'post-Fordism', and 'postmodernism' are the best known of these. There are key differences between such scenarios, yet they share the common message that present experiences of uncertainty will be repeated by continuing uncertainties in the future. Within organizational studies itself, significant shifts in focus have taken place in recent years, in part reflecting this broader climate of change. For example, interest in job design has been replaced by interest in the management of new technologies, interest in group psychology by an emphasis on organizational cultures; and interest in decision-making has been overtaken by interest in corporate strategy. New exemplars have appeared in the popular management literature for managers. Often inspired by Japanese approaches to management, these include suggestions for 'flexible labour', 'the flexible firm', for 'human resources management', and that managers should endeavour to manage the culture of their organizations.

It is advisable, however, to treat the simplified prescriptions that are so often associated with such fads with some caution. Much of significance has been written on why the demands on organizations to change have outstripped their ability to respond but, taking into account all the interest shown in this field, I would judge that rather less of significance has been produced to help people decide what approach to take to the relevant problems. This should not be thought surprising, however. Anxieties associated with continuing social and economic changes have been well summarized by a number of writers (see the discussion by Dunphy and Stace, 1988) who suggest that incremental (or 'evolutionary') change in organizations must now give way to more rapid adjustments. Disjunctive (or depending who is writing, 'transformative', even 'revolutionary') changes are, according to this view, the order of the day. Although there are problems with the detail of such formulations (when does 'incremental' change become 'transformative'?) the idea of disjunctive change is helpful, drawing attention as it does to the problems associated with social upheavals. Disruptive social changes are undoubtedly very difficult to manage effectively. They present organizational studies with some of the central practical and theoretical issues of our time.

Requirements of a Theory of Organizational Change

The theoretical and practical challenges that disruptive social changes present are well illustrated by the momentous developments of recent years in Eastern Europe. For example, at the time of writing this article, something approaching a 'Catch 22' has emerged for the Soviet economy. The Soviets cannot reform their economy until the collective economic assumptions of tens of millions of Russians begin to change, but such assumptions cannot be expected to shift until the economy itself is reformed. A free economy will not, however, follow the precisions of the planner's timetable for it requires that people should possess a liberal psychology and temperament, a way of living that for most of the twentieth century Soviet institutions have sought to repress. According to this view, despite what would appear to be a widespread wish to change the (man-made) way of life followed in the Soviet bloc, Central and Eastern Europe have by no means yet seen the last breath of communism.

Similar issues have been illustrated by the tragic developments in China in Tiananmen Square in 1989. On 2 June, a day before the troops moved in, four of the student leaders who were on hunger strike issued a Strike Declaration. Liu Xiaobo, Zhou Dou, Gao Xim and Hou Dejian affirmed their search for life, their desire for democracy, their distaste for repression, the need for personal honesty, and the value of equity. They listed their main tenets (as reported in the *Independent*, 10 June 1989):

- We have no enemy. Don't poison our wisdom and the democratization of China with hatred and violence
- We all need introspection. Everyone is responsible for the fact that China has been left behind by many other countries
- We are first and foremost citizens
- We are not in search of death – we are looking for real life

At one level it seems extraordinary that sentiments such as these could have so terrified the Chinese government that, before the eyes of the whole world, it would massacre its own people. No detailed plan for insurrection was proposed in the students' declaration, though their courageous statement was no less profound for that. It is only when the students' aspirations are seen in their broader context that their significance becomes clear. China's history of isolation, its Confucian traditions, reliance on a strong central State, peasant values, bureaucratic control and suppression of the individual, as well as recent events such as the 'cultural revolution', had all created a powerful institutional and cultural framework which was, unexpectedly, being threatened by economic liberalization in general and the sentiments of the students in particular.

Both the Russian and the Chinese instances provide examples, therefore, of the pressures for disjunctive social changes and the difficulties of bringing them about. What both demonstrate clearly is that an understanding of the processes of social upheaval requires a theoretical framework that will illuminate key issues simultaneously at different levels of analysis. If commentators are ignorant of social theory they run the risk of being reductionist in their explanations of social events. Similarly, if they are ignorant of psychology they are liable to be naive in their explanations of behavioural matters. To understand complex social changes, links have to be forged between social, economic, political and historical analysis on the one hand and people's beliefs, imaginations and aspirations on the other. Moreover, if such understanding is to be translated into action, relevant theory must do more than simply explain the past trends of history. Retrospective analysis is clearly essential, but through its treatment of key institutions, values, behavioural repertoires, and so on, the theory of social change should endeavour to develop a prospective orientation. In practice this means that such theory should explore the role of human agency in social events and the opportunities that can be taken to encourage new, perhaps unanticipated, trajectories of social development.

These requirements are exactly paralleled by the need within organizational studies to understand disjunctive organizational changes. Here, too, it is not possible to understand the problems of widespread change through theories that separate studies of the social and institutional from those of the cognitive and emotional. What is required are theories which take the relationship between such levels of analysis as a major focus for attention. Moreover, such theories should not stand apart from the phenomenon which they examine. Given how important it is that disjunctive organizational changes are managed satisfactorily, the maxim that 'theories are useful if they are useful' seems particularly apposite in this case.

Proposals made by Kenneth Gergen in this volume illustrate the importance of these points. Gergen suggests, correctly in my view, that theories gain importance not from how well they match the way things are but from the activities that they facilitate. He then suggests that organization theory and management practice has been restricted by too heavy a reliance on romantic and modernist forms of discourse. At the present time, he argues, it is important to combat the processes by which new meanings and possibilities in social life are stifled. Gergen suggests:

> The ideal of the organization as a smoothly running machine, clean and austerely effective, becomes dangerous. Rather, from the present perspective, organizational survival depends ultimately on the insinuation of polyglot, immersion in metaphor, and the prevalence of creative confusion. Rather than autonomous, self-directing managers, we find the emphasis on thoroughgoing interdependence, and the quality of relatedness replacing the character of the individual as the centre of concern.

The uncertainties of the present age mean that it is, I think, difficult to overrate the importance of this suggestion that new ways of interacting should be explored; and the exhortation that people should embrace confusion, immerse themselves in metaphor, become polyglot, is impressive, even inspiring. However, as with the Russian and Chinese cases already touched upon, Gergen's prescription raises key questions about the practicality of attempts to introduce rapid transformations in the shared cognitive schemas and institutional frameworks which people have become skilled in using. I do not question the need for what Gergen proposes. What I do ask, however, is how feasible is it? The mutual impact of institutional structures, symbols, ideologies, modes of discourse, beliefs, imaginations, behavioural skills and opportunities for actions needs to be better understood. A central task for organization theory must be to focus on the processes that link cognitions with social contexts, the ways in which taken-for-granted assumptions influence social imaginations, and the opportunities that can be created to manage significant infrastructural changes.

Unger's Theory of Social Reconstruction

Processes associated with disjunctive organization change clearly need to be understood in their totality, but the social sciences are notorious for their tendency to fragment, either into separate levels of analysis or into mutually suspicious paradigmatic groups. In recent years, however, theorists from very different disciplinary backgrounds have, independently, begun to address the issue of human agency in complementary ways. From within organization studies institutional theory (Scott, 1987; Zucker, 1987) has emphasized the dependence of organizations on social norms and has explored the ways in which environments influence organizational resources and goals. From sociology Giddens' (1984) conception of structuration has gone further, offering an ontological basis for understanding the mutual relationship between the rules and resources that society makes available to its members and the ways social actors reproduce that society. Arguing from a philosophical perspective, Realist philosophers of the social sciences such as Bhaskar (1986) and Outhwaite (1987) have developed similar positions. From a different perspective social anthropologists, for example Bourdieux (1977), have proposed approaches to link structure and process. Amongst psychologists too, interest is currently being shown in relevant cognitive approaches developed from Vygotsky's activity theory. Later in this chapter I wish to comment on this last approach, but it is appropriate to begin by reviewing the ideas of Roberto Unger, a leading figure in the American critical legal studies movement and a political activist in his native Brazil. Unger writes from a political science perspective, explicitly seeking to develop new constitutional and institutional forms. Yet he criticizes the fragmented nature of the social sciences, and proposes a theory that offers the basis for a more integrative approach.

The origins of critical legal theory help to introduce Unger's ideas. These lie in a particularly significant failure of expectations of social change to match institutional realities. American law students involved in the protest movements of late 1960s and Vietnam war period were deeply impressed with the contrast between their campaign experiences and the constitutional and legal theories they were being taught in the classroom. For a number of them the nature of conventional legal discourse was to emerge as a burning theoretical issue. To illuminate the problems they turned to Lévi-Strauss, Gramsci, Habermas, Foucault and others. An orientation to the issue emerged which, in part, attempted to replace conventional understandings of the law as realist and as a benign science of technocratic policy by an account locating legal argumentation within a broader system of beliefs legitimating the prevailing social order.

In a series of recent publications, Unger (1987a, 1987b, 1987c) has developed this tradition into a broader thesis which accords well with the general shift towards culturalism in social theory. He offers a strongly political vision of social life. Societies are supported by conflicts, he argues; tensions and vulnerabilities are hidden by mechanisms of stabilization and constraint. As conflicts are temporarily resolved, solutions become supported by particular organizational and technological styles, by emerging group interests, patterns of privilege, and the ways in which a basic grammar of social interactions becomes articulated in official dogmas. The imaginative schemas of participants interact with the institutional frameworks in which they operate. The resulting 'formative context' provides a set of pragmatic but unreflective routines. According to this view, conventional wisdom can be thoroughly misleading as a guide to action; the social arrangements that people are familiar with may be deeply entrenched in their minds; all that is arbitrary in social life can be obscured, as bases of authority, legal dogmas, divisions of roles, technologies and styles of organizing come to be seen as normal and inevitable. The status quo is attributed with a false necessity and, mistakenly, a consistency is attributed to its component parts. According to this view also, social arrangements which are unsupported by their institutional context may fail, not because (as is usually assumed) there are intrinsic flaws in the ideas upon which they are based but because of the hostile environments in which they were located.

Unger's theory of change develops this perspective. He believes society 'always stands at the edge of a cliff'. Despite their resilience, formative contexts are only more or less arbitrarily held together and real opportunities exist for promoting change. Unger takes the view that 'everything in society is frozen or fluid politics'. He describes social life in terms of an agitation that is both contained and irrepressible.

Unger's key theoretical concept is, therefore, the notion of 'formative context'. Through this he focuses on the arrangements and beliefs that people take for granted, and on the ways in which they identify and pursue their interests. Such assumptions are pervasive in their effects for they give coherence and continuity to the roles that people enact in everyday life. Normally unrecognized by those who are affected by them, formative contexts are an accepted set of pragmatic (and potentially, compulsive) institutional and imaginative assumptions that guide the ways in which interests are defined and problems are approached. Through the roles they enact, people behave as if their social worlds are coherent, intelligible and defensible; the biased, indeed arbitrary, nature of the terms upon which different interests have come to be understood are overlooked and social practices assume a 'false necessity'.

Unger recognizes, of course, that generalizations about social ideals are necessarily drawn from the dominant assumptions of particular classes. No society is composed of universally held belief systems and, indeed, Unger's theory of social change draws its force from the point that people do not always agree. None the less he maintains that, to an extent, formative contexts are shared, for without them social life would reduce to an endless bickering between different interest groups. Moreover 'the weight of established institutional arrangements as well as the privileged hold that certain groups and traditions have upon the mass culture' exert a unifying influence over expectations and ideals. Thus, although the process is by no means complete, the strategic premises of different groups tend to converge around a core set of assumptions that provides an essential background condition for action and interaction.

While formative contexts can be deduced from the outcomes they support, they are not, it should be emphasized, self-evident entities that present themselves for easy scrutiny. Several factors conspire to conceal the structure of formative contexts; Unger mentions the proven pragmatic utility of established roles, the security that familiar scripts give to those who enact them, and the vanity of leaders who like to assume that their commands articulate the wishes of those commanded. A formative context exists

> because (and in the sense that) it is hard to disturb and even grasp in the course of ordinary activities. Its power to shape a world of routine, deals and quarrels depends upon the extent to which it gains immunity – or rather immunizes itself – against the possibility of challenge and revision.

Moreover the 'false necessity' of formative contexts is resilient. Formative contexts are not

> just factitious entities that cease to exist as soon as people stop taking them seriously. They may not long be able to survive a decisive withdrawal of consent. But they can often induce in those whose life chances and daily routines they shape a blank and despairing resignation that muddles the clarity of the distinction between consent and coercion. (1987b: 61)

Unger recognizes that the 'naturalistic fallacy' is weaker in industrialized societies than in traditional ones. Moreover, a central plank of his analysis is the suggestion that particular institutions can be compared in terms of their responsiveness to criticism and their ability to

Table 14.1 *Key aspects of the formative context of North Atlantic countries*

Institutional aspects	Imaginative aspects
Constitutional arrangements that provide for representation without militancy. A fragmentation of government power ('checks and balances' of eighteenth-century origins) coupled with class rivalry (with its origins in the nineteenth century).	Images of civic equality and of official accountability for government practices. Democratic forms of organization for government and political parties.
	Acceptance that most citizens are passive in political life.
Market economies with property rights the primary instrument of economic decentralization.	Acceptance of the primacy of property rights (rather than trust and responsibility) in economic life.
Relevant control exercised by bureaucrats and judges.	Images of voluntary employment/personal employment contracts.
Within business organizations task-defining and task-executing activities are separated. Such organizational styles are reinforced by technologies and by legal rules.	Acceptance of impersonal hierarchies to govern the organization of work and economic exchange. Professionals and managers expected to act in the name of technical and economic rationality. Unconvivial work borne by an underclass.
Large organizations have privileged relations with government, and legal rights which insulate them from market, labour and capital instabilities.	Acceptance that occupational status correlates with relative social advantage.
The workforce is fragmented into distinct groups.	Basic conflicts of purpose and values absent from community life. Separate private life for family and friendship.

Source: Summarized from Unger, 1987.

change, a capacity he terms 'negative capability'. None the less, even within the heterogeneity of modern societies, Unger maintains that emancipation from false necessity is only partial. To summarize the points made earlier: to those who work within them, social institutions come to appear less the outcomes of various political disputes and more as acceptable if, perhaps, imperfect approximations to the ideals of efficiency and good sense. Unger's basic point is that any stable system of rights and powers operates as a 'practical expression of a certain way of imagining society'. Formative contexts thus contain strong prescriptive elements. They imply a conception of 'what the relations among people can and should be like in different areas of existence'. Understood in this way, formative contexts are 'the hardest of social facts' for they 'are the most resistant to transformation and the richest in the range of their effects'.

Aspects of the formative context that Unger describes for North Atlantic countries are illustrated in Table 14.1. Institutional frameworks and interacting imaginative preconceptions (or 'models of human association') are identified in four key areas: the organization of government, private rights, the organization of work, and the structure of occupations.

Central to Unger's approach is his analysis of how social changes occur and the insights that an understanding of this process can provide for promoting significant social changes. He distinguishes between 'context supporting routines' and 'context transforming conflicts'. The former occur as people enact the conception of human relationships implicit in their formative context; the latter lead to its modification. Unger's approach to change is not merely to encourage reformist tinkering, nor does he favour a revolutionary strategy of exploiting structural crises. His theory seeks to develop the opportunities of a middle route. Given the nature of formative contexts piecemeal changes can, over time, amount to significant change, he argues. To achieve this, people can be encouraged first to recognize and then to review the acceptability of their formative context: anomalies and inconsistencies within an existing context help expose its general nature, disputes about roles and priorities can escalate to highlight the 'taken-for-granted' character of social life. His basic aim is to help people find new ways of relating to their contexts; as they become more proactive in this the distinction between 'context supporting routines' and 'context transforming conflicts' would, Unger argues, be eroded. Changes in formative contexts can, according to this view, be introduced piecemeal. Cumulatively such changes can significantly change a formative context. Yet because of their multi-faceted nature, formative contexts do demonstrate both inertia and resilience and the process is likely to be slow.

Formative Contexts and Organization Change

Unger's work is highly polemical and is not without its problems, some of which are mentioned below. Moreover, his concerns are broader than the ones that organizational theorists would normally address. Yet both the issues that he focuses upon and the style of analysis he develops are particularly relevant to organization studies. Hierarchy, power, the importance of rationality, problems of employee control and commitment and the need for organizational flexibility are commonplace themes in this area.

General Applications of the Theory

A general indication of how Unger's style of theorizing can be adapted for organizational analysis can be provided by reference to Table 14.2 which summarizes key aspects of Unger's theory of social change. Here the terms 'social arrangements', 'social structure' and 'social theory' might rather plausibly be replaced by 'organizational arrangements', 'organizational structure' and 'organizational theory'. Unger rarely uses the word 'culture'. None the less his approach is strongly interactionist and his general social theory is consistent with accounts of organizations as bodies of thought, of the loose relationships that may be found between social/structural components and ideational/symbolic ones, and

Table 14.2 *Key aspects of Unger's theory of social change*

---

1 The origins of social arrangements lie in past social conflicts and the institutional and imaginative arrangements which followed their resolution.

2 Such 'formative contexts' are deep seated and pragmatic in their effects on everyday life. They provide an implicit model of how social life should be led. Taken for granted as they are, they are rarely recognized by those whose actions are informed by them and they can quickly assume an aura of inevitability.

3 Formative contexts are not the product of any single factor but of a number of factors, each of which has its own history.

4 Although people may assume that different elements of their formative context stand and fall together, different elements may be replaced at different times.

5 Changes in formative contexts do occur over time. Minor arguments about the propriety of various arrangements inevitably arise and, though the character of the whole shows a resilience, 'shifts and drifts' in the character of a formative context are always taking place.

6 There are important functional benefits associated with flexible social structures but, though the institutions of modern societies are not as entrenched as within traditional ones, emancipation from 'false necessity' has been only partial.

7 People are able to break with their contexts and build new ones, and it is appropriate that they should. Neither individuals nor societies are pre-determined.

8 Institutional supports are needed to facilitate 'context making'. What is important is that people should be encouraged/enabled to develop new unconstrained relationships with their contexts.

9 Because of the influence formative contexts have over the way disputes are expressed and resolved, past events continue to influence the present developments. Social theory can help to identify appropriate ways forward for different situations.

Source: Summarized from Unger, 1987a.

of the opportunities provided by exceptions and conflicts for social and intellectual reconstruction.

At the descriptive level, Unger's approach points towards the different kinds of explanation of organizational life that are possible. First, it suggests that participants will tend to describe organizational arrangements in rational terms as a possibly flawed, but none the less acceptable, approximation to an uncontroversial way of getting things done. Second, his account of the political basis of social arrangements indicates that the logic and good sense that is assumed within such accounts is likely to be misleading; organizational arrangements are essentially arbitrary. This insight implies that what happens within an organization is likely to be best explained in terms of such factors as the accidents of history, institutional norms, demarcation disputes, control battles, technological choices, the sedimentation of successive decisions, 'tinkering', 'muddling through', and so on. Third, the idea of formative contexts predicts that, none the less, the roles and routines enacted by participants will feel 'natural' to them. The ways they account for social events are likely to be oversimplified, yet, through their everyday actions participants will rediscover the meanings that inform their roles and will reaffirm the context that informs their behaviour.

Regarding the implications of the theory for the management of change, the approach can be taken to imply that formative contexts are reproduced by the behaviours of those affected by them, but that this process involves a process of improvisation and compromise that will be poorly recognized, articulated or planned for. The theory suggests that shifts in formative contexts tend to occur anyway, but the development of new contexts could be assisted by analysis intended to locate behavioural routines in their broader normative contexts. Stereotyping such contexts would provide a start. Consideration of what is revealed by naturally occurring disputes and incongruities would help build on this process. Examples of exceptions to prevailing norms should also be explored. As I discuss further below, given the strong emphasis he places on the prescriptive aspects of formative contexts, Unger himself emphasizes the value at this stage of close debate about alternative possibilities. The process of developing new social forms would be greatly enhanced by the development of institutional arrangements that encourage behavioural experimentation and diversity.

Formative Contexts and the Theory of Organizational Archetypes

The distinctiveness of the theory of formative contexts when it is applied to organizations can be illustrated by comparing it to theories developed by writers on organizations who also work within a social constructionist perspective. Hinings and Greenwood (1988) provide a good comparison. Setting out to develop a holistic approach to describing organizations they analyse meanings and structures in organizations through Miller and Friesen's (1980, 1984) notion of 'organizational archetypes'. Hinings and Greenwood suggest that the consistency of different organizational forms is best explained in terms of the 'provinces of meaning and interpretive schemes' that are shared by organizational members, that these bind structures and processes in an 'institutionally derived normative order'. They define archetypes in terms of shared values and beliefs in three related areas: the domain of activity considered appropriate for the organization to be active within, the principles believed appropriate for its internal structures and processes, and the criteria considered appropriate for its evaluation. At first sight, therefore, their general approach seems consistent with Unger's notion that, to those who lie within them, social systems assume a coherency which itself provides a model for adequate performance.

Yet there are important differences between the approaches. The notion of organizational archetype (like so much writing on organizational culture) emphasizes coherence and consistency within an organization. This is not to say that it denies the possibility of change, simply that it focuses on the tendencies organizations demonstrate towards inertia. While the theory of formative contexts also acknowledges tendencies to inertia, it emphasizes the significance of the inconsistencies, incoherences and disputes that are also everyday features of organizational life. Greenwood and Hinings agree that prevailing archetypes will be supported by the exercise of power and politics, but the theory of formative contexts attributes a primacy to such processes. As we have seen, Unger proposes that the origins of interpretive schemas and institutional structures lie in the ways in which resolutions to past disputes became institutionalized and continue to be supported through familiar routines. Applied to organizations, this line of reasoning does not take the experienced coherency and good sense of social life at face value, but emphasizes its origins in politics and influence processes.

Formative Contexts, New Technologies and Organization Choices

Developments in the use of advanced information technologies in the UK since the early 1980s provide a specific example of the insights that Unger's approach can yield. The introduction to work organizations of systems based on advanced information and communication technologies has presented a number of distinctive management problems. It is now commonplace in the information technology literature, for example, for commentators to emphasize the indeterminism of these technologies and the range of goals and organizational forms they can be used to pursue. Such technologies are exceptionally flexible in their applications and varied in their effects and, as a result, the impacts that they have within organizations can be both complex and difficult to predict. Much speculation has been published in recent years about the social and organizational impact that these technologies will have. What is now clear is that because of their extraordinary performance characteristics, technologies based on microelectronics *could* be used to support wholly new ways of organizing. Conventional orthodoxies about the functional superiority of familiar heirarchies, departments, professions, job demarcations or geographical constraints may therefore no longer be easily defensible.

None the less, in the vast majority of cases to date, new office and factory systems based on microelectronic technologies have mostly been built along rather conventional lines. Despite the increasing familiarity people have with these technologies little progress seems to have been made in using them to rethink conventional assumptions about organizing. Although the new information technologies offer considerable scope for strategic choice, in practice such 'choices' either have not been recognized or they have been exercised in favour of familiar solutions. In the main, these new technologies have been absorbed within existing organizational archetypes.

Detailed studies of how new work systems have been designed help to indicate why this has happened. Analysis of how systems designers work, for example, has shown that the ways in which they approach the design task are strongly Tayloristic, giving primacy in their actions to technological, not behavioural or organizational, considerations. It is clear that the ways design engineers regard projects differ from the perceptions of those who are asked to live with the result. One study (Jensen, 1988), for example, recorded key differences in attitudes between the designers of a computer-mediated learning system for use in class-rooms and those of the teachers expected to use it. The designers of the system:

described the project in terms of its engineering specification not its
   impact on the classroom;
had more specific and numerous descriptions of it than the teachers;
viewed the project as more important than did the teachers;
overestimated its chance of success; and
underestimated the uncertainty and conflict that the teachers experienced.

This study confirmed the findings of other studies that many design engineers work from technological possibilities, rather than from user needs, skills, abilities, and problem-solving requirements. Put most simply, systems are built because 'we have the technology'. The views of computer experts are, time and again, taken more seriously than those of experienced user groups. The questions that a user-oriented approach would encourage, answers to which would stimulate creative approaches to organizing, are only rarely asked in the design of such systems. There are a number of such questions: for example, How do people ask for advice? What is the best way for a computer to present it? How will the needs of novices differ from those of experts? Do people trust computers? How should tasks be divided between people and the machine? How can communications with a machine adequately be achieved? How can the technologies be used to support more convivial social arrangements? How can they be used to support involved, capable staff?

Paradoxically, social scientists who have worked with design engineers on problems such as these report that design engineers often *do* take observations about the inadequacy of their approaches rather seriously. It is not, in other words, that engineers generally turn their backs on such questions altogether, dismissing the very idea of a user-centred approach. In practice, however, even when they are sympathetic towards a user-centred approach, they usually do not display much ability to adopt one. Design engineers need, it would seem, constant reminders and guidance about what such a human-centred approach means. What they *do* feel familiar with are structured design methods that encourage an analysis of the logic of information characteristics. They are far less well equipped to appreciate the need to build design around an understanding of how users might interact around or through machines, improvise to solve problems, and so on. Translating this analysis to the jargon of Unger's theory, design engineers work within their own distinctive formative context.

Their behavioural routines and their cognitive and imaginative modes of thought have been shaped and reinforced by the institutions and practices of the professional group which gives them identity and legitimacy.

Formative Contexts and Activity Theory

Earlier I argued that disruptive social changes need to be studied in their totality and that relevant theory should adopt a forward-looking, action-oriented perspective. Unger's approach is sympathetic to these aims but, designed as it was primarily for political and constitutional theorists, the application of his theory to organization studies requires a change of emphasis. In this section I first outline where this is needed and secondly introduce complementary notions derived from activity theory.

Reviewing Unger's Approach

First, while Unger is acutely aware of the need to reform interpersonal relations, his theory of change says very little about how the distinctive characteristics of a formative context may be learned and internalized by those affected by them. This is a crucial issue. The processes by which people learn and unlearn the institutional norms of their societies are obviously central to an understanding of the relationships of dominant structures, symbols, ideologies and resources, to beliefs, imaginations, and behaviour. An understanding of such processes and of the significance of possible individual differences would significantly inform judgements about the likely effectiveness of strategies for change.

Second, emphasizing that formative contexts provide unrecognized exemplars for acceptable performance, Unger pointed out that once people have been alerted to the nature of such assumptions they may begin to design alternatives. In his book *False Necessity* he assumes that, unshackled by conventional assumptions, visions of alternative social orders can be explored, and new formative contexts built which will eradicate conventional patterns of domination and hierarchy. Alternatives to the formative contexts of North Atlantic countries listed in Table 14.1 could, for example, include: a system of government made up of overlapping rather than separated powers to encourage argument which, if unsolved, could be put to general referendum; decentralized markets; the abolition of absolute property rights and the introduction of a rotating capital fund; and a system of constitutional and welfare rights. As Perry Anderson (1989) has noted, this approach has a dreamlike quality about it. Building alternative scenarios of what might be possible may be an interesting and worthwhile exercise, but complex social scripts are notoriously difficult to rewrite. The point has been well recognized in the organizational literature. For example, Argyris and Schon (1974) among many others have pointed out how difficult it can be to match the theories of social behaviour that people espouse with the theories that seem to guide their actual behaviour; Weick's (1969) concept of enactment points to many of the limitations of a simple goal-directed model of human behaviour; and Suchman's (1987) analysis of human–machine interactions has emphasized the importance of improvisation in human behaviour by developing the notion that actions are 'situated'. Putting this another way, the basis of formative contexts lies in pragmatism.

The third criticism is related to this point and concerns Unger's conception of human agency. Unger certainly does recognize that taken-for-granted assumptions are necessary prerequisites for social life, but he dwells heavily on the negative aspects of this insight. Repeatedly he alerts people to the tendencies to attribute a false necessity to established societal patterns and to assume that proposals for social change can only be realistic if they remain close to the status quo. He has good reasons for doing this, of course. Like Harré (1979), he accepts that people are social agents because they are capable of turning away from one principle of action to embrace another, and he is concerned to highlight how, by limiting imaginations and ambitions, formative contexts are disempowering. Yet within the existing contexts of complex societies there may be more scope for emancipation than Unger acknowledges. Mention has already been made of Giddens' notion of structuration, and of Bhaskar's transformational model of human activity. Both of these theorists recognize that societies can liberate as well as constrain. They take as their starting point the 'duality' of social structures: societies provide the conditions for human agency, yet are also produced by it. Any theory of agency must acknowledge the significance of this interaction, for it provides a framework for understanding the preconditions of social life.

One implication of this perspective is that in complex, differentiated and relatively flexible societies, formative contexts are likely to offer a variety of possible resources. Some citizens will undoubtedly be more advantaged than others, but modern societies offer opportunities for the enactment of a plurality of social rules and provide a variety of resources that citizens may exploit. 'False necessity' should certainly be attacked by the development of new institutional forms, but formative contexts can also be modified if people exploit the often unrecognized opportunities that already exist for promoting changes. I am suggesting that the distinctions between 'context supporting routines' and 'context transforming conflicts' are already eroded to some degree within modern societies.

To summarize: despite its strengths, Unger's approach does not explore the central processes of socialization and cultural learning, it places too heavy a reliance on debate and planning, and it offers a somewhat restricted account of human agency. These various criticisms are related. To respond to them it is helpful to review certain recent developments in cognitive theory. While the approaches I review have developed independently from Unger, they demonstrate a striking convergence of ideas.

Vygotsky's Activity Theory

In looking for ways of understanding further how cognitions are linked to social contexts it is correct to note that traditional psychological theory does not help much. Western learning theory has been dominated by an interest in how people process information, the assumption being that learning is largely a passive process of information absorption, with research suggesting that information-processing abilities decline with age. It is perhaps surprising, therefore, that recent developments in the field of learning and memory have provided an interesting set of notions. Many of the advances in this area have followed ideas associated with the Russian psychologist Lev Vygotsky, working in the 1920s and 1930s, and those of his followers, Luria, Leont'ev and Davidov, who sought to develop Vygotsky's notions into 'activity theory'. Like Unger, Vygotsky was impressed by the social changes of his day; he was an ardent supporter of the Russian revolution. His ideas were to incur the displeasure of the Soviet orthodoxy, however, and publication of his books was to be banned for many years. But since the late 1970s a number of commentaries on his writings have appeared in the West, and his work is now becoming increasingly influential (Brotherton, 1990). Two recent developments of his approach, by Wertsch and Engestrom, are particularly relevant to the present discussion.

Vygotsky's ideas can be introduced by identifying different levels of explanation of behaviour. His analysis points to the distinction between actions and operations, a fairly standard split, but also between these and activities. Vygotsky's notion of 'activity' is closely analogous to Goffman's mid-range concept of 'frames'. That is, activity is a sociocultural interpretation imposed on the context by the participants themselves (examples of activity would be 'work', 'instruction', 'play'). 'Action', on the other hand, is specific goal-directed behaviour. An individual might make the same action, for example moving from one place to another, when participating in different activities. Finally, analysis at the level of 'operations' reveals detail of the circumstances under which action is carried out. Crucial to the Vygotsky approach is the idea that explanation of how 'activities' occur must link the institutional and the cognitive levels of analysis.

Vygotsky's belief was that higher mental processes have their origin in social processes and that such processes can only be understood by an understanding of the tools and signs that mediate them. Through the use of tools (including 'social tools'), people alter their environments; similarly, Vygotsky argued, through the employment of signs people alter themselves. Actually he does not want to differentiate too much between behaviour and thought. Higher psychological functioning emerges, Vygotsky thought, 'first between people (interpsychologically) then inside the individual (intrapsychologically)'. For him, learning is essentially an active, voluntary, process; it occurs as a result of actions and concepts which are themselves only to be fully understood within the context of social interactions.

Vygotsky's approach thus provides the possible link between culture and thinking that Unger assumes but does not examine. The approach resonates with a number of contemporary developments in Western psychology. These include recent approaches that define intelligence in terms of interaction with environments, and the finding that, although information-processing abilities decline as people get older, people may become ever more skilful within 'encapsulated' areas of cognitive functioning; that is, within certain styles of thought. The two recent developments that are particularly relevant to the present discussion, however, are the notions of 'activity setting' and 'activity system'.

The notion of 'activity setting' (Wertsch, 1985) has clear affinities with the notion of the 'formative context'. Activity settings are not determined by physical contexts but are brought to the situation by participants themselves. To illustrate, Wertsch uses as an example the point that, when given the same task to work on with a child, teachers and parents may approach the situation very differently: teachers may interpret the activity setting as a learning opportunity and prompt the child only to solve the problem for itself by experiment; parents, on the other hand, may understand the setting in terms of goal achievement and prompt the child rapidly towards the correct solution. Like formative contexts, activity settings are often not readily recognized or accessible to conscious reflection by those participating in them. None the less, people are extremely skilful in acting in accord with their, often tacit, definitions of their situation. Activity settings are, of course, socially defined, and to develop his analysis Wersch adds the concept of 'motives'. By this he does not mean individual motives in the conventional psychological sense, rather, as participants' understandings of the goals that are socially defined as appropriate in any particular activity setting.

The second, related, development is the notion of 'activity systems' (Engestrom, 1987, 1989). Engestrom uses the term in part to debunk a number of common misconceptions about the nature of expertise and to help professionals respond to changing public expectations of their services. In the Vygotsky tradition Engestrom emphasizes the historical and cultural origins of expertise. It is unrealistic, in his view, to assume that experts in any given field all practise the same skills; expertise should not be understood as the property of individuals who, after long periods of apprenticeship, have absorbed a standard repertoire of explicit knowledge and tacit skills. Rather, analysis of expertise in its historical and cultural context points to significant changes of priority and style. Moreover, the behaviour of specific experts has to be understood as part of the broader social, technical and organizational system within which they operate. Engestrom suggests that the exercise of expertise is a collective activity with individual experts enacting their priorities through the activity system of which they are a part. This will include their colleagues and co-workers (who are themselves part of a broader community), the recognized roles they enact, their shared conceptions, their shared tools, and so on.

To illustrate this style of analysis Engestrom describes his work with a medical practice. The various contrasting views the doctors held of appropriate priorities for their work (in Wersch's terminology, their activity settings) were explored by interviews with them. It emerged that medical expertise was being practised in a range of ways. The primary object of medical practice could be taken to be the treatment of somatic diseases (an ontological–biomedical view); or the provision of health care services (an administrative–economic perspective); or the patient as a psychosomatic whole (a psychiatric orientation); or the patient's social life situation (a sociomedical perspective); or the patient as a collaborator (a systemic–interactive approach). Engestrom quotes Arney and Bergen (1984) to support the view that these five frames of reference broadly correspond to five historically distinct ways of thinking about disease.

The analysis was further developed by videotaping the doctors in consultation with their patients, later obtaining their reflections on what had happened. Analysis revealed a number of discoordinations between the doctors and patients. (These included: complex patient problems versus restricted biomedical concepts and practices; patient needs that required flexible treatment versus the actual operation of rigid administrative rules; and patient needs that required a collaborative response from different health care providers versus the fragmented division of labour that was actually in operation.) It emerged that the doctors had developed distinctive personal strategies to cope with these difficulties; for example, a doctor working with a biomedical perspective might send a patient with ambiguous symptoms for more tests to rule out all possible somatic causes, thus postponing consideration of possible psychic issues, while a doctor working within a psychosomatic orientation might prescribe sick leave while trying to make it possible for the patient gradually to begin to discuss underlying stress factors.

Finally, Engestrom comments on his efforts to help the doctors change their activity system. The style of analysis he describes has clear relevance to Unger's theory of formative contexts. He notes that the key task was to help participants learn what is not there. Activity systems are not well recognized by their participants, however, so the first task is to provide 'a collective mirror'. Historical analysis, interviews and, above all, the identification of the tensions and contradictions which were daily features of the operation of the activity system provided his basic data set. From this he was able to model the activity system, illustrating its tensions, and thus helping those working within it to recognize and debate their situation and articulate an alternative way of working. In helping them develop semi-autonomous, multi-professional teams oriented towards psychosomatic and community medicine, Engestrom's experiences indicate that the process of building an innovative, unfamiliar, activity system is a complex and iterative affair. People need time to experiment with the contradictions of old and new systems. Regressions to the old as well as innovations to the new are bound to occur. Different groups will show different capacities to learn. Overall, the process is more likely to be a cyclical process of development rather than a linear one.

Conclusions: Postmodernism and Planned Organization Change

Before concluding this discussion it will help to summarize the main themes of the argument. The changes of recent years have created a climate of some uncertainty for organizations which seems unlikely to diminish in the foreseeable future. A range of new approaches to the management of change have been popularized during the 1980s but, as the dramatic events in Eastern Europe and China have revealed, disjunctive social and organizational changes are not easily understood or managed. Relevant theory must develop from the recognition that social arrangements are artefacts. As far as possible, such theory should endeavour to explain disjunctive changes in their totality by focusing on the links between institutional and social structures on the one hand and cognitive and behavioural factors on the other. Moreover, it should develop an action-oriented perspective.

Two, potentially complementary, approaches and their implications for organization studies have been presented as relevant to these aims. Unger's theory of social reconstruction differentiates societies in terms of their formative contexts; that is, in terms of their particular historical and institutional characteristics and related values and behaviours. To those living within them, formative contexts appear both rational and necessary, but Unger attacks such complacency. It is both possible and desirable, he argues, to plan and build alternatives that will be more efficient, egalitarian and convivial. Applied to organizational analysis the theory of formative contexts highlights the pressures that exist towards inertia, but emphasizes the possibilities of developing visions of alternatives.

Vygotsky's approach to understanding the cultural origins of higher mental processes develops the notion of 'activity', emphasizing the close relationship of behaviour and thought. Vygotsky's approach stresses that the significance of behavioural routines can only fully be appreciated by those participating in them. Engestrom's notion of activity systems develops such an approach, noting the cultural and historical origins of expert skills, and suggesting that the exercise of expertise must be understood as a social process.

Although these approaches were designed from very different perspectives they share a number of similarities. Both propose rather similar mid-range concepts to establish the link between individuals and their social and cultural contexts. Both emphasize the limited understandings that people have of the origins and nature of these contexts and of their relationships to them. Both emphasize the significance of conflict or inconsistencies for efforts to explore new social or organizational forms, but both acknowledge the resilience of existing systems.

There are significant differences between Unger's and Engestrom's approaches, of course. In particular, Unger's concerns are broader than Engestrom's. Yet when the approaches are applied to organization change, their differences complement each other rather well. The theory of formative contexts clearly locates individuals and their organizations in their broad historical and social contexts, emphasizes the power of existing institutional arrangements over taken-for-granted practices, and highlights both their arbitrary nature and the opportunities that could be exploited to build alternative organizational forms. The strategic influences that formative contexts exercise over organizational life usually, of course, remain understood only implicitly and are managed only tacitly. Unger's writings emphasize how important it is to review the context that informs the details of everyday life and to consider alternatives. Engestrom's theory of activity systems is similar in the way it locates cognitions in their broader cultural context, but this approach focuses explicitly on how detailed analysis of the internal contradictions of activity systems can provide opportunities for their modification. While Unger emphasizes the power of plans and visions in transcending the institutional limits of formative contexts, Engestrom explores the significance of engagement and the value of experimentation for learning and behaviour change. Unger's analysis indicates that people need to find ways to modify the cognitive, social and material foundations of the contexts that inform their actions. Engestrom's approach demonstrates how this might be done.

Reference was made earlier to Gergen's suggestion that organization theory should move into the postmodern era. The arguments I have been presenting here point in the same way. At a time of considerable social and organizational upheaval, conventional assumptions about the management of 'planned change' in organizations must be discarded, for it is a mistake to assume that disjunctive social changes can be managed in a rational, ordered and consistent way. A different series of expectations is required and the theories introduced in this chapter go some way to providing one. They emphasize the arbitrary cognitive and institutional bases of organizations, explain their inertia, point to the insights that careful study of internal conflicts and inconsistencies can provide, and underline the joint significance of debate, engagement and experiment. In short, the ideas discussed in this chapter provide the basis for a postmodern theory of the management of change.

Acknowledgement

Many thanks to Chris Brotherton for alerting me to recent developments in activity theory.

References

Anderson, P. (1989) 'Roberto Unger and the politics of empowerment', *New Left Review*, 173: 93–108.

Argyris, C. and Schon, D. (1974) *Theory in Practice: Increasing Professional Effectiveness*. San Francisco: Jossey-Bass.

Arney, W. and Bergen, B. (1984) *Medicine and the Management of the Living: Taming the Last Great Beast*. Chicago: University of Chicago Press.

Bhaskar, R. (1986) *Scientific Realism and Human Emancipation*. London: Verso.

Bourdieux, P. (1977) *Outline of a Theory of Practice*. Cambridge: Cambridge University Press.

Brotherton, C. (1990) *New Developments in Research in Adult Cognition*. Nottingham: Nottingham University Department of Adult Education.

Dunphy, D. and Stace, D. (1988) 'Transformational and coercive strategies for planned organisational change: beyond the O.D. model', *Organisational Studies*, 9: 317–34.

Engestrom, Y. (1987) *Learning by Expanding: An Activity Theoretical Approach to Developmental Research*. Helsinki: Orienta-Konsultit Oy.

Engestrom, Y. (1989) *Developing Thinking at the Workplace: Towards a Redefinition of Expertise*. San Diego: University of California Center for Human Information Processing.

Etzioni, E. and Etzioni, A. (eds) (1964) *Social Change: Sources, Patterns, and Consequences*. New York: Basic Books.

Giddens, A. (1984) *The Constitution of Society: Outline of the Theory of Structuration*. Cambridge: Polity Press.

Harré, R. (1979) *Social Being*. Oxford: Basil Blackwell.

Hinings, C. and Greenwood, R. (1988) *The Dynamics of Strategic Change*. Oxford: Basil Blackwell.

Jensen, K. (1988) *Designerens Roll, et Casestudy i Skolesystemet*. Copenhagen: Nielsen.

Lash, S. and Urry, J. (1987) *The End of Organised Capitalism*. Cambridge: Polity Press.

Miller, D. and Friesen, P. (1980) 'Archetypes of organisational transition', *Administrative Science Quarterly*, 25: 269–99.

Miller, D. and Friesen, P. (1984) *Organisations: A Quantum View*. Englewood Cliffs, NJ: Prentice-Hall.

Outhwaite, W. (1987) *New Philosophies of Social Science: Realism, Hermenuetics and Critical Theory*. Basingstoke: Macmillan.

Scott, W. (1987) 'The adolescence of institutional theory', *Administrative Science Quarterly*, 32: 493–511.

Suchman, L. (1987) *Plans and Situated Actions: The Problem of Human–Machine Communication*. Cambridge: Cambridge University Press.

Unger, R.M. (1987a) *Social Theory: Its Situation and Its Task*. Cambridge: Cambridge University Press.

Unger, R.M. (1987b) *False Necessity*. Cambridge: Cambridge University Press.

Unger, R.M. (1987c) *Plasticity into Power*. Cambridge: Cambridge University Press.

Weick, K. (1969) *The Social Psychology of Organising*. Reading, MA: Addison-Wesley.

Wertsch, J. (1985) *Vygotsky and the Social Formation of Mind*. Cambridge, MA: Harvard University Press.

Zucker, L. (1987) 'Institutional theories of organization', *American Review of Sociology*, 13: 443–64.

CONCLUSION

Decluding Organization

Michael Hughes

Prologue

The introduction to this volume has clearly delineated the theoretical and substantive continuities and disjunctures between the contributors. It *concluded* that theorizing 'organization' is experiencing an upheaval which can be perceived as an exciting plurality of contending positions or evidence of terminal disarray. However, there is still a search for theoretical coherence within the field of organization studies which underpins these contributions, though each perspective manifestly parades in the cortège of orthodoxy. This quest to establish conceptual integrity has some way to go in terms of resolving the current clash between opposing approaches to knowledge and disarticulated arenas of discourse. The most significant differences arise between the so-called Modernist and Postmodernist projects, which erupted in organization theory during the late 1980s. These positions have somewhat reluctant champions since it is not at all clear that the labels accurately or unambiguously attribute any coherence. They are not fully accepted or agreed by those engaged in the debates, and remain highly differentiated, as the chapters in this volume demonstrate. But there seems little doubt that organization theory is either alive but enduring a metamorphosis, or wandering as the living dead following the multiple blows delivered by postmodernist deconstructionism and linguistic barbs. Thus, this final chapter will attempt a measured, but concise, speculative assessment of possible theoretical directions in organization theory which might emanate from these views. There is a need to open out rather than conclude, commenting on the challenge to post-Weberian conceptualizations of organization and rational organizational forms, whilst avoiding another account or summary of the positions expressed within the preceding pages.

Loss of Theoretical Direction

The obituary of 'functionalism' and system-theoretic models has been written in whole or in part since the mid-1960s (Cicourel, 1964; Silverman, 1970; Benson, 1975). Two fundamental weaknesses were exposed and the literature subsequently crystallized into competing arenas of theoretical contest. First, the attempt to import and subordinate psychosocial representations of the 'self' into the 'social' failed to provide a convincing answer to the problems of the attribution of meaning to social behaviour and the treatment of subjectivity, despite the surge of interest which this created in organization theory. However, the resultant 'interpretive' approach to organizational behaviour did provide the field with a critical dimension which subsequently spawned variations based on selective borrowings from philosophy, anthropology and linguistics. The 'action frame of reference' (Silverman, 1970) clearly set an agenda which placed agency and actor at the centre of theoretical discourse. Second, contingency approaches which had consolidated a system-theoretic orthodoxy came under sustained attack for inadequate theorization of the 'environment'. This critique was mainly driven from positions derived from Marxist analyses of political economy which denied analytical primacy to the organization–environment interface. Consequently, the arena of debate refocused organizational analysis by theoretically subordinating 'organization' to social and economic production, power and control (Clegg, 1975; Clegg and Dunkerley, 1980). Thus, organizations could no longer be considered as hermetically sealed, adapting their structure and practices through rationally constructed exchanges with the 'environment' across a featureless boundary. This vulnerability was only partially repaired by a proliferation of refinements and breaches of the organization–environment boundary. Contingency approaches developed these responses in survivalist and dependency modes, and with the extension of evolutionary-ecology concepts such as those in population ecology models (Aldrich, 1979).

The loss of direction evident in the 1980s was due partly to the proliferation of frameworks which had spun on from these attempts to provide alternatives or to plug theoretical holes, but the suggestion that organization theory was imprisoned in a set of ontologically delimited paradigms which were essentially incommensurable (Burrell and Morgan, 1979), plunged the field into 'relative chaos'. If this analysis of the field were accepted, then there could no longer be an uncontested orthodoxy, yet neither was there a clear alternative, only a plurality of theoretical options with no apparent transparadigmatic discourse. This blinding clarity was further attenuated with the proposition that organization theorizations were 'metaphorical' and characterized by complete relativism (Morgan, 1986), and thus ways of understanding or imagining organization were a matter of consumer choice.

Despite the implied or explicit dual subordination of analytical primacy, and theoretical relativism, 'organization' had not lost its status as a theoretical or substantive problematic – order, control, change, culture and meaning were concepts still in the service of a 'modernist' project. More importantly, organization was still a necessary empirical category though theoretical developments clearly rejected the centrality of and focus on 'the organization'. Organizations were now theorized as being institutionally embedded in social and cultural practices, and this would have to be understood from contending theoretical corners.

A Critical Thread

Each chapter in this collection articulates a dimension which locates and establishes an 'authored' difference and distancing from a system-theoretic orthodoxy. Through consideration of theory, organizational form and problematic, they reflect the current diversity, innovation and incoherence of organization studies. But within this loose array there is a shared critical thread. The naivety of reasoned certainties and reified objectivity, upon which organization theory built its positivist monuments to modernism, is unceremoniously jettisoned. Although this 'certainty' is occasionally, and vigorously, defended elsewhere (Donaldson, 1985) and frequently reproduced (in most OB/OT textbooks), these articles of faith are unlikely to form the axioms of any rethinking or new theoretical directions latent within present critiques. This is not surprising since the scientism upon which organizational 'rationality' rested was never fully determined, as the 'realist' debates in social theory revealed (Bhaskar, 1975; Keat and Urry, 1975). The anthropocentric nature of social theory and epistemological conventions formed an important element and focus in 'realist' arguments against positivism. This recast the status of theory and the role of agency and social context in the production of knowledge. More recently, the analysis of organization theory as a gendered and thus flawed product, can also be placed within an anthropocentric critique, as Calás and Smircich's 're-writing' demonstrates. These arguments can only further disable orthodox axioms in organization studies.

The system-theoretic position was always weak and vulnerable when confronting the paradoxical nature of *inter alia* actor and agency, meaning and interpretation, structure and process, goal and purpose. If this indeterminacy cannot be resolved – and to borrow Gergen's 'playful' imagery – does it merely change the field of organization theory into an adventure playground where academic discourse resembles the firing of well-aimed paint pellets at any 'construct' that stays still long enough? And does organization theory eventually emerge with a more resplendent conceptual hue; or are some of the players deadly serious, loading up with heavy-calibre theory-tipped and destructive projectiles? It would appear that the putative modernist–postmodernist engagement bears both likely outcomes and little promise of there being an incremental incorporation of one by the other.

The tension placed on this shared thread is revealed by the locations of the 'problematic' in organization theory. As the chapters in this collection attest, these theoretical tensions and developments have occurred not least through disciplinary permeability in attempts to make organization intelligible. The theoretical traffic, however, has an osmotic quality since it is predominantly one-way into organization theory from other fields. The results of selective conceptual transplants and the outcomes of trans-disciplinary discourse is also a 'field' of inquiry, in terms of the social construction of organizational knowledge, as accounts of producing organizational knowledge and cultural transitivity. Despite the fads and fashions of elliptically exotic theoretical mutations introduced into organization theory, continuity in the narrative has been maintained through the retention of organization as the theoretical core and problematic. However, with the more recent challenge posed by post-modernist approaches to knowledge, an 'overturning' of modernist think-ing, the concept of 'organization' itself is now at issue, though none of the authors writing in this mode, or assessing its impact on organization studies, explicitly abandons it (Thompson and McHugh, 1990; Hassard and Pym, 1990). Perhaps not surprisingly the vocabulary employed still rests heavily upon 'organization', but the constitutive elements of the reality which it represents seem to be changing from empirical categories to communicative constructs. Grand narratives eschew the counterfactual evidence which is central to the development of an organizational theory in social formations characterized as postmodern.

A Line of Theoretical Asymmetry

The longer-term direction of organization theory cannot be easily gleaned from the theoretical mist that hangs over the current struggle to comprehend postmodernist re-writing (Cooper and Burrell, 1988). It is most unlikely that there will be *a* direction since the field is evidently fragmented, and has remained precariously poised on a catastrophic cusp since the death rattle of 'functionalism' was first heard. This state of disorder will not readily be resolved, but there is a bold line of asymmetry which can be drawn between two broad and opposing trajectories. This asymmetry lies between the attribution of theoretical centrality to either *organization* or *language*, and the counterpoise appears to be very unstable. The trajectories which this asymmetry fuels can be traced by noting the two fundamental issues which are addressed: socially constructed organizational realities versus organization as a linguistic construct.

Organization: Socially Constructed Realities

For most readers of organization studies literature there should be nothing particularly startling about this side of the line. Theoretical developments have 'spiralled' and folded back on themselves whilst grappling with criti-ques of rational organizational forms, power, negotiated order, culture and 'practice'. Unless organization theory is permanently mesmerised by the next 'fad', it will continue this uncomfortable and turbulent journey. It is acknowledged that people construct and construe, reproduce and destroy their social settings in a multitude of ways. As a constitutive part of this construction/destruction, organizations are socially located and fabricated as institutional forms, but are not culturally determined. Therefore, organization is theorized as an outcome of activity which is differentially engaged, experienced, sustained and 'known'. Competing analyses of these outcomes will create and reproduce a plurality and diversity of accounts since each will theoretically privilege a 'reality' and agency. However, the mediation of socially constructed organization by language in attempts to theorize organizational behaviour has undermined attempts to establish certainty, coherence or singular direction. Thus each aspect of our understanding has to be regarded as culturally transitive. Hence, the chapters in this volume offer only a limited prospect for *a* theory of organization and would seem to resign the field to a more or less permanent cycle of re-thinking *organization*. There can be no new dawn of orthodoxy, coherence or synthetic solutions to de-differentiate the field despite attempts at reductionist analyses which revive ethnography and symbolic interactionism in a postmodern guise, as Turner argues.

Language: Organization as a Linguistic Construct

Postmodernism, when represented as an alternative 'gaze' or critical analysis of overdetermined social realities and certainty, can propel organization theory along its social constructionist trajectory. However, if the propositions derived from postmodernist texts are that language enslaves any attempt to theorize, or must be enslaved to this end, rather than the reflective deconstruction of concepts of organization, then they reduce the representation of organization to a play on words, signs, utterance or 'saying' and a retreat into 'text'. This is clearly the point at which organization theory is subsumed along with other approaches to knowledge, although the role of language in communicating or articulating an ideological framework, and in the attribution of meaning in a social setting, cannot be seriously contested. However, it is equally clear that even though social constructs are not impervious to language, and that there are communicative orders, language does not fully delimit or determine the social settings in which we live. The radical ontological and epistemological disjuncture latent within this mode of re-thinking is most clearly posed by Gergen's chapter, which comes closest to de-theorizing organization and subordinating it to intransitive discourse. A linguistic–constructionist 'overturning' treats organization as a non-discrete theoretical, or empirical, category and requires no agency. Should organization theory embrace the discordant voices of linguistic conjury, the narrative will be deprived of a narrator. On this side of the line of asymmetry there is no direction or theory of organization.

Declusion: Decomposition or Conclusion?

Acknowledging that 'organization' is conceptually problematic and attending to this by confronting theoretical challenges, projects organization theory into transformation. The theoretical compression placed on 'organization' within bounded disciplinary discourse leads to an unravelling and recombination of its conceptual core, a sort of theoretical parallel to Cooper's analysis of 'control at a distance', whereby *organization* remains as the problematic. Re-thinking but not abandoning the field of play.

References

Aldrich, Howard E. (1979) *Organizations and Environments*. Englewood Cliffs, NJ: Prentice-Hall.

Benson, J. Kenneth (1975) 'The interorganisational network as a political economy', *Administrative Science Quarterly*, 20 (June): 229–49.

Bhaskar, Roy (1975) *A Realist Theory of Science*. Leeds: Leeds Books.

Burrell, W. Gibson and Morgan, Gareth (1979) *Sociological Paradigms and Organisational Analysis*. London: Heinemann.

Cicourel, A. (1964) *Method and Measurement in Sociology*. New York: Free Press.

Clegg, Stewart R. (1975) *Power, Rule and Domination: A Critical and Empirical Understanding of Power in Sociological Theory and Organisational Life*. London: Routledge.

Clegg, Stewart R. and Dunkerley, David (1980) *Organisation, Class and Control*. London: Routledge.

Cooper, Robert and Burrell, W. Gibson (1988) 'Modernism, postmodernism and organisational analysis: An introduction', *Organisation Studies*, 9 (1): 91–112.

Donaldson, L. (1985) *In Defence of Organisation Theory: A Response to the Critics*. Cambridge: Cambridge University Press.

Hassard, John and Pym, D. (1990) *The Theory and Philosophy of Organisations*. London: Routledge.

Keat, Russell and Urry, John (1975) *Social Theory as Science*. London: Routledge.

Kuhn, Thomas S. (1962) *The Structure of Scientific Revolutions*. Chicago: University of Chicago Press.

Morgan, Gareth (1986) *Images of Organisation*. London: Sage.

Silverman, David (1970) *The Theory of Organisations*. London: Heinemann.

Thompson, Paul and McHugh, David (1990) *Work Organisations: A Critical Introduction*. London: Macmillan.

Index